A Re-definition of Belonging?

Immigration and Asylum Law and Policy in Europe

VOLUME 20

Editors

Elspeth Guild
Kingsley Napley Solicitors, London,
Centre for Migration Law, Radboud University Nijmegen

Jan Niessen
Migration Policy Group, Brussels

The Series is a venue for books on European immigration and asylum law and policies where academics, policy makers, law practitioners and others look to find detailed analysis of this dynamic field. Works in the series will start from a European perspective. The increased co-operation within the European Union and the Council of Europe on matters related to immigration and asylum requires the publication of theoretical and empirical research. The series will contribute to well-informed policy debates by analyzing and interpreting the evolving European legislation and its effects on national law and policies. The series brings together the various stakeholders in these policy debates: the legal profession, researchers, employers, trade unions, human rights and other civil society organizations

A Re-definition of Belonging?

Language and Integration Tests in Europe

Edited by

Ricky van Oers
Eva Ersbøll
Dora Kostakopoulou

MARTINUS
NIJHOFF
PUBLISHERS

LEIDEN • BOSTON
2010

This book is printed on acid-free paper.

Library of Congress Cataloging-in-Publication Data

A re-definition of belonging? : language and integration tests in Europe / edited by Ricky van Oers, Eva Ersboll, Dora Kostakopoulou.
p. cm. — (Immigration and asylum law and policy in Europe, 1568-2749 : v. 20)
Includes index.
ISBN 978-90-04-17506-8 (hardback : alk. paper)
1. Naturalization—European Union countries. 2. Language policy—European Union countries. 3. Acculturation—European Union countries. I. Oers, Ricky van. II. Ersbøll, Eva. III. Kostakopoulou, Theodora.
KJC6044.R4 2010
342.2408'3—dc22

2010001600

ISSN 1568-2749
ISBN 978 90 04 17506 8

PRINTED IN THE NETHERLANDS

Contents

About the authors

Eva Ersbøll is a Senior Research Fellow at the Danish Institute for Human Rights in Copenhagen. She is a lawyer and formerly a legal assistant to the Danish Parliamentary Ombudsman and an analyst to the Commissioner of the Council of the Baltic Sea States on Democratic Institutions and Human Rights, Including the Rights of Persons belonging to Minorities. Her PhD is on Danish Nationality in an International and Historical Perspective. She has published on a number of other topics, including Union citizenship, nationality law in Europe, equality and non-discrimination, the rights of the child and the rights of elderly persons suffering from dementia.

Marie-Claire Foblets Marie-Claire Foblets, Lic. Iur., Lic. Phil., Ph. D. Anthrop. (Belgium). Professor of Law and Anthropology at the Universities of Leuven (Louvain), Brussels and Antwerp. She held various visiting professorships, i.a. at ParisI/Sorbonne. She is member of the Royal Academy of Sciences and Arts in Flanders, honorary member of the Brussels bar, and currently chair of the Institute for Migration Law and Legal Anthropology at the Law Faculty in Louvain (Leuven). She has done extensive research and published widely on issues of immigration, integration and nationality law in Belgium. In the field of anthropology of law, her research focuses on the application of Islamic family laws in Europe, and more recently on accommodation of cultural and religious diversity in State law (i.a.: FOBLETS, M.-C., *Les familles maghrébines et la justice en Belgique. Anthropologie juridique et immigration*, Paris, Karthala, 1994; FOBLETS, M.-C. (ed.), *Familles – Islam – Europe. Le droit confronté au changement*, Paris, L'Harmattan, 1996 (coll. Musulmans d'Europe); FOBLETS, M.-C. (ed.) *Femmes marocaines et conflits familiaux en immigration. Quelles solutions juridiques appropriées?*, Antwerp, Maklu, 1998; FOBLETS, M.-C. & J.Y. CARLIER, *Le nouveau Code marocain de la famille. Son application en Europe* [The Family Code in Morocco. Its application in Europe], Brussels, Bruylant (2005); FOBLETS, M.-C., Recht op maat. *Culturen in de rechtbank.* [Culture(s) in the courtroom. Justice made to measure], Antwerp, Maklu (forthcoming).

Dora Kostakopoulou is Jean Monnet Professor in European Law and European Integration at the University of Manchester.

Kristine Kruma has obtained a master degree in international law at Lund University and is currently doctoral student at this university. Since 1999, she has been lecturer at the Riga Graduate School of Law and since May 2007 judge of the Constitutional Court of Latvia. She has participated in different courses in the universities of Arhus, Umeo, Oslo, Helsinki, Galway and Turku. She has been stagiaire in the Legal Service of the European Commission and visiting-scholar at both the Max Planck institute in Heidelberg and the Centre for Migration in Nijmegen. She is a member of the editorial board of the Baltic Yearbook of International Law. Since 2006, she has been a member of the Odysseus Network of experts in migration and asylum law. She has published on issues of citizenship, migration and general international and EU law issues.

Ines Michalowski is a senior researcher at the Social Science Research Center in Berlin (WZB). She holds a joint PhD from the Institute for Political Science in Paris and from the University of Münster in Germany. During the academic year of 2008–2009 she was a fellow at the Transatlantic Academy in Washington, D.C. Her publications include *Integration als Staatsprogramm. Deutschland, Frankreich und die Niederlande im Vergleich*, Münster: LitVerlag, 2007 and, together with Uwe Hunger, Can M. Aybek & Andreas Ette (eds.) *Migrations- und Integrationsprozesse in Europa. Vergemeinschaftung oder nationalstaatliche Lösungswege?*, Wiesbaden: VS-Verlag, 2008.

Ricky van Oers is a PhD researcher at the Centre for Migration Law of the Radboud University of Nijmegen, the Netherlands. Her research concerns the introduction and effects of formalised citizenship tests in Germany, the Netherlands and the United Kingdom. She participated in the NATAC-project, coordinated by Rainer Bauböck, which focused on comparing the way in which 15 EU Member States regulate the acquisition and loss of nationality. Furthermore, she conducted research into the implementation of the Directives on family reunification (2003/86/EC) and on long term residents (2003/109/EC) in the EU Member States. For a list of publications please consult www.ru.nl/rechten/oers.

Yves Pascouau has obtained a Ph.D. in law from the University of Pau et des Pays de l'Adour and research assistant at the Centre for European Studies (Centre de documentation et de recherches européennes) at the faculty of Law in Bayonne. His main researches deal with European Migration and Asylum Issues. He is also conducting a research within the Institut d'Etudes Européennes de Bruxelles (ULB-Université Libre de Bruxelles). This study, financed by the Communauté française de Belgique through an ARC project, concerns mandatory integration measures in the Member States of the European Union.

Bernhard Perchinig (PhD, University Vienna) is a political scientist and Senior Research Fellow at the Institute of Urban and Regional Research of the Austrian Academy of Sciences and lecturer at the Institute for Political Sciences at Vienna University. His main research interests are citizenship policies, antidiscrimination policy, European migration policies and urban integration. Next to his academic work he has served as a consultant to i.a. the European Commission, the Council of Europe, the Fundamental Rights Agency, the Migration Policy Group (Brussels) and the International Organisation for Migration (IOM).

Judit Tóth (PhD) is Associate Professor of Law at the Department of Constitutional Law, University of Szeged. As partner in the CHALLENGE research project (www.libertysecurity.org), she is leading the research on enlargement of the European Union and its ramifications. She has rich experience in academic work as research fellow at the Hungarian Academy of Sciences, at the Institute for Political Sciences from 1990 to 2001, and since 2002, the Institute for Minority and Migration Issues. She has been teaching in Szeged since 1995, and as law practitioner she has been giving legal advice to the Parliamentary Committee, the Prime Minister, and the Minister of Justice since 1986 and currently also to the Ombudsman. She has published widely on comparative constitutional law, migration law and enlargement policy.

Zeynep Yanasmayan is a PhD candidate at the Faculty of Social Sciences of the Catholic University of Leuven (KUL). She holds an MscEcon degree on Security and Citizenship from the University of Wales, Aberystwyth and an MA degree on European studies from the Free University of Brussels (ULB). Her major research interests revolve around integration and citizenship policies, Turkish minorities in Europe and diaspora politics.

Preface

Language and integration tests are a topical issue in various European Union Member States. Several Member States have introduced language and integration courses in their domestic legislation. Immigrants have to pass language and integration tests in order to prove that they have acquired a certain level of knowledge, sometimes even before entering the country. Although the modalities of the integration tests and courses vary among the Member States, the introduction of the tests reflects a change in ideas about the relationship between legal status and integration. Furthermore, there appears to be a trend in several Member States towards formalisation of the language and integration tests before naturalisation. Between 2002 and 2008, Austria, Denmark, France, Germany, the Netherlands and the UK introduced 'knowledge of society' as a condition for naturalisation. In certain Member States, the informal language test upon naturalisation has recently been replaced by a formalised test, prepared and conducted by language institutions.

Since these developments are rather recent, little is known about the effects of the introduction of the formalised testing schemes on the behaviour of potential applicants and on the selective effects of those new tests. Whether the introduction of such new ways of testing has in fact contributed to the integration of immigrants into the host society, which is often the official aim of these policies, or whether the tests function as a mechanism for selection and exclusion is unknown. Knowledge of these effects is all the more relevant since the formalisation of the tests has often coincided with an increase in the level of required knowledge of the language and of the host society or with the introduction of other obstacles, such as high fees or a six-month waiting period after a candidate has failed a test. The aim of this book is to exchange information concerning the reasons for introduction, the content and the effects of the language and integration tests. Experts from Austria, Belgium, Denmark, France, Germany, Hungary, Latvia, the Netherlands and the UK have analysed the policies affecting the integration of newcomers and/or future citizens in their respective countries. Is the introduction of the language and integration tests the result of a redefinition of belonging?

This book is the outcome of the seminar, '*Language and Integration Tests for Newcomers and Future Citizens*', organised by the Centre for Migration Law of the Radboud University Nijmegen on 15 February 2008. The book forms part of CHALLENGE, a research project financed by the European Commission under its sixth framework programme. Publication of this book has been made possible with financial support from the European Commission, for which we are grateful.

Introduction

*Dora Kostakopoulou**

Integration programmes and tests have emerged and proliferated in Europe in the new millennium. These are not merely citizenship tests, in other words tests required for acquisition of the citizenship of the host state (Bauböck, Groenendijk, Ersbøll & Waldrauch 2006, Bauböck, Perchinig & Sievers 2007). Migrants are also required to attend language tuition and civic orientation or education courses, intended to provide information about the history of a country, its legal system, culture, values and way of life, and to sit integration examinations in order to enter European countries, obtain temporary or permanent residence and to gain access to social benefits. Furthermore, integration programmes and tests have migrated abroad; they are part of a pre-departure phase that commences in the states of origin for spouses seeking reunification with their loved ones in the Netherlands, Germany, France and, soon, in the UK. Whereas, in the past, integration policy was aligned with (a liberal) citizenship policy and non-discrimination and governments insisted on the distinction between integration and migration, in the new millennium we have so far witnessed a deliberate alignment of migration and integration in official discourses and policies and the revaluation of national norms and values. Multiculturalism and the politics of recognition have been superseded by a model of integration that shifts the attention away from issues such as equal treatment, non-discrimination and social inclusion towards conditional socio-political membership, the preservation of core national norms and values and towards social cohesion. In the eyes of governmental elites, social cohesion, national unity and belonging can be bolstered by requiring migrants to learn to speak the language of the host state and by re-educating them so that they can embrace a country's history and institutions, its values and the national way of life.

---

* Dora Kostakopoulou is Jean Monnet Professor in European Law and European Integration at the University of Manchester.

Van Oers, Ersbøll and Kostakopoulou, A Re-definition of Belonging?, pp. 1–23.

In official discourses at the national and, increasingly, at European levels, civic integration is presented as the required antidote to the alleged failures of multiculturalism and the alleged creation of 'parallel worlds' within societies owing to increasing ethnic and cultural heterogeneity. Critics, mainly on the right of the political spectrum, have accused multiculturalism of essentialising culture, undermining social trust and creating 'multiple enclaves' that have little mutual interaction (Barry 2001, Levy 2000). The risk of political fragmentation is counteracted by an emphasis on social cohesion and the acceptance of national values by newcomers. In Sweden, a partial retreat from multiculturalism occurred in 1986 with Proposition 1986, but this was short-lived (Schierup, Hansen & Castles 2006: 222). In 1997 the Government pursued a policy of mainstreaming integration by focusing on the provision of equal rights and opportunities for everybody in all sectors of society. Proposition 1997 thus affirmed diversity and called for the development of an integrated multi-ethnic society. In the Netherlands, integration displaced the multiculturalist paradigm in the late 1990s. Following the entry into force of the *1998 Newcomer Integration Act*, migrants were obliged to attend integration courses, that is, language and 'social orientation' courses, and non-completion resulted in administrative fines or reductions in social benefits. In the UK, integration tests were first introduced in the domain of naturalisation. The *Nationality, Immigration and Asylum Act 2002* sought to end the 'mail order' approach to the acquisition of citizenship by requiring applicants to demonstrate 'sufficient knowledge about life in the United Kingdom', in addition to language proficiency. A modernised oath of allegiance and a citizenship pledge, to be taken during citizenship ceremonies, were deemed to enhance both the symbolic significance of citizenship and the integration of migrants. Influenced by Sir Bernard Crick and Robert Putnam, the former Home Secretary, David Blunkett, sought to revalue national citizenship and to foster a strong sense of 'British identity'. The linguistic and civic education integration requirements have now become mandatory for those seeking to settle in the UK and for newcomers. However, government officials also wish to revisit the citizenship framework and to require migrants to demonstrate good behaviour and a willingness to integrate.[1] Citizenship reform is clearly linked to strengthened border protection and a reformed

[1] Compare Tony Blair's speech on 'the duty to integrate'; *The Duty to Integrate: Shared British Values*, Speech on Multiculturalism and Integration delivered at 10 Downing Street, London, on 8 December 2006, for the 'Our Nation's future', available at http://www.number-10.gov.uk/output/Page10563.asp.

immigration system'.[2] Within this context, a Green Paper entitled, 'The Path to Citizenship: next steps in reforming the immigration system', was published on 20 February 2008 (Kostakopoulou 2010).[3] The basic premise of the Green Paper was that migrants have to 'earn' their residence in Britain and, subsequently, British citizenship. As the former Home Secretary, Jacqui Smith, has stated, 'It is against this backdrop that we will now implement the next phase of reform: creating a new path to citizenship, one in which the expectation will be on newcomers to 'earn' the right to stay by learning English, paying taxes, obeying the law and contributing to the community. This reform is part of the wider work being conducted across Government to reinforce our shared values and to increase the cohesiveness of our communities'.[4] 'Earned' residence and citizenship are based on a multiple gateway approach; that is, individuals' settlement is broken into distinct phases, including a phase entitled 'probationary citizenship', which are clearly differentiated by gates that open or close depending on the migrants' success or failure in tests of language and knowledge of life in the UK and the absence of a criminal record (Kostakopoulou 2010).

In much of the present integration discourse and policy, governments have assumed the role of independent observers endowed with a duty to diagnose problematic symptoms and to prescribe the right remedy by changing law and policy (Entzinger & Biezeveld 2003). From this standpoint, they can make impartial judgements about the state of society, the desirable level of diversity and about migrants' responsibilities. Little attention, however, is devoted to the fact that politicians are not only implicated in diagnostic exercises and representations about the state of social affairs, but they also tend to play a leading role in the construction of narratives about the alleged decline of national citizenship, the potential of ethnic diversity to undermine social cohesion, and the advantages or disadvantages of greater cultural heterogeneity. Without a doubt, civic integration policies have been state-led projects; governments have played a key role in defining and redefining political belonging and in refashioning national identity within varied environments. In this respect, governmental elites are part of the 'integration issue' or the 'integration problem' and, certainly, something may be gained, in terms of capturing headlines and voters' attention, from portraying integration tests

---

[2] Jacqui Smith, Foreword, in: Home Office, UK Border Agency, *The Path to Citizenship: Next Steps in Reforming the Immigration System – Government Response to Consultation*, July 2008.

[3] Home Office 2008.

[4] Home Office 2008: Foreword.

and social cohesion as rightful responses to, rather than indicators of, anxiety and confusion in host societies about the meaning of national identity in the wake of internal differentiation and almost unstoppable globalisation.

What is also overlooked in policy circles, as well as the recent academic literature, is the concept of integration itself. Indeed, in the process of examining integration programmes and the civic integration discourse in Europe, one often gains the impression that integration is a stand-alone concept. Accordingly, civic integration programmes are officially justified on the basis of the need to impart skills, prepare people for citizenship and to make them self-sufficient and compliant with the integration contract. In reality, however, integration is a second order or derivative concept; it always presupposes something else, in other words the entity into which something is to be integrated and the reason mandating the process of integration. More importantly, without the basic or first-order concept, integration makes very little sense; it is an empty concept. We are told that we need to integrate into a social context, whether this be a specific community, the broader society, a working environment, a locality, etc. In turn, integration is deemed to be necessary because, without it, the broader context remains less than whole: incomplete, imperfect, divided, fragmented, unstable and thus insecure. As Joppke and Morawska have pointed out, the integration of migrants presupposes the subjective vision of an already integrated and unified receiving society (Joppke & Morawska 2003). It thus follows that not only does integration make sense by being linked to and, in turn, building on those first-order concepts, but its very meaning is also shaped by the meaning we assign to those concepts. To quote another example here, the concept of 'spouse' is also a derivative concept; it makes little sense without the concept of 'marriage'. In addition, the way we define and think of marriage to a large extent determines the way we think about the role and responsibilities of spouses. The transmission of meaning from first-order to second-order concepts is thus significant, since the relationship between the two is unavoidable. If the first-order concept is approached through an ideological lens or is reinterpreted in a particular way, this will activate corresponding shifts of meaning in the derivative concept. More precisely, if community is conceived of as a cohesive, homogeneous entity consisting of 'autochthonous' individuals of a shared ancestry or of like-minded individuals united in a patriotic attachment to certain values, or if diversity is seen to undermine the national culture or the 'specialness' (of national citizenship),[5] then integration will 'imitate' those interpretations, which will then become embedded in every-

[5] Goodhart 2008, *The Independent*; 2004, 'Too Diverse?', *Prospect*, February, pp. 30–37.

day discourse and in the legislative framework. In this respect, 'stereotypes of how to be 'national' will serve as a model test to evaluate if the immigrant is well-integrated' (Carrera 2006a: 3). For all these reasons, civic integration is not an innocent concept and is in need of conceptual refinement. The subsequent chapters examine the ideas, assumptions and conceptual frameworks underpinning civic integration initiatives in a number of European countries and unravel the multi-layered scripts that sustain them.

Notwithstanding the existence of specific visions of society or community underpinning integration, as well as the fairly inevitable variation in civic integration discourses and their institutional manifestations in European countries (discussed in the various chapters of this edited collection), three common themes characterise the new civic integration paradigm. These are discursive isomorphism in favour of integration and assimilation as the preferred modes of ethno-cultural minority incorporation (Joppke 2007), a unidirectional outlook and the predominance of an approach based on law enforcement and sanctions. It might be worth examining these isomorphic similarities briefly at this point.

In the migration and citizenship literature we find a number of modes of migration incorporation, which in turn correspond to citizenship models (Parekh 1998, Parekh 2000, Kostakopoulou 2002). The first is the mode of separation. This centres on primordial or ethno-nationalist conceptions of community, in other words on notions of community based on blood ties, common ethnic origin and a homogenous culture. It tends to exclude minority groups from formal membership, political participation and respectful settlement. It is accompanied by restrictive migration and citizenship policies and tends to emphasise that migrants 'are not here to stay'. Citizenship acquisition, in this mode, is based on *ius sanguinis* and opportunities for the naturalisation of long-term resident non-nationals are slim. The second mode, assimilation, requires the minority community to abandon important aspects of its identity, whether ethnic, cultural or religious, and to embrace the culture and values of the host community. Acculturation is necessary for political belonging, for the enhancement of national cohesion and for the preservation of a country's national identity. The traditional concept of the US at the turn of the 20th century, as a melting pot in which the 'old' traits disappear and a 'new' American identity prevails, is a typical example. The communitarian model of citizenship requires assimilation since it places the emphasis on the maintenance of a community's distinctive identity, as articulated by the majority community. Since, in this model, communities are essentially communities of trust, cultural commonalities play an important role in giving rise to loyalties and sustaining social relations. Applicants for naturalisation have to assimilate into the majority culture and to meet a set of strict conditions, such as long-term residence, a display of allegiance to the state in citizenship ceremonies, linguistic competence, knowledge of the host society and its history, renunciation of the nationality of origin, and so forth.

Integration, on the other hand, requires minority groups to identify with the common culture of citizenship in the public arena, while maintaining their cultural differences in the private sphere. As Parekh and others have noted, the common culture of citizenship is not ethnically and culturally neutral (Parekh 1998). The fourth mode, proceduralism, is based on a mutually agreed framework founded on liberal democratic principles, which provides space for the development of diversity and the promotion of a civic national sense of belonging. This mode accommodates diversity within certain bounds set by the dominant culture (Parekh 1998: 80). The third and fourth modes of minority incorporation are congruent with civic republican and liberal conceptions of citizenship respectively. The former relies on citizens' active participation in the polity and their zealous commitment to the common good. In this model, communities are built on values rooted in historical settings and sustained by a culture of civic duties. Applicants for naturalisation would have to demonstrate their commitment to the pursuit of the common good and their knowledge of the history and constitutional configuration of the polity. The latter, liberal conception of citizenship is less demanding; applicants for naturalisation should embrace the values of the host community, without necessarily abandoning their particular ethnic identifications and cultural identities. By contrast, the fifth mode, pluralism, protects and enhances diversity and does not make political belonging conditional upon conformity (Young 1990, Kostakopoulou 2001, Parekh 2000, Bauböck 1994, Tully 2002, Castles & Davidson 2000, Castles & Miller 1998, Connolly 1996, Rubio-Marin 2000). Since the bonds that hold communities and individuals together are political in nature and institutional in scope, minority groups feel that they are both respected and protected in a society characterised by openness, equality, intercultural dialogue and opportunities for all stakeholders. This mode reflected the model of multiculturalism that prevailed in Sweden and in the Netherlands until the late 1990s, but it also has a broader normative appeal in so far as it sketches a vision of community based on equal citizenship, partnership arrangements and reciprocal learning among minority and majority communities. Accordingly, ethnic politics is neither a problem for nor a fundamental weakness of political systems, but a 'manifestation of a broader process of liberalisation and democratisation' (Kymlicka 1997: 587). True, both the modes of minority incorporation and types of citizenship mentioned above are imperfectly correlated with national models but, like all typologies, they are useful and insightful. They enable comparative reflections and a deeper understanding of existing policy options and provide normative points of reference for evaluating current policies and evolving legal-political frameworks.

Secondly, in the new civic integration paradigm integration is defined as two-way process or a contractual agreement between the migrant and the host society, from which a number of obligations ensue. Migrants must be loyal and respectful of the values, culture and traditions of the host society. In turn, the host society will authorise their residence, endow them with protection against arbitrary expulsion and facilitate their involvement in the socio-economic and cultural spheres. Interestingly, whereas in the past the host society had to facilitate settlement and to adapt to the presence of newcomers, the emphasis has now shifted to the migrant, who has the responsibility to integrate, or to assimilate, into the mainstream culture, which is often depicted as a unified ensemble, and to prove his commitment to the host society.[6]

In framing integration as an obligation on the part of the migrant, implicit equivalences – such as indigenous/superior/complete and foreign/inferior/lacking – and ethnocentricity resurface, thereby rendering integration a unidirectional processes. This is because, to a varying degree, integration programmes logically presuppose the existence of deficits on the part of migrants, which must be overcome through learning the language, history, civic traditions and culture of the host state. It is very doubtful whether this is an objective and value-free presupposition, as it carries within it the traces of a certain ideological configuration which associates foreignness with 'objective deficiencies' in need of remedy. The lack of impartiality becomes evident if one thinks more deeply about the transformation of multilingualism, which is, generally speaking, a resource worthy of appreciation, into a handicap or an impediment if it does not include knowledge of the language of the host society. The justification for the latter does not have to be based on assumptions about the alleged intellectual inferiority of migrants – as it was the case at the turn of century in the US. The semantic shift from resource to disadvantage can be explained on the basis of the problems that newcomers may have in participating in social life or their alleged inability to make political judgements – as is the case with the justifications offered for the contemporary civic integration programmes. Ethnocentricity has underpinned previous integration policies and to a large extent explains the

[6] Home Office 2008; Lord Goldsmith 2007; Joppke 2003, 2007.

considerable criticism levelled at integration and assimilation in the 1980s and the 1990s.[7]

However, the 'one-way method' of old and new assimilation and integration frameworks reflects more ideology than reality (Rumbaut 1994, 1999), because cultures and institutions are mutable in reality. Indeed, a cursory look at the countries with long migration history and sizeable migrant populations reveals processes of change, the combination of many national and ethnic elements, fusion, hybridity, the constant flow of influences and the interweaving of diverse elements derived form local, ethnic, national, transnational and international spaces in socio-political and cultural life. Unidirectional integration also leaves very little room for reciprocal relations, dialogue, mutual learning, mutual adaptation and co-evolution and interdependence between majority and minority communities. It is true that, under the model of assimilation, the broader national culture remains broadly unchanged, whereas integration permits dialogue and some adjustments. But unidirectional integration is consistent with the ideological narrative of one nation surrounded and sustained by a coherent and organic culture, as well as processes designed to cement hierarchy, power and control over newcomers.

The third element, which will be discussed extensively by the contributors to the collection, concerns the fact that most European states have adopted integration programmes that are mandatory, sanction-oriented (fines, no entry, no family reunification, non-renewal of residence permits, deportation and unsuccessful naturalisation) and test-based. If the migrant does not take part in and successfully complete integration programmes, his status and entitlement to social benefits will be affected. Although scholars, such as Joppke, would view compulsory integration as the pursuit of liberal goals through illiberal means and an instance of repressive liberalism (Joppke 2007), the vital role of civic integration in the process of the management of migration should not be overlooked (Carrera 2006b). By relying on enforcement, punishment and disciplinary techniques, such as a test-based rather than a project-based approach to language acquisition and civic education, integration programmes reveal the link between integration and restrictive migration and citizenship policies. Indeed, it is very rare to find an answer to the question of why it is presumed that 'shared belonging' is something that can be obtained by testing one's fluency in the host language and the accumulation of factual information about civics, history or life in the coun-

[7] This lends credence to Brubaker's argument that we are witnessing a return to assimilation (Brubaker 2003).

try, which may well be forgotten a few months after the test, rather than on the basis of shared common experiences, working and contributing to the common good and enhancing the welfare of society. Here, we can discern the influence of ideological assumptions about the constitution and membership of political communities associated with nationalist ideology, since important qualities, such as a desire to succeed and to create a home, to work hard, to persevere, to make a long-term commitment to living in and contributing to the country are given less weight than fluency in the host community's language and knowledge of its traditions and values for the purposes of determining entry to the country and belonging. In the eyes of governmental elites making and remaking the nation, language, knowledge of history and the constitution, lists of national values – i.e., the traditional markers of national identity – determine who deserves to reside in the country and become a member of the political body.[8]

Additional support for the argument that integration programmes foster migration aims is derived from the shift from integration in the host country to pre-departure integration, or integration in the country of origin. The justifications offered are not persuasive enough. Indeed, we may wonder whether it is actually possible to talk of integration or preparing for integration when the person concerned has not yet joined the entity into which (s)he is supposed to be integrated. In the light of the remarks above about the necessary links between integration and the society that requires it, it is plausible to conclude that integration cannot take place if the links have not been established. Physical proximity and an interactive relationship must exist between an individual and the group in question, in order to safely assume that what may be called an 'integration process' has started. Otherwise, the individual is still a stranger, a non-resident and a non-member. This applies to other domains, too. If, for example, a person wishes to change his or her job, the issue of 'integration' in the new professional environment does not arise before that person joins the organisation. Similarly, when a person joins the new organisation and starts feeling at home there, (s)he can no longer consider himself integrated into the old one. (S)he may think fondly of it, have nice memories or simply miss his or her former colleagues, but the term 'integration' could not capture such feelings and thoughts. In this respect, one might argue that integration cannot be de-territorialised, nor can it be activated by remote control. This is precisely why, in EC law, integration is firmly situated within the host Member State and is intimately linked to residence, since it

[8] As Smith (1986: 206) has noted, 'Creating nations is recurrent activity which has to be renewed periodically'.

is designed to ensure that Community nationals who have crossed borders become part of the fabric of the host society by being treated as equals. Integration has never leaked outside the host society, nor has it ever been associated with entry, since this would create unjustified interferences with the right to cross-border mobility (Kostakopoulou, Carrera & Jesse 2009).

In this respect, one might call into question the extent to which pre-entry or pre-departure conditions and procedures can be conceptualised as legitimate integration measures. They are, essentially, admission requirements or conditions for entry authorisation. They are means of implementing restrictive migration policies. For example, how can a spouse be convinced that, in order to obtain a visa to join a loved one, (s)he must take and pass a language or civic orientation test because potential failure will lead to refusal of a leave to enter, and that all this amounts to 'preparation for integration'? How could such admission requirements be seen as means of increasing trust and cohesion in the host society? In their eyes, such requirements represent a hurdle designed to delay or even to deter their entry. Indeed, if the conditionality of visa acquisition is overemphasised and spouses find themselves unable to join their partners, then it is quite likely that states will fail to honour international commitments relating to the right of respect for family life (Article 8 ECHR). Such normative infringements, which would make it virtually impossible to exercise the right or impair the very substance of the right, enshrined in Article 8 ECHR, could potentially breach EC law, since, as a fundamental right, Article 8 is part of the general principles of EC law.[9] After all, a distinguishing characteristic of Article 8 is that it has an inbuilt duty to protect; it clearly requires respect for the rights enumerated in it. If, on the other hand, integration measures, such as language and civic orientation tests, are deemed to be simply arrangements governing the exercise of the right to family reunification and do not jeopardise its very existence because, for example, failure to pass the examination does not preclude the spouse from being granted temporary leave to enter or because spouses can retake the tests in the host member state, then such interferences, falling within the states' margin of appreciation, could possibly be justified according to Article 8(2) ECHR if they are in accordance with the law, pursue a legitimate aim and are necessary in a democratic society.[10]

---

[9] See Case C-413/99 *Baumbast, R v. Secretary of State for the Home Department* [2002] ECR I-7091; Case C-60/00 *Mary Carpenter v. Secretary of State for the Home Department* [2002] ECR I-6279; Case C-109/01 *Hacene Akrich* [2003] ECR I9607; Case 5/88 *Hubert Wachauf* [1989] ECR 02609, Case C-200/96 *Metronome Musik GmbH v. Musik Point Hokamp GmbH* [1988] ECR I-1953, para. 21.

[10] Compare Case C-540/03 *EP v. Council* [2006] ECR I-5769.

The contributors to this volume tease out the three features of the civic integration programmes identified above: their unidirectional, mandatory and sanctions-based character. They also comment on the reasons for their introduction as well as on their capacity to deliver the intended outcomes.

1.1 *The European Dimension*

Any in-depth examination of national integration laws and policies would be incomplete if it were not accompanied by an analysis of the European Union integration framework, which has developed incrementally over the last six years.[11] This is not because we wish to argue that European processes have led to policy convergence at the national level. Such a claim would be incorrect not only because a single and unified integration agenda does not exist in the EU, but also because the Member States have shaped and continue to shape the EU integration framework since 2003. Before studying the latter in more detail, however, it might be worth mapping the evolving European integration agenda.

Although states have traditionally viewed issues concerning third-country nationals as matters within their sovereign jurisdiction, in Maastricht national executives agreed to bring this policy area within the Community's formal structure by designing the separate intergovernmental pillar (the 'third pillar') of the Treaty on European Union (1 November 1993). Participation in such a framework of 'diluted' intergovernmentalism enabled them to experiment with cooperation in this area without ultimately losing control. A few years later, at the Amsterdam Intergovernmental Conference (1997), they agreed to transfer migration-related issues, including policies towards third-country nationals and judicial civil cooperation, from the third pillar into the EC Treaty under certain conditions.[12] The transfer led to the emergence of a different, rights-based logic concerning the treatment of third-country nationals, which found concrete expression at the Tampere special summit in October 1999. At Tampere, the Heads of State and Government agreed to set forth a number of policy trends and priorities for the 'area of freedom, security and justice' (AFSJ), which included: a) partnership with the countries of origin; b) a common European asylum policy; c) the fair treatment of TCNs; and d) the fair management of migration flows.[13] The fair treatment

[11] The discussion in this section is more fully developed in Kostakopoulou 2009.

[12] The Amsterdam Treaty entered into force on 1 May 1999.

[13] Tampere Presidency Conclusions, European Council, 15–16 October 1999, SN 200/99 Brussels.

of resident TCNs entailed a vigorous integration policy and the granting of rights and obligations comparable to those of EU citizens. According to the Tampere conclusions, long-term resident third-country nationals should be granted a set of uniform rights in the host Member State that are as near as possible to those enjoyed by Union citizens.

This commitment led to a rethinking of the position of TCNs in the Community legal order and the weakening of the hierarchical and security-based post-Maastricht paradigm. A new rights-based integration template was taking root and the Commission responded to it by proposing two directives, on *family reunification* (1999) and on *the status of long-term resident third-country nationals* (2001) respectively. The former Directive[14] was based on Article 63(3)(a) EC and sought to harmonise national legislations in this area by granting the right to family reunification to all third-country nationals, including refugees under the Geneva Convention of 1951 and persons enjoying temporary protection, who reside lawfully in a Member State and hold a residence permit for at least a year regardless of the purpose of their residence. The draft Directive *on the status of third-country nationals who are long-term residents* was based on Articles 63(3)(a) and 63(4) EC and sought to provide a uniform framework for the granting of long-term resident status in the EU and to grant long-term resident third-country nationals the right of residence in the other Member States.[15]

Both draft Directives viewed integration as a matter of equal treatment and had isomorphic similarities to the EC rules concerning the free movement of persons. Certain Member States, however, such as the Netherlands, Denmark, Austria and Germany, expressed reservations and managed to dilute the Commission's proposed provisions in order to make them fit with their own migration rules (Carrera 2005). Accordingly, provisions on integration conditions and measures were added to both Directives.[16] In the family reunification Directive, children over 12 years old, arriving in a Member State unaccompanied by their family members have to meet an integra-

[14] COM (1999) 638 final CNS 1999/0258, Amended Commission Proposal COM (2000) 624 final.

[15] European Commission, *Proposal for a Council Directive concerning the status of third-country nationals who are long-term residents*, COM (2001) 127 final, Brussels 13.3.2001.

[16] See Articles 4 and 7 of Council Directive 2003/86 (OJ L 251/12, 3.10.2003) and Articles 5 and 15 of Council Directive 2003/109 (*OJ* L 16/44, 23.1.2004). Compare also Directive 2004/114 on the conditions of admission for third-country nationals for the purposes of studies, student exchange, unpaid training or voluntary service (*OJ* L 375, 23.12.2004) and Directive 2005/71 on a specific procedure for admitting third-country nationals for the purpose of scientific research (*OJ* L 289/15, 3.11.2005).

tion 'condition' provided for under domestic legislation (Article 4(1)), while third-country nationals' rights to family reunification are conditional upon compliance with 'integration measures', which may be required for ordinary migrants before they have been granted family reunification (i.e., probably in the country of origin) (Article 7(2)). Similarly, the long-term residents' Directive includes provisions on 'integration conditions' that third-country nationals have to meet in order to enjoy long-term resident status and residence in other Member States.

By that time, integration had become a prominent theme in certain national arenas and, in 2002, the Justice and Home Affairs Council called for coordinated action and more policy coherence at the national and European levels. More specifically, it proposed the establishment of National Contact Points on Integration, in other words, a network of experts designed to promote the exchange of information and best practice in this area and to monitor progress.[17] The European Council meeting in 2003, in Thessaloniki, stressed the need to develop a coherent framework for migrant integration policy, based on a set of common basic principles, and invited the Commission to present annual reports on migration and integration.[18]

The Commission responded to the JHA Council's call for a common policy framework by issuing a Communication on *Immigration, Integration and Employment*.[19] The Communication reflected the liberal-multiculturalist paradigm of equality and the Tampere discourse on the fair treatment of TCNs. It called for the development of 'a holistic approach' to integration which would include a consideration of the socio-economic aspects of integration as well as other issues, such as cultural diversity, citizenship, participation and political rights. In this respect, tackling racism, strengthening anti-discrimination and promoting family reunification[20] were regarded as important components of a comprehensive integration policy. The Communication also highlighted the need for a closer dialogue with third countries, concerning the mutual recognition of professional qualifications acquired by TCNs prior to their arrival in the EU based on the principle of reciprocity.[21] Taking

[17] Council Meeting 2455, Luxembourg, 14–15 October 2002. The NCPs contributed to the compilation of the first edition of the *Handbook on Integration for Policy-Makers and Practitioners*. The second edition (2007) focused on the issues derived from the Common Basic Principles and a third edition is forthcoming.

[18] Thessaloniki European Council, 19–20 June 2003. Presidency Conclusions 11638/03. The first report was published in 2004: COM(2004) 508.

[19] COM (2003) 336 final, 3 June 2003.

[20] *Ibid.*, p. 25.

[21] COM (2003), note 26 above, p. 34.

an overall view, the Commission's communication embraced the positive aspects of migration and highlighted its future role in sustaining productivity and economic growth in Europe.[22] The positive impact of migration and the worrying prospect of an ageing workforce in the EU was also discussed in the Commission's First Annual Report on *Immigration and Integration in Europe*.[23] The Report called for the development of comprehensive integration policies and created a conceptual link between migration and integration by stating that, 'admission and integration policies are inseparable and mutually reinforce each other'.[24] It also reflected national concerns about the migrants' responsibilities to 'understand and respect the fundamental norms and values of the host society' and to speak the language of the host state.[25]

The Hague Programme, the successor to the Tampere Programme, set forth the policy objectives in the Area of Freedom, Security and Justice (AFSJ) for the period 2005–2010 and was adopted by the European Council on 4 and 5 November 2004.[26] It emphasised the need for greater coordination in national integration policies and EU initiatives and for the development of a clear framework on integration, based a set of common principles (CBPs) that were adopted by JHA Council on 19 November 2004.[27] These were aimed at assisting the Member States in designing their integration policies and the Council in devising supporting initiatives.

Although the principles refer to the dynamic process of integration and 'the two-way process of mutual accommodation by all immigrants and residents of MS' (CBP 1), they nevertheless reflect national priorities and con-

[22] Having said this, irregular migration is the subject of a law-enforcement approach; 'the only coherent approach to dealing with illegal residents is to ensure that they return to their country of origin'; p. 26.

[23] COM (2004) 508, p. 5.

[24] *Ibid.*, p. 9.

[25] *Ibid.*, p. 9.

[26] On 4 November 2004, the European Council adopted the Hague Programme, which set forth the objectives to be implemented in the area of freedom, security and justice for the period 2005–2010. This was followed by the Commission's Action Plan (May 2005), which outlined ten priorities for action, a set of implementing measures and a timetable for their adoption. The priorities cover fundamental rights and citizenship, counter-terrorism, a common asylum area, migration management, integration, internal borders, external borders and visas, privacy and security, organised crime, civil and criminal justice, sharing responsibility and solidarity. The Commission's effort to strike a better balance between freedom and security is evident in the Action Plan, which was approved by the Council on 2 June 2005. See European Commission Communication to the Council and the European Parliament, *The Hague Programme: Ten Priorities for the next five years – the Partnership for European Renewal in the filed of Freedom, Security and Justice*, COM(2005) 184 final, Brussels 10 May 2005.

[27] Justice and Home Affairs Council Meeting 2618, 14615/04 of 19 November 2004.

ceptions by placing the emphasis on migrants' responsibilities to respect the basic values of the EU (CBP 2), learn the language, history and institutions of the host society (CBP 4.1), be active societal participants (CBP 5) and on the possibility of conflict involving cultural and religious practices with European rights or national law (CBP 8.2). Notably, the Common Basic Principles incorporate no reference to access to citizenship as a condition for 'integration'. The conditionality accompanying the 'two-way process' of integration has been grafted on to the EU framework on integration, which includes benchmarking, i.e. the use of indicators and indices that would enable policy coordination, soft policy adjustment, their evaluation and the exchange of information and best practice among the Member States. According to Carrera (2008), this has resulted in the application of a quasi-open method of coordination in the field of integration policy (see also Carrera 2009). The Commission's Communication on *a Common Agenda for an Integration Framework for the Integration of TCNs in the EU* (2005)[28] sought to flesh out the CBPs by suggesting concrete actions at both national and EU levels and the establishment of a European Integration Forum, consisting of a number of stakeholders in this area, thereby ensuring the involvement of civil society. This body would facilitate the exchange of information and expertise, promote consultation and facilitate the making of policy recommendations. The Communication also highlighted the need for a more coherent approach to integration at EU level and contained a visible external dimension; it referred to the strengthening of 'the integration component of admissions procedures, through pre-departure measures, such as information packages and language and civic orientation courses in the countries of origin' with a view to promoting the implementation of CB4, which states, 'basic knowledge of the host society's language, history and institution is indispensable to integration; enabling immigrants to acquire this basic knowledge is essential to successful integration.' The Commission's Second Annual Report noted the 'new emphasis on obligatory integration courses, containing both language instruction and civic orientation',[29] whereas the Third Annual Report[30] called for the exploration and clarification of various concepts of citizenship participation and 'the added value of common European modules for migrant integration'.[31] It acknowledged that the CBPs impacted upon integration

[28] COM (2005) 389 final, Brussels, 1 September 2005.

[29] SEC (2006) 892, p. 5.

[30] COM (2007) 512, 11 September 2007.

[31] *Ibid.*, p. 10. Compare the Commission's Communication, *The Global Approach to Migration one year on: Towards a Comprehensive European Migration Policy*, COM (2006) 735 final, Brussels, 30 November 2006.

policies in certain Member States and noted the trend towards mandatory integration in the European Union. The embeddedness and close interaction between the national and European levels generated ambivalence, but the conceptual coherence and justifiability of the integration paradigm was not called into question.

The informal meeting of the Ministers responsible for integration in Potsdam (May 2007) addressed the need to make the 'two-way process' of integration more balanced by highlighting the responsibilities – and involvement – of the host society. Promoting unity in diversity was stressed at Potsdam and at the JHA meeting in June 2007.[32] In the Communication on *A Common Immigration Policy in Europe: Principles, Actions and Tools*[33] integration is seen as 'the key to successful immigration'.[34] '…the positive potential of immigration can only be realised if integration into host societies is successful. This requires an approach that does not only look at the benefit for the host society but takes also account of the interests of the immigrants: Europe is and shall continue to be welcoming environment for those who have been granted the right to stay, be they labour immigrants, family members, students or persons in need of international protection'.[35] The Communication's third common principle, namely 'prosperity and integration', however, bestowed legitimacy on integration tests and programmes by stating that, 'immigrants should be provided with opportunities to participate and develop their full potential. European societies should enhance their capacity to manage immigration-related diversity and enhance social cohesion'.[36] Although we are left with the impression that diversity is seen as an exogenous feature resulting from migration, rather than as an intrinsic characteristic of European societies, the Communication, nevertheless, included a number of positive recommendations, such as the need to pay attention to the participation of migrant women in the labour market, to ensure non-discriminatory access to health care and social protection and to assess the implementation, and the need for modification, of Council Directive 2003/86/EC on the right to family reunification. The third

[32] In June 2007 the European Fund for the Integration of Third-Country Nationals was established; Council Decision 2007/435/EC, OJ L 168/18, 28 June 2007. The Fund had a budget of 825 million euros, which would be distributed among the Member States for the development and implementation of national integration strategies (768 million). The remaining 57 million euros will be devoted to Community actions.

[33] COM (2008) 359 final, SEC (2008) 2026, Sec (2008) 2027, 17 June 2008.

[34] *Ibid*., p. 8.

[35] *Ibid*., p. 4.

[36] *Ibid*., p. 7.

section of the Communication, entitled 'Governance of Migration', invited the European Council to endorse these principles.

The European Pact on Immigration and Asylum submitted by the French Presidency in autumn 2008 mirrored national trends, thereby lending legitimacy to the unidirectional conception of integration featured in national arenas. In a draft version, the 'two-way process of mutual accommodation' (CBP 1) was clearly shown as a 'one-way process', since migrants would have to enter into a compulsory integration contract that would require them to conform to the national identity of the Member State in order to obtain permission to settle in the EU. Following several drafts,[37] agreement on the text of the European Pact was reached at the JHA Council on 25 September 2008; it was then adopted by the European Council on 16 October 2008 in Brussels.[38] The Pact endorsed the 'Global Approach' to migration, which was adopted in 2005, and the Commission's Communication on *a Common Migration Policy*, and proposed the implementation of five political commitments which include the organisation of legal migration so as to take into account the priorities, needs and reception capabilities determined by each Member State and to encourage integration and the development of a comprehensive partnership with the countries of origin and transit in order to encourage synergy between migration and development. Evidently, none of these principles is new. With respect to the former commitment, the Pact refers to integration policies founded on a balance between migrants' rights and duties and their obligation to respect the national identities of the Member States and the EU. Although it is alleged that the Pact strikes 'the right balance Europe needs' and 'demonstrates that Europe is able to protect its citizens, honour its traditions and develop partnerships', in reality it legitimises the Member States' restrictive migration agenda and the retreat from multiculturalism and pluralism: 'legal immigration policy must be selective and concerted'; 'family immigration must be more effectively organised…must be in accordance with the acceptance capabilities of the Member State and the integration capabilities of migrants'.[39] Clearly, in the evolving area of freedom, security and justice, the paradigm of migration control and law enforcement continues to be dominant. Governments will define the parameters within which selective and controlled migration will

[37] See Version II of the European Pact on Immigration and Asylum, 4 July 2008. Available at www.libertysecurity.org.

[38] The final text is more conservative in both tone and content than the draft dated 4 July 2008.

[39] The draft dated 4 July defined integration capabilities on the basis of a) families' resources and accommodation in the host country and b) knowledge of that country's language.

take place, notwithstanding the deployment of the notion of a pact. Like migration, integration tends to be defined by governmental elites as a matter relating to agents' abilities and responsibilities and the host societies' acceptance capabilities. The structural dimensions of integration and the characteristics of the contexts of reception tend to be sidelined. Integration is no longer regarded as a matter of ensuring equal treatment and removing barriers to inclusion and participation for all residents irrespective of their nationality. However, if such considerations are not brought back to the integration agenda, its present narrow frame risks creating schisms and divisions in European societies, thereby usurping the goals pursued by an integration policy.

1.2 *Plan of the Book*

This volume examines integration tests in 'old' and 'new' Europe and presents research spanning a range of methodologies and perspectives. We seek to provide a comprehensive overview of integration tests by focusing on the requirements imposed on newcomers and on persons seeking settlement, family reunification and, finally, naturalisation in the host country. The first two chapters of this book address integration requirements for naturalisation in Austria (Chapter 1) and Germany, the Netherlands and the UK (Chapter 2), respectively. Five chapters focus on integration programmes aimed at newcomers, as well as on citizenship tests in Europe. The final chapter of this book, by Marie-Claire Foblets and Zeynep Yanasmayan, shows that the Belgian federal system, notwithstanding its limitations, can offer a more progressive approach to integration by highlighting the importance of citizenship and the vision of a plural and more equal society.

In the first chapter of this book, entitled *All you need to know to become an Austrian: naturalisation policy and citizenship testing in Austria*, Bernhard Perchinig reflects on the political function of citizenship tests before embarking upon a detailed empirical analysis of the content of federal and provincial citizenship tests. Drawing on Foucault's differentiation between 'technologies of power' and 'technologies of the self', Perchinig makes the case for understanding citizenship testing as a symbolic act of subjugation to state power that needs to be communicated to the public and as a means of controlling membership of the polity. This is achieved by raising income thresholds, requiring proof of legal residence in, not just registration with, the municipality for a certain period of time and the introduction of naturalisation tests. In addition, Perchinig argues that the main political goal of the nationality law reform of 2005 was to make the conditions for family reunification with spouses from abroad more stringent. Since family reunification for third-country nationals is restricted by an annual quota, the spouses of Austrian citizens can join their partners without quota – representing restrictions. This legal difference was one of the reasons for soaring naturalisation figures in the early years of the 21st century. By restricting access to naturalisation, the government sought to reduce the family reunification of naturalised immigrants, thereby making nationality law reform an instrument for migration control. Perchinig then examines the substantive content of federal as well as provincial tests and argues that, while tests at the federal level reflect a predominantly republican understanding of nationality, at the provincial level a communitarian notion of nationality prevails that is deeply rooted in the provincial historical legacy.

Ricky van Oers' chapter on *Citizenship tests in Germany, the Netherlands and the UK* (Chapter 2) focuses on the introduction, rationale and effects of citizenship tests in the three countries under consideration. Through an analysis of the political debates leading to the introduction of the tests and using the typology of the liberal, libertarian, republican and communitarian concepts of citizenship in order to interpret and categorise the arguments expressed by participants in the political debates, van Oers sheds light on the reasons for the introduction of the tests and the changing perceptions of citizenship in Germany, the Netherlands and the UK in the past ten to fifteen years. She then guides the reader through the formal tests and compares and contrasts their content and their effects. In order to investigate the potential exclusionary effect of citizenship tests, van Oers examines the naturalisation rates before and after the introduction of the civic education test in the Netherlands and UK and the pass rates per nationality in the Dutch, British and German tests. Whereas the civic education requirement in the UK does not appear to have had a permanent negative effect on naturalisation rates in general, it nevertheless has a negative effect on the naturalisation of certain migrant groups. The Dutch naturalisation test, on the other hand, has led to falling naturalisation rates and to the exclusion of the most vulnerable section of the migrant population.

In the third Chapter, *On Trial in Denmark*, Eva Ersbøll examines the integration requirements for naturalisation, permanent residence and, in the future, entry to Danish territory. Although knowledge of the Danish language has been an explicit condition for acquisition of Danish nationality for more than 150 years, since 2002 an examination certificate has been required as documentation of the applicant's language proficiency. The latter involves reading and writing proficiency, coupled with knowledge of Danish society, culture and history. In 2005 the Danish language requirement was tightened and a supplementary naturalisation test was introduced. Then, in

2007, following the Dutch example, the Aliens Act was changed in order to provide for both immigration tests as a condition for permanent residence and integration tests as a condition for obtaining an entry visa. Furthermore, within the past five years, the possibilities provided by nationality legislation for exempting certain groups from the knowledge requirements have been reduced, while expanding to include the second generation of migrant descent. Eva Ersbøll examines these changes and investigates how applicants and language schools have looked upon the naturalisation test since its implementation in 2007. This leads her to reflect on the justification of the various tests and their compatibility with democracy and human rights.

Yves Pascouau sheds light on the French integration agenda that has prevailed since 2000. In Chapter 4, *Integration measures in France: an evolving process between integration and migration concerns*, he analyses the French integration programme and the integration agreement signed between migrants and the French Republic. Initially perceived as a two-way process of mutual accommodation, French integration policy has become more akin to a one-way process, which places a number of responsibilities on migrants. From the creation of an integration contract to the adoption of integration measures that have to be fulfilled from outside the territory, French legislation has widened the scope of integration measures and strengthened their mandatory character. Pascouau examines the sanctions that accompany failure to fulfil the integration contract that applies to residence permit applications and those that apply to the integration contract for the purpose of family reunification, thereby exposing the link between integration measures and the management of migration.

In *Integration tests in Germany. A communitarian approach?* (Chapter 5), Ines Michalowski discusses the German framework for integration and its underlying justifications. She ponders the distinctive characteristics of the framework and the usefulness of the concept of cultural assimilation in explaining the adoption of integration requirements. She argues that the introduction of elaborate integration tests is much less of a break with German legal and political tradition, as studies of other countries have suggested, and that it reflects a trend towards a more republican, rather than a communitarian, understanding of citizenship.

In Chapter 6, Judit Tóth analyses the legal rules regarding migrants' integration and naturalisation and official debates on kin-state legislation in Hungary. Since the Hungarian Constitution requires that acts regarding entry, residence and nationality have to be passed by qualified majority in the Parliament, continuous political consensus has prevailed on ethnic preference since 1990. The homogeneity of the Hungarian population, which can be explained by the fact that the majority of migrants have, so far, come from adjacent regions, may explain the low acceptance of migrants in Hungary. Tóth examines the ethnic foundations of Hungarian nationality law and the naturalisation requirements of the constitutional examination and Hungarian language test.

In terms of the reception and integration of permanent residents, a new component of the migration regulations consists of mandatory participation in integration courses and co-operation with the employment department as a precondition for protected persons to obtain social security benefits. Since active support or community services are lacking, the reception and integration policy has been rigid in comparison to other Member States. Legislation adopted in 2007 subjects the granting of allowances to refugees and the preservation of their residence status to their attaining a certain level of integration.

In *Latvian Integration Policy: Lost in Translation* (Chapter 7), Kristine Kruma examines the integration policy of another 'new' EU Member State. After a period of Soviet occupation, Latvia regained its independence in 1991. Guided by the principle of State continuity, decision-makers reconstituted the body of citizens by recognising only those who were citizens at the time of the occupation and their descendants. Soviet-era migrants could apply for the special status of 'non-citizen', which was intended as a temporary status until they qualified for naturalisation. Kruma discusses the reasons for the adoption of the Programme entitled, 'The Integration of Society in Latvia' in 2001 and its ramifications for citizenship attribution, language policy and education policy. She highlights the ambivalence that exists in Latvian integration policy owing to the combination of the concept of the nation-state, based on elements of republican and communitarian democracy, with a multi-cultural society that does not necessarily share the same values as the titular nation.

In the final chapter of the book, Marie-Claire Foblets and Zeynep Yanasmayan reveal the competing modes of minority incorporation and integration in Belgium. While Flanders has, since 2004, required newcomers to follow a citizenship path accompanied by civic integration courses, the two other regions, i.e. Wallonia and Brussels-Capital, are characterised by a civic-political conception of belonging and policies aimed at enhancing the participation and inclusion of migrants. Against the background of the instruments and institutions of the federal State and, in particular, the Nationality Code and its impact on the conceptualisation of citizenship, Foblets and Yanasmayan critically examine the Flemish policy of mandatory civic integration, *inburgering*, and reflect on its implementation and ramifications for Belgium. By comparing the Belgian case to countries that make use of similar instruments, the authors show that the dynamics (in this case the rivalry between

Flemish and French-speaking Communities) shaping the Belgian political system also generate 'peculiarities' for integration policy. These 'peculiarities' have allowed Belgium to pursue a double-edged integration policy, one that is both multicultural and assimilationist. However, they also provide resources for the separation of citizenship policy, regulated at federal level, and integration policy. The disentanglement of these policies appears to offer more credibility to both, whereas their conflation leads to restrictiveness, as attested by the examples of other European countries.

Bibliography

Barry, B., *Culture and Equality*, Cambridge: Polity Press 2001.

Bauböck, R., Transnational Citizenship. Membership and Rights in International Migration. Aldershot: Edward Elgar Publishing 1994.

Bauböck, R., E. Ersbøll, K. Groenendijk & H. Waldrauch (eds.), *Acquisition and Loss of Nationality, Volumes I and II*, IMISCOE Research, Amsterdam: Amsterdam University Press 2006.

Bauböck, R., B. Perchinig & W. Sievers (eds.), *Citizenship Policies in the New Europe*, IMISCOE Research, Amsterdam: Amsterdam University Press 2007.

Brubaker, R., The Return to Assimilation? Changing Perspectives on Immigration and its Sequels in France, Germany and the United States, in: C. Joppke & E. Morawska (eds.) *Toward Assimilation and Citizenship: Immigrants in Liberal Nation-States*, Basingstoke: Palgrave Macmillan 2003, pp. 39–58.

Carrera, S., Integration as a process of inclusion for migrants? The case of long-term residents in the EU, in: H. Schneider (ed.), *Migration, Integration and Citizenship: A Challenge for Europe's Future*, Maastricht: Forum Maastricht 2005, pp. 699–721.

Carrera, S., *A Typology of Different Integration Programmes in the EU*, Briefing Paper IP/C/LIBE/ FWC/2005-22, 2006a.

Carrera, S., (ed) *The Nexus between Immigration, Integration and Citizenship in the EU*, CHALLENGE, Brussels: CEPS 2006b.

Carrera, S., *In Search of the Perfect Citizen? The Intersection between Integration, Immigration and Nationality in the EU*. Leiden: Martinus Nijhoff Publishers 2009.

Castles, S. & M. Miller, *The Age of Migration. International Population Movements in the Modern World*. Basingstoke: Macmillan Press 1998 [1993].

Castles, S. & A. Davidson, *Citizenship and Migration: Globalisation and the Politics of Belonging*. Basingstoke: Macmillan Press 2000.

Connolly, W., Pluralism, Multiculturalism and the Nation-State: Rethinking the Connections, *Journal of Political Ideologies*, Vol. 1, 1996, pp. 53–73.

Entzinger, H. & R. Biezeveld, *Benchmarking in Immigration Integration, European Research Centre on Migration and Ethnic Relations*, Rotterdam: Erasmus University of Rotterdam 2003.

Joppke, C. & E. Morawska, Integrating Immigrants in Liberal Nation-States: Policies and Practices, in: C. Joppke & E. Morawska (eds.), *Toward Assimilation and Citizenship: Immigrants in the Liberal Nation-States*, London: Palgrave 2003, pp. 1–26.

Joppke, C., Beyond National Models: Civic Integration Policies for Immigrants in Western Europe, *Western European Politics*, 30(1) 2007, pp. 1–22.

Kostakopoulou, D., *Citizenship, Identity and Immigration in the European Union: Between Past and Future*. Manchester: Manchester University Press 2001.

Kostakopoulou, T., Integrating Non-EU Migrants in the European Union: Ambivalent Legacies and Mutating Paradigms. *Columbia Journal of European Law*, 8(2) 2002, pp. 1-21.

Kostakopoulou, D., The Area of Freedom, Security and Justice and the Political Morality of Migration and Integration, in: H. Lindahl (ed.), *A Right to Inclusion and Exclusion? Normative Fault Lines of the EU's Area of Freedom, Security and Justice*, Oxford: Hart Publishing 2009.

Kostakopoulou, D., S. Carrera & M. Jesse, Doing and Deserving: Competing Frames of Integration in the European Union, in: E. Guild, C. Groenendijk & S. Carrera (eds.), *Illiberal, Liberal States: Immigration, Citizenship and Integration in the EU*, Ashgate 2009.

Kostakopoulou, D., Matters of Control: Integration Tests, Naturalisation Reform and Probationary Citizenship in the UK, *Journal of Ethnic and Migration Studies* (forthcoming, 2010).

Kymlicka, W., Multicultural Odysseys, *Ethnopolitics*, 6(4) 1997, pp. 585–597.

Levy, J., *The Multiculturalism of Fear*, Oxford: Oxford University Press 2000.

Parekh, B., Integrating Minorities in a Multicultural Society, in: U. Press & F. Requejo (eds.), *European Citizenship, Multiculturalism and the State*. Baden-Baden: Nomos 1998, pp. 67–85.

Parekh, B., *Rethinking Multiculturalism: Cultural Diversity and Political Theory*. London: Palgrave 2000.

Rubio-Marin, R., *Immigration as a Democratic Challenge*. Cambridge: Cambridge University Press 2000.

Rumbaut, R., Origins and Destinies: Immigration to the United States Since World War II, *Sociological Forum* 9(4) 1994, pp. 583–621.

Rumbaut, R., Assimilation and Its Discontents: Ironies and Paradoxes, in: Hirschman et al. (eds.), *The Handbook of International Migration: The American Experience*. New York: Russell Foundation 1999, pp. 172–195.

Schierup, C.-U., P. Hansen & S. Castles, *Migration, Citizenship and the European Welfare State*, Oxford: Oxford University Press 2006.

Smith, A., *The Ethnic Origin of Nations*, Oxford: Blackwell 1986.

Tully, J., The Unfreedom of the Moderns in Comparison to the Ideals of Constitutional Democracy, *Modern Law Review*, 65(2) 2002, pp. 201–28.

Young, I.M., *Justice and the Politics of Difference*. Princeton: Princeton University Press 1990.

Chapter 1

All You Need to Know to Become an Austrian: Naturalisation Policy and Citizenship Testing in Austria

*Bernhard Perchinig**

1.1 *Introduction*

This chapter analyses the introduction and implementation of 'citizenship testing' in Austrian nationality legislation. The first part gives an overview about the debate on naturalisation; the second part of the chapter analyses the content of the tests at federal and provincial levels and the dominant understanding of citizenship they reflect. Finally, the impact of testing on naturalisation behaviour will be discussed.

Several European countries have introduced compulsory language and civic integration courses and tests in recent years, as a precondition for either permanent residence status and/or naturalisation. Reflecting a shift from a rights-based understanding of integration to an understanding focusing on the duties of immigrants, this tendency has been criticised as 'repressive liberalism' (Joppke 2007: 14), shifting the balance of rights and duties of liberal contractualism decidedly in favour of duties. In this line of reasoning, the introduction of civic integration requirements should not be understood as a rebirth of nationalism or racism, but as inherent to a liberal understanding of society, which presupposes that, '...members of the polity possess the necessary reasoning powers or abilities to (....) plan for their future (King 1999: 8, cited in Joppke 2007: 14). In parallel to a Rawlsian style of liberalism focusing on rights, equality and protection from discrimination, a 'liberalism of power and disciplining' (Joppke 2007: 16) would soon coerce individuals into

* Senior Research Fellow at the Institute of Urban and Regional Research of the Austrian Academy of Sciences and lecturer at the Institute for Political Sciences at Vienna University.

Van Oers, Ersbøll and Kostakopoulou, A Re-definition of Belonging?, pp. 25–50.

releasing their capacities for self-production and self-regulation. As in labour market policies, work-fare programmes have largely replaced welfare and unemployment payments, civic integration courses seek '...to make people both self-sufficient and autonomous by illiberal means' (Joppke 2007: 16).

Joppke's argument is based on the crucial assumption that language and civic integration courses genuinely do provide immigrants with the competencies needed for autonomy that they do not yet possess. With regard to naturalisation, naturalisation tests should thus function as a reliable measure of achievement in the competencies necessary to participate in political decision-making. After all, a stable residence status including the right to return, a passport allowing visa-free entry into most states of the world, and voting rights at all levels of the polity are the main privileges of citizenship of an EU Member State today. Access to civil rights has been extended to foreign citizens thanks to the development of human rights and the Long-term Resident Directive has granted stable residence and access to social rights, which remained closely connected to nationality until the end of the 20th century, to most resident third-country nationals in Europe. Nationality of an EU Member State today is much more focused on the political element than in previous years. Of the three dimensions mentioned, only voting rights may be meaningfully associated with competencies, which means that naturalisation tests should reliably measure the competencies needed to participate in politics and the exercise of voting rights.

Regarding language, Joppke's assumption implies that knowledge of the *lingua franca* of the state of residence is a necessary condition for political participation and voting rights. Although it is true that politics is conducted in the vernacular (Kymlicka 2001) and that, in nearly all cases, it will be necessary to speak the language of the country of residence in order to participate actively in a party or NGO, this is not true of voting. A sound knowledge of English, the de facto *lingua franca* of the world, is sufficient in all EU states for obtaining sufficient overview of parties, their programmes and candidates. Nearly all parties nowadays have websites informing the public of their activities in English and some even publish their party manifestos in this language. In many EU countries, radio and even TV news programmes are available in English. Furthermore, many parties in countries with a large immigrant population also publish information material in the languages of the major immigrant groups. Finally, nationality – including out-of-country voting rights – is granted to descendants of emigrants living abroad in many EU Member States. Some Member States, e.g. Austria and Italy, grant nationality *iure sanguinis* without any residence conditions to all descendants of emigrants, so that the grandchildren and great-grandchildren of emigrants, many of whom will not be fluent in their parents' or grandparents' language, may acquire the nationality of the state of origin of their ancestors and will therefore hold voting rights. They also will rely on political information in English or another language when participating in elections at the embassies. And furthermore, Union citizens are enfranchised at the local level independent of their knowledge of the local language.

We therefore see that knowledge of the national language of the country of residence as a condition for naturalisation cannot be argued as a necessary condition for participation in elections. Obviously, this argument is fuelled not by a functional understanding of language as a tool of communication, but by a communitarian understanding of language as a sign of cultural belonging. This recontextualisation of language as a sign of belonging to the political community stands in sharp contrast to a liberal understanding of citizenship and points towards an ethno-cultural demand for assimilation framed in liberal terms. As Blackledge (2006) has shown in the British case, language can easily become a marker of racialist 'otherness' in the implementation of citizenship testing, replacing 'outdated' and socially unacceptable features such as skin colour or race.

As has been argued by MacNamara (2005) and Shohamy (2001), tests never measure simply knowledge and competencies, but they are tools of power embedded in historical, cultural, social and political contexts. Tests not only create 'winners' and 'losers' and disguise a disciplinary measure as a scientific exercise, they also define what knowledge is deemed socially recognised as legitimate (Shohamy 2001, 18). Citizenship tests transcend language or knowledge tests: they test knowledge deemed essential in order to become a fully-fledged member of the polity by the state. In a republican understanding, testing the 'political maturity' of a candidate would be a legitimate condition for granting voting rights.

In political science, a long tradition of debate can be observed concerning civic and political education. In this debate, a knowledge of institutions is seen merely as an element of democratic learning, which focuses on the understanding of political processes, the development of critical thinking and the ability to make informed decisions. Modern concepts of civic education focus on active participation and democratic learning. For instance, the edict of the Austrian Ministry of Education and Culture on the Education Principle of Civic Education states:

> The educational principle of civic education is based on the reasoning that learning is based on experience and understanding and that insight and knowledge are related to relevant activities. Thus, the teaching of political knowledge has to be supported by the experience of democratic attitudes and behaviour. (....)

> The social experiences of the pupils are an important point of reference for civic education. Teaching thus has to be connected to their experiences.[1]

In this sense, the Austrian naturalisation tests, which simply ask about factual knowledge of the constitution and the institutional framework of the Austrian political system, are by no means a measure of the capabilities deemed necessary for political participation by modern standards of civic education. So why are they employed?

In a Foucaultian understanding of 'governmentality', 'the art of government' is not limited to state politics, but includes a wide range of control techniques, including self-control. Foucault transcends the traditional, state-centred, notion of power by including social control in disciplinary institutions as well as internalised knowledge guiding the individual's behaviour. Foucault differentiates between 'technologies of power', which 'determine the conduct of individuals and submit them to certain ends or domination', and 'technologies of the self, which permit individuals to effect by their own means or with the help of others a certain number of operations on their own bodies and souls, thoughts, conduct, and way of being, so as to transform themselves in order to attain a certain state of happiness, purity, wisdom, perfection, or immortality' (Foucault 1988, 16).

Naturalisation tests match both technologies: staged as a disciplinary procedure following the ritual of an examination, they belong to traditional 'technologies of power', but are legitimised in terms of a 'technology of the self', intending to prepare the individual to function as a citizen in a democratic polity.

In his seminal deconstruction of the myth (Barthes 1964: 92), Roland Barthes analysed the front page of an issue of *Paris Match*, displaying the photo of a black French soldier who, deeply moved, is saluting before the tricolour, the French flag. According to Barthes, the primary sense of the picture – a black soldier saluting the tricolour – conveys a second message, its significance, central to the secondary semiotic system of the story, which says: 'France is a big empire, all her sons, independent of skin colour, are loyal servants, and there is no better argument against the critics of colonialism than the enthusiasm of this black soldier to serve his supposed oppressor' (Barthes 1964: 95).

---

[1] Austrian Federal Ministry of Education, Culture and the Arts, *Grundsatzerlass zum Unterrichtsprinzip Politische Bildung in den Schulen*. Available from http://www.bmukk.gv.at/medienpool/15683/pb_grundsatzerlass.pdf, last accessed 27 March 2009. Translation by the author.

By analogy to Barthes' analysis, the significance of naturalisation tests is subjugation. In taking tests, the content of which is neither a preparation for participation in the polity nor does it enhance one's capability to take part in the everyday life of a society, the presumptive citizens symbolically affirm their readiness to obey the state power in their future life. Naturalisation tests neither prepare a person for more autonomy nor enhance self-sufficiency; their main function is a symbolic message to the citizens that access to their privileged status has to be earned by general subjugation under the coercive powers of the state.

1.2 *The Political Debate on Naturalisation*

Testing language proficiency and knowledge of Austria as a precondition for naturalisation became a political issue in Austria at the end of the 1990s. Until 1998, the nationality law did not explicitly demand a certain level of knowledge of German, but simply spoke about the need to prove the candidate's 'knowledge of German', which was interpreted by the provincial authorities in charge of naturalisation in rather different ways. In some provinces, the official in charge decided the case simply by talking to the applicant; in others, the candidates had to translate newspaper articles or other publications. In general, naturalisation practices were only known to experts and hardly discussed in public.

In the mid-1990s the debate on naturalisation intensified when the 'Freedom Party' (FPÖ; *Freiheitliche Partei Österreichs*) of the late Jörg Haider started to campaign against 'premature naturalisation', allegedly practised mainly in Vienna. The conservative ÖVP (*Osterreichische Volkspartei*) soon came out in support of the FPÖ, arguing that Austrian nationality was a 'valuable asset' not to be granted to immigrants 'lacking the will to integrate' (Çinar & Waldrauch 2006: 40). In 1996, the ÖVP presented a proposal to reform the Nationality Act. Naturalisation should only be granted after 15 years of residence (instead of the average ten years) and proof of sufficient integration and a certain level of knowledge of German should be made a precondition. The Social Democratic Party (SPÖ, *Sozialdemokratische Partei Österreichs*), which at this time controlled the Ministry of the Interior, rejected these proposals, in particular the introduction of comprehensive integration requirements and instead suggested reducing the waiting period for naturalisation to eight years. Talks with the smaller coalition party on presenting a joint proposal for a reformed Nationality Act started. In the negotiations, the coalition partners agreed to introduce a more stringent language requirement. The joint draft bill for a nationality law amendment presented in 1998 by the government defined naturalisation as the culmination of successful integration and made naturalisation dependent on proving a 'sufficient knowledge' of German. In practice, the provincial governments continued to implement different language standards.

The main aim of the amendment, however, was to eliminate differences in the administration of the Nationality Act with respect to the facilitated naturalisation of immigrants. Until the 1998 amendment, the regional authorities were relatively free to make use of facilitated naturalisation after four years instead of the regular ten years of residence, for 'special reasons'. The City of Vienna, which also has the status of a federal province under the Austrian constitution, made broad use of this facility, since in 1989 the governing SPÖ had decided to foster facilitated naturalisation as compensation for not introducing local voting rights for immigrants. Also in Vienna the waiting period was extended to six years in reaction to the increase in naturalisations in 1994.

Between 1980 and 1990, the number of naturalisations in Austria had remained more or less stable at around 8,000–10,000 a year. Since the 1990s naturalisations rose steadily – partly due to the growing number of immigrants residing in Austria for more than 10 years, partly due to the much more flexible rules for family reunification for Austrian citizens: family reunification with a legally resident third-country national was capped at a maximum number of around 8000 residence permits for family members per year, but no quota restriction was imposed for family reunification with Austrian citizens. Thus, naturalisation became an alternative to family reunification or family formation under the quota regime for long-term resident immigrants eligible for naturalisation. Against this background, the debate on naturalisation continued to rank high on the political agenda even after the 1998 Nationality Law amendment. The reform of 1998 was not accepted as sufficient by the FPÖ, which continued to demand restrictions on naturalisation legislation, focusing on the imposition of compulsory language tests for the applicant and the family members to whom naturalisation was to be extended. When, in 1999, the coalition government was formed between the ÖVP and the FPÖ, the governmental programme gave notice of a planned amendment to the existing Nationality Law. In the subsection entitled 'Comprehensive Integration', 'verifiable proof of knowledge of German' and of 'a basic knowledge of Austria and Europe' was introduced as a new precondition for naturalisation.

In practice, however, the nationality law was not amended, but 'integration requirements', i.e. the requirement of attendance at a German language course of 100 hours as precondition for a permanent residence permit, were introduced into the amended Residence Law in 2002. The regulation not only targeted newly arrived immigrants, but also all third-country nationals who settled after 1998. These courses had been suggested for the first time by the FPÖ during a press conference in April 2000 and gained instant support from the ÖVP (Rohsmann 2003: 69), Two main arguments surfaced in the public debate: whereas the FPÖ stressed the need to prove '... the immigrant's willingness to integrate', the ÖVP-led Ministry of the Interior referred to the success of the Dutch model. The opposition, as well as humanitarian NGOs, dismissed the suggestion as a threat to resident migrants. Since the law contained a wide variety of exceptions, only 10% of the target group actually attended these courses until 2003 (Die Presse, 17.3.2005, p. 3).[2] Interestingly, there was nearly no public debate to extend the language requirements and to include 'integration' issues or societal knowledge into the tests at this time.

After the division of the FPÖ into two parties (FPÖ and BZÖ) in 2002, the ÖVP formed a coalition with one of its offspring, the 'Coalition for the Future of Austria' (BZÖ).[3] Again, the government programme explicitly mentioned further restrictions in naturalisation legislation, particularly the reduction of facilitated naturalisations before a person completes 10 years of residence, the rejection of dual nationality, as well as improvements in reacquiring Austrian nationality. Until 2005, however, reforming immigration legislation was the main political focus of the government.

Between 2002 and 2005, Austria's immigration and settlement legislation was reformulated from scratch. In 2005 a new Alien Law, a new Residence and Settlement Act, a New Alien Police Law and an amended Asylum Law passed parliament. In public, these new regulations were presented as a success of the Conservatives (ÖVP), who presented themselves as the party most competent to manage migration and integration. In response and in order to regain its image as the leading party in the field of immigration, the BZÖ increased the pressure also to amend the existing nationality legislation. In February 2005, the then Deputy Chancellor Hubert Gorbach (BZÖ) announced an amended Nationality Law for the first time, to be presented in 2005. According to the draft bill, not only the applicant for naturalisation,

[2] In the reform of the Alien Law of 2005 the rules for the 'new integration agreement' were redefined: the language course was redefined as a 'language and integration course' and extended to 300 hours and a compulsory 'integration test', a de facto test of proficiency in German with regard to speaking, listening, reading and writing, was introduced. The test can be replaced by a certificate of basic proficiency in German as part of the 'Austrian Language Diploma' examination. Immigrants accepted under the quota for 'key personnel' and persons holding certain qualifications, e.g. an Austrian high school graduation diploma or an Austrian final apprenticeship examination, are exempt from taking the test, as are persons over the age of 65, children or persons with medical conditions preventing them from taking the test.

[3] Although chaired by Peter Westenthaler, the late governor of Carinthia, Jörg Haider, was an important architect of this new coalition.

but also the family members to whom naturalisation was to be extended should have to prove their knowledge of German by taking a test. Children would not have to take the test until they completed primary school education; minors attending secondary school would not need to take the test as long as they obtained positive grades for German (Bruckner 2006, 149). Thus, the test mainly would target applicants and their spouses.

This move was supported by the ÖVP, which suggested even harsher demands. On 1 March 2005, the Mayor of Innsbruck, Mr. Van Staa (ÖVP), also suggested extending the waiting period for naturalisation for third-country nationals to 15 years and for European Union citizens to 13 years. Further he demanded that all naturalisations be made public and that a right of veto be granted to the municipality of residence of the applicant. Now, the BZÖ again tried to defend its image as the leading anti-immigrant party. In July 2005 the newly-installed Minister of Justice of the BZÖ, Karin Miklautsch, demanded the introduction of harsher naturalisation requirements, such as a minimum waiting period of 12 years, a higher level of knowledge of German and proof of 'sufficient adaptation'. Similar suggestions were also made by the 'association of civil servants responsible for nationality', a private association of the heads of the regional government departments for nationality, meeting once or twice a year for an exchange of experiences and ideas (Perchinig 2005: 307).

An additional argument now entered the public debate: whereas 'proof of integration' had been the major argument for restricting access to naturalisation when the ÖVP-FPÖ coalition was formed in 1999, the link between naturalisation and immigration control now became important. Cutting back on immigration had been one of the main programmatic points when the ÖVP-FPÖ government was formed in 1999, thus the immigration quota had been lowered to around 8000 persons per year. However, the figures from 'Statistics Austria', derived from the newly-created population register, presented a different picture: in 2002, 78,000 third-country nationals had settled in Austria and this figure rose to 80,000 in 2003 and 88,000 in 2004 – about ten times the agreed immigration quota, which should serve as the major tool for migration control.

Although a certain percentage of the figures could be explained by changes in the way short-term migration, asylum-seekers and seasonal employees were counted, about 28,000 new immigrants per year originated from the traditional recruitment areas – the former Yugoslavia and Turkey. Most of these were family members of Austrian citizens. In 2004 alone, around 23,300 persons received a first-time residence permit as a family member of an Austrian citizen (Perchinig 2005: 310).

Combined with the massive rise in naturalisations between 1999 (25,000) and 2002–2003 (around 45,000), the growing number of family reunifications with Austrian citizens might also be taken as a sign of an unintended effect of the restriction of family reunification through the annual maximum number of residence permits set for family members of third-country nationals. Since no restriction was imposed on family reunification with an Austrian citizen, naturalisation obviously had become the 'second option' for uniting with one's spouse and/or children residing abroad.

The empirical data were presented to the cabinet of the then chancellor Wolfgang Schüssel (ÖVP) in spring 2005 by the staff of Statistics Austria. They explained that, despite a restrictive immigration quota, de facto immigration to Austria had soared since 1998 and reached a peak in 2004. According to their data, the period from 1999–2004 – the time of the ÖVP-FPÖ coalition and its strict anti-immigrant programme – had witnessed the highest migration since the end of the 1980s. Following their lecture, family reunification with newly-naturalised immigrants was identified as a major problem related to uncontrolled migration flows by the Chancellor's cabinet. Since restricting family reunification for nationals was seen as legally impossible in view of human rights' obligations and a large number of decisions by the Constitutional Court regarding the right to family life based on the European Convention on Human Rights, the cabinet decided to make naturalisation more demanding in order to reduce the number of target persons eligible for family reunification.[4]

Publicly, this move was sold as a labour market measure: in an interview with the weekly *Trend* (12/05, 24), Chancellor Schüssel depicted naturalisation as one of the main problems related to migration and as a major reason for growing unemployment,

> Our target is full employment. We would have full employment without such high immigration. Imagine what it means for a small country to naturalise, as it did last year, 40,000 foreigners. 25,000 partners, children and parents can accompany them who, simultaneously, have the right of residence and of access to the labour market.

1.3 *The Nationality Act of 2006*

The Nationality Act of 2006 (BG *BGBl.* 37/2006), which passed parliament against the votes of the SPÖ and the Greens and under harsh criticism from the City of Vienna and NGOs, again seriously restricted access to naturalisation. Naturalisation was made dependent on ten years of legal settlement and at least five years of settlement according to the Law on Settlement and Residence of 2005, which excluded, for instance, rejected asylum-seekers enjoying

[4] Personal report by Mr. Gustav Lebhart of Statistics Austria, 12 November 2006.

subsidiary protection from naturalisation. The possibilities for facilitated naturalisation were reduced and the naturalisation of foreigners married to Austrians was made dependent on six years of uninterrupted legal residence by the target person and a marriage duration of at least two years. Furthermore, the income thresholds were raised and certain types of income (social support payments) were excluded. Finally, fees were raised considerably (Çinar & Waldrauch 2006: 52 ff.).

According to § 10 of the Law, applicants for naturalisation now also have to prove their knowledge of German and their 'basic knowledge of Austria's democratic order and the history of Austria and the respective province.' Certain categories of former nationals (including survivors of the Holocaust, minor children who do not yet have to attend compulsory schooling, persons who are not able to comply with the requirements of language proficiency because they are elderly, are chronically ill or lack the legal capacity) are exempted. With respect to minor children attending a primary school, no proof of language proficiency is required. However, minor children attending a secondary school shall provide proof of a positive grade or positive 'achievements' in the subject of German.

Knowledge of German is demonstrated either by fulfilment of the requirements of the 'integration agreement' regulated in § 14 of the Law on Settlement and Residence of 2005, which requires 300 hours of attendance of a course in German, or a document proving a knowledge of German at proficiency level A-2 of the Common European Framework of Reference issued by a recognised examination centre.[5] Knowledge of the 'democratic order and history of Austria and the respective federal province' is demonstrated by taking a multiple-choice test to be organised by the provinces. According to § 10.5, the content of the test shall cover a basic knowledge of the structure and institutions of the Republic of Austria, fundamental civil rights and liberties including the right to legal protection, electoral rights and the historic development of Austria and the respective province on the basis of the curriculum for the fourth grade of secondary school (*Hauptschule*). The naturalisation exams may be repeated.

The technical implementation of the Nationality Law is organised in a separate by-law.[6] According to this by-law, the examinations have to be organised by the respective provincial governments at least every six months (§ 1.1). The examination covers three areas (§ 2.1):

---

[5] For an overview of the levels of language proficiency in the Council of Europe's Common European Framework of Reference, see annex 1.

[6] 138. Verordnung der Bundesministerin für Inneres über die Prüfung zum Nachweis der Grundkenntnisse der demokratischen Ordnung sowie der Geschichte Österreichs und des jeweiligen Bundeslandes (Staatsbürgerschaftsprüfungs-Verordnung – StbP-V).

1. Basic knowledge of the democratic order of the Austrian Republic,
2. Basic knowledge of the history of Austria,
3. Basic knowledge of the history of the respective province

The examination consists of 18 questions, six in each area, organised as a multiple-choice test with three choices. Each applicant may be given a separate set of questions drawn from a set of sample questions published by the federal and respective provincial government. Two hours should be allocated for sitting the examination (§ 3). The test can be passed by answering at least half of the questions in each area or at least two-thirds of all questions correctly (§ 5).

1.4 *Empirical Analysis*

Soon after the Nationality Law and the respective by-law had passed parliament, the Ministry of the Interior published a preparatory script for the test, containing information about the topics and sample questions, on its website and in print. The brochure covers the area of 'basic knowledge of the democratic order of Austria' and the area of 'basic knowledge of Austria's history', it is 53 pages long and only available in German. The script contains 91 sample questions and is available on the website of the Ministry of the Interior.[7]

All nine provincial governments also published teaching material and sample questions on their websites in the subsequent months.[8] Both the length of the scripts and the number of sample questions vary considerably. All scripts are written in plain, clear German using short and easily comprehensible sentences. With the exception of Salzburg, Styria and Upper Austria, all scripts use illustrations such as photos, maps or graphics. In five of the nine provinces, the provincial archives have been given responsibility for developing the teaching material and the test questions. In the province of Burgenland, the provincial Department for Municipalities and Schools was responsible for drafting and, according to a statement in the script, copied most of the material from a history book used in secondary schools. In Vienna, the Department for Immigration, Nationality and Civil Registration

[7] http://www.bmi.gv.at/staatsbuergerschaftswesen/Default.asp.

[8] The scripts and sample questions for Burgenland, Carinthia, Lower Austria, Upper Austria, Salzburg, Tyrol and Vorarlberg can be downloaded from http://www.bmi.gv.at/staatsbuergerschaftswesen/Default.asp, for Styria from http://www.verwaltung.steiermark.at/cms/beitrag/10264763/89739/, and for Vienna from http://www.wien.gv.at/verwaltung/personenwesen/staatsbuergerschaft/allgem.html.

drafted the test questions and the information brochure in cooperation with the provincial archives. In the province of Vorarlberg, drafting of the brochure and the development of test questions was outsourced to a private association (*Okay-Zusammenleben*), which has been developing and implementing local integration programmes for immigrants on behalf of the provincial government for several years.

According to the Nationality Law and the By-Law on the Implementation of the Naturalisation Tests, the third area of the test concerns 'basic knowledge of the history of the respective province.' In practice, both the preparatory scripts and the sample questions cover many more topics than history alone, e.g. regional symbols and the provincial anthem, the provincial governmental institutions and names of politicians, the names of prominent artists or scientists from the province, as well as asking about items on display at provincial museums, natural, architectural or tourist landmarks, regional food and customs, the number of subway lines or the use of the health care system. Historical questions stretch back far into the middle ages, asking about the names of archdukes, bishops and counts from provincial history.

Table 1: Test material used in the Austrian provinces

Province	Provincial government department responsible for the script
Burgenland	Department for Municipalities and Schools[9]
Carinthia	Carinthian Provincial Archives
Lower Austria	Lower Austrian Provincial Archives and Governmental Department for Nationality and Elections
Salzburg	Salzburg Provincial Archives
Styria	Styrian Provincial Archives
Tyrol	Provincial Archives of the Tyrol
Upper Austria	Department for Municipalities
Vienna	Department for Immigration, Nationality and Civil Registry Office
Vorarlberg	*Okay-Zusammenleben*. Project for Immigration and Integration. Scientific Counselling: Provincial Archives of Vorarlberg and Department for Home Affairs of the Government of Vorarlberg.

[9] 'Most of the content of the script was copied – with the consent of the authors – from the following books: *Lehrbuch für die Unterstufe 'Geschichte des Burgenlandes*,© LSI Mag. Dr. Günther Stefanits, ARGE 75, 7000 Eisenstadt; *Festgabe des Landes Burgenland anlässlich des Jubiläums 75 Jahre Burgenland*; Mag. Dr. Günther Stefanits, *Endonymische Minderheitennamen im Bundesland Burgenland, Österreich*, Herausgegeben von der Nomenklaturkommission des Landes Burgenland 2006.

1.5 *Methodology*

For the empirical analysis, the following categories were deduced from the sample questions:

- History
- Geography and Economy
- Political Institutions and Politics
- Regional or State Symbols
- International and European Union
- Culture, Science, Landmarks
- Rights (Human Rights, Social Rights, Minority Rights)
- Food, Customs and Other
- Cultural and Religious Diversity

The category 'History' covers questions regarding historical events and persons, the category 'Geography and Economy' deals with questions about geographical or economic facts, such as the highest mountain in a province or the most important industry. The category 'Symbols' covers the colour of the provincial flag, for instance, or the animals depicted in the coat of arms. The category 'Political Institutions and Politics' cover questions about institutions as well as the political process and the names of the president, the chancellor or the provincial governor. Several questionnaires also contained questions about the rights of women or how to gain access to social rights, e.g. where to apply for rent subsidies or what institution to contact in the event of unemployment. In four provinces, a few questions also concern minority rights or the rights of religious groups. All questions dealing with the rights of persons or groups, or questions mentioning the existence of minorities were assigned the heading 'Rights'.

Most questionnaires also contain questions about important composers, poets, painters, sportsmen or scientists or about important natural or architectural landmarks. These questions were grouped into the 'Culture' category. Questions concerning food or customs were grouped into a separate category. Finally, specific attention was given to the issue of cultural and religious diversity, which was mentioned by a few provinces, mainly with regard to the so-called *Volksgruppen* settled in those provinces.[10]

---

[10] Austrian legislation grants specific cultural rights to six so-called *Volkgsruppen*: Slovenes in Carinthia and Styria, Croats and Magyars in Burgenland, Czechs and Slovaks in Vienna and the Roma. A *Volksgruppe* is defined by traditional settlement in Austria for at least

Coding was carried out by the author according to plausibility. Whenever a question could be coded for more than one category, the preparatory script was consulted and the question was coded according to the semantic context in which it was mentioned in the script.

In the introduction to the book, the editors differentiate between a liberal, a republican and a communitarian understanding of citizenship. Liberal theory sees citizenship mainly as the legal expression of belonging to a society and as a set of rights of the individual vis-à-vis the state. In liberal thinking, citizenship tests can scarcely be legitimised, as long as citizens by birth do not have to take them. Nevertheless, citizenship test questions about knowledge of human rights, women's rights, social rights or minority rights could be understood as an indicator of a liberal understanding of citizenship, since preparation for the questions informs the applicant about his/her individual rights.[11] In contrast to a liberal approach, a 'republican' understanding requires knowledge of political institutions and the political process as a core condition for taking part in the polity. Questions concerning the institutional structure of the state, the political process or the name of political representatives thus can be understood as indicator of a republican understanding. A communitarian understanding is reflected in questions about remote historical events, customs and culture, landscape and symbols – in short, elements designating a common narrative and culture, not a common polity.

Following this method, the questions were assigned to the different concepts of citizenship. Questions about the use of rights and questions touching on minority rights and cultural diversity were interpreted as indicators of a liberal understanding, those relating to the functioning of international, national or provincial institutions and politics as 'republican' and those focusing on natural or cultural landmarks, history, symbols and customs as 'communitarian'. The categories 'geography' and 'economy' are ambiguous, since either might refer to part of the common narrative of identity (highest mountain, name of the longest river in several provincial sample questions)

three generations, a specific language or culture and possession of Austrian nationality. For the Slovenes in Carinthia and the Croats and Magyars in Burgenland, these rights include the right to use their language in court and in contacts with the administration in certain districts and the right to bilingual schooling. For the other groups, the law mainly protects their right to preserve their identity and to receive funding from the state. Immigrant minorities are not covered by the respective regulations (see Baumgartner/Perchinig, 2006).

[11] Etzioni makes a further distinction between a libertarian approach, which limits testing to basic information about how to vote or the context of basic laws, and a liberal approach focusing on knowledge of individual rights with regard to the state (Etzioni 2007, 358).

or simply touch on knowledge needed to participate in society (e.g. number of subway lines in Vienna). Geographical and economic questions associated with narratives were thus coded as 'communitarian', and questions regarding knowledge useful for everyday life as 'republican'. In a final step, all historical questions were analysed with regard to the historical phase to which they refer in order to gain a better understanding of the historical reference points of the state and the provincial narratives of the tests.

1.6 *The Content of the Test*

1.6.1 *The Federal Level*

The preparatory script by the Ministry of the Interior contains some rather straightforward information about the political and legal structure of Austria and Austria's history. The brochure is divided into two parts. Under the heading 'The Democratic Order', the first part (39 pages) provides information about state institutions, the political process and the government, law-making, fundamental rights, women's rights and antidiscrimination and the basic features of the European Union. This part contains 54 sample questions. The second part (11 pages) provides basic factual information about Austria's history and its involvement in international organisations. A further chapter of 2 pages touches on the economy and environmental issues; the final chapter (one page) provides basic information about the recognised minorities (*Volksgruppen*) in Austria. The second part of the script contains 37 sample questions.

As the following graph shows, the federal sample questions focus strongly on politics, international relations and the European Union. According to the pattern developed above, a republican understanding of citizenship dominates the test: nearly 70% of all sample questions cover knowledge of political institutions, the political process, international relations and economic and geographical facts. About 22% of all questions concern history or state symbols, which can be read as an indicator of a communitarian view. Only 8% relate to fundamental, minority and women's rights and are thus indicative of a liberal understanding. The issue of women's rights is presented in an ambivalent way, focusing on the prohibition of forced marriage and honour killings and thus implicitly suspecting candidates of being sympathetic to these crimes.

The historical part of the script is presented in five chapters covering different time periods: the time before the Bourgeois revolution in 1848, the period form 1848 to the end of World War I, when Austria was part of

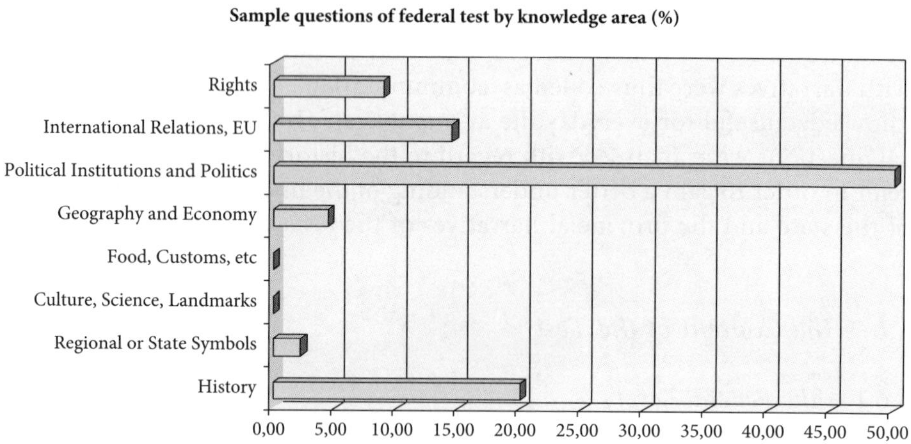

Diagram 1: Sample questions of the federal test by knowledge area

the Habsburg empire, the period 1918–1945 (including the 'First Republic', 1918–1934), the authoritarian semi-fascist *Ständestaat* (1934–1938) and the national-socialist dictatorship from 1938 to 1945. A further chapter covers the founding period of the Second Republic from Austria's liberation in 1945 to the state treaty granting independence in 1955, and the last chapter covers the period since 1955.

As the graph shows, about half of the historical questions refer to the time after World War II, the vast majority to the founding period of the Second Republic from 1945–1955. The other periods mentioned in the script each account for around 15% of the questions. The federal test thus displays a clear focus on the post-WW II founding period and the present state.

1.6.2 *The Provincial Level*

As Diagram 3 shows, the sample questions at the provincial level present a startling variety of issues. Nearly all the provincial information scripts and sample question sets vastly transcend the historical realm they should cover according to the Nationality Law and venture widely into the fields of geography, politics, culture and knowledge of social institutions.

In most provinces, historical questions amount to between 20% and 30% of the set of sample questions, with the exceptions of Salzburg (less than 10%) and Styria (more than 50%). The second most important knowledge area concerns geography and the economy. Knowledge of the political institutions and politics and of culture, the sciences and landmarks also play an important role in some provinces, although the share represented by 'culture' differs markedly from province to province. Only in Vienna and the Tyrol do some questions also concern international organisations with offices in the

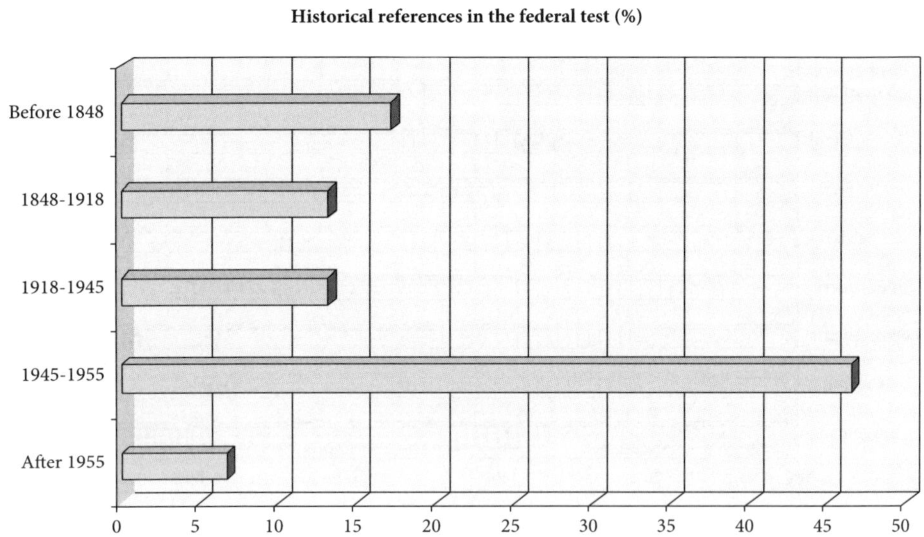

Diagram 2: Historical period of reference in the federal test

province (Vienna) or the European Union, in particular the Euro-Region of Tyrol-Alto Adige (Tyrol). In five provinces, questions concerning social rights and access to social services (unemployment insurance, rent subsidies) also play a certain role. Only in Carinthia and Vorarlberg are local food or customs mentioned. In the Carinthian question set four questions concern traditional local food[12] and, in Vorarlberg, one question mentions a game of cards not known elsewhere in Austria (*Jazzen*).

Again, the questions were grouped according to the understanding of citizenship they reflect. As Diagram 4 shows, most provinces favour a mix of the communitarian and republican understandings of nationality; liberal traits are sparse. Questions relating to communitarian elements range from 40% to more than 70% (Styria) and, in six of the nine provinces, these aspects cover more than 50% of the sample questions. The republican element also accounts for between 40% and 50% of all questions. It is interesting to note

[12] One of these questions concerns the ingredients of the local cider, which, according to the information script, is made from apples and pears. However, local producers of cider might well disagree with this description: Since I own a house inherited from my grandfather in a village in Carinthia, I used to buy cider from my neighbour, who grows fruit and is a regionally well-known producer of cider and pear and apple brandies. Having read the Carinthian test questions, I approached him and asked how he produces his cider. Seemingly dumfounded, he stared at me and answered, 'From apples, what else?' Confronted with the information from the test, he answered, 'That is wrong – that's how they make cider in Styria', the neighbouring province.

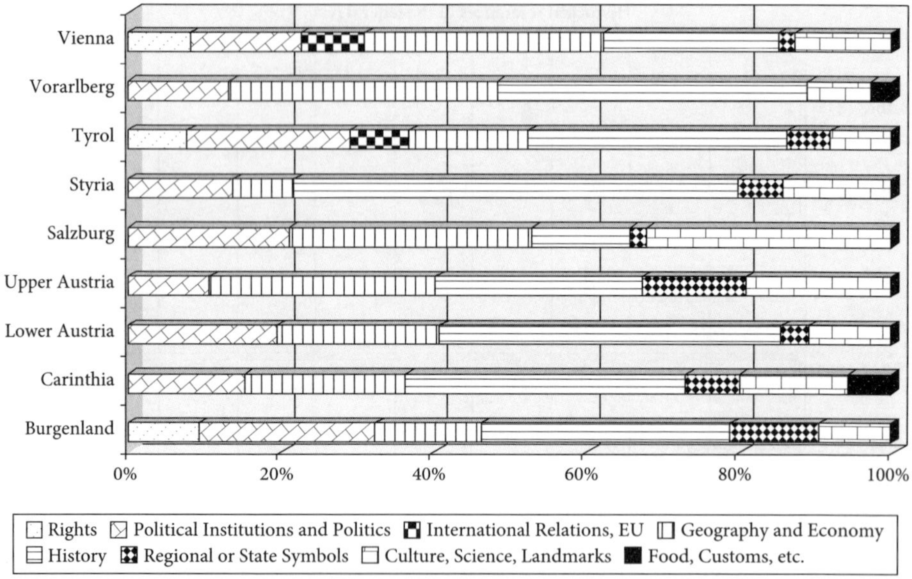

Diagram 3: Sample questions from the provincial tests by knowledge area

that four provinces (Burgenland, Carinthia, Tyrol and Vorarlberg) explicitly mention the diversity of culture and religion – in Burgenland and Carinthia solely in connection with the ethnic groups (*Volksgruppen*) traditionally resident there. One of the sample questions in Tyrol concerns the percentage of foreign residents in Tyrol. Only the sample questions from Vorarlberg mention the history of immigration and the main immigrant groups and thus include them in the common narrative.

Whereas the historical identity depicted in the federal test focuses on the founding period of the Second Austrian Republic, the historical references of most provinces are deeply rooted in pre-modern times. As shown in Diagram 5, in all provinces except Burgenland the main historical reference period (more than 40% of all historical questions) concerns the time before 1848. In Carinthia and Salzburg, more than 60% of all historical questions concern this era. Only in the province of Burgenland the majority of questions covers the time after World War I, and this is the only province in which the historical questions are fairly evenly distributed. The second most important period mentioned in the provincial tests concerns the First Austrian Republic (1918–1933); followed by the period of the authoritarian *Ständestaat* (1934–1938). The period of the National-Socialist dictatorship is mentioned in all provinces except Carinthia and Salzburg, with a share of between 7% and 17%. The Second Austrian Republic (1945 onwards) is covered by approximately one quarter to one third of the historical questions in Burgenland, Tyrol and Vienna, and by less than 20% in all other provinces. Most provinces obviously draw most of their historical self-understanding

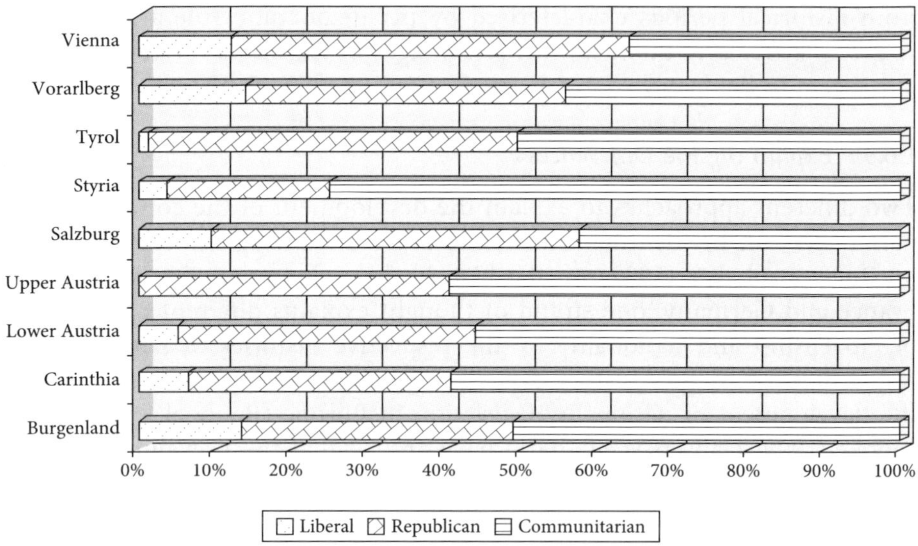

Diagram 4: Citizenship Models reflected in the provincial naturalisation tests

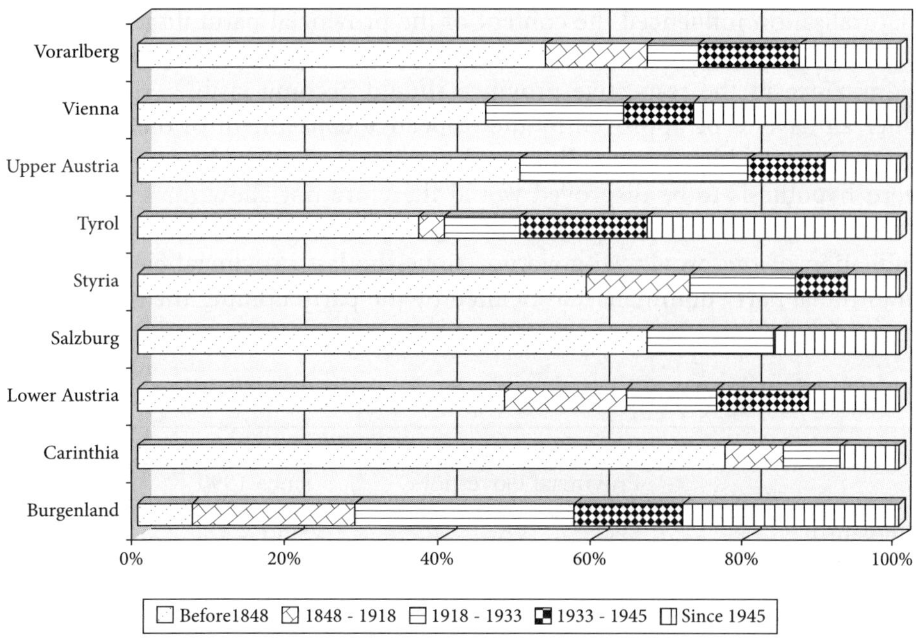

Diagram 5: Historical questions by period and province

from historical periods characterised by pre-democratic rule and a feudal society. Particularly the historical self-images of Carinthia, Styria and Salzburg seem to be deeply rooted in ancient and mediaeval history.

1.6.3 *Explaining the Differences*

Two different approaches to explain the development of the conceptions of nationality can be identified in the literature. Following the seminal study by Roger Brubaker (1992) on the historical development of nationality in France and Germany, one strand of thought explains different conceptions of citizenship and nationality by the respective histories of nation building. Contrary to this history-driven explanation, comparative studies of the development of nationality legislation in Europe (Bauböck et al., 2006; Joppke, 1999; Hansen/Weil, 2001) have argued that the prevailing conceptions of nationality have become policy-driven and are subject to international policy learning and changes in the party composition of the respective governments. We will test both hypotheses with regard to the content of the provincial nationality tests in Austria.

If the different ideological stances of the parties in government towards naturalisation influenced the content of the provincial naturalisation tests, a systematic correlation between the content of the provincial test and party dominance in the respective province should become visible. The tests do after all have to be approved by the respective department of the provincial government, which gives politicians leeway to influence their content. The zero hypothesis to be disproved would therefore not allow for a systematic correlation. To test the hypothesis, party dominance is defined by the party affiliation of the provincial governor since the last provincial elections and traditional party dominance, as defined by the party holding the seat of governor for the most years since 1990.

Table 2: Party affiliation of provincial governor since 1990

	Party affiliation of Provincial Governor	Dominant party since 1990
Burgenland	SPÖ	SPÖ
Carinthia	FPÖ/BZÖ	FPÖ/BZÖ
Lower Austria	ÖVP	ÖVP
Upper Austria	ÖVP	ÖVP
Salzburg	SPÖ	ÖVP
Styria	SPÖ	ÖVP
Tyrol	ÖVP	ÖVP
Vorarlberg	ÖVP	ÖVP
Vienna	SPÖ	SPÖ

Source: Own calculations based on Fallend, 2005, 980

Party dominance in the provinces has been fairly stable. In Lower Austria, Upper Austria, Tyrol, Vorarlberg and Vienna the party affiliation of the provincial governor has not changed at all since 1945. In Burgenland, a swing from the Conservatives to the Social Democrats (SPÖ) took place in 1964; since then the governor has always been a party member of the SPÖ. In Salzburg, a swing took place from the Conservatives (ÖVP), which had held the office of provincial governor from 1945 to 2004, to the SPÖ in 2004 and in Styria in 2005. Only Carinthia shows a different pattern. Following the rule of the SPÖ from 1945 to 1989, the late Jörg Haider of the Freedom Party (FPÖ) was elected governor from 1989–1991, followed by Christoph Zernatto (ÖVP) from 1991–1999. He then lost his position to Jörg Haider in 1999. Haider changed his party affiliation from the Freedom Party to the *Bündnis Zukunft Österreich* (BZÖ), which split from the FPÖ in 2005.

As can be seen from Diagram 6, there is no strict correlation between party dominance in a province and the composition of the tests. The distribution of the questions to the different knowledge areas is fairly diverse, although the share of historical questions tends to be higher in provinces with a conservative or BZÖ party dominance than in provinces where the Social Democratic Party takes the lead. A similar picture emerges in the analysis of the proportion of historical questions devoted to the time before 1848 as an indicator of a pre-modern historical self-image. In the (historically) conservatively dominated provinces (including Salzburg), the percentages for this period range from 36% to 67%, in Carinthia (BZÖ) the share is highest (77%). In provinces dominated by the SPÖ, between 7% to 45% of all historical questions cover this period. Overall, historical party dominance or the party affiliation of the provincial governor does not seem to play a decisive role, although provinces where the Social Democratic party dominates present a slightly more 'modern' understanding of nationality testing.

Do different historical conceptions of provincial identity define the self-understanding depicted in the tests? In order to answer this question, the information scripts were analysed with regard to the presentation of history and key historical events. No significant differences emerged in this respect. All the scripts go back to mediaeval history as the founding era of the *Länder*, which later formed Austria, and provide information about the most important historical persons and events.

With the exception of Vorarlberg, all scripts focus on elite and event history and do not attempt to deliver a historical analysis. Only the scripts from Vienna and Vorarlberg differ insofar as most of the information presented in the scripts covers the 20th century – with Vienna strongly focusing on the social policy of 'Red Vienna' in the 1920s (e.g. the novelty of a toilet and running water in council houses), and Vorarlberg concentrating on emigration

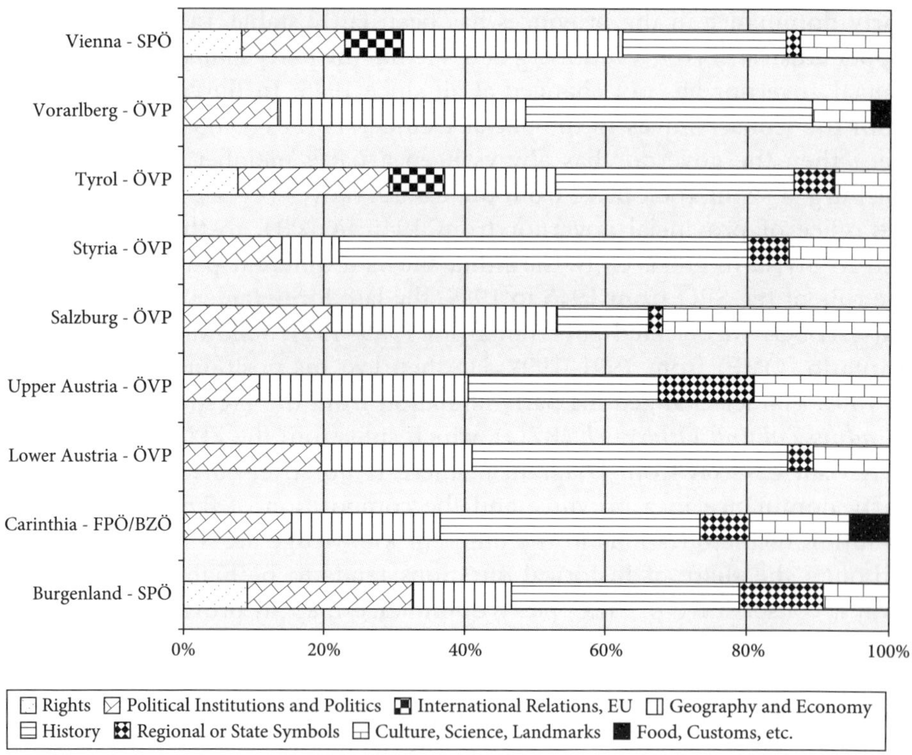

Diagram 6: Knowledge areas in provincial samples by provincial party dominance

from and immigration to the province. In the other provinces, however, earlier periods dominate the historical narrative. Governed by a Social Democratic government, the City of Vienna has opposed the introduction of naturalisation tests, this opposition seemingly is reflected in the simplicity of most of the questions of the provincial test, many of which concern tourist attractions (Schönbrunn Castle, St. Stephen's Cathedral) or information useful in everyday life (e.g. the number of subway lines). The script from the provincial government of Vorarlberg is strongly biased towards social history and the history of migration and thus symbolically includes immigrants in the provincial narrative. Whereas all the other brochures follow a widely superficial presentation of historical events to be learned by heart, the script from the provincial government of Vorarlberg gives historical analysis and explanations and reads as a historical essay, facilitating an understanding of local history.

These differences lend support to a Brubaker-style explanation: Vienna and Vorarlberg are also the two provinces with the highest proportion of immigrants. Both dispose of established institutional models to deal with integration. In Vienna, the local administration includes a Department for Integration and Diversity with a staff of around 100 and, in Vorarlberg, integration activities have been outsourced by the provincial government to the association *Okay-Zusammenleben*, which has developed an integration strategy for the province. In the Viennese case, the history of dealing with migration and the political protest against the introduction of naturalisation tests has led to the test becoming as easy as possible, whereas the authors of the tests and information material in Vorarlberg have taken the opportunity to include immigrants in the regional narrative. In all other provinces, the development of the test obviously did not lead to reflections about their link to integration.

However, the final explanation for the differences might even be significantly simpler: whereas, in most provinces, the staff of the provincial archives or the department for naturalisation (mostly historians not used to writing for a broad public) wrote the scripts, in Vorarlberg this task was outsourced to the association developing local integration programmes on behalf of the (conservative) provincial government, who hired a locally well-known, liberal left-wing journalist to write the script and develop the sample questions. The institutional setting for the development of the tests and the capabilities of the authors might explain the differences better than theoretically driven scientific explanations.

1.7 *Naturalisation Statistics and Citizenship Testing*

Did the tests influence naturalisation behaviour? Tests have been implemented since 1 April 2006, thus providing about three years of experience. According to the Ministry of the Interior, neither the numbers of candidates nor the success rates are published. According to newspaper reports, about 90% of the candidates pass the test at the first attempt (Kurier, 25.1.2009), making testing a rather symbolic exercise.

Nevertheless, the new Nationality Act of 2006 had dramatic consequences for the development of naturalisation, particularly as a result of stricter requirements with regard to income and residence. The high success rate in the tests makes it rather unlikely that they are an important explanation for the decline, but no empirical studies available concerning the effects of testing on naturalisation behaviour. Adult education centres involved in the organisation of integration courses report deterrent effects on naturalisation in particular for immigrants settled for more than ten or twenty years not well capable of speaking German. According to a report by Statistics Austria published on 13 February 2008, naturalisations declined by 46.5% in 2007

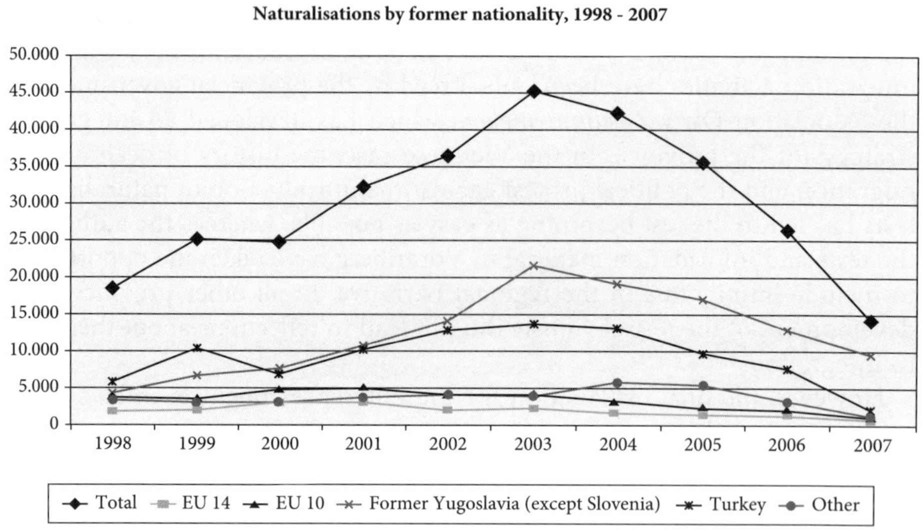

Diagram 7: Naturalisations by former nationality 1998–2007

compared to 2006. From 2005 to 2006 a decline of about 20% had already been observed.

As the graph shows, naturalisations increased markedly between 1998 and 2003 – mainly involving citizens of the former Yugoslavia and Turkey; the huge group of Bosnian refugees residing in Austria since the early 1990s had fulfilled the ten-year residency requirement by the early years of the new decade and a large group of Turkish immigrants had also come to Austria in the early 1990s.

The most dramatic decline took place between 2006 and 2007. Most of the decline can be accounted for by the naturalisation of the spouses of Austrian citizens (-64.5%) and the extension of naturalisation to spouses and children (-52.9%), which is a clear effect of the restrictions imposed on these groups under the Nationality Act of 2006. The number of facilitated naturalisations after four or six years respectively declined by 26.9% (Statistics Austria: Press Release 9.060-029/08, 14 February 2008).

Analysed by country of origin, the number of naturalisations of Turkish citizens declined by 72.5%, of Croatian citizens by 46%, of Bosnian citizens by 23.7% and of citizens of Serbia and Montenegro by 11.9%. The steep decline between 2006 and 2007 is a clear indication that the intended effects of the Nationality Law of 2006 – a reduction in naturalisations – have become a reality.

1.8 *Conclusions*

Naturalisation testing was introduced within the framework of an amendment to the Nationality Act, restricting access to naturalisation in many ways, including by introducing stricter language requirements and naturalisation tests. The debate about testing focused on issues of integration, but the main rationale for the restrictions in the naturalisation law were based on migration control, as explained above. Since family reunification with third-country nationals was limited by a yearly maximum, but family reunification with Austrians was not limited at all, for many immigrants naturalisation became the easiest way to (re)unite with or form a family. The reforms of 2005 were mainly intended to reduce the number of naturalised immigrants eligible for family reunification. Naturalisation thus became a means of migration control.

In this respect, naturalisation testing plays a mainly symbolic role. The main restrictions contained in the reforms of 2005 concern the legality of residence prior to naturalisation – previously, registered residence alone was sufficient. Furthermore, the need to proof an income exceeding the minimum pension in the three years before the application had been introduced.

Whereas the federal test depicts a clearly republican understanding of citizenship and focuses on the founding period of the Second Austrian Republic, the provincial tests and preparatory scripts not only differ widely with regard to content and quality, but also show a strong bias towards a communitarian understanding of belonging and a self-understanding deeply rooted in mediaeval history. The differences in the provincial tests can be explained neither by party dominance in a province, nor by a different understanding of provincial history. The best explanatory variables are the institutional setting and the capabilities of the institutions in charge of writing and developing the test.

Both the low level of institutional investment in the development of the test and the high success rate of around 90% show that citizenship testing in Austria is also a symbolic exercise intended to demonstrate to the general public that the naturalisation regime is more strict. Obliging candidates to learn historical and other facts that relate neither to everyday life nor to the knowledge necessary for political participation mainly is a public orchestration of the power of the state to demand a sign of subjugation from future citizens.

The sharp decline in naturalisation is not the result of testing, but of more restrictive conditions with regard to the income and residence of applicants. The message to the public, however, speaks of 'readiness for integration', proved by testing.

Bibliography

Bauböck, R. et al., *Acquisition and Loss of Nationality. Policies and Trends in 15 European States*, Amsterdam: Amsterdam University Press 2006.
Baumgartner, G. & B. Perchinig, Minderheitenpolitik, in: Herbert Dachs et. al., *Politik in Österreich. Das Handbuch*, Vienna: Manz 2006, pp. 686–701.
Barthes, R., *Mythen des Alltags*, Frankfurt/Main: Suhrkamp 1964.
Blackledge, A., The Racialisation of Language in British Political Discourse, *Critical Discourse Studies* Vol. 3/1, 2006, pp. 61–79.
Brubaker, R., *Citizenship and Nationhood in France and Germany*, Boston/MA: Harvard University Press 1992.
Bruckner, René, Neuerungen im Staatsbürgerschaftsrecht, *Öffentliche Sicherheit* 5–6/2006, pp. 146–149.
Çinar, D. & H. Waldrauch, The Acquisition of Nationality in Austria: Legal and Political Overview, in: R. Bauböck et al., *Acquisition and Loss of Nationality. Policies and Trends in 15 European states. Vol. II: Country Studies*, Amsterdam: Amsterdam University Press 2006, pp. 19–61.
Etzioni, A., Citizenship Tests: A Comparative Communitarian Perspective, *The Political Quarterly*, Vol. 78 (2007), pp. 353–363.
Fallend, F., Landesregierung und Landesverwaltung, in: Herbert Dachs et al. (eds.), *Politik in Österreich. Das Handbuch*, Vienna: Manzsche Verlags- und Universitätsbuchhandlung 2006, pp. 974–990.
Foucault, M., Technologies of the Self, in: Martin, L.H. et al., *Technologies of the Self: A Seminar with Michel Foucault*. London: Tavistock 2001, pp. 16–49.
Hansen, R. & P. Weil, Introduction: Citizenship, Immigration and Nationality: Towards a Convergence in Europe?, in: R. Hansen & P. Weil (eds.), *Towards a European Nationality. Citizenship, Immigration and Nationality Law in the EU*, Basingstoke: Palgrave 2001, pp. 1–24.
Joppke, C., How immigration is changing citizenship: a comparative view, *Ethnic and Racial Studies* Vol. 22 (1999), pp. 629–692.
Joppke, C., Beyond National Models: Civic Integration Policies for Immigrants in Western Europe, *West European Politics* Vol. 30/1, 2007, pp. 1–22.
King, D., *In the Name of Liberalism*, Oxford: OUP 1999.
Kymlicka, W. (2001): Politics in the Vernacular: Nationalism, Multiculturalism, and Citizenship. Oxford: OUP 2001.
McNamara, T., *21st century shibboleth: language tests, identity and intergroup conflict, Language Policy*, Vol. 4 (2005), pp. 351–370.
Perchinig, B., Einwanderungs- und Integrationspolitik, in: E. Talos (ed.) *Fünf Jahre Schwarz-Blau. Eine Bilanz des 'Neu-Regieren'*, Münster: Litt-Verlag 2006, pp. 295–312.
Rohsmann, K., *Die 'Integrationsvereinbarung' der Fremdengesetznovelle 2002. Integrationsförderung durch Sprach(kurs)zwang?*, Diploma Thesis, University Vienna 2003.
Shohamy, E., *The power of tests: A critical perspective on the uses of language tests*, London: Longman 2001.

Chapter 2

Citizenship Tests in the Netherlands, Germany and the UK

*Ricky van Oers**

In order to gain an insight into the effects of citizenship tests, this contribution will examine the situations in Germany, the Netherlands and the United Kingdom. Between 2003 and 2008, these countries introduced citizenship tests as a condition for the acquisition of citizenship. This means that in all three countries, in order to become citizens, immigrants have to prove that they are sufficiently integrated by demonstrating that they have a command of the language and knowledge of the society which might accept them as full members.[1] Before the tests were introduced, a local or municipal state representative would conduct an interview with the naturalisation applicant in order to test whether the prospective citizen had sufficiently integrated. Only linguistic knowledge was tested. The introduction of the formalised tests hence reflects a change in ideas about the relationship between legal status and integration. Whereas naturalisation used to be perceived as a means for integration, it nowadays is seen as the finalisation of a completed integration process, or, in the words of former Dutch Minister for Aliens Affairs and Integration Verdonk, the 'first prize'.

The erection of higher barriers to naturalisation, such as the introduction of citizenship tests, is often seen as a means to control immigration via nationality law. According to Etzioni, 'this can be gleaned from that (a) it is almost exclusively immigrants or their children who are subject to these tests and that (b) historically, citizenship exams have been introduced or modified

* Centre for Migration Law, Radboud University Nijmegen, The Netherlands.

1 A citizenship test also forms part of the naturalisation procedure in Austria, Denmark, Hungary and Latvia. See the contributions by Bernhard Perchinig, Eva Ersbøll, Judit Tóth and Kristine Kruma in this volume.

Van Oers, Ersbøll and Kostakopoulou, A Re-definition of Belonging?, pp. 51–105.
 ISBN 978 90 04 17506 8. Printed in the Netherlands.

in line with changing attitudes towards immigration in those nations that utilise them' (Etzioni 2007: 353).[2]

Even though the three countries under consideration have chosen to reinforce the integration requirement for naturalisation, the way in which the new membership tests have been put into practice varies considerably. Whereas the Netherlands and Germany require a uniform level, which needs to be attained by all immigrants, this is not the case in the UK. Furthermore, the level of the German test is higher than the level of the Dutch test. These differences provide a useful means of gaining an insight into the effects of the new requirements. Do the new ways of testing indeed function as a mechanism for selection and exclusion, or do they serve the goal of improving immigrant integration and participation, often the official aim of the policies?

In this contribution, three different aspects of the new methods of integration testing will be examined. Firstly, the reasons for introduction of the naturalisation tests in the countries under consideration will be discussed through an analysis of the political debates leading up to the introduction of the tests in the three countries (section 2). What were the aims of the proponents of the test, and which arguments were put forward against the introduction of a formalised citizenship test? Was the target group of immigrants who are required to take the test defined and, if so, how? Was the question addressed of what future citizens have to know for successful integration? The liberal, libertarian, republican and communitarian concepts of citizenship, as elaborated in section 1, will be used to interpret and categorise the arguments expressed by participants in the political debates, in order to define where the centre of gravity lies in the arguments used in the debates leading up to the introduction of the citizenship tests. Analysing the political

[2] Etzioni and Neuman point out that, historically, the requirement of English language ability has been introduced into US citizenship law as a means of reducing immigration from Eastern and Southern Europe (Etzioni 2007: 354, Neuman 1994: 236). A civics test was later used to complement the literacy test, to serve as a tool to limit immigration from non-Western Europe and Asia. The 1952 Immigration and Nationality Act clearly defined both tests that were used as a barrier to admission, not just to Asian immigrants but also to known communists or communist sympathisers. The 1986 Immigration Reform and Control Act was aimed in part at preventing illegal Latin American immigrants becoming citizens (Etzioni 2007: 354). A similar pattern was followed in Canada, which enacted literacy requirements for naturalisation designed specifically to exclude Chinese immigrants who often did not speak English or French (Etzioni 2007: 355). Etzioni stresses that the citizenship tests which have more recently been introduced in Germany, the Netherlands and the UK are 'significantly more rigorous than previous ones or their US counterpart' (Etzioni 2007: 356).

debates by using the concepts of citizenship will improve the comparability of the political debates in the countries under consideration. More importantly, using these concepts will show that the way in which citizenship is perceived in the countries under consideration has significantly changed in the past ten to fifteen years.

Secondly, the tests in the countries under consideration will be described and analysed (section 3). What are immigrants required to know in order to become Dutch, British, or German citizens? Do the tests serve the goal for which they were introduced?

Lastly, for each country, in order to examine whether the tests have the effect of excluding some of the immigrant community from full membership rights, the effects of the citizenship tests will be analysed (section 4). For this purpose, the numbers of naturalisations before and after the introduction of the knowledge requirements will be discussed. Furthermore, the pass rates per nationality will be examined in order to see whether the tests affect certain immigrant categories more than others. The effects of the Dutch naturalisation test are also discussed via an analysis of interviews conducted in 2006 with those responsible for implementing the test, on the one hand, and immigrants on the other.

2.1 *Concepts of Citizenship*

Before discussing the various concepts of citizenship that will be used as an instrument to analyse the political debates in Germany, the Netherlands and the UK, it is useful to describe the different dimensions of citizenship, which can refer to virtually every aspect of the relationship among citizens or between the citizen and the state (Fermin 2001: 67).

The literature generally identifies three different meanings of the concept of citizenship: citizenship as legal status, citizenship as activity and citizenship as identity (Carens 2000, Bauböck 2001, Entzinger 2008, Fermin 2001, Kostakopoulou 2003).

Citizenship as legal status (*what you get,* Kostakopoulou 2003: 86) is the most 'minimal' concept of citizenship, referring merely to a legal position (Pluymen 2008: 17). In this dimension, citizenship equals 'nationality', which needs to be understood as a vertical relationship between a person and a state. A citizen in the legal sense benefits from a privileged relationship with the state, in which she enjoys a number of (civil, political and social) rights, but may be obliged to fulfil certain duties towards that state.

Citizenship as activity (*what you owe*, Kostakopoulou 2003: 86) concerns the participation of citizens in the life of the polity. Participation not only means political behaviour, such as exercising one's voting rights, it can also refer to economic or social participation, for example doing voluntary work or maintaining social contacts. In this dimension, citizenship is therefore an attitude, requiring citizens to contribute to the common good of the community by exercising civic virtues.

Citizenship as identity (*what you feel*, Kostakopoulou 2003: 86) refers to an exclusive social status of membership of a polity and identification with it. Carens has called this dimension of citizenship the 'psychological' dimension (Carens 2000). This dimension cannot easily be captured in legal terms and procedures. On an individual level, it focuses on issues regarding the identification with and loyalty and commitment to the culture and tradition of the society of which one forms part.

In the concepts of citizenship that will be described below, the dimensions of citizenship are interpreted in different ways and combined to create elaborate and coherent theoretical perspectives of citizenship (Fermin 2001: 70). These perspectives do not need to be seen as mutually exclusive concepts of citizenship. Each country is *sui generis* and the perspectives are inaccurate as descriptions of national practices of citizenship (Bellamy 2004: 7). Hence, the concepts do not exist in a pure, clearly distinguishable form in individual countries (Kostakopoulou 2003: 94). In practice, societies combine aspects of the different concepts in their naturalisation policies (Neuman 1994: 241, Bellamy 2004: 7). Citizenship policies in modern democracies are therefore numerous, since liberal notions of civil and political rights have often been combined with, for example, communitarian notions of belonging and republican ideas of participation.[3]

2.1.1 *Liberal Citizenship*

Liberal theory stresses the development of individuals, who are regarded as autonomous. The principles of freedom and equality are of great importance, since these principles are regarded as conditions for the exercise of personal autonomy (De Vries 2008: 4).

The liberal theory uses a 'thin' concept of citizenship. The perspective of citizenship as legal status prevails. Membership is considered merely a legal status that equals 'nationality', as it is used in international law (Bauböck 2000: 40). Citizens have no responsibilities towards society and the emphasis lies on developing personal goals in life. Citizenship is not seen as involving any particular pattern of activity or requiring any form of identification with the community.

[3] Bauböck calls this 'recombinant citizenship' (Bauböck 2000).

Since the principles of freedom and equality are liberal core values, naturalisation is seen as a right for long-term residents and as a means of improving integration, rather than as the culmination of a completed integration process. From a theoretical point of view, admission criteria should generally not go beyond a reasonably short period of residence (Carens 1998).[4]

It is hard to defend a citizenship test under the liberal model. However, in cases where a state guarantees that the requirement of success in a citizenship test does not stand in the way of an immigrant's right to citizenship, such a test might be justified under the liberal model. Hence, ample and low-cost possibilities for immigrants to learn the language and to obtain the necessary knowledge of society need to be provided.

A difference can be made between different versions of liberalism. From an egalitarian liberal perspective, full equality will only occur where everyone has equal opportunities (De Vries 2008: 4). From this point of view, integration policy needs to focus primarily on equipping newcomers with the skills and tools necessary for equal participation in society. It is however doubtful whether obligatory integration requirements, such as taking a citizenship test, can be defended using egalitarian liberal arguments.

Whereas egalitarian-liberalism focuses on the equality aspect of liberal theory, libertarianism places the accent on individual freedom by focusing on minimal state interference in private life and requiring a high level of respect for individual liberty. In a right-wing approach to libertarianism, the liberal model of passive citizenship underestimates the extent to which fulfilling certain obligations is a precondition for being accepted as a full member of society. Failure to fulfil common obligations, in particular the obligation to support oneself, is as much of an obstacle to full membership as the lack of equal rights (Kymlicka & Norman 1994: 356). Hence, instead of an unconditional right for immigrants, the granting of citizenship is based on the calculation of the relevant costs and benefits associated with the admission of applicants into the demos (Kostakopoulou 2003: 94). The state will select future citizens on the basis of the net benefits its society might gain from the acceptance of an immigrant as a member.

Another distinction that can be made within liberal theory is the difference between emancipatory liberalism and liberal-egalitarian multiculturalism. Liberal-egalitarian multiculturalism acknowledges that membership of a cultural community can be of vital importance to an individual's well-being and provides the basis of effective exercise of individual autonomy.

[4] Bauböck realises that certain virtues, competences and knowledge express the idealised self-image of a free political community and that they should be shared as widely as possible (Bauböck 1994: 102).

Therefore, as well as promoting individual freedom, this form of liberalism contends that the Government should also protect an individual's choice to form part of a (cultural, religious or ideological) collective, while respecting the liberal context of the host community (Kymlicka 1995). Emancipatory liberalism, on the other hand, strongly emphasises individual freedom. In this approach, individuals need to free themselves from cultural, religious or other associations, if necessary forced by the government, in order to be able to develop fully into autonomous individuals (De Vries 2008: 4). Once liberalism transmutes into an identity, an ethical way of life everyone is expected to be conformant with, Joppke speaks of 'repressive liberalism' (Joppke 2007, 2010). Since state abstention from regulating only the external behaviour of people, not their inner motivations, is a key precept of liberalism, a test that examines an individual's true values is 'pernicious from a liberal point of view' (Joppke 2010). Following this line of reasoning, citizenship tests requiring only objective knowledge can, under circumstances, be defended under the liberal model, whereas tests scrutinising the candidates' 'inner dispositions' need to be disqualified from a liberal point of view.

2.1.2 *Republican Citizenship*

Republicans criticise the passive concept of citizenship in the liberal model. In the republican model, rather than a mere legal status, the perspective of citizenship as activity prevails. A citizen is someone who plays an active role in shaping the community through political debate and decision-making (Miller 1995: 443).

Since political participation features at the heart of republican citizenship, a regime founded on republican principles would appear to have the greatest stake in encouraging aliens to seek naturalisation. Higher rates of naturalisation mean increasing the number of people able to fully participate and deliberate (Schuck 1994: 330). However, before they can be admitted as full and equal citizens, people need to have certain minimum-required qualities for the exercise of citizenship. In the republican tradition, residence is certainly not enough for admission as a member of a political community, since the community is thought of as sharing fundamental political values and judgments rather than just co-residence (Bauböck 1994: 97).

A citizenship test requiring future nationals to be familiar with the language and society could be defended in the republican model. Linguistic competence is seen to encourage political participation and to serve as a common medium of political discourse (Neuman 1994: 265). It is therefore an indispensable requirement for future citizens. One could also argue that knowledge of society will foster effective political participation (Kostakopoulou 2003: 101). The 'knowledge of society' tests may however not require more than is necessary to participate in a democratic society. Testing knowledge regarding a country's constitution and political system can hence be considered justified in the republican model.

'Classic' republicanism has been criticised for its idolisation of dedication to the public cause, which contrasts sharply with the contemporary practice in which people chiefly look for happiness in their private lives (Fermin 2001: 72). Citizens might have other loyalties that should not necessarily be inferior to loyalty to the republic (Van Gunsteren 1998, Miller 1995). The *neo-republican* approach to citizenship does not demand overarching or total claims of allegiance to the republic, but something less than this (Van Gunsteren 1998: 26, Miller 1995: 448). According to Van Gunsteren, the 'duty' of a citizen is to 'transform a community of fate into a republic that can be willed by all who are involved as citizens' (Van Gunsteren 1998: 26). In order to achieve this, individual perfection is not implied, 'what is required is [...] that citizens act so as to (re)produce citizenship' (Van Gunsteren 1998: 26). That is why, in the neo-republican model, the most important condition of citizenship is its actual exercise, which could, alongside political participation, also imply social and economic activity.

2.1.3 *Communitarian Citizenship*

In the communitarian model, states are seen as the legal embodiment of a national community. This community has arisen and grown from a shared history and has a common identity and culture that has traditionally been defined by the majority community and that needs to be maintained (Kostakopoulou 2003: 95, Vermeulen 2007). The community's continuity depends on a minimum of unity and solidarity. A basic consensus regarding the principles uniting the community hence needs to be sustained, which requires a certain moral solidarity (Vermeulen 2007: 110).

In the communitarian model, citizenship as identity hence is the most important dimension. In order to become a member, an immigrant will need to share the national identity. Immigrants are required to absorb the main values and rules of conduct of the host society and to show a sufficient degree of loyalty before they can be admitted as citizens (Entzinger 2008: 182). This requires far-reaching adaptation or even assimilation on the part of the immigrant (Fermin 2001: 74, Neuman 1994: 264). The communitarian model thus considers naturalisation to be the end point of a completed integration process (Entzinger 2008).

The requirement of possession of sufficient knowledge of society in order to qualify for naturalisation fits in with the communitarian model. As

Kostakopoulou (2003: 102) has observed, in the communitarian model 'resident aliens must learn and appreciate the traditions and values of the majority community, and must earn their membership by showing commitment and working hard in order to familiarise themselves with the constitutional history and the nation's traditions.' The content of a 'knowledge of society' test may therefore comprise questions regarding the future citizen's acceptance of the values of the host community and detailed questions regarding history, geography, culture, sports and cuisine.

Since language is seen as a prominent defining factor in national identity (Neuman 2004: 264), linguistic competence is also essential for the maintenance of national identity and culture. It is an obligation for citizenship and a sign of allegiance to the nation's identity. A language requirement can thus be justified on the firm communitarian grounds that only speakers of the language can share the national identity (Neuman 1994: 264–265).

2.2 *Towards More Demanding Ways of Integration Testing*

In this section, the various concepts of citizenship described above will be used as an instrument for analysis, in order to identify a structure and create clarity in the ideas about citizenship that become apparent from the arguments used in governmental policy documents and in the political debates leading up to the introduction of the British, Dutch and German citizenship tests. When describing the political debates in the countries under consideration, I will adopt a chronological approach, starting with the country that first introduced a citizenship test.

2.2.1 *From a Liberal to a Communitarian Understanding of Citizenship: The Case of the Netherlands*

2.2.1.1 *A proposal for amending the Dutch Nationality Act*

In the Netherlands, the discussions regarding a more demanding integration test for naturalisation started in the early 1990s, when a proposition to alter the Dutch Nationality Act (DNA) was tabled in Parliament by the third Ruud Lubbers government, composed of the Christian Democratic CDA (Christian Democratic Appeal) and the Social Democratic PvdA (Partij van de Arbeid/Labour Party). One of the central elements of the integration policy at that time, the so-called 'Minorities' policy', was that a strong legal position would further immigrant integration. Naturalisation was seen as a means of achieving integration, as a step towards complete integration. This was explicitly stated in the Manual for Application of the DNA.[5] According to the government, strengthening an immigrant's legal position would improve his integration. Hence, the need to provide rights and opportunities and to facilitate access to nationality became evident. Therefore, the bill provided for the abolition of the renunciation requirement and a reformulation of the language and integration requirement. At the time, a municipal official would test, in a short interview, whether an immigrant had sufficient language skills and was sufficiently integrated into Dutch society. According to the Manual, applicants who spoke Dutch adequately and who had social contacts with Dutch nationals were regarded as fulfilling the language and integration requirement. Written language skills were explicitly not demanded.[6] Research conducted in 1988 had, however, pointed out that the requirement was not applied in the same way in the municipalities. In more than 10% of cases, not only were speaking and understanding tested, but reading and writing in Dutch were also included in the tests (Heijs 1988). In the opinion of the government, a more concrete formulation of the requirement would lead to a more uniform application, which would enhance equality and fairness in handling the language and integration requirement upon naturalisation. When drafting the proposals for amendment of the DNA, the Dutch Government clearly had a liberal understanding of citizenship.

The Christian Democrats in Parliament were unhappy with the proposed reformulation of the language and integration requirement, which, in their eyes, did not demand enough of future Dutch citizens. They proposed also requiring written language skills and a knowledge of Dutch society. Such knowledge was deemed necessary, since new Dutch citizens should be able to effectuate their newly acquired rights.[7] Instead of a means for integration, the CDA in the Parliament saw naturalisation as the 'legal and emotional completion of the integration', thereby deviating from the position the government had so far held.[8] The focus on the ability of future Dutch nationals to effectuate their newly acquired rights shows that emancipatory liberal concepts of citizenship started to influence the ideas of citizenship of the Christian democrats in Parliament. Since they designated naturalisation as the emotional completion of the integration process, communitarian ideas started to play a role as well.

---

5 Manual for the Application of the Dutch Nationality Act 1985, A1- Article 8, p. 19.
6 Manual for the Application of the Dutch Nationality Act 1985, A1- Article 8, p. 20.
7 TK 1995–1996, 26 September 1995, pp. 4–219.
8 Hand. TK, 16 February 1995, 49–3150.

Other political parties in Parliament (the liberal democratic D66, Green Left and the social democratic PvdA) strongly opposed a stricter language and integration requirement.[9] According to the Christian Democratic Minister of Justice, demanding written language skills would discriminate against the illiterate, persons who received little education, the elderly and the handicapped. He did support the idea of demanding that future citizens have a knowledge of Dutch society. In opposing the requirement of written language skills, the Minister expressed the wish for Dutch nationality to remain open to 'weaker' groups living in the Netherlands. The Government hence still favoured a liberal understanding of citizenship.

2.2.1.2 *1998: a new bill is proposed*

In 1998 the government, which by then consisted of the social democratic PvdA, the conservative liberal VVD (People's Party for Freedom and Democracy) and the progressive liberal D66 (Democrats 66), submitted a new proposal to amend the DNA. The previous bill was withdrawn because the political parties could not agree on the abolition of the renunciation requirement. Since 1992, the requirement had not been applied in practice and the numbers of naturalisations had risen considerably, which clearly indicated to conservative liberal and Christian democratic MPs that naturalisation had become too easy (Böcker, Groenendijk & De Hart 2005). The requirement was reintroduced in 1997. In the meantime, the Government had introduced the 'Alien's Policy', which replaced the Minorities' policy and which emphasised the immigrant's own responsibility to integrate. In 1998, the Newcomers Integration Act (NIA) obliged newcomers to participate in integration courses, culminating in a test. Although the test was intended simply as a measurement of the level of Dutch language knowledge that had been attained, the first step in subjecting immigrants to formalised integration tests had been taken.

In the discussions regarding the 1998 proposal for amendment of the DNA, the Christian Democrats and the Conservative Liberals increasingly began to express the importance of acquiring Dutch nationality in ideological, communitarian terms. According to the Christian Democrats, a report by the Social and Cultural Planning Office dated 1996 had shown that immigrants had been obtaining Dutch nationality for pragmatic reasons, not because they actually felt Dutch, which they viewed as worrying. Dutch nationality should

[9] *Hand. TK*, 21 February 1995, 50–3200.

be something to be proud of.[10] The conservative liberal VVD argued that Dutch nationality should not be something seen merely as an added bonus. These arguments can be categorised under the communitarian model.

With the renunciation requirement being reintroduced, the language and integration requirement became the main subject of discussion. The Christian Democrats now had the support of the conservative liberal VVD and the small Christian parties, which shared their desire to demand written language skills of immigrants who wanted to become Dutch nationals. Together, they argued in favour of a higher proficiency in the Dutch language than the level targeted under the NIA, which in practice was often not achieved. The level of language proficiency of the NIA hence exerted upwards pressure on the level of language proficiency for naturalisation.

In their reaction, MPs from the Green Left and the social democratic PvdA wondered whether someone who was not able to read or write Dutch was less Dutch than someone who could.[11] According to Secretary of State Job Cohen (PvdA), future Dutch nationals needed to be able to participate in society, instead of being qualified for a certain type of education or able to function in certain posts. Advanced language proficiency is therefore not required, but knowledge of Dutch society is, since, according to Cohen, without that knowledge, an immigrant cannot be considered integrated.

When the Progressive Liberal D66 proposed demanding a certain level of reading skills of naturalisation applicants, it became clear that a majority in Parliament was in favour of a stricter language and integration requirement. In 2000, the bill was adopted. A Royal Decree concerning the Naturalisation Test required that naturalisation applicants pass a naturalisation test, in which they have to prove sufficient knowledge of Dutch society and demonstrate that they could speak, understand, read and write Dutch at level A2 of the Council of Europe's Framework of Reference. By adding writing skills, the Decree goes further than the desire expressed by Parliament. Parliament did however not make use of the possibility of commenting on the Decree before its entry into force. The new Dutch Nationality Act (nDNA) entered into force on 1 April 2003.[12]

From a liberal understanding of citizenship, in which the dimension of citizenship as legal status prevails, under the guidance of the Christian Democrats and the conservative liberals in Parliament, citizenship policy in

---

[10] MP Verhagen (CDA), *Hand. TK*, 17 February 2000, pp. 51–3185.

[11] *Hand. TK*, 16 February 2000, pp. 50–3636.

[12] Act of 21 December 2000 (*Staatsblad* 618).

the Netherlands started to shift in a communitarian direction, which centres around the dimension of citizenship as identity. Whereas naturalisation until the first half of the 1990s was primarily seen as a step towards completed integration, obtaining citizenship, in the course of the 1990s is more and more perceived as the final step in the integration process. The conservative liberal Minister for Foreigners Affairs and Integration, Rita Verdonk, who was in charge of the execution of the naturalisation test after its introduction in 2003, often referred to naturalisation as the 'first prize'.

Since the introduction of the test, the question of whether the level and content of the test have a value matching the acquisition of Dutch citizenship has hardly been addressed. Such a discussion is hampered by the fact that the content of the test is undisclosed. The dramatic decrease of 70% in applications for naturalisation following the introduction of the test (see paragraph 2.4) has not led to any debate in Parliament. In 2003 Christian Democratic and Christian Union MPs did ask the Minister for Foreigners Affairs and Integration to raise the level of language proficiency for naturalisation.

2.2.1.3 *Replacement of the naturalisation test*

On 21 September 2005, a proposal for a new Integration Act, which was meant to replace the Newcomers' Integration Act of 1998, was introduced in Parliament.[13] According to the centre-right government, consisting of Christian Democrats, Progressive Liberals (D66) and Conservative Liberals (VVD), a more obliging and result-oriented integration policy was required in order to combat the supposedly failed integration of 'large groups' of immigrants.[14] In the explanatory memorandum to the Bill, the government stated that in order 'for immigrants to catch up and to allow them to successfully participate in the social markets', they need to have a knowledge of the Dutch language and to know and accept Dutch norms and values (Spijkerboer 2007:39):[15]

> Consensus regarding the basic values and the prevailing norms, and command of the Dutch language are, in the Government's opinion, necessary. [...] The Government thinks that the continuity of society is threatened if communities come to be opposed to each other, if social institutions are insufficiently effective for ethnic groups, and large parts of the population do not actively participate in society and the economy.[16]

---

[13] *TK* 2005–2006, 30 308, nos. 1 and 2.
[14] *TK* 2005–2006, 30 308, no. 3, p. 13.
[15] *TK* 2005–2006, 30 308, no. 3, p. 14.
[16] *TK* 2005–2006, 30 308, no. 3, p. 40.

When drafting the proposals for a new integration policy, the government was guided by several citizenship concepts. Firstly, with the focus on participation, the (neo-)republican citizenship concept becomes apparent. A trace of communitarianism becomes apparent from the focus on the acceptance of Dutch norms and values and the continuity of the community.

The new Act, which came into force on 1 January 2007, introduced the integration examination as a condition for permanent residence.[17] Since the level of the integration examination is equal to the level of the naturalisation test, it was decided that passing the integration examination would provide exemption from the naturalisation test. During the Parliamentary discussions of the Act, it was eventually decided that the integration examination would replace the naturalisation test altogether. Hence, since 1 January 2007, the Netherlands has required newcomers to meet the same standards as future citizens.

The Franssen Commission, an Advisory Commission on the standardisation of the integration requirements, advised on the content of the new integration examination.[18] The Commission saw participation in society as the goal of integration. Integration policy should be aimed at increasing the possibilities for immigrants to actively participate in society, since this benefits both the immigrant and society. Hence, when drafting its recommendations regarding the integration requirement, the Commission had a (neo-) republican concept of citizenship in mind.

According to the Commission, integration consists of several different aspects that each play a role in integration policy. The first meaning of integration is full participation in society. Everyone should be able to acquire a full social position as free and autonomous citizens. Dutch language skills and knowledge of social relations, norms and values are mentioned as requirements for achieving this goal, which can be described as emancipatory liberal. Secondly, integration implies that every citizen should respect the rules and norms of the Dutch constitutional state. The Commission mentioned values such as freedom of speech, freedom of religion and equality between men and women. Thirdly, integration and 'the proper functioning of a migrant' implies knowing and living up to unwritten rules, codes and agreements. This aspect of integration requires the immigrant to assimilate

[17] Act of 30 November 2006 (*Staatsblad* 625).

[18] *Advice regarding the level of the new integration examination by the Franssen Commission*, The Hague, June 2004.

For the advice, see http://www.degeschiedenisvaninburgering.nl/docs/advies-franssen.pdf, site visited on 20 March 2009.

into Dutch society by prescribing the way he is supposed to behave. The Commission hence advised the introduction of a test which goes further than testing merely objective knowledge. Whether the new integration examination is an example of 'repressive liberalism' will be discussed in paragraph 2.3.1. Lastly, the Commission mentioned that integrated citizens are required to be active in societal life in one way or another. The Commission mentioned voluntary activities at a community centre, in a sports club or as a member of the school board as examples.[19] This last aspect of integration can be described as neo-republican because of its focus on participation.

2.2.2 *Encouraging Community Cohesion: The Debate in the United Kingdom*

2.2.2.1 *The Nationality, Immigration and Asylum Bill*

The discussions regarding a stricter language and integration requirement for naturalisation in the United Kingdom started on 12 April 2002, when the Nationality, Immigration and Asylum Bill was introduced in the House of Commons. Although nationality is mentioned first in the Bill's title, 89% of the text concerns immigration and asylum. As a result, the parliamentary debates rarely touched upon the nationality provisions (Dummett 2006: 574). The Bill contained a proposal to add as a requirement for naturalisation 'sufficient knowledge of life in the UK' to the British Nationality Act (BNA) 1981 and a proposal to draw up regulations to determine whether a person has sufficient knowledge of English, Welsh or Scottish Gaelic. Knowledge of one of these languages was already a requirement for naturalisation under the BNA 1981 for all applicants for naturalisation, other than spouses. The language test consisted of an interview with a police officer. If the naturalisation applicant and the police officer could understand each other, all was well (Dummett 2006: 571). The requirement was not applied strictly in practice (Hansen 2001: 82).

The Bill was drafted to implement the proposals contained in the government White Paper, *Secure Borders, Safe Haven* dated February 2002 (Home Office 2002), which aimed to offer a response to the riots which took place in three northern English towns in the summer of 2001. According to the White Paper, these could be ascribed to the 'lacking [of] a sense of common values or shared civic identity to unite around' (Home Office 2002: 10). Knowledge of British life and language could support the objective of

[19] *Advice Franssen Commission*, p. 11. The Commission also mentions the fact that immigrants feel at home in their new society as a requirement for integration.

developing a sense of civic identity and shared values (Home Office 2002: 32). Hence, the White Paper announced that specific evidence of knowledge of the language was to be required for naturalisation in all cases (Ryan 2008: 303).[20] The language requirement would be extended to spouses to ensure that everyone in British society could take a full and active part in society (Home Office 2003: 34). Furthermore, 'light touch education for citizenship for those making a home in the UK, with a view to an examination for citizenship applicants' would also be required.

The new integration requirements were not only meant to strengthen the sense of community belonging, which can be considered a communitarian argument for amending the naturalisation provisions, but also to allow immigrants to take their full place in society. Furthermore, having knowledge of life and language in the UK would help people better understand their rights and duties. Lastly, the new requirements would promote the individual's economic and social integration (Home Office 2002: 11). The latter arguments can be described as emancipatory liberal.

The government stressed that it had no wish to discourage naturalisation and that immigrants were not required to give up their own identity: 'British society is based on cultural difference, rather than assimilation to a prevailing monoculture' (Home Office 2002:10). It is doubtful whether this statement is consistent with the proposals for a citizenship ceremony and a pledge, contained in the Bill. By making this statement, however, the government explicitly rejected a communitarian understanding of citizenship.

2.2.2.2 *The Nationality, Immigration and Asylum Bill in Parliament*

On 24 April 2002, the House of Commons discussed the bill. Several MPs feared that the requirement of having 'sufficient knowledge about Life in the United Kingdom' was too broadly formulated. In Standing Committee on 30 April, amendments were put forward to explore what 'sufficient knowledge' of life in the UK means. Conservative MP Humfrey Malins asked for a requirement concerning a 'basic' knowledge of the history and government of the UK. The Immigration Advisory Service put forward an amendment to require sufficient knowledge of 'political, civic and multicultural' life in the UK, since it deemed that demanding mere knowledge of 'life in the UK' would leave this aspect open to wide interpretation.[21]

[20] *Secure Borders, Safe Haven*, paragraph 2.13.

[21] The Immigration Advisory Service (IAS) is the UK's largest charity, providing representation and advice in immigration and asylum law, www.iasuk.org, site visited on 28 April 2009.

Several MPs stated that the test should, in practice, not form a barrier to naturalisation. According to Liberal Democrat MP Simon Hughes, conventional tests are inappropriate for some people. He feared the requirement would act as a barrier to citizenship.[22] These arguments can clearly be categorised under the liberal model, which views naturalisation as a right for permanent residents, which should not be blocked by integration requirements. We will see that passing a conventional citizenship test would eventually not be the only way to fulfil the British knowledge requirements.

In the House of Lords, the vagueness of the new Life in the UK requirement also gave rise to concerns. The parliamentary Under-Secretary of State for the Home Office alleviated concerns by stating that expert advice will be taken on what an applicant should be expected to know. The Home Secretary had asked Sir Bernard Crick to chair an advisory group of external experts. The Under-Secretary acknowledged the fact that the word 'sufficient' was imprecise and that it might imply a more onerous requirement than the Government intended.[23]

The Bill received Royal Assent on 7 November 2002. The different sections of the Act had different effective dates. From 28 July 2004, the standard of knowledge of English that applicants for naturalisation need has been defined as ESOL (English for Speakers of Other Languages) Entry 3. This level corresponds to level B1 of the Common European Framework of Reference, which is the lowest stage of the 'independent user' level.[24] The requirement of sufficient knowledge of Life in the UK entered into force in November 2005.

2.2.2.3 *The New and the Old*

In September 2003, the independent 'Life in the United Kingdom' advisory group published its report, 'The New and the Old', containing advice on how the provisions of the Nationality, Immigration and Asylum Act concerning knowledge of life in the UK and of the English language should be implemented (Home Office 2003). The advisory group saw its work as falling within the broader policy aim of the government to encourage community cohesion. The communitarian idea that enhancing knowledge of society and language will create a sense of shared civic identity is still upheld (Home Office 2003: 8).

---

[22] House of Commons Standing Committee E, Column 024.

[23] House of Lords, 8 July 2002, Column 453.

[24] For an overview of the levels of language proficiency in the Council of Europe's Common Framework of Reference, please see annex 1.

According to the report, the variation in the application of the language requirement called for a stricter application of the requirement. Furthermore, the Crick group saw the common use of English as the most important means of creating a common identity. The group advised that assessments of language skills should demonstrate progress which has been made from the applicant's starting point, rather than aiming for a uniform level of command of English for all applicants. Those applicants who already had sound English language skills at ESOL Entry 3 level (B1) would only have to take a citizenship assessment. This would also apply to the 'Knowledge of Life in the UK' requirement.

The advisory group suggested publishing a free handbook. People who already possess a sufficient level of English can study the handbook themselves, after which a short written test has to be taken. The expert group recommended that everyone should be able to pass the test and that free tuition and assessments should be offered. These recommendations can be categorised under the liberal model. As regards the content of the handbook, the advisory group thought future British citizens should be equipped with the knowledge needed to participate actively, that is knowledge relevant to the everyday problems of settling in and practical information about UK society and civic structures (Home Office 2003: 10). However, when defining what it means to be British, the advisory group went further: to be British, for instance, also means respecting the laws, values, beliefs and traditions of the country and pledging allegiance to the state (Home Office 2003: 11). Furthermore, in order to 'create a sense of Britishness' some knowledge of the history of the UK should be included in the curriculum. These recommendations speak in favour of a more communitarian view of citizenship.

2.2.2.4 *Sufficient knowledge of life and language in the UK*

The government accepted most of the Crick recommendations.[25] The requirement that sufficient knowledge of life in the UK be demonstrated eventually entered into force on 1 November 2005. As of that date, in order to fulfil the knowledge requirements, naturalisation applicants can either sit the 'Life in the UK test', developed by the commercial agency Ufi (University for Industry) on the basis of a handbook written by members of the advisory group, or follow a language with citizenship course at an adult education centre.[26]

---

[25] Lords Hansard text for 2 February 2004, Columns WS13 and WS14.

[26] The knowledge requirements are considered fulfilled when a course participant shows that reasonable progress has been made, which is assumed if he has progressed by one ESOL level. Those with no workable English need to acquire at least a basic level of competence.

To ensure that those with a long-term future in the UK have the right skills to fully participate in the community, it has been decided that, as of 2 April 2007, immigrants who apply for indefinite leave to remain (ILR) have to pass the Life in the UK test as well. They do not have to fulfil the knowledge requirements again when applying for naturalisation.[27]

At the beginning of 2008, official figures showed that more than 13,000 immigrants per month succeeded in passing the 'Britishness test'.[28] In response, Conservative MP James Clappison stated that '[p]eople who come here should integrate into our society, so I welcome the fact that people are learning about our country. [...] But I continue to have concerns about the volume of migration, and the strains which this is placing on public services. I personally also think it would be worthwhile for people to have to learn something about British history.' The high success rate hence led to the desire to increase the difficulty of the test.

2.2.2.5 *Path to citizenship*

In February 2008, the British government published a Green Paper entitled *The Path to Citizenship: Next Steps in Reforming the Immigration System*, in which it announced changes in the immigration system (Home Office 2008a). Routes to naturalisation should be provided for highly skilled and skilled workers, family members and refugees. By offering the right to citizenship to those 'with the skills and the talents, the assets and ideas that we need to remain one of the world's leading nations' (Home Office 2008a: 6) and to two categories of immigrant who cannot be denied access to British territory on the basis of international obligations, it became apparent that the British Government only intended to accept as full members those immigrants who would contribute (economically) to British society. Since in the future, the British Government aims to select immigrants on the basis of the benefits British society will gain by accepting them as citizens, libertarian ideas of citizenship started to influence the British Government's policy on immigration and naturalisation. In order to achieve this aim, the Government intended to introduce the concept of 'earned citizenship': in future, immigrants would need to show they merit the benefits of citizenship by learning the language, paying taxes and becoming self-sufficient, obeying the

---

[27] This does not mean that the requirements are redundant at the naturalisation stage (Ryan 2008: 305). Persons who have been exempt from fulfilling the requirements when applying for ILR, EEA and Swiss nationals and those who acquired ILR before April 2007 will still have to fulfil the requirements when applying for naturalisation.

[28] 'The test that's letting in one migrant every three minutes', *Daily Mail*, 22 January 2008.

law and participating in the British way of life by playing an active part in the community (Home Office 2008a: 7).[29]

The government's libertarian proposals in 'The Path to Citizenship' were confirmed in the Borders, Citizenship and Immigration Bill, which was sent to in Parliament in January 2009. The Bill introduced 'active citizenship' as a new test for citizenship by shortening the residence requirement for naturalisation for those immigrants who have showed to have been active participants in UK life.[30] The libertarian concept of citizenship furthermore becomes apparent from the introduction of an economic naturalisation requirement: in order to qualify for naturalisation, immigrants who have come to the UK for work purposes will be required to have been employed until the application for naturalisation.[31]

Traces of other citizenship concepts can, however, also be found in the latest government proposals relating to naturalisation. Firstly, by focusing on 'participating in the British way of life by playing an active part in the community', earned citizenship could also be seen as a neo-republican concept.

The reform of immigration and naturalisation policy is also defended with communitarian arguments, since the Green Paper states that:

> We need to work harder to strengthen the things – the values, the habits, the qualities – that we have in common, and thereby strengthen our communities. (Home Office 2008a: 12)

---

[29] As examples of 'active citizenship', the Government mentions volunteering within a recognised organisation, fund-raising activities for charities or schools and running or helping to run a playgroup which encourages the different communities to interact (Home Office 2008a: 29–30).

[30] Proposed amendment to paragraph 4a of Schedule 1 of the British Nationality Act 1981, clause 39 of the *Borders, Citizenship and Immigration Bill*. In *The Path to Citizenship*, the Government mentions volunteering within a recognised organisation, fund-raising activities for charities or schools and running or helping to run a playgroup which encourages the different communities to interact as examples of 'active citizenship' (Home Office 2008a: 29–30). From the Borders, Citizenship and Immigration Bill, it becomes apparent that payment is inconsistent with active citizenship (Ryan 2008: 308).

[31] Proposed amendment to paragraph 4a of Schedule 1 of the British Nationality Act 1981, clause 37 of the *Borders, Citizenship and Immigration Bill*. Probationary citizenship is a new category of legal residence. Together with the equally new stage of 'permanent residence', probationary citizenship will replace the Indefinite Leave to remain stage.

The promotion of these 'things' implies convergence in outlook and behaviour and, hence, confirms the government's communitarian understanding of citizenship.[32]

The Borders, Citizenship and Immigration Act was given Royal Assent on 21 July 2009. It is expected that the sections giving effect to earned citizenship will be introduced in July 2011.[33]

2.2.3 *Failed Liberalisation: The German Debate*

2.2.3.1 *A Red-Green proposal for reform*

In Germany, the debates regarding the reinforcement of the integration requirements for naturalisation started in the late nineteen-nineties, when a new coalition government between the Social Democratic Party (SPD) and the Greens (Bündnis 90/Die Grünen) replaced the long-time governing coalition of Christian Democrats (CDU/CSU) and Liberal Democrats (FDP), following the federal elections of September 1998. The new coalition envisaged fundamental German citizenship law reform as one of its most important reform projects (Gerdes, Faist & Rieple 2007: 46). To this end, the coalition, supported by the FDP, presented a Bill for reform of nationality law to the German *Bundestag* on 16 March 1999.[34] This Bill proposed an extension of the exception clauses to the requirement relating to renouncing one's original nationality upon naturalisation and birth right citizenship for children born on German territory, if at least one of the parents had lawful habitual residence in Germany for at least eight years and if he or she had been in possession of a permanent residence permit for at least three years.[35] The Bill

---

[32] See also the response to the Government consultation by the Migration and Law Network: http://www.kent.ac.uk/law/migration/documents/Path%20to%20Citizenship.doc, site visited on 3 April 2009.

[33] http://www.ukba.homeoffice.gov.uk/sitecontent/newsarticles/2009/september/transitional-arrangements-earned?area=Citizenship.

[34] *Entwurf eines Gesetzes zur Reform des Staatsangehörigkeitsrechts*, Bundestag Drucksache (BT-DS) 14/533.

[35] An earlier proposal for a law reform proposed the full acceptance of dual nationality and automatic acquisition of German nationality for children of non-German parents in cases where at least one of the parents had immigrated to Germany before the age of 14. These proposals were fiercely opposed by the Christian Democratic CDU/CSU. After the coalition lost the majority in the *Bundesrat* (the upper house of Parliament) following the elections in the *Land* of Hesse, it was forced to amend the Bill to gain support from the FDP. For more detailed information see: Green 2004: 95–103 and Gerdes, Faist & Rieple 2007: 46.

furthermore reduced the residence requirement for ordinary naturalisation (Article 85 Residence Act) from fifteen years to eight years.

According to the explanatory memorandum, the Bill pursued two aims; firstly, to increase the number of naturalisations of the large number of permanent residents in Germany. The drafters of the Bill viewed congruence of residents (*Wohnbevölkerung*) and citizens (*Wahlbevölkerung*) as a precondition for democracy. The second goal was to improve the integration of immigrants living permanently in Germany and of their German-born children, by facilitating access to German nationality.[36] Nationality law should hence be used as a means of pursuing an integration policy.[37] According to the memorandum of the Bill, integration implied acquiring knowledge of the German language, which opened up the possibility of participating in the process of political democratic opinion-forming. A lack of 'sufficient' knowledge of the German language was presented as a reason for denying a naturalisation application. Furthermore, applicants needed to have an 'inner leaning towards the Federal Republic of Germany', to be documented by the acceptance of the free and democratic basic order and a declaration of loyalty.[38] The new Bill thus put an 'integration price tag' on the liberalisations it offered (Hartnell 2006: 391).

The drafters of the Bill were guided by both republican concepts – facilitating access to nationality in order to increase the number of people able to participate in the political process and making sure they master the language so they can effectively exercise their new political rights – and by egalitarian-liberal concepts of citizenship – giving permanent residents equal rights in order to improve their integration. At the same time, requiring future citizens to have an inner leaning towards Germany reflects a communitarian concept of citizenship.

2.2.3.2 *Discussion of the coalition Bill in Parliament*

During the discussions in Parliament, most of the attention was devoted to the issues of birthright citizenship and dual nationality, since these were the most controversial. Far less attention was therefore paid to the introduction of the requirement relating to possession of a sufficient command of the German language.

---

36 BT-DS 14/533, p. 2.

37 BT-DS 14/533, p. 10.

38 BT-DS 14/533, p. 18. As before, an applicant for naturalisation may not depend on social assistance, unless the applicant is not responsible for this dependence (Gerdes et al. 2007: 47).

At its first reading left-wing PDS (Democratic Socialist Party) and CDU/CSU MPs criticised the Bill by putting forward liberal and communitarian arguments respectively. The PDS MPs feared that the vagueness of the language requirement would open the door to arbitrariness and would place an excessive burden on elderly immigrants, for whom the ability to express themselves in a simple way should suffice.[39] Green MP Cem Özdemir (Bündnis 90/Die Grünen) agreed with the PDS group that the language requirement will introduce a new hurdle but, in defence, he suggested that requiring people to know the language used by the official authorities (*Amtssprache*) is intended to protect rather than to frustrate them. Furthermore:

> Anyone who does not master the official language will never experience what is understood by an employee council, a trade union or consumer protection.[40]

This remark by Özdemir can be described as a stance of emancipatory liberalism: making immigrants independent and autonomous individuals by forcing them to learn the language.

PDS MP Ulla Jelpke criticised the introduction of a paragraph requiring an oath to the free and democratic basic order by qualifying it as an opportunity to poke one's nose into someone's convictions (*Gesinnungsschnüffelei*).[41] Furthermore, the PDS did not understand why applicants for naturalisation need to sign a declaration of loyalty, while those who receive German nationality at birth are not required to do so. Guido Westerwelle (FDP) disagreed with the PDS MPs by showing a communitarian idea of citizenship, when he stated that anyone wishing to obtain German nationality via naturalisation needed declare loyalty to Germany, because:

> the German passport is not just a paper, which one can additionally accept, but requires a conscious shift towards German society.[42]

Unlike the PDS MPs, the CDU/CSU politicians criticised the Bill for not requiring enough of an immigrant's integration and for giving away 'naturalisation for free' (*Einbürgerung zum Nultarif*). In a counter proposal, they stated that naturalisation is the expression of successful integration and socialisation in Germany and that only those immigrants who have obviously adapted to the German way of life can become German via naturali-

[39] Amendments put forward by the PDS, aimed at removal from the Bill of the declaration of loyalty (BT DS 14/992) and the language requirement (BT DS 14/993), were rejected.

[40] Plenarprotokoll (Plepro; Minutes of the plenary session) 14/40, 3431 (C).

[41] Plepro 14/28, p. 2296.

[42] Plepro 14/40, 3436 (C).

sation. Alongside knowledge of the German language, they required future German citizens to have knowledge of the constitutional order of the Federal Republic of Germany.[43]

Otto Schily, SPD Minister for the Interior, and several Green MPs defended the bill by putting forward the liberal argument that changing the nationality law is required by democracy, which requires giving immigrants who have been living in Germany for a long time and who will continue to live in Germany equal rights and obligations. Green MPs furthermore pointed out that future German citizens are not required to give up their identity. According to Özdemir (Bündnis 90/Die Grünen):

> To us, a German citizen is not someone who, as it were, has had a blood transfusion. To us, a German citizen is not someone who has certain habits regarding music, clothing or food, or has adopted other habits as his own.[44]

Hence, the Green MPs opposed a communitarian concept of citizenship. At the same time, Özdemir required future Germans to obey the liberal values of the German Constitution:

> To us, a German citizen is someone who belongs to this society, who supports the Constitution of this country and who shares the values of this society with us, values such as the equal treatment of men and women. We do not make any exceptions in this matter. [...] Anyone who lives here must accept the right to the inviolability of the human body and all the principles of our Constitution.[45]

While stressing the fact that immigrants, even though they were not required to give up their identity, needed to adapt to the liberal values of the Constitution, the liberal-egalitarian multicultural idea of citizenship becomes apparent.

The Bill was adopted in the *Bundestag* on 7 May 1999. Most CDU/CSU and PDS MPs voted against the Bill, while some abstained from voting.

The Bill was discussed in the *Bundesrat*, the upper house of Parliament representing the German states (*Länder*) a few weeks later.[46] In the discussion Edmund Stoiber, then President of the *Land* of Bavaria and later CSU president, stressed that, whereas naturalisation does not require a renunciation of one's original cultural nature, it should be the culmination of the

[43] BT-DS 14/535, *Entwurf eines Gesetzes zur Neuregelung des Staatsangehörigkeitsrechts (Staatsangehörigkeitsneuregelungsgesetz – StANeuG).*

[44] Plepro 14/40, 3431 (B).

[45] Plepro 14/40, 3431 (B).

[46] *Bundesrat*, 738th session, 21 May 1999. Bavaria votes against the Bill.

integration process. Stoiber furthermore stated that citizenship law needed to serve the goal of maintaining German identity and of integrating foreign citizens, in order to promote a *Miteinander* (a situation in which citizens live with each other) instead of a *Nebeneinander* (a situation in which citizens live alongside each other). According to the CSU politician, nationality law is of great importance for the identity and cohesion of German society, established by a common history, culture and coherence of nation and homeland (*Heimat*). A conscious feeling of belonging together lies at the basis of the inner peace in Germany and the systems of social security. Since citizenship is the expression of this 'belonging together', it cannot be the object of arbitrariness. When making his remarks, Stoiber clearly had a communitarian idea of citizenship in mind.

With the *Land* of Bavaria abstaining from voting, the *Bundesrat* adopted the Bill. The new, reformed Citizenship Act (*Staatsangehörigkeitsgesetz*) came into force on 1 January 2000.

2.2.3.3 *The debates surrounding the Immigration Act*

Roughly three years after the entry into force of the reformed Citizenship Act, the government put forward a proposal for an Immigration Act (*Zuwanderungsgesetz*), which envisaged minor changes to nationality law.[47]

One of the major features of the Immigration Act has been the emphasis upon integration requirements (Hailbronner 2006: 225). The discussion surrounding the adoption of the Immigration Act has taken the requirement relating to knowledge of the German language out of the context of naturalisation: knowledge of the language became the 'key to integration' in general. Many MPs hoped that knowledge of the German language would hinder the creation of 'parallel societies' (*Parallelgesellschaften*, Davy 2008: 34).

Following the integrative goals of the new Immigration Act, which entered into force on 1 January 2005, the requirement relating to having 'basic knowledge of the legal and social order and the living conditions in Germany' was introduced as a condition for obtaining a permanent residence permit.[48] The requirement to have a 'basic' and subsequently 'sufficient' command of the German language already applied since 1978. In 2005, the requirement to have 'sufficient' command of the German language was laid down in the Residence Act.[49] Hence, immigrants who wish to obtain permanent residence are required to attend an integration course (*Integrationskurs*), consisting

[47] 7 February 2003, BT-DS 15/420, p. 115.
[48] Residence Act (*Aufenthaltsgesetz*) Article 9, paragraph 2, number 8.
[49] Residence Act Article 9, Paragraph 2, number 7.

of 600 hours of language tuition and 30 hours of civic education, called an 'Orientation Course' (*Orientierungskurs*).[50] The successful attendance of an integration course, defined as reaching level B1, reduced the required time of lawful residence for naturalisation from 8 to 7 years (Hailbronner 2006: 225). Research has shown that, in the early years, only between 38% and 53% of participants reached level B1 (Rambøll (2006: 34; 54–55) and that these were mainly more highly qualified migrants (Rambøll, 2006: 57).[51]

2.2.3.4 *Introducing citizenship tests in certain* Länder

Starting in 2006, Baden-Württemberg introduced and Hesse proposed introducing formalised tests based on the requirement of acceptance of the free and democratic basic order of the Constitution. Both *Länder* deemed the declaration of loyalty insufficient for determining the applicant's inner leanings (*innere Hinwendung*) towards the German state and society, as required by the Nationality Act.

On 1 January 2006, the *Land* of Baden-Württemberg introduced a controversial formalised integration test in the form of an interview guide (*Gesprächsleitfaden*). The interview guide consists of 30 questions. Examples of questions are:

- What is your attitude towards criticising a religion? Do you think that is permissible?;
- What do you think about the statement that a woman should obey her husband and that her husband is allowed to beat her if she is disobedient?; and
- What is your opinion of forced marriages? Do you think such marriages are compatible with human dignity?

[50] Since January 2008, immigrants who need more extensive training can take 900 hours of language education. The number of hours dedicated to civic education increased from 30 to 45 hours. Furthermore, a permanent residence permit can only be obtained by those immigrants who have participated successfully in the integration course, in other words those who pass a language test at level B1 and who pass the test at the end of the civic education course. See Michalowski's chapter in this book for more information regarding the requirements for permanent residence.

[51] Due to the fact that taking the language test at the end of the course remained optional until January 2008, a precise evaluation of the numbers is difficult. Owing to the mechanism of self-selection, 70.8% of all test candidates passed the test, whereas only between 38% and 53% of all participants who finished the programme reached level B1 (see Michalowski in this volume).

If the answers given by the applicant are not in line with the German values addressed in the test questions, the application will be denied. The test, which was soon labelled the 'Muslim test', was heavily criticised both in the press and in the *Bundestag*, especially for its focus on immigrants with an Islamic background.[52]

Since the test employed in Baden-Württemberg examines whether an applicant for naturalisation has the right convictions and values to become a German citizen, it can be classified as a stance of repressive liberalism.[53]

At the initiative of the CDU Minister of the Interior, Volker Bouffier, the *Land* of Hesse proposed introducing a naturalisation test in March 2006, based on a test bank consisting of 100 questions. In addition to questions to check an applicant's acceptance of German liberal values (*Werte*), this test also contained questions regarding the applicant's knowledge (*Wissen*) of the German constitution, history and society, the German political, legal and social order, as well as culture, science and sports in the Federal Republic.[54] In Bouffier's opinion, 'Only those persons who know how the state and the society operate can understand, judge and accept its values'.[55]

The *Wissen* part of the test clearly fits in with the communitarian model for it demands a very detailed knowledge of a whole range of topics, including German history and geography. The *Werte* part of the test can, like the interview guide in Baden-Wüttemberg, be qualified as a stance of repressive liberalism, for it seeks to question a test candidate's inner motivations.

The test developed by Hesse was never put into practice, but merely served as a basis for discussion at the Conference of Senators and Ministers of the Interior (*Innenministerkonferenz, IMK*) which took place in May 2006 and

---

[52] See for instance 'Deutschland: Streit um Einbürgerungsleitfaden', *Migration und Bevölkerung*, Ausgabe 1, February 2006.

[53] See also the contribution by Ines Michalowski in this volume.

[54] *Leitfaden Wissen & Werte in Deutschland und Europa*, Hessisches Ministerium des Innern und für Sport, 14 March 2006. Examples of questions are: 'The German painter Caspar David Friedrich depicted, in one of his most famous paintings, a portrait of Rügen, an island in the Ostsee. What is shown on this painting?' and 'Please name three German low mountain ranges'.

[55] See *Innenminister Bouffier legt Konzept für Einbürgerung vor, 'Wissens- und Wertetest' soll für alle Bewerber Pflicht werden'*, [Minister for the Interior Bouffier presents concept for naturalisation, 'Knowledge and values test' shall be required of all applicants], press release of the Ministry of the Interior of Hesse of 14 March 2006; *Einbürgerungstest-Fragenkatalog in Hessen*, Innenminister Bouffier, www.migrationsrecht.net, 16 March 2006, visited on 2 September 2008.

during which the topic of uniform naturalisation requirements was to be addressed.[56]

2.2.3.5 *Testing integration: the proposals of the* Länder

One of the main purposes of the IMK of 4 and 5 May 2006 was to formulate uniform requirements for naturalisation, in order to prevent 'naturalisation tourism': avoiding the strict naturalisation policy in the *Land* of residence by applying for naturalisation in a more liberal *Land*.[57] The language requirement, for instance, was not applied uniformly in practice. Although the application instructions stipulated that an applicant for naturalisation, as well as the ability to hold a conversation in daily life and with the authorities, taking one's age and level of education into account, also needed to be able to read and understand a German text on everyday matters, some *Länder* also required writing skills (Renner 2002).[58] Knowledge of language was normally tested in an interview between the applicant and an official of the municipal foreigner's office but, in some *Länder*, language skills were tested at an adult education centre (*Volkshochschule*).

In the future, naturalisation applicants were to be required to have both an oral and a written command of the German language at level B1 of the Common European Framework of Reference. It was furthermore decided that all *Länder* would, under their own responsibility, offer those interested in acquiring German citizenship a naturalisation course, in which basic civic knowledge as well as the basic principles and values of the German constitution would be taught.

Until the last day of the conference, the participants argued about the organisation of the naturalisation courses. Whereas certain SPD-led *Länder* objected to an extensive knowledge and values test following the examples of Hesse and Baden-Württemberg, the CDU/CSU-administered *Länder*

---

[56] *Innenminister Bouffier legt Konzept für Einbürgerung vor, 'Wissens- und Wertetest' soll für alle Bewerber Pflicht werden'*, press release of the Ministry of the Interior of Hesse of 14 March 2006. See also 'Einbürgerungstest: Hessen will Einigung für ganz Deutschland' [Naturalisation test: Hesse wants unity for all of Germany], *Frankfurter Rundschau*, 4 May 2006 and 'Hessen will bundesweiten Fragenkatalog', *Spiegel Online*, www.spiegel.de, 14 March 2006.

[57] Due to Germany's federal structure, the *Länder* are left to implement the Nationality Act. This has led to different naturalisation practices in the *Länder* and, consequently, substantially different naturalisation percentages and procedures (See Dornis 2001, Tränhardt 2008).

[58] Temporary Application Instructions (*Vorläufige Anwendungshinweise*) of December 2004, No. 11.1.1.1.

maintained that mere participation in a naturalisation course would not suffice for the acquisition of German citizenship.[59] Eventually it was unanimously decided that an obligatory naturalisation test would not be introduced and that the test could take place orally or in writing, or in another form, such as role-play.[60]

A Bill regarding the amendment of the Nationality Act, incorporating the decisions made during the conference of May 2006, was adopted in the *Bundesrat* in March 2007.[61] The aim of the Bill was to ensure that only those persons who are integrated and who endorse the German social and legal order become naturalised.[62] Naturalisation can therefore only be the culmination (*Schlussstein*) of successful integration.

By introducing a civic knowledge test, increasing the level of language required, and by labelling naturalisation as the culmination of an integration process, the *Bundesrat* favoured a communitarian concept of citizenship.

2.2.3.6 *Testing integration: the government proposals*

On 23 April 2007, the government, consisting of CDU/CSU and SPD as of November 2005, introduced a Bill for the implementation of eleven EU Directives on asylum and migration (*Richtlinienumsetzungsgesetz*).[63] The implementation of the EU Directives did not require an amendment of the nationality law, since nationality law is still an area for the exclusive competence of the EU Member States. However, in its Article 5, important amendments to the provisions of the Nationality Act were proposed.

During the parliamentary debates, relatively little attention was paid to the proposed amendments to the nationality law, since the focus was on important changes to the Residence Act. For this reason, Berlit has criticised the law implementing the EU Directives for being merely a mantle that veils heterogeneous changes to nationality law. In the wake of the regulations that require implementation and numerous controversial themes, changes to

---

[59] See 'Innenminister einigen sich nicht auf Einbürgerungstest', *Hamburger Abendblatt*, 2 May 2006, 'Noch mehr Hürden; SPD gibt nach: Einbürgerungswillige müssen künftig eine Prüfung zur Staatsbürgerkunde ablegen', *Die Tageszeitung*, 6 May 2006 and 'Einbürgerung; Testfrage Integration; Nach kurzem Wahlkampf-Streit suchen Union und SPD einen Kompromiss bei der Prüfung von Neubürgern', *FOCUS*, 13/2006, and 'Kompromiss beim Einbürgerungstest', *Frankfurter Allgemeine Zeitung*, 7 May 2006.

[60] 'Innenministerkonferenz einigt sich auf Einbürgerungsverfahren', *REGIERUNGonline* (www. bundesregierung.de), 5 May 2006, site visited on 7 March 2008. See also 'Kompromiss beim Einbürgerungstest', *Frankfurter Allgemeine Zeitung*, 7 May 2006.

[61] Bundesrat Druchsache 137/07(B).

[62] BT-DS 16/5107, p. 1.

[63] BT-DS 16/5065.

the nationality law will be accepted, which would have less chance of being adopted if discussed separately (Berlit 2007: 457).

In the explanatory memorandum to the Bill, the government stated that the proposals for an amendment of the Nationality Act were based on the decisions reached at the IMK.[64] By choosing level B1 as the required level of language skills, the government aimed to tie in with the knowledge of language required for a permanent residence permit, which is also B1. According to the Government, the required knowledge for obtaining German nationality cannot be lower than the level required for permanent residence.[65] The new language requirement would also apply to spouses of German nationals, who were previously required only to be able to 'express themselves in daily life without experiencing considerable difficulty'.[66]

The government Bill furthermore requires applicants for naturalisation to have 'knowledge of the legal and social order and of living conditions in Germany'. By requiring 'knowledge', rather than 'basic knowledge', which is required for obtaining a permanent residence permit, the gradual intensification of integration policy is observed.[67] An applicant for naturalisation would need to prove this knowledge by producing a certificate of successful participation in a naturalisation test.[68] By way of preparation, naturalisation courses will be offered, participation in which is not compulsory. The government proposal therefore goes further than the proposal decided upon by the Interior Ministers in May 2006, which provided the possibility for the *Länder* to choose how they would test whether a naturalisation applicant had acquired the required knowledge. The Bill empowered the Ministry of the Interior to regulate the naturalisation test and the structure and content of the course in a Decree, which does not require the prior consent of the *Bundesrat*.

During the discussions in the *Bundestag*,[69] MPs from the Left Party (*Die Linke*), the FDP, as well as several SPD MPs, criticised the tightening of the conditions for naturalisation. According to the Left Party, the 'numerous stricter measures' in nationality law are not required by the EU Directives the Bill is supposed to implement and will only have the effect of excluding

64 BT-DS 16/5065, p. 155.

65 BT-DS 16/5107, p. 13.

66 Temporary Application Instructions (*Vorläufige Anwendungshinweise*) of December 2004, No. 9.1.2.1.

67 BT-DS 16/5065, p. 227.

68 But the required knowledge can also be demonstrated in another way, such as via equivalent German schooling. BT-DS 16/5065, p. 229.

69 Plepro 16/103, 103rd Session of the *Bundestag*.

people further from democratic involvement through voting.[70] The FDP opposed a test of civic skills, which would especially deter older foreigners from submitting an application for naturalisation and proposes deleting the reference to level B1. In opposing the exclusionary effects of the tightening up of nationality law, the Green and FDP MPs show that they favour a liberal concept of citizenship.

Liberal ideas regarding citizenship also become apparent from declarations made by SPD MPs, who believe that the tightening up of the conditions for naturalisation is counterproductive from an integration perspective. Naturalisation is a condition for and an important milestone in the integration process and should not appear at the end of this process. These MPs did not understand why new hurdles for naturalisation were introduced, despite the numbers of naturalisations returning to their pre-1999 level.[71]

The Law implementing EU Directives on asylum and migration entered into force on 19 August 2007, with the requirement of knowledge of the legal and social order and of the living conditions in Germany entering into force on 1 September 2008.[72] In cases where the naturalisation applicant has fulfilled special integration achievements, the residence requirement may be reduced to six years. In the application instructions (*Anwendungshinweise*), the possession of language skills *exceeding* level B2 of the CEF qualifies as a 'special integration achievement'. The instructions furthermore refer to long-term activity as a volunteer in a non-profit organisation. Requiring persons to be active in the social life of the community can best be categorised under the republican concept of citizenship.[73] It does however also fit the libertarian model, which requires citizens to contribute to the well-being of society.

In order for the test to remain 'beyond the scope of any criticism', the German government gave the Institute for Quality Development in Education (IQB) of the Humboldt University Berlin the task of preparing a questionnaire.[74] A proposal from MPs of Bündnis 90/Die Grünen entitled 'Involving Parliament in the Development of the Naturalisation Test', in which

[70] BT-DS 16/5634, pp. 3–4. See also Plepro 16/103, 10592 (A). The fact that the proposals concerning nationality law do not serve the purpose of implementing an EU Directive and hence did not form part of the negotiations that took place before the start of the legislative procedure was also criticised in the *Bundesrat* (Bundesrat Drucksache 15/5527, p. 12).

[71] Plepro 16/103, p. 10640 ff.

[72] Gesetz zur Umsetzung aufenthalts- und asylrechtlicher Richtlinien der Europäischen Union vom 19. August 2007 (*BGBl.* 2007, Part I, No. 42).

[73] Temporary Application Instructions (*Vorläufige Anwendungshinweise*) of 10 December 2004, No. 10.3.1.

[74] Peter Altmaier, parliamentary secretary for the Ministry of the Interior, in answer to a question from MP Keskin (Die Linke), Plepro 16/168, p. 17796 (C).

they recommended that Parliament not vote on a decree for the execution of the naturalisation test without prior approval from the parliament, was rejected.[75]

2.2.4 *Conclusions*

In this section, the Parliamentary debates in the Netherlands, the UK and Germany on the introduction of a citizenship test are described, starting from the moment when introducing stricter language and integration requirements for naturalisation was first proposed. We have seen that, in all three countries, the changes proposed to the language and integration requirements have always been overshadowed by changes that were considered more important: the abolition of the renunciation requirement in the Netherlands and Germany, and changes to the immigration law in the UK and Germany.

As we have seen, arguments that can be described within each of the citizenship concepts have been used by MPs in the discussions regarding the reinforcement/introduction of language and knowledge of society requirements. Generally, proponents of more demanding ways of testing integration put forward arguments derived from a communitarian or republican understanding of citizenship: only those sharing the values and ways of life of the majority community or who are able to participate in the life of the democracy should be allowed to obtain full membership. Reinforcing the requirements to acquire nationality, however, is also defended by using libertarian arguments: by having knowledge of the language and ways of life, future citizens are more likely to contribute to the (economic) well-being of the host society. Those opposing to more demanding ways of integration testing, on the other hand, apply a liberal understanding of citizenship: access to nationality is seen as a right for long-term residents and acquiring the nationality of the country of residence as a means for integration.

Before the introduction of the citizenship tests, Germany, the Netherlands and the UK favoured a liberal understanding of citizenship, since in all three countries naturalisation was seen as a step in the integration process. Originally, the idea behind the reforms of the nationality law in the Netherlands in 1992 and Germany in 1999 was to facilitate access to nationality. In Germany, facilitating access to German nationality was also defended using a republican argument: this would increase the number of persons able to participate in the democratic process. Furthermore, in Germany, a republican argument was used in order to introduce a language requirement: this would enable

75 18 June 2008, BT-DS 16/9602.

people to take part in the process of political decision-making. The idea of tightening up the language requirement and demanding knowledge of society as a condition for naturalisation in the Netherlands was initially defended using emancipatory liberal arguments: such knowledge would enable people to make better use of their rights and obligations.

In the meantime, all three countries have witnessed a shift away from the liberal citizenship concept towards republicanism and communitarianism. Opponents of liberalisation in both the Netherlands and Germany formulated communitarian arguments in order to reinforce the conditions for obtaining nationality. In the Netherlands, applicants for naturalisation needed to 'feel' Dutch and to 'be proud of' Dutch citizenship. In Germany, the proponents of the test required future Germans to have adapted to the German way of life. In both the Netherlands and Germany, the proponents of the test clearly saw naturalisation as the culmination (*Schlussstein* or 'first prize') of complete integration, not as a step in the integration process.

In the UK, the importance of community cohesion, which needed to be promoted by encouraging a sense of common values and shared citizenship, was the most important reason for introducing the knowledge requirements in the Nationality, Immigration and Asylum Bill in 2002. Concerns about community cohesion also played a role in Germany. The latest reform of the German nationality law aims to accept as citizens only those who are integrated and who endorse the German social and political order.

With the increased focus on the importance of an immigrant's active participation, it becomes apparent that, lately, (neo-)republican concepts of citizenship have started to play a more important role in the debates surrounding citizenship in the countries under consideration. Since the focus is also placed on the contribution an immigrant will make to society, the libertarian citizenship concept equally applies. In recent years, we have seen that being an active, contributing citizen is increasingly being emphasised and, in the case of Germany and the UK, even rewarded. In the UK, this is all the more apparent since an economic requirement for naturalisation has been added. In Germany, such a requirement had already been in force for some time.

In the Netherlands and Germany, another, more pragmatic, reason for stricter citizenship tests was formulated. In both countries, the different application of the language requirement was a reason for formalising the requirement. In the Netherlands, this formalisation was intended to increase equality and fairness in handling the language and integration requirement. The fact that the reformulation of the language requirement eventually led to the introduction of the naturalisation test was not the intention of the drafters of the 1992 Bill. The most important reason for formalisation in Germany was the prevention of 'naturalisation tourism'. For this reason, the more liberal *Länder* had to adapt to the practice of the *Länder* that operated a stricter naturalisation policy.

In Germany and the Netherlands, before the introduction of the citizenship tests, a formalised test had already been introduced at an earlier stage in the integration process. The introduction of the citizenship tests can thus be seen as the result of a path-dependent process: once the road to presenting formalised integration tests to newcomers had been taken, it was considered logical that a test also be presented to immigrants who wanted to become citizens. In both countries, the level of the integration tests exerted upward pressure on the level of the citizenship tests. The fact that, in practice, these levels were not attained in many cases hardly played a role in the discussions.

2.3 *The different citizenship tests*

When introducing the citizenship tests, the governments of the countries under consideration explicitly claimed that these tests were not intended to hinder naturalisation or at least they did not use the use the reduction in the number of naturalisations as an argument for introducing the tests. All those applying for naturalisation should, in principle, be able to pass the test. Whether these statements are correct and whether the tests match the purpose for which they were introduced will be discussed in this section.

Table 1 presents certain characteristics of the Dutch, German and British citizenship tests.

Table 1: Citizenship tests in the Netherlands, Germany and the UK

Country	Netherlands		Germany	UK	
Citizenship test	Naturalisation test.	Integration examination (1 April 2007).	*Einbürgerungstest* and language examination.	Life in the UK test.	Language with citizenship course.
Level[76]	A2.	A2.	B1.	B1.	All levels under B1.
Possibilities for preparation	No.	Certain categories of immigrant can follow integration course.	Language and naturalisation course, handbooks and DVD published by commercial publishers, all test questions are published on the internet.	Handbook published by Government.	Not applicable.

[76] For an overview of the levels of language proficiency in the Council of Europe's Common Framework of Reference, please see annex 1.

Table 1 (*cont.*)

Country	Netherlands		Germany	UK	
Price	€260 (in case no re-examination required).	€230 (in case no re-examination required).	*Einbürgerungstest*: €50 Language examination: costs vary between €100 and €120.	£34.	Prices vary, but courses can cost up to £1200. Free for people on benefits.
Developed by	Commercial agency (ICE+CITO).	Commercial agency (ICE+CITO).	Institute of the Humboldt University Berlin (Institute for Quality Development in Education, IQB).	Commercial agency (Ufi).	Commercial agency (NIACE).
Exemption based on qualifications	Yes.	Yes (list slightly extended as opposed to list of diplomas granting exemption from naturalisation test).	Yes.	No.	No.
Exemption based on physical or mental impediment	Mentally and physically handicapped persons can be exempted. Condition needs to be proven by medical certificate.	Mentally and physically handicapped persons can be exempted. Condition needs to be proven by medical certificate.	Persons suffering from a physical or mental illness or impediment will be exempted. Handicap needs to be proven by doctor's certificate if not visible.	Persons suffering from a long-term illness or disability or a mental impairment will be exempted. Handicap needs to be proven by doctor's certificate.	Persons suffering from a long-term illness or disability or a mental impairment will be exempted. Handicap needs to be proven by doctor's certificate.
Exemption based on age	No.	No.	Yes, for persons who cannot fulfil the language and integration requirements due to their age (*altersbedingt*).	Yes, persons aged 65 or over.	Yes, persons aged 65 or over.
Illiterates	Possibility for exemption after 'feasibility investigation'.	Possibility for exemption after 'feasibility investigation'.	No reference is made to exemption for illiterates.	No possibility of exemption.	No possibility of exemption.

The level of the German knowledge tests is the highest in the countries under consideration in this chapter: level B1. Although the level of the British 'Life in the UK' test is also B1, naturalisation applicants in the UK whose knowledge of the English language is below that level can also choose to fulfil the knowledge requirements by successfully completing a language course with citizenship content.[77] Courses are offered at all different levels. Hence, the recommendation of the Crick Group has been adopted, that assessments of language skills should demonstrate progress made from the starting point of the applicant, rather than striving for a uniform level of command of English for all applicants.

There is a sharp contrast among the countries under consideration as regards the modes of preparation for the tests. Until 1 April 2007, the Dutch government did not offer any means of preparing for tests for immigrants who needed to pass the naturalisation test. According to an official from the Ministry of Justice, 'there will not be a booklet containing sample questions, as is the case for example for the driver's license, since we do not only aim at testing whether a naturalisation applicant has the right knowledge, but also whether he has the right attitude. And this cannot be learnt by heart.' (Groenendijk 2005: 30). Since the content of this test was undisclosed, publishing agencies were unable to develop preparation materials.

The replacement of the naturalisation test by the integration examination did not significantly change the situation, since the content of this examination remains undisclosed. Newcomers, meaning immigrants who arrived in the Netherlands after 1 January 2007 and who have an obligation to integrate, are now however able to follow an integration course which will prepare them for the examination.[78] Furthermore, the 'final achievement levels', a description of the content of the knowledge of society test in the integration examination, have been published.

In Germany, test candidates have the possibility of following a naturalisation course.[79] Furthermore, all 300 federal and 10 regional test questions,

---

[77] Successfully completing a language course means proceeding to the next level.

[78] These immigrants will have to pay for the courses themselves, but they can be reimbursed in the event of successful participation. Municipalities may offer to pay for the integration course for immigrants who are obliged to integrate.

[79] It should however be noted that, in January 2009, these courses had only been set up in a couple of *Länder* because of very limited demand. Hauke Friederichs 'Deutscher in drei Minuten', *Die Zeit*, 6 November 2008, no. 46–10. See Ines Michalowski's contribution in this volume.

including the multiple choice questions, are published on the internet.[80] Future candidates can take a sample test on the internet, after which they will immediately get the results and can obtain information about the correct answers.[81] Commercial publishing agencies have in the meantime published numerous learning materials in the form of books and a DVD (Hanschmann 2008: 393).

In the UK, the government published the handbook, *Life in the UK, A Journey to Citizenship*, which costs £9.99.[82] Sample test questions can be found on a web site, which enables future candidates to see whether they have sufficient knowledge to pass the test (www.lifeintheuktest.gov.uk/htmlsite/self_10.html).

Another significant difference among the tests in the countries under consideration lies in the prices of the tests. Taking the Dutch naturalisation test, in use until 1 April 2007, cost at least €260. The new integration examination is a little cheaper: €230. These prices differ significantly from those of the German *Einbürgerungstest* (€50) and the British *Life in the UK* test (£34). It has to be borne in mind, however, that future British citizens who choose to follow the course route instead of the test route will have to make a greater investment in order to fulfil the knowledge requirements, since language courses can cost up to £1200. In addition, in Germany, the price of the language test for obtaining the *Zertifikat Deutsch*, which varies between €100 and €120, needs to be added to the costs of the *Einbürgerungstest*. Those who have obtained a German qualification at high school level or higher are not required to take the language examination or the *Einbürgerungstest*.[83] In the Netherlands, those in possession of a secondary or higher education qualification are also exempt from proving that they have sufficiently integrated by taking the integration examination. Hence, in all three countries, those

[80] For the federal questions, see: http://www.bmi.bund.de/cae/servlet/contentblob/123028/publicationFile/13216/Einburgerungstest_Allgemein.pdf (site visited on 24 April 2009). For the *Länder* questions go to: http://www.bmi.bund.de/cae/servlet/contentblob/123030/publicationFile/ 13217/Einburgerungstest_Laender_Zusammen.pdf, site visited on 24 April 2009.

[81] http://oet.bamf.de/pls/oetut/f?p=512:1:4493717440784429, site visited on 6 May 2009.

[82] The first edition of the handbook, published in 2004, became a best-seller. The second edition was published in 2007, when the content of the study guide needed to be revised after passing the test became a condition for settlement.

[83] *Vorläufige Anwendungshinweise des Bundesministeriums des Innern* of 19 October 2007, points 10.1.1.6 and 10.1.1.7. Persons who have successfully (meaning moving up to the next grade) attended a German school or who have successfully participated in the integration course (meaning those who have passed the examination at the end of the integration course) are also exempt from taking the language test. They are, however, required to pass the *Einbürgerungstest*.

with poorer language skills will have higher costs to bear in order to fulfil the language and integration requirements.

Exemptions have also been made for persons suffering from mental or physical disabilities. In the Netherlands, an exemption will only be granted in cases where the handicapped person is unable to learn an adequate level of Dutch within a period of five years. This needs to be proven by a statement from an independent specialist, appointed by the municipality. Applicants in the UK will also need to prove they suffer from an impediment by submitting a doctor's certificate. In Germany, this certificate is only necessary in cases where the handicap is not visible.[84] In Germany and the UK, an exemption can also be granted on the basis of age. While German law stipulates that persons who cannot fulfil the language and integration requirements because of their age (*altersbedingt*) are exempt from these requirements, all those aged 65 and over are exempt from fulfilling the knowledge requirements in the UK.

In the Netherlands, the elderly are not exempt from the citizenship test. This country, however, does provide for exemption for illiterates, provided they can prove their inability to learn Dutch at level A2 within a period of five years in a 'feasibility investigation' at the adult education centre in Amsterdam. This investigation costs €208. In the other countries, no exemption is granted for illiterates.

2.3.1 *Content of the knowledge of society tests*

As we have seen in section 2, the content of the citizenship tests in the countries under consideration has not been subject to parliamentary debates. In the Netherlands, it was decided to hire ICE and Cito, commercial agencies specialised in testing and examining, to develop the naturalisation test and the integration examination.[85] In the UK, the Home Office concluded a commercial contract with the University for Industry (Ufi) to design the *Life in the UK* test, based on the topics determined by the Crick group and explained in the study guide. In Germany, the government contracted the IQB (Institute for Quality Development in Education, *Institut zur Qualitätsverbesserung im Bildungswesen*) of the Humboldt University Berlin to draw up a questionnaire containing the questions in the *Einbürgerungstest*.

The questions in the IQB test are geared towards the themes of 'Living in a democracy' (150 questions), 'History and Responsibility' (90 questions)

[84] *Vorläufige Anwendungshinweise*, 19 October 2007, No. 10.6.1.

[85] http://www.bureauice.nl/, site visited on 6 April 2009.

and 'Man and Society' (60 questions). Detailed knowledge of history is not required and the test does not contain questions about social norms. Questions about individual lifestyles, gender equality and homosexuality all relate to legal principles applicable in Germany, not to opinions and convictions (Michalowski, 2008). The questions regarding German culture focus on customs and traditions, such as putting up a tree at Christmas, hiding eggs at Easter and wearing costumes for Carnival.[86] As promised during the discussions in Parliament and during the IMK 2006, the test clearly differs from its predecessors in the *Länder* of Hesse and Baden-Württemberg.

Each test consists of 33 questions, ten of which are taken from the federal questionnaire and three from the regional questionnaires. Each regional questionnaire consists of 10 questions about the colours of the flag of the *Land*, its coat of arms, its administration and its geographical position. Since all *Länder* questionnaires have similar contents, there is no difference in difficulty between the *Länder* questionnaires, as is the case in Austria.[87] In order to pass the test, a candidate needs to answer 17 questions (51%) correctly. The test is not taken using a computer; instead, the candidate has to tick the appropriate box with a pencil on a paper questionnaire.

Since the decision to introduce the German citizenship test was made during the IMK of 2006, the minutes of which have not been published, it is difficult to see what the exact goals are which the *Einbürgerungstest* is supposed to attain. The goal of the Bill, introduced by the *Länder*, was in any case to ensure that only immigrants who are integrated and who endorse the German social and legal order are naturalised. Whereas this goal can be described as communitarian, the German test focuses on the working of democracy and can therefore be categorised under the republican model.

In order to pass the computer-based *Life in the UK* test, candidates need to study the chapters of the handbook entitled 'A changing society', 'UK today: a profile', 'How the UK is governed', 'Everyday needs' and 'Employment'. In each of the chapters, information that is relevant for everyday life is given. The information given is merely descriptive and value-free: in the book, candidates can learn what the most popular sports in the UK are and how many people say they have no religion. The book does not aim to impose social norms and values. In the short section on customs and traditions, the main festivals and events, such as New Year's Eve and Guy Fawkes Night, are explained. The information on UK history contained in the handbook is not tested. The handbook hence contains information relevant to 'the everyday

[86] See Michalowski in this volume.

[87] See Perchinig in this volume.

problems of settling in UK society' and practical information on this society and civic structures, which means that the recommendations of the Crick Group, which was also responsible for the content of the handbook, have been followed. The test consists of 24 questions, 18 of which (75%) need to be answered correctly.

The UK test was introduced to make sure that future British citizens have practical knowledge of British life and language, in order to create a sense of civic identity and shared values. The test indeed consists of questions relating to practical and general knowledge of the UK. It is doubtful whether this knowledge helps fulfil the communitarian goal the test is supposed to attain. This also applies to the other goals of the test: making sure that immigrants are able to take their place fully in society by reinforcing their ability to participate in society and to engage actively in British democracy and helping people to better understand their rights and duties and promote their economic and social integration. Since the immigrants following the test route to citizenship will already have a sound knowledge of language and life in the UK, it might be that the goals of the knowledge requirements will rather be achieved in the language courses for those with little or no English language skills, since these courses aim to make sure that participants at least acquire a basic level of competence. This will enable them to participate in society and understand their rights better than before.

In order to pass the Dutch naturalisation test that was in force until 1 April 2007, a candidate had to pass the so-called 'societal orientation' test. This involved a multiple choice test taken on a computer in order to prove that the candidate had sufficient knowledge of society. Furthermore, future citizens had to pass a language test that consisted of four elements: speaking, understanding, reading and writing. In order to pass the societal orientation part, a candidate needed to answer 28 of 40 questions (70%) correctly.

The integration examination also consists of two parts: a 'central' part and a 'practice' part. In the 'practice' part, immigrants have to prove, in various assessments or by submitting a portfolio, that they have enough knowledge of the Dutch language to get by.[88] The content of the 'central' part, which consists of an oral language test, an electronic practice test and a societal knowledge test, is undisclosed, but an impression of the test can be gained from the list of final attainment levels. The following topics are listed: work

---

[88] A portfolio consists of 30 proofs that a candidate has dealt with a particular situation in practice. In order to fill her portfolio, an applicant can, for instance, use a letter of application or a completed form to prove that he or she has spoken to a teacher at the school the children attend.

and income; manners, norms and values; housing; health and health care; history and geography; authorities; polity and the rule of law; and education and upbringing. Subsequently, for each of the themes, the practices and knowledge essential for functioning adequately and the norms for 'acting successfully' are described. Hence, all the themes are described in a normative way. Instead of merely requiring knowledge of the liberal rights, norms and values applicable in the Netherlands, the questions in the Dutch knowledge of society test aim at the test candidates' acceptance of these liberal norms and values. Future Dutch citizens are not only required to know that homosexuality is not forbidden in the Netherlands, they may neither bother persons who openly come out for their homosexuality. They must know what 'freedom of opinion' entails, but are also required to respect those having a different opinion. In the theme 'manners, norms and values', it is indicated that the test candidate needs to be able to 'keep to appointments made or cancel these in time'. In the more value-neutral, theme of 'polity and the constitutional state', candidates are not only required to have a knowledge of basic rights, such as freedom of religion and opinion, but they also need to act according to these principles, meaning that they 'do not bother people who act in an unknown or undesired manner in the field of religion. As regards the topic of 'health and health care', 'playing sports, being active and eating healthily in order to stay healthy' is formulated as a norm for acting successfully.

The goal of the Dutch naturalisation test as formulated in the Parliamentary debates was mainly to enable future citizens to make full use of their rights. Since the content of the naturalisation test was undisclosed, it is hard to say whether this test served the goal for which it was introduced. When looking at the effects of the test, it is highly doubtful whether the test has achieved this aim, since the test appears to form a barrier to naturalisation and hence leads to exclusion (see section 2.4.1). Unlike the naturalisation test, the introduction of the integration examination was not debated within the context of the amendment of Dutch citizenship law, but in the context of the introduction of the Integration Act, which regulates the conditions for permanent residence. According to the commission which advised on the content of the integration examination, integration equalled participation, which implied that immigrants needed to have knowledge of social relations and norms and values. Furthermore, in the eyes of the advisory commission, integration also meant respecting the rules and norms of the Dutch constitutional state and knowing and living up to unwritten rules, codes and agreements. The themes of the integration examination do indeed focus on these issues. However, the integration examination goes much further than the emancipatory liberal goal for which the naturalisation test was originally introduced. Since the final attainment levels of the test imply that the test aims at imposing social norms and values, the test in this respect shows a remarkable similarity to the interview guide applied in Baden-Württemberg, and might hence be qualified as an expression of repressive liberalism.

Since this was decided upon outside Parliament, the content of the citizenship tests was not discussed in Parliament in the countries under consideration. Since their introduction, however, these tests have still not been the subject of extensive debate.[89] In the Netherlands, such a discussion has been 'avoided' because the content of the test has been kept secret (Groenendijk 2005: 30). Especially in the Netherlands the fact that the effects of the test have not been subject to debate is striking, since the number of naturalisations dropped dramatically after the introduction of the tests. In the section below, the effects of the tests will be described and analysed.

2.4 *Effects of the Knowledge Requirements*

In order to examine the effects of the introduction of the citizenship tests in the countries under consideration, the numbers of naturalisations before and after the introduction of the citizenship tests will be described and analysed. In this way, it will be possible to determine whether the tests have the effect of excluding part of the immigrant community from full citizenship rights. Information about the pass rates for the tests per nationality is also analysed. In the Netherlands, statistical information on the effects of the naturalisation test will be supplemented with empirical data collected in 2006.

2.4.1 *The Netherlands: Falling Numbers*

In the table below, the numbers of naturalisations in the Netherlands from 1994 until 2008 are represented.

The entry into force of the nDNA has led to a dramatic decrease in the number of naturalisations. The numbers reached an all-time low in 2004 and 2005 (respectively 14,752 and 14,893 naturalisations), when more than 50% fewer persons were naturalised compared to 2002 (29,299 naturalisations), the year before the new DNA entered into force. The total number of naturalisations in 2008 is still 44% lower than the level reached in 2002.

[89] Since the test was only introduced in Germany fairly recently, such a debate might take place in the future. For the time being, only the Green party seems to have taken up on the issue, when it criticised the test's content and level in a motion (Drucksache 16/10183).

Table 2: Number of applications for naturalisation by adults in the Netherlands 1994–2008

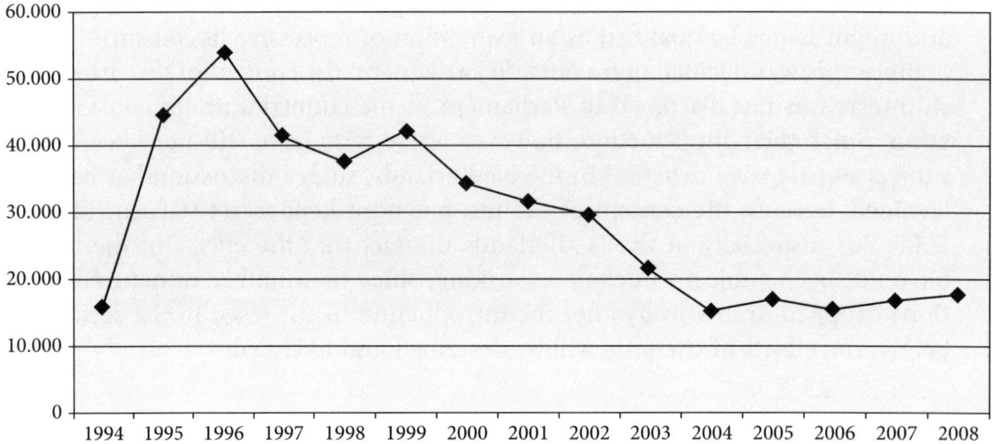

Source: IND.

The language and integration requirement is not the only requirement changed by the nDNA. The residence requirement also became harder to fulfil.[90] Despite the fact that the naturalisation test is not the only explanation, it plays an important role in the fall in the numbers of naturalisations. This becomes apparent when numbers relating to the test itself are examined.

Eighteen months after the test was introduced, a spot check revealed that only 12% of all applicants had taken the naturalisation test, the rest being exempt due to language or medical impediments (3%) or based on possession of a diploma (85%).[91] In 2004 and 2005, 6,684 persons passed the naturalisation test, while a total of slightly fewer than 28,000 applications for naturalisation were filed. Broadly speaking, this means that, in the years 2004 and 2005, fewer than 25% of all applicants for naturalisation had taken the test before applying for naturalisation. Whereas more recent statistics show that the percentage of persons who successfully passed the naturalisation test before applying for naturalisation has risen to between 25 and 29 per cent, the conclusion can still be drawn that, since the introduction of the test, most

[90] Instead of five years of 'normal' residence, under the new Act residence must have been lawful, which means residence on the basis of a residence permit, for the entire five years. Furthermore, residence must be uninterrupted.

[91] Evaluation Naturalisation Test, INDIAC, June 2005, p. 33.

applications for naturalisation are made by immigrants with qualifications (INDIAC 2007: 71).[92]

Obviously, if more immigrants passed the naturalisation test, the number of candidates among the number of applicants for naturalisation would be higher. Out of the 19,669 persons who presented themselves as prospective candidates in the period April 2003 to September 2006, 46% passed both parts of the test. This low pass rate is partly due to the fact that one-third of the immigrants who presented themselves as potential candidates eventually did not participate in the first part of the test. One of the reasons for potential candidates backing out was that they were not willing or able to pay for a test, the outcome of which was uncertain (Van Oers 2006: 63).

When immigrants who do not even apply to take the test for fear of failing it are taken into account, it becomes clear that the existence of the test constitutes a major barrier for many immigrants who want to become Dutch nationals.

Few data are available regarding the integration examination. In a letter to Parliament of 9 December 2008, the Minister for Integration stated that 611 persons took the integration examination in 2007, of whom 568 (93%) passed.[93] In 2008, 4,956 (79%) of the 6,281 test candidates passed the exam.[94]

Results of the Dutch naturalisation test

In order to see which groups are most affected by the introduction of the naturalisation test, the table below illustrates the pass rates of the test per nationality. Persons holding the nationalities in the table below represent the categories with both the highest absolute number of test candidates and the absolute number of candidates who passed the test. Persons from these countries can therefore not generally rely on possession of a diploma to qualify for exemption.

From the table below it becomes apparent that those of Moroccan (2,118 participants) and Turkish nationality (1,145 participants) represent the largest groups of test candidates. The pass rates for the Moroccan and Turkish candidates (64% and 61.5% respectively) are however lower than the pass rates of those holding Surinamese or Chinese nationality. At the same time, 316 test were taken by persons holding Ghanaian nationality (not visible in

[92] Since accurate data on the number of persons passing the test before applying for naturalisation were not available, the percentage was based on an estimate using available numbers.

[93] *TK* 2008–2009, 31 143, no. 35.

[94] It is not clear how many of the test candidates took the test in order to apply for Dutch nationality.

Table 3: Top nationalities participating in Dutch naturalisation test (April 2003–August 2006)

Nationality	Tests taken	Passes	Failures	Pass rate
Surinamese	295	224	71	75.9%
Chinese	640	421	219	65.8%
Moroccan	2118	1356	762	64%
Turkish	1145	704	441	61.5%
Afghan	1059	645	414	60.9%
Sudanese	337	202	135	59.9%
Iraqi	801	470	331	58.7%
Egyptian	372	214	158	57.5%
Somali	460	233	227	50.6%

Source: IND.

table 3). Although this is more than the total number of test taken by persons holding Surinamese nationality (295 tests), Ghanaian nationality does not figure in the top nine nationalities with the highest absolute number of test candidates.[95] This implies that a large proportion of the candidates of Ghanaian nationality failed the test.

Although the nationalities in the table above represent the categories with the highest absolute number of candidates who passed the test, the relative number of persons passing the test is generally low. Whereas less than a quarter of all Surinamese candidates fail the test, this is more than one-third in the case of all the other nationalities mentioned. Almost half of all persons participating in the test of Somali nationality failed the test. The pass rates for Afghan, Sudanese and Iraqi candidates are roughly 60%. This implies that the naturalisation test is difficult to pass for persons originating from 'refugee-producing countries'.

2.4.1.1 *'Problem Categories'*

From interviews with those charged with implementing the test, on the one hand, and with immigrants on the other hand, conducted in 2006, it appeared that two groups were particularly affected by the introduction of the naturalisation test (Van Oers 2006: 130-132). A vulnerable group of immigrants, such as the elderly, those with little or no education and women who had fallen behind in their integration gave up their desire to become a Dutch national due to the requirement to pass the naturalisation test. They were particularly put off by the level of the test and the requirement relating to possession of

[95] For that reason, there is no information available on the number of Ghanaian nationals who pass the test. Ghana could hence not be included in table 3.

written language skills. Also, the price of the test, its undisclosed content and the lack of opportunity for preparation played a considerable part in their decision not to take part in the naturalisation test.

The lack of opportunity to prepare for the test and the high fees were also reasons for immigrants experiencing fewer problems integrating into Dutch society not taking part in the test. In particular, immigrants who had learned to speak good Dutch at work or by participating in Dutch society, but who had never learned to read or write Dutch properly, were deterred from taking the test.

The price and level of the test were the main reasons why immigrants in this 'problem category' were deterred from taking the test. Instead of becoming Dutch nationals, they continued to reside in the Netherlands as aliens. The test clearly discriminated against weaker groups in society as opposed to groups who had little or no trouble integrating. However, this category of immigrants also regarded the existence of the naturalisation test as a requirement for naturalisation as problematic. Well-integrated immigrants who did not hold a Dutch diploma viewed the obligation to take the naturalisation test as very frustrating.[96] Due to the narrow formulation of the exemption grounds, those who had resided in the Netherlands for a very long time, who had worked and raised their children in the Netherlands and who, in other words, were generally very well integrated into Dutch society, were faced with the expensive and, in their eyes, insultingly easy naturalisation test the moment they wanted to become Dutch nationals. With the introduction of the integration examination in 2007, the possibilities of exempting obviously integrated immigrants have been extended. Since 1 April 2007, immigrants with a Flemish or Surinamese diploma do not have to pass an integration examination in order to become a Dutch national, as they are shown to have adequate knowledge of the language. Moreover, immigrants who have spent at least eight years in the Netherlands during their school years are presumed to speak enough Dutch and have sufficient knowledge of Dutch society to become a citizen without having to prove this by passing the examination. Consequently, the feeling of unfairness among the category of evidently integrated immigrants who felt that they were treated unfairly has been reduced.

Since the level and price of the integration examination are similar to the level and price of the naturalisation test and the content of the integration examination remains largely undisclosed, the harmful consequences of the naturalisation test for the category of immigrants who face problems integrating into Dutch society will continue to exist.

---

96 Examples of such diplomas are qualifications as a beautician, a welder, or a security guard.

Table 4: Numbers of naturalisations in UK 1994–2007

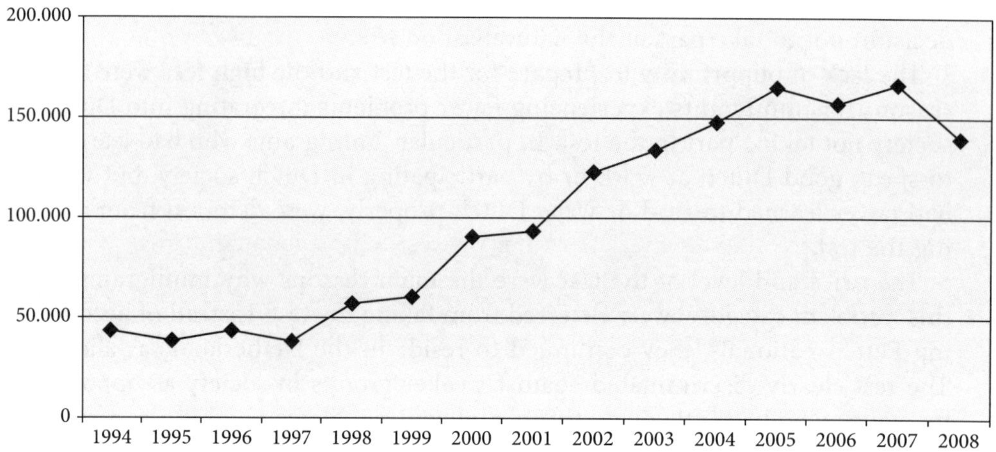

2.4.2 *The United Kingdom: steady rise*

The numbers of naturalisations in the UK in the years 1994 to 2007 are presented in the table above.

Starting in 2000, the number of naturalisations has been steadily increasing. The reading and subsequent entry into force of the Nationality, Immigration and Asylum Act has had an effect on the number of naturalisations granted. Firstly, the reading in 2002 and subsequent passing of the Act, introducing new conditions for obtaining British nationality, led to a higher number of applications in 2003, which was translated into an increase in the number of naturalisations granted in 2003 and 2004.[97] Although the requirement relating to knowledge of *Life in the UK* entered into force in 2005, the number of naturalisations that year rose by 10%, compared to the year before. By way of explanation for this rise, the Home Office refers to the considerable increase in the number of applications in October 2005, which suggests that prospective British citizens filed their applications early in order to avoid the new requirement, which entered into force in November 2005.[98]

The number of naturalisations in 2006 decreased by 5%, but the number of naturalisations for that year was still 4% above the number of naturalisa-

[97] *Home Office Statistical Bulletin*, Persons Granted British Citizenship UK, 2002, published 28 August 2003, p. 3 and Home Office Statistical Bulletin, Persons Granted British Citizenship UK, 2003, published 25 May 2004, p. 3.

[98] *Home Office Statistical Bulletin*, Persons Granted British Citizenship UK, 2005, published 23 May 2006, p. 3.

tions in 2004, the year before the knowledge of *Life in the UK* requirement was introduced.

It can be concluded that, even though the stricter language requirement and the introduction of the *Life in the UK* requirement have had a certain effect on the number of immigrants granted nationality, this effect was only marginal and not permanent.

Results of the Life in the UK *test*

What do the results of the *Life in the UK* test tell us about the effect of the introduction of the knowledge of language and *Life in the UK* requirements? According to the second annual report of the Advisory Board on Naturalisation and Immigration (ABNI), 367,712 tests were taken between October 2005 and July 2007. In total, 69% of the test candidates passed the test. From this number, we can conclude that a significant proportion of applicants for naturalisation and settlement (since 1 April 2007) is being held back by actual test failures (Ryan 2008: 313). In addition, we have to consider the unknown number of potential applicants who do not even participate in the *Life in the UK* test (Ryan 2008: 313). This method of reasoning, however, fails to take account of the option for naturalisation applicants to fulfil the knowledge requirements by following the ESOL-with-citizenship course trajectory. The number of persons applying for citizenship after having followed the ESOL-with-citizenship trajectory is unfortunately unknown. However, since interviews conducted with persons working at the Nationality Checking Services in June 2008 showed that most applicants for naturalisation followed the test route, we can draw firm conclusions from the results of the test.

In order to see which groups of persons are affected most by the introduction of the *Life in the UK* test, the pass rate of the test per nationality is examined. A list of selected nationalities is presented in the table below:

Table 5: Pass rates *Life in the UK* test per nationality (November 2005–November 2008)

Nationality	Tests taken	Passes	Failures	Pass rate
USA	10,347	10,145	202	98.1%
Australia	9,424	9,238	186	98.0%
South Africa	28,546	26,888	1,658	94.2%
Russia	6,112	5,564	548	91.0%
Ukraine	3,642	3,142	500	86.3%
Romania	3,555	3,033	522	85.3%
Kenya	7,373	6,202	1,171	84.2%
Nigeria	24,005	19,819	4,186	82.6%
Ghana	14,184	11,575	2,609	81.6%

Table 5 (*cont.*)

Nationality	Tests taken	Passes	Failures	Pass rate
India	65,605	52,078	13,527	79.4%
Pakistan	46,455	29,707	16,748	63.9%
Kosovo	10,023	4,923	5,100	49.1%
Iraq	32,598	15,875	16,723	48.7%
Afghanistan	25,797	12,380	13,417	47.9%
Bangladesh	26,759	12,031	14,728	45.0%
Turkey	23,157	10,327	12,830	44.0%

Source: Second report of the Advisory Board on Naturalisation and Integration and the Final Report of the Advisory Board on Naturalisation and Integration.

From the table above, it is clear that the pass rates for the test vary significantly per nationality. The pass rate is almost 100% for applicants holding the nationality of a country where English is the majority language (USA, Australia). Furthermore, countries with a relatively high level of development (Russia, Ukraine, Romania, India) have a high success rate. Relatively high pass rates are also achieved by those holding the nationality of a former British colony (South Africa, Kenya, Ghana, Nigeria and, again, India). Countries which have produced large numbers of refugees (Iraq, Kosovo and Afghanistan) appear at the bottom of the list, with a success rate of less than 50%. Bangladesh and Turkey, both at the bottom of the list, produce many applicants for family reunification. According to Ryan, the provisional conclusion can be drawn that pass rates are likely to vary significantly in line with the initial basis for admission to the UK: pass rates for economic migrants are high, while refugees and family migrants on average find it harder to pass the *Life in the UK* test (Ryan 2008: 305, 313). Hence, the impact of the 'knowledge of life' tests is highly differentiated by nationality and is probably differentiated by immigration category (Ryan 2008: 303).

2.5 *Effects of the German Knowledge Requirements*

In order to find out whether the introduction of the language requirement in German nationality law in 2000 has had an effect, the number of naturalisations from 1994 to 2007 is shown in the table below.

It is apparent that, following a peak in the number of naturalisations in the year 2000 (184,000), this number has been falling, contrary to expectations that the number would rise following the entry into force of the amended Nationality Act on 1 January 2000. This means that one of the most important goals of the 1999 reform has not been attained. On the contrary:

Table 6: Number of naturalisations in Germany 1994–2007[99]

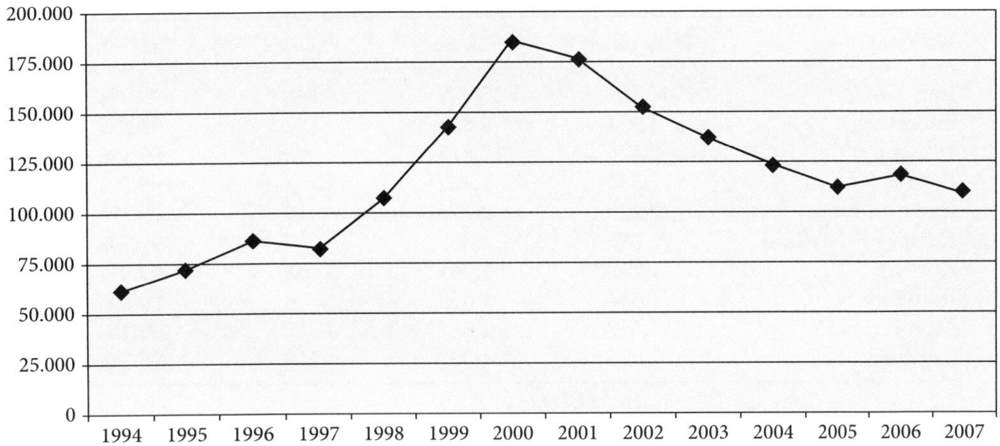

Source: NATAC and Migrationsberichten 2006 and 2007.

since 2000 numbers have been decreasing following a considerable increase in the years prior to the reform. The peak in the year 2000 can be ascribed to the fact that those who were interested in naturalisation applied in order to avoid new barriers for naturalisation, such as the introduction of the language requirement (Anil 2006: 458).[100]

Following a decrease in the number of naturalisations since the year 2000, figures rose slightly in the year 2006. However, this increase was not permanent, since the number of naturalisations declined again in 2007, reaching their lowest point since the amendment of the nationality law in 2000. This might be explained by the introduction of a stricter language requirement in August of that year. At the time of writing of this contribution, the numbers of naturalisations of certain *Länder* showed that a further decrease of between 10 to 15% was expected in 2008.[101]

---

99 Excluding the naturalisations of ethnic Germans.

100 Furthermore, in 2000, many children benefited from a transitional provision, 40b of the Nationality Act introduced by the reform of 1999. On the basis of this provision, children under ten years old who fulfilled the requirements for *ius soli* acquisition of nationality at the time of birth were able to naturalise as German citizens. On the basis of Article 40b, more than 20,000 children received German nationality in 2000. In 2001, this number rose to 23,400. In the years after 2001, these numbers decreased considerably, to fewer than 50 children in 2007.

101 *Newsletter Migration und Bevölkerung*, 5th edition, June 2009, p. 3.

Table 7: Pass rates of the *Einbürgerungstest* per nationality (1 September 2008–31 March 2009)

Nationality	Tests taken	Passes	Failures	Pass rate
Iraq	46,266	45,679	136	97.3%
Turkey	4,954	4,818	92	96.8%
Ukraine	2,424	2,818	2	99.9%
Poland	2,381	2,422	8	99.7%
Iran	2,225	2,373	19	99.1%
Russian Federation	2,096	2,089	7	99.7%
Kosovo	1,779	1,741	38	97.9%
Romania	1,634	1,630	4	99.8%
Morocco	1,632	1,617	15	99.1%
Germany	1,075	1,057	18	98.3%

Source: German Bundestag, Drucksache 16/13558.

Results of the German Einburgerungstest

Since the *Einbürgerungstest* was officially introduced quite recently, it is hard to say anything about the effects it has had on the number of applications for naturalisation. Four months after the introduction of the test, various media sources reported that the vast majority of all test candidates (98%) passed the citizenship test.[102] Several sources concluded that the test was too easy.[103] When looking at the pass rates of the ten countries of birth of the largest immigrant groups in Germany (table 7), it appears that the difference between the nationality with the highest pass rate (Ukrainian) and the nationality with the lowest pass rate (Turkish) is very small: only 3,1%.

Looking at the high pass rates, the impression is created that the *Einbürgerungstest* is not a hurdle for immigrants. According to the German Government, the high pass rates rather show that the demands of the test are not insurmountable and are not perceived as such by the possible naturalisation applicants.[104] When comparing the number of candidates who took the test

[102] See, for example, 'Deutsch werden ist voll leicht; Fast alle einbürgerungswilligen MigrantInnen bestehen den Einbürgerungstest. Dessen KritikerInnen ist das Beleg dafür, dass es Überflüssig ist. Die Mehrheit der Eingebürgerten stammt aus dem Libanon' [Becoming German is very easy; almost all immigrants wishing to becoming German nationals pass the citizenship test. According to critics, this proves the test is redundant. A majority of naturalised persons originate from Libanon], *Die Tageszeitung*, 2 January 2009.

[103] See contribution by Michalowski in this volume.

[104] BT-DS 16/13558.

to the number of naturalisations in the previous year, the effect of the test on the number of naturalisations can, however, be expected to be negative.[105]

2.6 *Conclusions*

The countries under consideration in this contribution have witnessed a profound change in the dominant concept of citizenship applied by Governments and policy makers. From a liberal understanding of citizenship, the centre of gravity in the debates surrounding changes in the rules governing naturalisation has gradually shifted towards a thicker, communitarian concept. At least in the Netherlands and Germany (and increasingly in the UK since the publication of the *Path to Citizenship* Green Paper) naturalisation is regarded as the culmination of a completed integration process, which can only take place when applicants have more or less assimilated into the majority culture. Consequently, applicants for naturalisation in the three countries under consideration have to meet a series of strict conditions, including linguistic competence, knowledge of the host society and, with the exception of the UK, history.

The formalisation of the language and integration requirements has led to a considerable rise in the required level of knowledge in the three countries under consideration. Furthermore, formalisation of the tests in the three countries implied that the tests were no longer administered by the state. Instead, the tests were contracted out to private companies, which are responsible for the development and administration of the tests. Faith in the discretion of local or municipal state officials has apparently been replaced by reliance on and confidence in private companies and educational institutions (Guild, Groenendijk & Carrera 2009). In addition, in the UK and Germany, alongside formalisation of the tests, it was decided that the spouses of citizens would be covered by the same language requirement as 'ordinary' naturalisation applicants. Apparently, the British and German governments no longer felt confident that the spouses and partners of nationals would integrate automatically.

In addition to formalising the language test, the political will was expressed in all three countries to test certain aspects of knowledge of society. Apart from very general qualifications reflecting the kind of knowledge future nationals needed to possess, national parliaments did not decide on the

---

[105] See Michalowski in this volume.

content of the new knowledge requirement. Delegating the responsibility for the content of the tests might have been based on the fear that members of parliament would never reach an agreement on the content of the test, which to a certain extent implies agreeing to the content of national identity. Dutch historian Ernst Kossmann once compared national identity to a large jellyfish that has drifted ashore: it is subjected to a thorough investigation but people do not even consider going and standing in the middle of it (Kossmann 1986).

In the Netherlands and Germany, applicants for naturalisation who hold certain diplomas or who have had several years of schooling will be (partially) exempt from fulfilling the new knowledge requirements. This means that most of the second generation will be free from the obligation to take the citizenship tests in both these countries. Empirical research in the Netherlands has shown that the test functions as an insurmountable barrier to the less well-educated half of first-generation immigrants and to school dropouts – both groups which already are in a weaker financial and socio-legal position. These empirical research results are backed by statistical evidence of the negative effect of the new Dutch integration requirements on the number of naturalisations, which have been decreasing since the introduction of the test. In Germany, naturalisations have been declining since the introduction of the language requirement in 2000. Numbers are expected to decrease even further now that the *Einbürgerungstest* has come into force. In both Germany and the Netherlands, reduction in the number of naturalisations was not (officially) a goal of the reforms of citizenship law. It appears, however, that in these countries, the tests have had the effect of excluding a considerable part of the immigrant population from full citizenship rights. For these immigrants, the obligation to integrate constitutes a threat rather than an expansion of their possibilities. This cannot be considered beneficial to their integration. The fact that the language and integration requirements for naturalisation were made stricter following a fall in the number of naturalisations in Germany and the Netherlands implies that there may be other reasons for the introduction of the tests than those put forward in the political debates.

The knowledge requirements do not appear to have had a permanent negative effect on the number of naturalisations in the UK, based on the data examined so far. When looking at the pass rates of the *Life in the UK* test by nationality, a negative effect on certain immigration categories can, however, be discerned. Formalised tests thus present new barriers to many migrants in all three countries under consideration. The conclusion can be drawn that, implicitly, the tests send out a message to the less well-educated immigrants that they are not welcome, or are at least less welcome. Despite the negative effect of the tests, in all three countries the desire was expressed to raise the level of the tests.

The formalisation of the language and integration requirements for naturalisation signals that policy makers and politicians have established an automatic link between the acquisition of knowledge and integration. The idea that knowledge of language and society is a reflection of someone's integration has become generally accepted. It is, however, at least questionable whether conclusions regarding someone's integration can be drawn from her test results (Bjornson 2009).

When judging the content of the tests on the basis of the sparse information given in this chapter, we are left wondering whether the ambitious goals the tests are meant to serve are achieved. For all three tests, we may indeed ask what the actual value of the questions is for the integration of immigrants in society, especially since the introduction of the tests stresses the idea that integration is primarily a cognitive process rather than an emotional process on both sides (Guild et al. 2009). Lastly, the idea has emerged that a test is the best way of ensuring that immigrants will acquire the knowledge which is supposedly essential for integration. This line of reasoning neglects the fact that tests also operate as a mechanism of selection and exclusion. They are a means to decide to which immigrants which rights are given.

Bibliography

Anil, M., The New German Citizenship Law and its Impact on German Demographics: Research Notes, *Population Research and Policy Review* 25(5) 2006, pp. 443–463.

Bauböck, R., *Transnational Citizenship. Membership and Rights in International Migration.* Aldershot: Edward Elgar Publishing 1994.

Bauböck, R., Recombinant Citizenship, in: A. Woodward & M. Kohli (eds.), *Inclusion and Exclusion in European Societies*, 38–58. London, New York: Routledge 2001.

Bellamy, R., Introduction: Modern Citizenship, in: R. Bellamy, D. Castiglione & E. Santoro (eds.), *Lineages of European Citizenship; Rights, Belonging and Participation in Eleven Nation-States*, Basingstoke (etc.): Palgrave Macmillan 2004, pp. 1–21.

Berlit, U., Änderungen im Staatsangehörigkeitsrecht durch das EU-Richtlinienumsetzungsgesetz', *Informationsbrief Ausländerrecht* 11/12/2007, pp. 457–470.

Böcker, A., K. Groenendijk & B. de Hart, De Toegang tot het Nederlanderschap. Effecten van twintig jaar beleidswijzigingen, *Nederlands Juristenblad* 80(3) 2005, pp. 157–164.

Carens, J., Membership and Morality, in R. Brubaker (ed.), *Immigration and the Politics of Citizenship in Europe and North America*, Lanham and London: University Press of America 1989.

Carens, J., *Culture, Citizenship, and Community: a contextual Exploration of Justice as Evenhandedness*, Oxford (etc.): Oxford University Press 2000.

Davy, U., Einbürgerung in Deutschland; Blinde Flecken in einem Rechtsstaat, *Die Verwaltung*, 2008(41): 31–62.

Dornis, C., *Einbürgerung in Deutschland; Ihre Rolle bei der Integration von Zuwanderern und die Verwaltungspraxis im Regionalvergleich*. Aachen: Shaker Verlag 2001.

Dummett, A., United Kingdom, in: R. Bauböck, E. Ersbøll, K. Groenendijk & H. Waldrauch (eds.), *Acquisition and Loss of Nationality; Volume 2: Country Analyses*, Amsterdam: Amsterdam University Press 2006, pp. 551–585.

Entzinger, H., Inburgeren op de Grens van Wetenschap en Politiek, in: A. Böcker, T. Havinga, P. Minderhoud, H. van de Put, L. de Groot-Van Leeuwen, B. de Hart, A. Jettinghoff & K. Zwaan (eds.), *Migration Law and Sociology of Law; Collected Essays in Honour of Kees Groenendijk*, Nijmegen: Wolf Legal Publishers 2008, pp. 177–184.

Etzioni, A., Citizenship Tests: a Comparative, Communitarian Perspective, *The Political Science Quarterly* 78(3) 2007, pp. 353–363.

Fermin, A., *Verplichte Inburgering van Nieuwkomers*. Utrecht: Ercomer 2001.

Green, S. (2004), *The Politics of Exclusion. Institutions and Immigration in Contemporary Germany*. Manchester: Manchester University Press.

Gerdes, J., T. Faist & B. Rieple, 'We are all 'Republican' Now': The Politics of Dual Citizenship in Germany, in: T. Faist (ed.), *Dual Citizenship in Europe; From Nationhood to Societal Integration*, Aldershot: Ashgate 2007, pp. 45–76.

Geyer, F., Anspruch auf Einbürgerung, in: R. Hoffmann & H. Hofmann (eds.), *Ausländerrecht, AufenthG – FreizügG/EU – AsylVfG – StAG Handkommentar*, Baden-Baden: Nomos Verlagsgesellschaft 2008.

Groenendijk, C., Integratie en Uitsluiting in het Nederlandse Vreemdelingenrecht, in: P. Boeles & G. Lodder (eds.), *Integratie en Uisluiting*, The Hague: SDU 2005, pp. 9–31.

Guild, E., K. Groenendijk & S. Carrera, Understanding the Contest of Community: Illiberal Practices in the EU?, in: S. Carrera et al. (eds.), *Illiberal, Liberal States: Immigration, Citizenship and Integration in the EU*, Surrey: Ashgate 2009.

Gunsteren, H. van, *A Theory of Citizenship: Organizing Plurality in Contemporary Democracies*. Boulder: West View Press 1998.

Hailbronner, K., Germany, in: R. Bauböck, E. Ersbøll, K. Groenendijk & H. Waldrauch (eds.), *Acquisition and Loss of Nationality; Volume 2: Country Analyses*, Amsterdam: Amsterdam University Press 2006, pp. 213–251.

Hanschmann, F., Die Einbürgerungstestverordnung – Ende einer Debatte?, *Zeitschrift für Ausländerrecht* 11/12/2008: 388–394.

Hansen, R., From Subjects to Citizens: Immigration and Nationality Law in the United Kingdom', in: P. Weil & R. Hansen (eds.), *Citizenship, Immigration and Nationality: towards a Convergence in Europe?*, Basingstoke (etc.): Palgrave 2001, pp. 69–94.

Hartnell, H., Belonging: Citizenship and Migration in the European Union and in Germany, *Berkeley Journal of International Law*, 24(1) 2006, pp. 330-400.

Heijs, E., *Selectie bij Naturalisatie: de rol van taalkennis als eis voor het Nederlanderschap*, undergraduate dissertation, Catholic University of Nijmegen 1988.

Heijs, E., *Van Vreemdeling tot Nederlander; de Verlening van het Nederlanderschap aan Vreemdelingen 1813–1992*, diss. Nijmegen, Amsterdam: Het Spinhuis 1995.

Home Office, *Secure Borders, Safe Haven*, 2000, accessible at http://www. archive2. official-documents.co.uk/document/cm53/5387/cm5387.pdf.

Home Office, *The New and the Old; the Report of the 'Life in the United Kingdom' Advisory Group*, 2003, accessible at http://www.ind.homeoffice.gov.uk/6353/about us/thenewandtheold .pdf.

Home Office, *The Path to Citizenship: Next Steps in Reforming the Immigration System*, 2008a, accessible at http://www.ukba.homeoffice.gov.uk/sitecontent/documents/aboutus/consultations/closedconsultations/pathtocitizenship/. Site accessed 3 April 2009.

Home Office, *The Path to Citizenship: Next Steps in Reforming the Immigration System; Government Response to Consultation,* 2008b, accessible via http://www.ukba.homeoffice.gov.uk/sitecontent/documents/aboutus/consultations/closedconsultations/pathtocitizenship/governmentreponsetoconsultation?view=Binary.

INDIAC, *Trendrapportage Naturalisatie; Naturalisatie, Opties en Naturalisatietoets 2000–2006,* Rijswijk: Ministerie van Justitie 2007.

Joppke, C., Beyond National Models: Civic Integration Policies for Immigrants in Western Europe, *Western European Politics* 30(1) 2007, pp. 1–22.

Joppke, C., *How Liberal are Citizenship Tests?*, contribution to EUDO citizenship forum, http://eudo-citizenship.eu/cit-forum/viewtopic.php?f=2&t=10.

Kossmann, E.H., *De Lage Landen 1780-1980. Twee eeuwen Nederland en België. Deel I 1780–1914.* Amsterdam: Agon 1986.

Kostakopoulou, D., Why Naturalisation, *Perspectives on European Politics and Society*, Leiden: Brill 2003, pp. 85–115.

Kymlicka, W. & W. Norman, Return of the Citizen: A Survey of Recent Work on Citizenship Theory, *Ethics* 104(2) 1994, pp. 352–381.

Kymlicka, W., *Multicultural Citizenship; a Liberal Theory of Minority Rights.* Oxford: Clarendon Press 1995.

Michalowski, I., Wissen entscheidet. Der neue, bundesweite Einbürgerungstest im internationalen Vergleich, *WZB-Mitteilungen* 121, 2008, pp. 35–36.

Miller, D., Citizenship and Pluralism, *Political Studies* 43(3) 1995, pp. 432–450.

Neuman, G., Justifying U.S. Naturalization Policies, *Virginia Journal of International Law* 35, 1994, pp. 237–278.

Oers, R. van, *De Naturalisatietoets Geslaagd? Een Onderzoek naar de Totstandkoming en Effecten van de Naturalisatietoets.* Nijmegen: Wolf Legal Publishers 2006.

Pluymen, M., *Niet Toelaten betekent Uitsluiten*, diss. Nijmegen, The Hague: Boom Juridische Uitgevers 2008.

Rambøll Management, E*valuation der Integrationskurse nach dem Zuwanderungsgesetz. Abschlussbericht und Gutachten über Verbesserungspotenziale bei der Umsetzung der Integrationskurse*, Berlin 2006.

Renner, G., Streitpunkte: Mehrstatigkeit und Deutschkenntnisse, *Zeitschrift für Ausländerrecht*, 2002(10), pp. 339–348.

Ryan, B., Integration Requirements: A New Model in Migration Law, *Journal of Immigration, Asylum, and Nationality Law*, 22(4) 2008, pp. 303–316.

Schuck, P., Whose Membership is it anyway? Comments on Gerald Neuman, *Virginia Journal of International Law* 35, 1994, pp. 321–331.

Spijkerboer, T., *Zeker Weten. Inburgering en de Fundamenten van het Nederlandse Politieke Bestel.* The Hague: SDU 2007.

Thränhardt, D., *Einbürgerung. Rahmenbedingungen, Motive und Perspektiven des Erwerbs der deutschen Staatsangehörigkeit*, Gutachten für die Friedrich-Ebert-Stiftung Bonn 2008.

Vermeulen, B., *Vrijheid, Gelijkheid, Burgerschap.* The Hague: SDU Uitgevers 2007.

Vries, K. de, *'Through the Looking-Glass'. Over inburgering en fundamentele rechten bezien vanuit verschillende concepten van 'burgerschap'*, paper presented at the *Tweede onderzoeksdag* of the Stichting Instituut Gak, Amsterdam, 1 December 2008.

Chapter 3

On Trial in Denmark

*Eva Ersbøll**

3.1 *Introduction*

Like several other European countries, Denmark has introduced formalised immigration, integration and naturalisation tests in the new millennium. For family migrants, passing an immigration test is a condition for family reunification; for resident immigrants, passing an integration test is a condition for obtaining a permanent residence permit and, for permanent residents, passing a language and citizenship test is a condition for naturalisation. The immigration test and the integration test were introduced under the Aliens Act in 2007, while the conditions of passing a (formalised) language test and a supplementary citizenship test were introduced in the nationality legislation of 2002 and 2006 respectively.

Denmark has, since the country became a constitutional democracy, always been concerned with the importance of future citizens being able to talk and understand the Danish language, whereas letting family reunification and permanent residence be conditional upon language skills, etc., is a new phenomenon.

Danish naturalisation policy has shifted from moderately restrictive to very restrictive, whereas Danish alien policy, including the criteria for family reunification and the permanent residence permit, has in the mean time been comparatively liberal: the Danish Aliens Act of 1983 has even been called 'the most liberal in the world'.[1] According to this Act, refugees had a legal claim to family reunification and a residence permit issued to a foreigner with a

* Senior Research Fellow at the Danish Institute for Human Rights.

[1] See, for instance, Lars Jørgensen 2006, p. 141; the then chairman of the Danish Refugee Council called it 'the most human of its kind in the world' (*FTF* (the official report of the parliamentary proceedings) 1984–85, sp. 376).

Van Oers, Ersbøll and Kostakopoulou, A Re-definition of Belonging?, pp. 107–152.
 ISBN 978 90 04 17506 8. Printed in the Netherlands.

view to permanent residence was irrevocable after two years of residence in Denmark. However, since then, rights and procedures connected with both asylum and family reunification have been restricted several times.

By way of introduction, this chapter presents trends in Danish migration and the development of integration law and language tuition for adult migrants. Subsequently, the chapter gives an account of different types of residence status and the related integration tests. The test requirements for naturalisation will be discussed in the most detail, as substantial experience with both immigration and integration tests is still lacking: the immigration test has not yet been implemented and the integration test has only been effective for a short period.

As a common feature, the legal framework and the content of the relevant legislation will be presented and the rationales behind the introduction of the tests will be analysed. Against this background, the effects of the tests, including statistical evidence, will be evaluated; notably, the potential value of the tests as a means of integration will be discussed. To conclude, the findings will be summarised and possible conclusions will be drawn.

3.2 *Danish immigration*

3.2.1 *Trends in Danish immigration*

After World War 1, Denmark had a rather restrictive immigration policy, limiting migration to persons with a specific connection to the country. The years 1969–1971 marked an exception to this policy. At that time, full employment permitted a net immigration of around 20,000 job-seeking foreigners from non-Western European countries. However, during the subsequent years immigration was restricted again and, in 1973, during the oil crisis, immigration as such was brought to an end by the so-called 'immigration stop'. At that time, the number of foreign residents in Denmark was around 91,000.

The subsequent increase in the number of foreign residents is the result, first and foremost, of family reunification, asylum-seeking and the exercise of free movement rights according to the EC/EU legislation(Ersbøll 2001: 246). From the mid-1970s to the mid-1980s, immigration was at a low level; however, in the second half of the 1980s immigration increased. Family reunification was still part of the explanation, but just as important was an increase in the number of refugees, mainly from Poland, Iran, Iraq, Lebanon and Sri Lanka. In 1986, this led to a restriction of the Aliens Act. Still, the 1990s were characterised by refugees coming to Denmark, this time mainly from the former Yugoslavia and Somalia (Pedersen & Smith 2001).

In 1980, the number of (first-generation) immigrants in Denmark was about 135,000 (out of a population of about 5 million). In 2000, the number had increased to 297,000 – corresponding to 5.6% of the Danish population.

3.2.2 *Danish Aliens Policy*

As mentioned in the introduction, the legal rights of refugees and resident immigrants were well-protected by the 1983 aliens law. However, the increasing number of immigrants in the second half of the 1980s led to restrictions. An influential factor in this context was the high and increasing unemployment rate in Denmark from 1974–75 onwards and the fact that immigrants from non-Western countries had particularly low labour market participation levels and a corresponding high dependency on the Danish welfare system.[2]

The Social Democrats had relinquished power in 1982 when a new coalition government came into power, under the leadership of a Conservative Prime Minister. In 1983, however, the opposition managed to get the new liberal Aliens Act adopted and disagreements between the government and the opposition regarding aliens policy were openly voiced. In the late 1980s, general elections were called at frequent intervals and refugee and immigration issues moved to the centre of the political debate. The political disagreements culminated in 1993, when the Conservative, longest-reigning Prime Minister since the end of the Second World War had to step down following an inquiry into the Conservative Minister for Justice's illegal inactivity concerning the handling of applications from Tamil refugees for family reunification (known as the 'Tamil case'). This paved the way for a new Social Democratic government coalition (Rerup & Christiansen 2005). The political atmosphere was severely affected by the preceding events and, again, frequent general elections were held – in 1994, 1996 and 1998 (the Cabinets of Poul Nyrup Rasmussen II, III and IV). Throughout this time, aliens and integration policies were on the agenda; motions for solutions were debated and legislative initiatives were taken.

However, the Social Democrats and the Social Liberals on the one hand and the Conservatives, the Liberals and the Danish People's Party on the other hand persistently disagreed on the aliens policy. Some borrowing of ideas from abroad was observed, such as the Danish People's Party's proposal

[2] See the OECD report: *The labour market integration of immigrants in Denmark*; DELSA/ELSA 82006)7/REV1.

to pay asylum seekers in goods instead of cash – as the Labour government did in the UK.

In 2001, a general election was called and, again, refugee and immigration issues took centre stage in the election campaign. The Liberals argued in their election manifesto, 'Time for Change', that it was imperative to limit the influx of foreigners coming to Denmark, which would release resources for better integration. Foreigners should master the Danish language and should work and be self-sufficient. A number of proposals were made, among them tightening up the right to family reunification and permanent residence. The Danish People's Party came up with their 'Aliens proposition', containing proposals for strengthening the requirements for family reunification and permanent residence; in particular, they wanted restricted naturalisation criteria.[3]

Following the 2001 election, the Social Democrats and the left-wing parties lost many of their mandates. The Liberals became Denmark's largest party and, together with the Conservatives, they formed a new government with support from the Danish People's Party. In order to fulfil their promises to strengthen the aliens policy and implement improved integration of foreigners, a new Ministry of Refugee, Immigration and Integration Affairs (the Ministry of Integration) was established, with responsibility for most of the legislation concerning foreigners, formerly within the sphere of other ministries (such as the Ministry of the Interior, the Ministry of Justice, the Ministry of Education and the Ministry of Social Affairs).

After the general elections of 8 February 2005 and 13 November 2007, the Liberal-Conservative governing coalition continued with support from a strengthened Danish People's Party.

3.3 *Integration programmes*

3.3.1 *The Introduction of An Integration Act*

It is claimed that Denmark was the first country in the world to introduce an Act regarding the integration of foreigners.[4] The preceding negotiations on the Act were rather conflict-ridden. While in opposition, the Social Democrats had, since the late 1980s, argued for legislation promoting the integration of immigrants. After 1993, when the Social Democrats had formed

[3] See *Udlændingeudspil*, 2001, 6 November 2001.

[4] Danish Ministry of Integration; http://www.nyidanmark.dk/en-us/Integration/a_comprehensive_integration_initiative/...

a government coalition, an integration committee was established (Holm 2007). In December 1997, the newly appointed (20 October 1997) Social Democrat Minister for the Interior presented a proposal for an Integration Act to Parliament. The new minister was an elderly, well-known mayor with a reputation for being restrictive in his immigrant integration approach. His appointment would meet with rather severe criticism of the government's immigration policy, especially from mayors (many of whom were Social Democrats) in the suburban municipalities of Copenhagen. The Bill passed in 1998.

The Conservatives and the Liberals abstained from voting on the Integration Act. The reason was that their proposal for an amendment of the Aliens Act, which was discussed in Parliament at the same time as the Integration Act, had been turned down. The Liberals and the Conservatives had argued that one condition for family reunification should be that the person living in Denmark (the sponsor) had a home of his own. The Social Democratic Prime Minister, however, who had formed a government coalition in 1996 with the Social Liberals, wanted to comply with this party's resistance to such an amendment. The result was, according to the Liberals, a cabinet crisis leading to prime ministerial pressure on the Minister for the Interior, resulting in his breaking his previous promise to the Conservatives and the Liberals. Against this background, the two parties had considered voting against the bills. However, they decided to abstain because the Prime Minister and the Minister of the Interior had invested a great deal in the Act's adoption with a wide-ranging majority in Parliament, 'as a national compromise' and because they were basically satisfied with the ideas in the Integration Act and with their own 'substantial negotiated achievements', including the introduction of non-automatic permanent residence (after three years of residence) and the abolition of the entitlement to family reunification.[5]

Another opposition party, the Danish People's Party, rejected some of the basic ideas behind the Integration Act, which they believed would confirm the development of Denmark towards a multi-cultural society; in their opinion, refugees were to be sent home when the conditions in their country of origin made this possible – they were not to be integrated. The party declared that the new Minister of the Interior undoubtedly had been appointed because of the success of the Danish People's Party. It was their educated guess that the adopted Integration Act was far from the result the minister had imagined when he came into office.

[5] http://www.ft.dk/Samling19972/salen/L59_BEH3_38_11_1.htm

The Act on the Integration of Foreigners in Denmark entered into force on 1 January 1999.[6] The stated aim of the Act was to make it possible, through an integration effort, for newly-arrived refugees and immigrants to become active participants in society as a whole, self-supporting and with an understanding of Danish fundamental values and norms.

The Integration Act received considerable attention because it departed from Danish alien policy so far. Until then, social legislation had provided for the integration of refugees for an integration period of one and a half years, but similar initiatives had not been taken regarding (non-refugee) immigrants. The Integration Act comprised both refugees and immigrants and extended the integration period to three years.

The Act assigned the municipalities overall responsibility for integration efforts (formerly handled by the Danish Refugee Council). Newly arrived foreigners were to be offered an introduction programme, normally lasting three years. The municipalities were responsible for providing housing for newcomers, who were to be spread geographically more evenly around the country, and who generally had to stay in the municipality where they were stationed after their arrival for the duration of the integration programme. Another controversial invention was the so-called 'introduction aid' for foreigners who were unable to provide for themselves; this aid was a cash benefit at a lower level than would normally be paid to unemployed Danish nationals. This lower cash benefit paid to newcomers should serve as an incentive for them to find a job. The arrangement's compatibility with international non-discrimination principles was questioned and eventually, in 2000, the introduction aid scheme was abolished.[7]

3.3.2 *Integration Programmes*

A central part of the integration arrangement is an 'integration programme' offered to adult refugees and immigrants covered by the Integration Act. The target groups are foreigners legally residing in Denmark. Nationals from the other Nordic countries and the EC/EEA are not covered, nor are foreigners who fall within EC rules on visa exemption and the abolition of entry and visa restrictions in connection with free movement rights.[8]

---

[6] Act No. 474 of 1 July 1998.

[7] See, however, 3.3.2 below concerning the re-introduction of a similar low introduction aid in 2002.

[8] Now see section 2(3) in Consolidation No. 1593 of 14 December 2007 of the Act on the Integration of Aliens in Denmark (the Integration Act).

As part of the integration programme, refugees and immigrants are offered 'employment-promoting options', such as qualification improvement and work experience. Another key element of the programme is a Danish course. According to the 1998 Act, the extent and content of the introduction programme, including the Danish course, were laid down in an individual 'action plan' based on the abilities and skills of each individual foreigner with the explicit objective of introducing him or her to the labour marked or to further education.

However, in 2002, the new Liberal-Conservative government, shortly after it came into power, adopted a 'new aliens policy'.[9] This policy was based on the following three fundamental pillars: Denmark's international obligations are to be respected; the number of immigrants is to be limited and the requirements of being self-supporting are to be strengthened; resident refugees and immigrants must be better integrated and their labour market participation accelerated; therefore, the incentive to take up employment is to be strengthened.

Accordingly, in February 2002, the new Minister for Integration presented a Bill amending the Integration Act (section 19) in order to implement the new aliens policy. With the adoption of the Act, foreigners and their local councils became obliged to enter into 'an individual contract' (instead of the former 'action plan') in order to secure the quality of the introduction programme. This contract clarified which offers foreigners were to be made as part of the introduction programme – conditional upon whether they received cash (unemployment) benefits: a low level of introduction aid was (re)introduced at the same time by an amendment to the Active Social Policy Act (§ 27).[10] Furthermore, it was specified that foreigners offered an introduction programme have a duty to participate actively in the different programme elements.[11]

For each individual foreigner, the elements of the programme were laid down in the contract drawn up between the foreigner and the local council, on the basis of an assessment of the foreigner's situation, skills, background and needs (section 16(3), cf. section 19). The contract would specify the sanctions applicable to the legislation in a situation where the foreigner failed to appear or rejected one or more of the activities agreed upon (or decided) in

---

[9] En ny udlændingepolitik (A new aliens policy), 17 January 2002.

[10] Act No 361 of 6 June 2002. According to the new scheme on 'start-up help', only persons who have resided in Denmark for at least seven of the past eight years are entitled to a regular cash benefit; the lower rates are about 50–70% of the regular rates.

[11] Act No. 364 of 6 June 2002.

the individual contract. The consequences included a reduction or suspension of the introduction aid (sections 30 and 31) and a lack of options for obtaining a permanent residence permit (section 11(7) (2) of the Aliens Act (as amended in 2002)).[12]

In 2005, under an amendment of the Integration Act, the local councils became obliged to inform foreigners who fail to acquire knowledge of the Danish language, in a systematic and targeted way and within the stipulated timeframe, of the potential consequences of their 'inadequate acquisition of skills in the Danish language' (§ 20(6)).[13]

On 11 May 2005, the government launched a new integration plan, 'A New Chance for Everybody', with a view to enhancing integration efforts through several new initiatives. According to the plan, the fundamental values of society, such as democracy and equality between the sexes, must enjoy general recognition. More immigrants shall be employed, young immigrants and descendants of immigrants shall be as well educated and trained as young ethnic Danes, and ghettoisation is to be addressed.

On 17 June 2005, the government entered into an integration agreement with the Danish People's Party and the Social Democrats with a view to implementing the 2005 plan. The basic idea was that foreigners are to meet the same expectations and requirements as other citizens and that foreigners and their descendants must have the same fair opportunities as others. Education was seen as a precondition for integration and the municipalities were expected to work in a targeted manner, not least with the business community. Additionally, foreigners should make an effort, take responsibility for and demonstrate their will to integrate, find employment and become self-sufficient.

With a view to implementing the plan, in November 2005 the government presented a Bill for amending the Integration Act and the Aliens Act. Among other things, the Bill introduced 'integration contracts' (instead of 'individual contracts'), 'declarations on integration and active citizenship' and included an obligation for young people to be educated. Foreigners must sign and thereby recognise the values stated in the 'Declaration on integration and active citizenship'. The declaration as such is not legally binding. Its purpose is to render Danish values visible and signal that the society expects foreigners to make an effort to integrate as participating and contributing citizens, equal to other citizens. The Bill was adopted in 2006 and implies

[12] Amended by Act No. 365 of 6 June 2002.
[13] Act 402 of 1 June 2005.

that a foreigner's integration contract will last until he or she has acquired a permanent residence permit (section 19(8)).[14]

Within one month of taking over responsibility for an adult foreigner, the local council is obliged to initiate the introduction programme. Foreigners who do not receive introduction aid will only be offered a Danish course. A foreigner who has finished a Danish course will be issued with a certificate of active participation (if the relevant conditions are satisfied). In 1998, this certification of active participation was made a condition for being granted a permanent residence permit. In 2002, an examination requirement was added and, in 2007, the requirement was extended to an examination at a fixed level (as part of an 'integration test'), see section 3.6 below.

In order to understand the rationale behind the integration programmes, etc., the various citizenship models presented in the introduction and in the first chapters of this book offer useful explanations. When the Integration Act was introduced, mostly republican arguments about fostering participation were put forward, but traces of other models appear subsequently, especially libertarian arguments emphasising the duty of immigrants to participate and the immigrants' contribution to the society. Finally, with the 2006 amendments placing the emphasis on immigrants' recognition of the values appearing in the integration contract, communitarian arguments come into play. Still, egalitarian viewpoints have followed the republican, libertarian and communitarian viewpoints all along, stressing the importance of immigrants being 'participating and contributing citizens *equal to other citizens*', and integration is seen throughout as a two-way process – although with increasing weight given to the responsibilities of the immigrant.

3.4 *Danish Language Courses for Adult Foreigners*

3.4.1 *Legislation on Danish Language Courses*

In 1998, together with the Integration Act, an *Act on Teaching Danish as a Second Language for Adult Foreigners and Others and Language Centres* was adopted.[15] Like the Integration Act, the Act on teaching Danish entered into force on 1 January 1999. Danish language tuition was to be provided at language centres with a view to securing appropriate educational options

[14] Another condition for obtaining this residence permit is that the foreigner sign the integration contract as well as a declaration on integration and active citizenship in Danish society (section 19(1) (1)), see Act No. 243 of 27 March 2006.

[15] Cf. Consolidation Act No 975 of 25 October 2000 from the Ministry of Education.

for participants with very diverse backgrounds, abilities and needs. The educational facilities were to be qualified and streamlined and the number of weekly periods increased.

According to the 1998 Education Act, the following tests could be taken at the language centres: General Examination 1, General Examination 2 and Danish Examination 2.

In 2003, the newly established Ministry of Integration presented a new Education Act to Parliament. The Bill was the second phase of the government's plan to make the Danish education system more effective with a view to securing the integration of foreigners into the labour market. The new *Act on Danish Courses for Adult Aliens and others* entered into force on 1 January 2004.[16]

The Act provides for the following language tests to be taken at the language centres: Danish 1 examination (new), Danish 2 examination (almost comparable to the former General Examination 1 – but with a slightly higher level of oral Danish), Danish 3 examination (comparable to the former General Examination 2) and, finally, the higher education examination (the Study Test comparable to the former Danish Examination 2).

According to section 1 of the Act, the purpose of the Danish language courses is to assist foreigners in understanding and using the Danish language and acquiring knowledge of the Danish labour market, enabling them to be employed and self-supporting. The courses are meant to assist foreigners in acquiring the skills and knowledge that are relevant for working life, education and life as citizens in a democratic society.

One of the latest inventions in Danish language tuition is a free online course in Danish, which is supposed to make it possible for foreign job seekers to learn Danish before coming to work in Denmark. It is the intention of the Ministry of Integration to introduce a complete Danish language training programme within a few years. The programme will be targeted at students with little or no knowledge of Danish. The aim is to make foreign students able to reach a level of Danish language proficiency where they can be regarded as independent language users.[17]

In order to proceed with this new invention, an Act amending both the Act on Danish Education for Adult Foreigners and the Integration Act was adopted – unanimously – by Parliament on 28 May 2009. Free, job-oriented online Danish language education is to be introduced with a view to attracting highly skilled foreign manpower. This online language education may

[16] Act No. 375 of 28 May 2003.

[17] http://www.nyidanmark.dk/en-us/Integration/online_danish/online_danish.htm.

also be used by foreigners staying in Denmark, possibly as a supplement to the Danish language education given by the language schools.

The establishment of online education is part of the government's Recruitment Plan of October 2007 and Job Plan of February 2008. Civil society has responded positively to the programme that will include granting EU frontier commuters the same rights to Danish education as foreigners residing in Denmark.

Finally, more flexible Danish education for foreign workers is to be expected. A new flexible form of Danish education, 'Intro-Danish', will be proposed in a Bill presented by the Minister for Integration in autumn 2009. This is conceived as a supplement to the current Danish educational options intended for employed foreigners. The proposal is based on recommendations from a working group appointed by the government. Among its 18 recommendations, the working group has proposed a more flexible right to education (spread over five years and providing more instruction for Danish Course 1 students who may be able to pass the Danish 2 Examination, see below).[18]

3.4.2 *Content of Danish Language Courses and Tests*

As a rule, foreigners are offered a Danish language course lasting three years: Danish Course 1 (DC1), Danish Course 2 (DC2) or Danish Course 3 (DC3). The scope of each of the three Danish courses corresponds to 1.2 years' full-time study. The courses are split into 6 six-month modules with specific targets; on average, each module corresponds to 0.2 years' full-time study. Enrolment in a module other than the first module of a course assumes that the targets of the preceding module(s) have been achieved.

DC1 attaches importance to oral Danish. However, students do have to learn how to read and write a simple text in Danish. Students are taught about the Danish labour market, education, daily life, society, geography, democracy, fundamental values and Denmark past and present. The object of DC1 is to qualify the students for unskilled labour and active citizenship.

In DC2, students learn to understand, speak and read Danish and to write some texts. They are taught about the labour market, education, daily life, society, geography, the environment, democracy, fundamental values and Denmark past and present. The object is to qualify the students for the

---

[18] http://www.nyidanmark.dk/da-dk/nyheder/pressemeddelelser/integrationsministeriet/2009/ juni/fleksibelt_danskundervisning_udenlandske_arbejdstagere.htm.

labour market, active citizenship and participation in qualifying labour market courses or other vocational training alongside Danish colleagues.

In DC3, the speed and level of Danish are higher than in DC2. Students are taught about the labour market, education, daily life, society, geography, the environment, democracy, fundamental values, Denmark past and present and other subjects relevant to the humanities, social science and natural science. They learn to put problems into perspective and to incorporate general cultural, historical and societal knowledge. They learn to vary their spoken and written Danish language in order to be able to argue in favour of their personal attitudes and viewpoints. The object of the course is to qualify students for the labour market or for further education – and active citizenship.

All three courses culminate in tests in oral communication, as well as reading comprehension and written presentation. The Danish 1 Examination (D1E) is comparable to ALTE level 1/Council of Europe level (CEF) A2.[19] The Danish 2 examination (D2E) is comparable to ALTE level 2/CEF B1. D2E includes an assessment of whether the students can express themselves in fluent, understandable and relevant language with a certain complexity and correctness. The Danish 3 Examination (D3E) is comparable to ALTE level 3/CEF B2. D3E comprises an assessment of whether the students can express themselves relevantly and understandably using fairly nuanced and complex language, with a relatively high degree of accuracy. In writing, the students must be able to discuss a subject, describe attitudes and viewpoints, elaborate, give reasons and summarise.[20]

3.4.3 *Target Group*

The Danish language courses target foreigners according to their previous schooling, i.e. no schooling, limited schooling and extensive schooling, respectively. DC1 is intended for students who have little or no educational background and have not learnt to read and write in their mother tongue (and Latin-script illiterates who do not understand European notation).

[19] For an overview of the levels of language proficiency in the Council of Europe's Common Framework of Reference, please see annex 1.

[20] See *Bekendtgørelse om prøver inden for danskuddannelse til voksne udlændinge m.f.* (Regulation No. 912 of 28 September 2005 on tests within Danish education for adult foreigners and others); D3E may be taken by students who have completed the first five modules of DC3. Students who complete all 6 modules can take the higher education examination (the study test); since success in this examination is not an 'integration requirement' it will not be commented on further.

DC2 is intended for students with some educational background in their country of origin who are expected to learn Danish as a second language rather slowly. DC3 is intended for students with lower or upper secondary or higher education in their country of origin (for instance vocational training, grammar school or long cycle higher education) who are expected to learn Danish as a second language rather rapidly.[21]

Students with particular needs, due for instance to dyslexia, other learning difficulties, post-traumatic stress syndrome (PTSD), other psychiatric diseases or brain injuries, etc., are offered tuition in small groups or – in very special cases – individual tuition; such students may also be offered special (compensatory) education before starting a Danish course, with the right to deferment of the three-year Danish education period.

Furthermore, foreigners have the option of extending the three-year period of free Danish language tuition if, for instance as a result of full-time work, illness or childbirth, they are prevented from participating in courses for the three-year period. In general, the courses are flexible in terms of time, place and content, in order to enhance interaction with students' employment, activation or training; among other things, students may follow classes outside normal working hours.

3.4.4 *Fees*

The Danish language courses are free of charge for foreigners covered by the Integration Act. However, as regards self-supporting foreigners who are not covered by the Integration Act, the local council may (choose to) charge a fee per module (section 14 of the Education Act). The amount to be charged differs according to the various groups of foreigners. For participants holding a residence permit issued with a view to permanent residence, the maximum fee is 500 DKR (about 65 euros) (see section 3.5 below) while, for participants holding a residence permit issued with a view to temporary residence, it is 1000 DKR (about 130 euros). Nonetheless, primarily self-financing foreign students may be charged up to 5000 DKR (about 650 euros).[22]

---

[21] The aim of the test is to ensure that students have sufficient knowledge of Danish language to render them capable of managing well in the Danish educational system. Thus, reading and writing are the main focus. The students are supposed to be able to express a reasoned opinion on public matters in fluent Danish.

[22] Act No. 375 of 28 May 2003 and Information Letter 3/2004.

For students who have not followed the language courses a fee of 1000 DKR (about 130 euros) may be charged for registering for a language exam (D1E, D2E and D3E).[23]

3.4.5 *Statistics*

In DC1 and (to a lesser extent) DC2, most of the students are unemployed and receive their Danish language tuition as part of their introductory programme or as part of an activation offer. In DC3, students are usually employed or otherwise supported, for instance by a spouse.[24]

In 2005, the language schools reported that, on a national basis, they referred around 25–30% of enrolled students to DC3.[25] However in 2006, on a national basis, 49% of enrolled students followed DC3, while 37% followed DC2 and 14% DC1.[26] According to the leader of the organisation of heads of language schools, the FLD, the present distribution of enrolled students is probably around 60% in DC3, 25% in DC2 and 15% in DC1.[27] One possible explanation for the development leading to a majority of enrolled students now following DC3 may be that the number of job-seeking foreigners has increased significantly in recent years, while the number of refugees and family-reunified immigrants has decreased; see section 3.5 below. All things being equal, the 'new workforce' is better educated than 'the Integration Act students'.

Women are generally in the majority in the language schools. In 2005 and 2006, as a total, women made up 64.5% [presumably] of all students. As for the origin of the students in these years, 2/5 came from a non-Western country.

In the first examination period of 2006, 4,249 students were enrolled for the final examination (at D1E, D2E and D3E); 85% sat it and, of those, 91% passed the examination. In the second examination period, 3,630 students were enrolled, 90% took the examination and, of those, 87% passed. The pass rate was highest for D1E (92%) and lowest for D3E (84%). The average marks were between 6 (pass) and 10 (very good) for most students; the

---

[23] *Ibid.*

[24] Thus, they are normally self-supporting and pay a fee for the tuition.

[25] See, for instance, *Nyhedsmagasinet Danske Kommuner*, nr. 1/2006, where the percentage mentioned is 20.

[26] In 2006, the total number of students was 35,569; see report of February 2009 by the Danish Ministry of Integration: *Aktiviteten hos udbydere af danskuddannelse for voksne udlændinge m.fl. i 2006* (Activity among suppliers of Danish courses for adult aliens and others in 2006).

[27] Personal estimate given by mail on 19 February 2009.

widest variation in the marks was found at D3E level, where many students obtained marks at the top (10–13) as well as at the bottom (below 6, which is 'fail').[28]

3.5 *Access to Permanent Residence and the Right to Family Reunification*

3.5.1 *Third-country Nationals*

With the amendment of the Aliens Act in 1998, the regulation involving the change from a time-limited residence permit to an unlimited residence permit was given a more prominent place in the Aliens Act. Until then, the possibility of acquiring a secure status had been regulated indirectly by the imposition of the (3-year) time limit to withdraw a residence permit. Following the 1998 amendment, the Aliens Act distinguished between residence permits issued for the purposes of both temporary and permanent residence. A permanent residence permit could be issued to a foreigner holding a residence permit issued with a view to permanent residence once that person had lived in Denmark for more than 3 years.

With the 1998 amendment, a number of supplementary conditions were introduced to emphasise that it was expected that a foreigner wishing to stay in Denmark on a permanent basis would make an effort to learn the Danish language and to adapt to Danish society (Vedsted-Hansen 2006). As mentioned in section 3.2, it was also decided that, in order to qualify for a permanent residence permit, a foreigner should have completed an integration programme (or a comparable course); only active participation was required – at that time there was no requirement regarding passing a test, etc.

In 2001, after the Liberals and the Conservatives had formed a new government with support from the Danish People's Party, thus forming a majority in Parliament, the necessary basis for introducing more strict requirements for family reunification and for being granted a permanent residence permit was created.

In 2002, in an amendment to the Aliens Act, the residence requirement for being granted a permanent residence permit was raised from 3 to 7 years (§ 11(3)). Furthermore – apart from completing an integration course (§ 11 (7) (1) – the applicant now had to pass a test in the Danish language (§ 11 (7) (2).

[28] Due to some technical difficulties, no statistics from 2007 or 2008 are yet available.

At the same time, the entitlement to family reunification was repealed; new provisions on access to family reunification replaced the former entitlement rule and a number of new requirements were introduced, including the famous Danish '24 years rule', stating that a residence permit will only be granted to a foreign spouse or partner on the basis of marriage or cohabitation if both parties are over 24 years of age. In addition, the scope of the so-called 'attachment requirement' was extended to include Danish citizens as well; the couple's aggregate ties to Denmark ('overall attachment') must be stronger than the couple's attachment to any other country.[29]

With the amendment, the target groups for the family reunification rules are Danish citizens, Nordic citizens and refugees, in addition to third-country nationals who have held a permanent residence permit for more than the previous 3 years. Thus, third-country national sponsors must normally have resided in Denmark for a total of 10 years (7 years before they qualify for a permanent residence permit and 3 years subsequently) in order to obtain family reunification (§ 9(1)).[30]

In 2003, with an amendment to the Aliens Act, the requirement of 7 years' residence as a condition for the issue of a permanent residence permit was modified. Libertarian viewpoints supported the change, which made it possible for foreigners to acquire a permanent residence permit after 5 or even 3 years; the possibilities depended on the foreigner's integration level (firm connection to the labour market, self-supporting and a substantial connection to Danish society, for instance through association or political activity or long-cycle higher education) (§ 11, 4 and 5).[31]

Later in 2003, the 'attachment rule' was amended following strong criticism of its consequences for Danish expatriates who could not re-settle in Denmark with their foreign family. The solution chosen was to exempt spouses and partners who have held Danish citizenship for at least 28 years (§ 9 (7)); foreigners who have lived continuously in Denmark for 28 years or more and who are born and raised in Denmark or who have been living in the country since childhood were also exempted.[32]

In 2005, in an amendment to the Aliens Act, family reunification was made conditional upon the applicant and the person living in Denmark sign-

---

[29] Denmark is not bound by the Family Reunification Directive due to the Danish opt-out concerning justice and home affairs.

[30] In the amendment, the rules were made to cover Danish nationals who apply for family reunification with third-country nationals.

[31] Act 425 of 10 June 2003.

[32] Act 1204 of 27 December 2003.

ing a declaration stating that, to the best of their ability, they will involve themselves actively in the applicant's and any accompanying foreign child's Danish course and integration into Danish society (§ 9(2)). It was furthermore established that the financial guarantee (almost 7000 euros), which the sponsors undertake in order to secure coverage of public expenses relating to the applicant, may be reduced by half once the foreigner has passed a final examination in Danish or has been issued with a certificate proving his or her active participation in the Danish course (§ 9(4)).[33]

After the government had entered into an integration agreement with the Danish People's Party and the Social Democrats on 17 June 2005, with a view to implementing its integration plan, 'A New Chance for Everybody', the Integration Act and the Aliens Act were changed again (see section 3.3.2 above). Apart from introducing 'integration contracts' lasting until the issue of a permanent residence permit, together with declarations on integration and active citizenship, etc., the purpose was to strengthen the conditions for obtaining a permanent residence permit. Thus, a new requirement for acquiring a permanent residence permit was that a foreigner – in addition to completing the introduction programme – complete the activities (regarding job plan, etc.) that, according to the Act on an Active Labour Market Policy, are laid down in the integration contract. Furthermore, in order to obtain a permanent residence permit, the foreigner must have signed the integration contract and the declaration on integration and active citizenship.[34]

On 20 June 2006, the government entered into a new agreement with the Danish People's Party on future immigration. On the same day, a broader welfare agreement had been secured and the immigration agreement was an extension of this agreement. The challenges to be met in order to secure future welfare and cohesion included the employment of immigrants and immigrants' descendents. Employment was seen as a better way to integrate. It was considered important that foreigners be met with a clear signal as to what was expected of them in Denmark. Immigration policy should contribute towards improving Denmark's position among the competition for highly qualified international labour. Increasing highly qualified labour would

---

33 Act 402 of 1 June 2005.

34 See Act no. 243 of 27 March 2006; among the additional conditions for permanent residence are that the foreigner not have overdue public debt and not have been sentenced to two or more years' imprisonment or other criminal sanctions for serious crimes; other (suspended or unsuspended) sentences of imprisonment will postpone the date on which the person concerned will be eligible for a permanent residence permit (from 3–15 years or more).

strengthen welfare and production and enhance employment possibilities for people with a limited education. Libertarian ideas prevailed, calling attention to the fact that immigrants with good qualifications could prolong the upturn in the economy, while a lack of labour could hinder its progress.

In addition to the extension of a job card scheme and the establishment of a green card scheme, the following elements were part of the agreement:

- an integration test (exam) as a condition for acquiring a permanent residence permit;
- an immigration test in the Danish language and societal knowledge for foreigners applying for family reunification and for religious ministers.

In November 2006 the Minister for Integration presented a Bill amending the Aliens Act and the Act on Active Social Policy, providing for an immigration test and an integration test (plus a green card scheme, residence permits for foreigners with an annual salary of 450,000 DKR (60,000 euros) and residence permits for foreigners with special qualifications, see below in sections 3.6 and 3.7).[35] The Act was adopted in April 2007.

At about that time, alien policy occupied a less prominent position. All political parties recognised that Denmark was in need of more skilled foreign labour. However, in the November 2007 general election, the changes to alien policy were modest. It became clear that political parties wishing to exert an influence had to support 'the world's most restrictive rules on family reunification'; even the Social Liberals and the Socialist People's Party declared that neither the '24 years rule' nor the 'attachment requirement' (which the Social Democrats wanted to pursue) should stand in the way of a change in the cabinet (Rasmussen 2007: 161).

3.5.2 *Union Citizens*

Union citizens are exempt from fulfilling the aforementioned requirements for family reunification (which might prevent them from exercising their free movement rights, etc.). It is significant that many Danish citizens try to bypass the strict requirements for family reunification by making use of their right to free movement as union citizens. Danish citizens do not – as it were – appreciate the idea of being subjected to reverse discrimination. Therefore, the so-called 'Malmø Model' has been invented.

A number of judgments from the European Court of Justice (ECJ) on Union citizens' rights to free movement have contributed to this model,

[35] Act no. 379 of 25 April 2007.

whereby Danish citizens move to Malmø in Sweden (or to another place abroad) in order to settle there with their third-country national family members and eventually, after a certain period of time, return to Denmark with their family, thus availing themselves of the EU free movement rights.

There has, however, been some uncertainty as to what it takes for citizens to be able to benefit from EU law in their own country. In 1992, the *Singh* case (C-370/90) established that community workers returning to their own country were covered by the free movement rights. In 2003, the *Ackrich* case (C-109/01) established that citizens' deliberate use of free movement rights is not an evasion of national law and, in 2007, the Eind case (C-291/05) established that also returning unemployed citizens are covered by the free movement rights.

However, the uncertainty subsisted, partly concerning what the 'necessary residence period in another country' is in order to be covered by the EU law. Following an (anonymous) request for information from the Danish authorities by a journalist in the summer of 2008 and the refusal by civil servants to provide information about 'loopholes in the national legislation', the Danish Parliamentary Ombudsman criticised the information given by the Ministry of Integration about the EU regime.[36]

Around this same time, the ECJ delivered its judgement in the Metock case (25 July 2008, C-127/08). The court maintained that Union citizens who have made use of their right to free movement pursuant to *Directive 2004/38/ EC on the rights of citizens of the Union and their family members to free movement* have a right to family reunification with third-country national family members irrespective of whether the family members have previously stayed legally in another EU Member State. The judgement caused strong reactions in Denmark. Among members of the ruling parties and, in particular, members of the Danish People's Party, it was widely held that complying with the judgement would lead to an undermining of the 'fair and consistent' Danish aliens policy.

The Danish People's Party raised the possibility of neglecting the judgment, but the government stood firm on its implementation. In return, the government accepted a political agreement with the Danish People's Party with a view to 'combating the possible negative consequences of the Metock judgment'. According to the political agreement of 22 September 2008, the principles underlying Danish immigration policy would be upheld. The government would implement the *Metock* judgment but, at the same time, work towards an amendment of Directive 2004/38/EC on the rights of citizens

[36] http://www.ombudsmanden.dk/adv_soeg/?mode=search&global=1&freetext=metock#Sager.

of the European Union and their family members to free movement. – Furthermore, new control mechanisms in immigration cases were to be established and some of the naturalisation criteria were to be strengthened. In the autumn of 2008, the legislation to implement the agreement was adopted, see below.

Albeit with some delay, the ECJ's case law has been implemented in Danish law. The Ministry of Integration provides information on its homepage about the content of the relevant case law and its implications for Danish aliens and migration law.[37] Union citizens and EEA nationals who believe they fall within the scope of the new practice following, for instance, the Metock judgement, may request a reopening of their case. According to the statistics, there has been some increase in the number of family reunification cases where the sponsor is Danish. Thus, while 43 residence permits and 2 refusals were issued in such cases from 1 January 2008–10 July 2008, the numbers for the rest of the year were 112 residence permits and 4 refusals (of the 112 persons reunified with families, 8% were EU/EEA nationals and 92% third-country nationals).[38]

3.6 *The Integration Test*

3.6.1 *Background*

As mentioned in the introduction, the integration agreement of 20 June 2006 between the government and the Danish People's Party was concluded with a view to strengthening future welfare in Denmark. The integration test (or 'examination' as it is called in Danish) was presumed to fuel immigrants' motivation for seeking employment. Hence, with the amendment of the Aliens Act adopted on 25 April 2007, it was established that an integration test (examination) had to be passed as a condition for acquisition of a permanent residence permit and cash benefit.[39]

---

[37] http://www.nyidanmark.dk/en-us/coming_to_dk/eu_and_nordic_citizens/eu-eea_citizens/family_ reunification_in_denmark/family_reunification_in_denmark_for_union_citizens_and_eea_ nationals.htm.

[38] Tal og fakta på udlændingeområdet (June 2009); http://www.nyidanmark.dk/NR/rdonlyres/5E7B0EAB-3819–4CF6–A824–4E57EBCC12FB/0/tal_og_fakta_paa_udlaendingeomraadet_2008.pdf.

[39] Act No. 379 of 25 April 2007.

3.6.2 *Target Group*

As already mentioned, foreigners may, as a rule, apply for a permanent residence permit after having held a temporary residence permit for 7 years.[40] A number of supplementary conditions must be fulfilled, including passing an integration test; the requirements apply to foreigners who have been granted or have applied for a residence permit since 1 July 2006 and foreigners who had not yet completed an integration programme as of 29 November 2006.[41]

Persons who resided in Denmark as children are exempt from the requirements, as are the following categories of foreigners:

- Those who, at the time of application, are of retirement age or have taken early retirement;
- Those over the age of 50 who are granted an initial residence permit on the grounds of family reunification and who, for ten years prior to this date, have been married to or lived in a permanent relationship with a person residing in Denmark;
- Those who cannot take the test for reasons beyond their control, for example physical or mental handicap, experiences of torture or violence, severe trauma or illness, or other reasons pertaining to the person's qualifications.

3.6.3 *Content of the Test*

In order to take the integration 'examination', a foreigner must have held a full-time job for two years and six months and have passed a Danish language test, either D2E (ALTE 2/B1) or D1E (ALTE 1/A2) together with an English language test at a level corresponding to D2E (ALTE 2/B1).[42]

---

[40] EU/EEA citizens can reside in Denmark under the EU regulations on the free movement of persons and services.

[41] The welfare Commission had suggested that an integration examination, for instance, full-time employment for two years and having passed a Danish or English examination, should replace residence as one of the conditions for being granted a permanent residence permit (and a cash benefit).

[42] If the initial residence permit was issued to a child, he must wait until he turns 18 before applying for a permanent residence permit. Moreover, if the parent is a foreign national, the parent must hold a permanent residence permit, or the child must have resided legally in Denmark for seven years. In addition, the child must meet similar conditions as those applicable to adults. However, the child does not have to pass an integration test, but must have passed a Danish language examination.

3.6.4 *Attitudes Towards the Test*

Language teachers have called the new integration test absurd. They have recapitulated that D1E is intended for students who have little or no educational background and who have not learnt to read or write in their mother tongue; thus, the target group comprises persons who, as adults in Denmark, have acquired sufficient basic reading and writing abilities through hard work and perseverance to pass D1E. Many are to be found in the unskilled labour force and requiring that they take an English language test at same level as D2E as a condition for obtaining a permanent residence permit is tantamount to excluding them from acquiring the permit (Fleisher 2006).

3.6.5 *Statistics*

Due to the operational rules of the Act, the test has only been effective for a short period and, unfortunately, generally accessible statistics on decisions relating to permanent residence permits are lacking.[43]

3.7 *The Immigration Test*

3.7.1 *Background*

In the amendment to the Aliens Act adopted on 25 April 2007,[44] it was decided, in addition to the integration test, to establish an immigration test for foreigners applying for family reunification and for religious ministers applying for a residence permit. According to the Minister for Integration, the Bill followed the Dutch example.

According to the preparatory report, the purpose of the immigration test is to strengthen the individual foreigner's possibilities for successful and rapid integration into Danish society; it is the perception that foreigners who have passed the immigration test will then be better prepared for the introductory programme. Thus, the immigration test is seen as a supplement to the ordinary language courses. Another aim of the test is to help ensure that foreigners take responsibility as early as possible for their own integration and are able to document their motivation and wish to become part of Danish society.

While the Bill on introducing the immigration test was debated in Parliament, the Parliamentary Standing Committee on Foreigners and Integration

---

[43] The question of making such information accessible is at present dealt with by the Ministry of Integration.

[44] Act no. 379 of 25 April 2007.

Policy asked the Minister for Integration whether she expected a decrease in the number of applications for family reunification, as had been the case in the Netherlands. The Minister stressed that the purpose of the test was not to limit the number of family reunification; she did not expect a distinct decrease in the number of applications.[45]

Another question from the Committee concerned the possibility of introducing a pre-recognition system, allowing for a postponement of the immigration test to be taken once the authorities had established whether the applicant fulfilled the other requirements for family reunification.[46] This question was dealt with by the working group set up to conduct a pre-analysis of the implementation of the immigration test.[47] Subsequently, as will appear from the Agreement on the Budget for 2008, the government and the Danish People's Party agreed that applicants for family reunification must receive pre-recognition regarding their fulfilment of the other conditions for family reunification before they can take the immigration test; at the same time it was agreed to abolish the possibility of taking the test abroad.[48] These amendments presuppose the adoption of an amendment of the 2007 Act; a Bill along these lines will be presented in Parliament in autumn 2009, with a view to bringing the immigration test into play spring 2010.

3.7.2 *Target Group*

The target group is broad; as a starting point, the test applies to all foreigners applying for reunification with a spouse or partner (for the reasons mentioned in section 5.2. EU/EEA citizens are exempt from taking the immigration test).

In the agreement of 20 June 2006 between the government and the Danish People's Party, it was decided to examine whether, within the framework of bilateral agreements, immigrants from the Western world could be exempted from the test, as the Netherlands has done. The agreement stated that as far as possible these country groups would be exempted. However, as already mentioned, the result is that, as a starting point, all foreigners (except EU/

---

[45] See also http://www.folketinget.dk/doc.aspx?/Samling/20061/MENU/01287268.htm – the Minister for Integration's 'Talepapir' (speech paper) on consultation question A concerning L 93, 22 March 2007.

[46] See the Minister's answer to question 81 regarding L 93; 26 March 2007: http://www.folketinget.dk/doc.aspx?/Samling/20061/MENU/01287268.htm.

[47] Rapport fra arbejdsgruppen vedrørende foranalyse om implementering af indvandringsprøve; September 2007.

[48] http://www.fm.dk/Publikationer/2008/Aftaler%20om%20Finansloven%20for%202008/1%20 Aftale%20om%20Finansloven%20for%202008.aspx.

EEA nationals) are covered – regardless of their educational background and regardless of whether their country of origin is closely related to Denmark or not.

Dispensation from the test requirement is possible under certain special circumstances, for instance where the sponsor is a refugee who cannot take up residence in his country of origin due to the risk of persecution or where the sponsor's personal conditions call for exemption due to serious illness. In all cases where a refusal will constitute a violation of the European Convention on Human Rights, dispensation must be granted. In general, the test requirement does not apply to foreigners who cannot fulfil the requirements due to serious illness or handicap, including post-traumatic stress syndrome (PTSD).

Besides, the requirement shall not apply to foreigners who are granted family reunification under a special practice, including where the sponsor has a residence permit granted for occupational or educational reasons.

3.7.3 *Test Level, Content and Procedures*

The immigration test is an oral test. It consists of a Danish language test and a societal knowledge test. The level of the Danish language test is A1-minus, corresponding to module 1 of DC1 and DC2. The test of knowledge of Danish society will be composed of 30 questions extracted from a publicly accessible question bank of 100 questions; the level will be higher than A1-minus but, on the other hand, the questions will be accessible beforehand.

The intention is that immigrants must be familiar with Danish norms, values and fundamental rights, including democratic principles, individual freedom, personal integrity, gender equality, freedom of religion and freedom of speech. Furthermore immigrants must be familiar with certain more practical facts such as the prohibition of female circumcision, forced marriages and the fact that parents are responsible for their children, education, health, work, etc.

For the purpose of the immigration test, a preparatory package is prepared: the key part of the package is an educational film. The film is supposed to give participants a realistic general picture of Denmark and daily life in Denmark. Thus, the film shall communicate both facts and values with a view to adapting the expectations of immigrants to Danish reality. According to the Ministry of Integration, the basic message of the film will be that prospects in Denmark are good for those who are willing to make an effort and take on responsibility for their life in that country.

The film is supposed to provide answers to the 100 test questions about Danish society; it will be produced in Danish and dubbed in 18 foreign languages. The film is not supposed to include language lessons, since the immigrants themselves are responsible for preparing for the language test. However, some expressions from the language test may be integrated and presented in the film.

Apart from the film, a picture book will be produced, containing stills from the film, and a CD of all the questions from the societal knowledge test; the questions on the CD will also be translated into 18 foreign languages. All material will be available in a spoken version.

Tenders have been invited for the educational film that will form the primary basis for the immigrants' preparation for the Danish societal knowledge test. The test will be arranged as a computer-based test system that will play the questions and record the answers on a sound track. For each question, the computer will show a relevant picture from the educational film; likewise, it will show a picture for each of the four out of five language test exercises. Both the societal knowledge and the language test will be conducted in Danish. The tests will be evaluated by external examiners.

A cost-based fee has to be paid to take the test. The level of the fee will be influenced by the number of applicants; according to the Finance Act, the fee is expected to amount to around 3,000 DKR (about 400 euros).

The test must be taken after the applicant has received recognition in advance of his application for family reunification. The applicant will be granted a temporary visa in order to take the test in Denmark; the test may be re-taken at any time but in this case the fee is also payable again. Family reunification may be refused if the applicant fails the test.

As already mentioned, the test system is expected to be implemented in 2010. Each year, 1500–2000 foreigners are expected to take the test – corresponding to the present number of family reunifications. It is an essential premise that *all* applicants must be able to pass the test, regardless of their educational background.[49]

The Danish test (as it has developed) differs from the Dutch test in several ways. The Dutch test is a pre-departure test to be taken in the country of origin, while the Danish test is to be taken in Denmark. The Dutch test results become obsolete after one year; the Danish test continues to be valid. The Dutch test is conducted with electronic speech-recognition, while the Danish computer-based test will be corrected by Danish external examiners. Unlike the Dutch knowledge test, the Danish test is translated into 18 foreign languages. The Danish examination result may be challenged, unlike the Dutch result.

[49] *Ibid.*, p. 7.

Using the speech-recognition system, Dutch participants have three chances to practise in order to pass; this possibility does not exist in Denmark. The preparatory package will be accessible (free of charge) on the internet in Denmark, unlike the Dutch test; the price of the Dutch preparatory package is €63.90. The Dutch test is to be taken before an application for family reunification can be submitted; in Denmark, an application for family reunification is to be pre-recognised before the immigration test can be taken. In the Netherlands, religious ministers need to pass the immigration test before being granted a residence permit; in Denmark, religious ministers need to pass the test within 6 months of being granted a residence permit.

The rationale behind the Danish immigration test seems to be liberal/liberal-emancipatory in character in so far as the purpose is to make foreigners better prepared for life in Denmark and the intention is to ensure that the test does not preclude foreigners from being granted a residence permit for family reunification. Still, it is assumed that foreigners do prepare themselves for the test, although, according to language school teachers, many will not be able to do so. Furthermore, the fee to be paid may present an insurmountable barrier, especially if it is to be paid more than once by immigrants on a low income. Thus, in order to avoid accusations of 'repressive liberalism', in other words pursuing liberal goals using illiberal means (Joppke 2007), possibilities for free Danish language lessons (for instance, module 1 of DC1 or 2) and a fee reduction – or waiver in certain cases – should be provided for in the legislation to be adopted in 2010.

3.8 *Language Test Requirements as a Condition for Naturalisation*

3.8.1 *Background*

In the eighteenth and nineteenth centuries, Denmark recognised the statuses of 'subject' and 'citizen', but, over time, the status of '*indfødsret*' increasingly came to be seen as 'the real citizenship status'. Therefore, in 1849, when Denmark became a constitutional democracy, electoral rights in parliamentary elections became attached to the status of *indfødsret*. Another novelty, according to the constitution, was that the Danish King lost his previous exclusive competence to grant naturalisation; since then, foreigners have only been able to acquire Danish *indfødsret* (citizenship) by statute.[50]

In 1849, when the first Danish constitution was adopted, Denmark was at war with Prussia. The large number of Germans in the Kingdom and

[50] See the present Constitution from 1953, section 44(1).

the ongoing Three-Year War may be seen as part of the explanation for the demand for affiliation to the Danish people, documented by knowledge of the Danish language as a requirement for naturalisation (Ersbøll 2008: 592 ff.).

Since that time, the requirement that applicants for naturalisation must be able to speak and understand Danish has been maintained. Traditionally, the applicants' language abilities were assessed by the (local) police during its preparation of cases for naturalisation. Based on an informal interview with the applicants, a police officer made a statement as to whether the person concerned was able to speak and understand Danish.

However, in the 1990s, while the Social Democrats were in power, some moves were afoot among the opposition parties for extending the language requirement for naturalisation. The Progress Party and later the Danish People's Party called for testing the applicants' reading and writing abilities. The Liberals and the Conservatives came up with similar proposals and, eventually, after the Liberals and the Conservatives had formed a new government in November 2001 with parliamentary support from the Danish People's Party, the naturalisation criteria were strengthened.

At that time, the Liberal Minister for Integration saw the naturalisation criteria as instrumental in the process of integration: citizenship was seen as something to strive for, an incentive for foreigners to adapt to Danish society. The Danish People's Party, however, argued explicitly for a reduction of the annual number of naturalisations through stricter naturalisation requirements (an annual quota of 2000 naturalisations to avoid a 'population replacement'). In their opinion naturalisation was the end point of a completed integration process (Ersbøll 2008: 698 ff.).

3.8.2 *The Naturalisation Procedure*

As mentioned, according to the Danish Constitution, foreigners can only acquire Danish citizenship by statute. A practice has developed since 1849, according to which the Ministry responsible for naturalisation (now the Ministry of Integration) drafts Bills on naturalisation, including applicants who fulfil the legislature's requirements for naturalisation. In principle, decisions on naturalisation are at Parliament's discretion. Therefore, traditionally, no legislation on the naturalisation criteria has existed; instead, the criteria are agreed upon by the (majority of) political parties in Parliament and afterwards published in a circular from the Ministry of Integration.[51]

[51] Now see Circular letter no. 61 of 22 September 2008.

Applications for naturalisation are still prepared by the police, who check on the formalities, e.g. whether the application form has been correctly filled in and whether the required documentation has been submitted. Afterwards, when the application is sent to the Ministry of Integration, the Ministry examines whether the naturalisation criteria are met and, if so, includes the applicant – by name – in a Bill on naturalisation. Bills on naturalisation are introduced in Parliament twice a year, normally in April and October. As a rule, their reading takes two to three months.

Like other Bills, the Bills on naturalisation are subject to three readings. After the first reading, the Bill is referred to a parliamentary standing committee, the Naturalisation Committee of the Danish Parliament (*Indfødsretsudvalget*). The Committee receives confidential information on the applicants' conduct, etc., and may ask questions of the Minister for Integration. When the Committee has dealt with a Bill, it submits a report to Parliament concerning its adoption.[52] Another task of the Committee is to grant dispensation from the general naturalisation requirements.

Once Parliament has adopted a Bill on naturalisation, the Ministry of Integration notifies the persons concerned and sends them proof of their acquisition of Danish citizenship.

Since 2006, once a year Parliament has invited new citizens and their relatives to a 'Citizens Day' with a view to emphasising that applying for Danish citizenship is an important event and that, in Denmark, the distance between citizens and politicians is short.

3.8.3 *The Language Requirements for Naturalisation*

In June 2002, the Liberals, the Conservatives and the Danish People's Party entered into an agreement about the naturalisation criteria, providing for a number of new elements. For instance, only two Bills on naturalisation (instead of three) were to be presented in Parliament annually. Applicants for naturalisation must sign a declaration of faithfulness and loyalty to Denmark. The general residence requirement was extended from 7 to 9 years, the conduct requirements were strengthened and an examination certificate became a necessary condition for documenting the applicants' knowledge of the Danish language.[53]

[52] The Committee may suggest that applicants be excluded from the Bill if they no longer fulfil the naturalisation criteria, for instance because they have committed a crime after the naturalisation Bill was presented in Parliament.

[53] Renunciation of the nationality of origin has always been a Danish naturalisation requirement.

At the same time, the language skill requirement was raised. It was agreed that if an applicant had not passed grade 9 or 10 of Danish public school (or a higher educational institution) with a mark of 6 or higher in each Danish discipline (a mark of 7 – 8 is considered an average), as a rule, the applicant should pass a test set by a language centre at the level of General Test 1.[54]

Subsequently, after having visited some language centres, the Danish People's Party demanded a language test comparable to the school-leaving examination from public lower secondary schools. Their viewpoint was that future citizens needed Danish language skills at a level that enables them to follow the public debate as a basis for the right to vote; the level agreed upon at the 2002 agreement was, in their opinion, insufficient in this regard.[55] The then Minister for Integration rejected their demand; he promised, however, in connection with the new language reform, to tighten up the requirements of General Test 1 (cf. above, section 3.4.1. about the amendment replacing General Test 1 with D2E (level B1), which has a slightly higher level for oral Danish). This did not, however, satisfy the Danish People's Party, which maintained its demand for intensifying the language requirement. The then Minister for Integration kept on insisting that Danish language at level D2E, which was comparable to the level of Danish public school grades 4–5, was sufficient. At this level, students would be able to take part in discussions on issues concerning the society, etc., at the level required by school-leaving examinations. In order to reach an agreement, the Danish People's Party lowered its requirement to D3E with a pass mark of 8, but this proposal was also turned down by the Minister for Integration, who could not accept that only well-educated people should qualify for naturalisation. He argued that practical and often even more useful people should also have the possibility of becoming Danish citizens.[56]

After the general election of 8 February 2005, when the Liberal-Conservative governing coalition continued with support from a strengthened Danish People's Party, the Danish People's Party declared that it was time for a second round of the aliens policy, including more stringent naturalisation requirements. The situation developed in such a manner that, in December 2005, the three parties reached a new agreement on the naturalisation

[54] See Circular No. 55 of 12 June 2002 on naturalisation, section 25, listing a number of other tests from language centres and other educational institutions that satisfy the condition.

[55] www.ft.dk/samling/20031/salen/L23_BEH3_102_16_(NB).htm.

[56] Minister Bertel Haarder, see www.ft.dk/Samling/20041/salen/L58_BEH1_17_8(NB).htm.

criteria, including the requirements of Danish language ability at the level of D3E (ALTE 3/CEFR B3).[57]

Still, the ruling parties had not fully complied with the Danish People's Party's wish for a higher examination mark, but an opportunity presented itself after the passing of the Metock judgement by the ECJ; see section 3.5.2 above.[58] In November 2008, according to the 'Metock agreement' between the Liberals, the Conservatives and the Danish People's Party, the language requirement was further raised. For applicants without a Danish education, the general language requirement is now possession of a certificate of a pass in D3E with an average mark of at least 7 (on a 13-point scale) or 4 (on a 7-point scale) (or another comparable examination).[59]

3.8.4 *Target Group*

As a rule, the language requirement applies to all applicants for naturalisation, regardless of age and regardless of which 'immigrant generation' they belong to: first, second, third, etc.. A former exemption for persons over the age of 65 was repealed in 2002 and a provision on entitlement to citizenship for immigrant descendants was repealed in 2004, with the implication that immigrant descendents who have not acquired Danish citizenship by extension upon the naturalisation of their parents are referred for naturalisation as adults under the general conditions.[60]

The exemption criteria are restrictive. Until 2005, the Ministry of Integration could, for instance, exempt applicants who were unable to learn Danish to an adequate level due to mental illness, for example as a result of torture. In 2005, it was decided that the exemption possibilities for mentally or physically disabled applicants would be reduced. Thus, today, exemption from the naturalisation criteria may only be granted by the Naturalisation Committee

---

[57] See Circular No. 55 of 12 January 2006 on naturalisation.

[58] Case C 127/08.

[59] Adequate language skills may still be proved by a certificate for the lower secondary school-leaving examination after 9th or 10th grade, with an average mark of at least 6 (on the 13-point scale) or 2 (on the 7-step scale) in the Danish disciplines; see Circular No. 61 of 22 September 2008. The restriction concerning D3E resulted from the agreement of 22 September 2008 between the government and the Danish People's Party on the handling of the EU legislation on free movement, see also section 3.4.1 below.

[60] Until 2004, second-generation immigrants who had spent 10 years in Denmark and had not been convicted of crimes were entitled to Danish nationality; however, pursuant to Act No. 311 of 5 May 2004, this right was repealed (with the exception of second-generation immigrants from other Nordic countries).

of the Danish Parliament and only under exceptional circumstances, such as documented physical or mental illness of a very serious nature, resulting in the applicant being unable to (or having no reasonable prospects of) satisfying the language requirement.

According to a note to the naturalisation circular's provision on exemption from the language requirements, etc. (section 24(3)), it is assumed that the Ministry of Integration submits applications for exemption from the language requirement to the Naturalisation Committee in cases where the applicants, for example, suffer from severe physical disabilities (such as Down's syndrome), are brain damaged, blind or deaf or suffer from severe mental disorders such as (paranoid) schizophrenia, psychosis or severe depression. The note explicitly mentions that it is assumed that the Ministry refuses applications from applicants who suffer from PTSD (post-traumatic stress disorder).[61]

For the Naturalisation Committee, exemption is a matter of discretion; decisions are taken behind closed doors (in camera) and in principle without justification. No public guidelines or appeal possibilities exist.

3.8.5 *Public and Political Debate*

Traditionally, agreements on naturalisation criteria have been supported by a comprehensive majority in Parliament, but only the Liberals, the Conservatives and the Danish People's Party have supported the latest agreements. The government wants the naturalisation criteria to respond to society's expectations of the individual making an effort to become part of Danish society. The Danish People's Party wants to reduce the overall number of naturalisation with a view to avoiding the creation of a multi-ethnic society.

In 1998, almost all political parties agreed on the importance of considering the possibility of acquiring citizenship as a crucial positive element in the process of foreigners' integration in Denmark, but the harmony has come to an end. Today, the governing parties reject – as the Danish People's Party has constantly done – the idea of access to citizenship as a means of integration. The attitude of the government is expressed as follows by the (former) Minister for Integration:

---

61 According to the note, the Ministry of Integration is 'further assumed to refuse the application of applicants who suffer from PTSD (post-traumatic stress disorder), including where the condition is chronic and this is documented by a certificate from a medical professional'. The rule has been heavily criticised by various experts, organisations and others as providing grounds for discrimination; see Ersbøll 2006: 132.

> The acquisition of citizenship presumes that the applicant is already integrated in Danish society; this means that the applicant can speak, read and understand Danish, participates in the democratic process through local elections, association activities, school boards etc., and on the whole gets along in Danish society.[62]

Thus, today the ruling parties have also moved towards communitarianism, while the Red-Green Alliance, the Socialist People's Party and the Social Liberals still favour a liberal citizenship concept arguing for relaxed criteria for naturalisation, since they consider access to citizenship part of the integration process and crucial for foreigners' integration.

The 2005 agreement on the demanding language and societal knowledge requirements has given rise to severe criticism from different organisations and from the language teachers. The viewpoint is, in brief, that the high requirements exclude less well-educated permanent resident immigrants from becoming Danish citizens.[63] Besides, D3E provides a poor basis for granting citizenship; partly because it does not focus on knowledge that is useful in normal everyday life (while more abstract issues such as the environment, globalisation, developing countries, ecology, etc., may be discussed).[64]

The governing parties and the Danish People's Party do not share a desire to change the requirements and one-sided initiatives are unlikely to be taken. This is partly related to the 'contract policy' developed by the former Liberal Prime Minister. The Prime Minister's strategy was to create a 'contract' with the voters based on clear pledges in a limited number of clearly identified fields.[65] He wanted his politics to be accomplished; it was vital that he should not break his word – as his Social Democrat predecessor had done (or was perceived to have done) with unfavourable consequences for his credibility. The government's safety net has been the support from the Danish People's Party, which in turn wants concessions in order to pursue its goal.

---

62 Translation of part of a letter of 7 June 2006 from the Minister for Integration, Rikke Hvilshøj, to the Danish Institute for Human Rights (2006/307–108).

63 In particular, the exclusion of applicants suffering from PTSD from seeking dispensation from the requirements has shocked many, including doctors and psychologists; even representatives of the Liberals and the Conservatives seem to have considered an amendment, but since the provision is based on a tripartite agreement, a change would require the consent of all three parties.

64 www.information.dk/print/153297.

65 See the website of the Liberal Party: http://www.venstre.dk/index.php?id=4620.

In this way, the Danish People's Party (DF) has exerted its influence. As the former Liberal Prime Minister said to a Danish newspaper, right before he left Danish politics in order to become the Secretary General of NATO: 'When the contract policy works, it is because the DF has been able to deliver'. He added that the DF and the government had not stood in each other's way. Obviously there had been 'matters remote from the other party's heart', but the government and DF had never 'forced each other into a case that had cost blood'.[66] As for acceptance of the latest restrictions of the citizenship law, this may be associated with the fact that the government does not consider citizenship a 'must' for immigrants: citizenship is to be earned. As explained by the chairman of the Naturalisation Committee: 'The fact that some immigrants work and function in the country makes no difference. They can stay here – many for the rest of their lives – on the basis of a residence permit. But citizenship is to be earned. It is an appreciation of goodwill – demonstrated, among other things, by having learned the language'.[67]

3.8.6 *Statistics*

At the beginning of 2008, the Danish population comprised almost 5.5 million inhabitants, with 5.5% foreigners. The rest (94.5%) are Danish citizens; 90.9% are Danish citizens by origin, and 3.6% are Danish citizens by acquisition; these include 124,786 immigrants and 81,879 descendants.[68] (Statistically, a person is Danish if he has at least one parent who is a Danish citizen and was born in Denmark; a non-citizen is an immigrant if born abroad and a descendant if born in Denmark.)

Among immigrant men, 33.1% have acquired Danish citizenship and, among immigrant women, 32.9% have acquired Danish citizenship. Among immigrant descendants, the corresponding numbers are 68.1% (men) and 69.2% (women).[69]

Most of the transitions to Danish citizenship have occurred through naturalisation. The numbers increased considerably during the late 1990s and until 2002; in 2003, the numbers decreased due to the implementation of the stricter 2002 rules, but increased again in 2004 and 2005 by which time more

66 *Berlingske Tidende* 14 May 2009.

67 23 December 2007, see http://avisen.dk/vk-vi-aender-ikke-et komma-i danskproeve_4975aspx.

68 Source: Statistics Denmark, *Nyt fra Danmarks Statistik*, www.dst.dk/nyt.

69 Source: *Numbers and facts, population statistics on foreigners (Tal og fakta)*, August 2008, p. 10.

Table 1: Number of persons listed in naturalisation Acts, including children

1996	1997	1998	1999	2000	2001	2002	2003	2004	2005	2006	2007*	2008*
4,917	3,532	10,113	11,759	15,925	8,484	17,727	6,184	9,485	10,037	6,960	2,902	9,049

Source: The numbers included in the naturalisation acts are taken from the Acts on naturalisation (accessible on the website of the Danish Parliament (*Folketinget*): www.ft.dk).

* In 2007, as a consequence of the general election, only one naturalisation Bill was adopted; consequently, in 2008, three naturalisation Bills were adopted. Therefore, in order to compare years, the number of naturalisations in 2007 and 2008 should be added together and divided by two.

and more immigrants had taken the necessary language examinations. However, with the (gradual) implementation of the 2005 requirements, a decrease has re-occurred, this time probably of a more permanent character.

In order to understand the figures, it must be borne in mind that, in 2002, only 1,045 cases out of 17,727 were dealt with after the new 2002 Circular. Therefore, the statistics for 2003 are the first to demonstrate the impact of the 2002 Circular's strengthened criteria for naturalisation. As mentioned, the strengthened criteria resulted in a decline in naturalisations, but to a large extent it was caused by the new documentation requirement that forced many applicants to put their applications on hold until they had passed a language examination. However, there is every probability that the strengthening of the language requirements in 2005 and 2008 will form an insurmountable barrier for many applicants and, therefore, that the decline will be more permanent. It is also noteworthy that, due to transitional rules, until 2008 many cases were still dealt with according to the 2002 criteria. Thus, the 2005/2008 criteria have not yet fully taken effect.[70]

At the same time as the number of naturalisations has decreased due to the applicants' lack of sufficient Danish language skills, the number of refusals of naturalisation has increased for the same reason.

The figures demonstrate that, since tightening up the language requirement, the number of refusals of naturalisation due to lack of sufficient Danish language skills has increased considerably. The requirements are now set so high that certain groups will be permanently excluded from fulfilling them – even if they do their utmost.

[70] The Naturalisation Act adopted in spring 2009 covered 1356 applicants with 471 children; among the applicants, 22 had their cases dealt with according to the 2002 criteria, 1120 according to the 2006 criteria and 471 according to the 2008 criteria.

Table 2: Refusals of naturalisation due to lack of Danish language proficiency

1999	2000	2001	2002	2003	2004	2005	2006	2007	2008[71]
537	840	778	503	2507	1632	1185	961	1498	3446

Source: Ministry of Integration

Table 3: Number of applications for dispensation from the language requirements, etc.

	2000	2001	2002	2003	2004	2005	2006	2007	2008
Applications	98	49	180	227	275	540	359	108	227
Dispensations	97	34	151	106	105	65	103	37	41
Refusals	1	15	29	121	170	475	256	71	186

Source: The Ministry of Integration

As already mentioned, all applications for exemption shall be submitted to the Naturalisation Committee of the Parliament that makes its decisions 'behind closed doors', and the Committee's practice with respect to granting exemption from the language requirements has been restricted in parallel with the restrictions of the requirements for naturalisation, see Table 3.

3.8.7 *To sum up*

For the Danish People's Party, a marked reduction in the number of naturalisations has been an explicit goal and the party has determined negotiated naturalisation criteria in order to produce this result. This has been possible because the government has been in need of agreements with the Danish People's Party in order to implement its general policy. The result is naturalisation requirements that have an exclusive effect, partly because those with little schooling or with learning difficulties and many elderly people are unable to pass D3E with a mark of 4 – regardless of the efforts they make. In this regard, it constitutes a special problem, in that severely traumatised

[71] The marked increase in refusals in 2008 might have to do with a new method, the 'lean process' the Ministry of Integration has implemented in order to make the handling of naturalisation cases more effective. The lean process implies that an application for naturalisation is refused if any required document is missing; if a missing document is subsequently submitted, the applicant may be granted naturalisation. However, according to the Ministry of Integration, the guidelines are so well-developed that, in practice, such situations will rarely occur and, therefore, the numbers must be assumed to reflect a genuine increase in refusals due to lack of the required language skills.

refugees and others suffering from chronic PTSD in all probability will be prevented, for this reason, both from passing the language examination and from seeking dispensation from the language requirements.

3.9 *The Citizenship Test*

3.9.1 *Background*

While foreigners enrolled on the Danish language courses learn about Danish society, culture and history, etc., the examinations that round off the language courses do not test societal knowledge, but only Danish language skills. Against this background, the Liberals, the Conservatives and the Danish People's Party agreed, in December 2005, that applicants for naturalisation should demonstrate their knowledge of Danish culture, history and society by taking a citizenship test. The test was introduced under the provisions of section 24(2) of the naturalisation circular of 12 January 2006. A new Act on a citizenship test authorised the Minister for Integration to draw up regulations regarding the establishment of the citizenship test and other arrangements for it. The Act was quite brief and did not say anything about the content of the test. The preparatory report explained that a multiple-choice test with questions on 'Danish society, Danish culture and history' was planned and that the Ministry of Integration would incorporate the necessary expert knowledge when drafting a textbook and the test questions. In spite of the opposition parties' criticism of the 'thin' content of the Act, it was adopted on 31 May 2006.[72] The citizenship test was implemented in May 2007.[73]

3.9.2 *The Citizenship Test*

The citizenship test is organised by the language schools across Denmark as a multiple-choice test with a list of potential answers to each questions – modelled on the Dutch societal knowledge test that formed part of the Dutch naturalisation test with a total of 40 questions to be asked. For each examination, a commission draws up suggestions for the 40 questions. Among them, five concern actual events, etc., in Danish society; the remaining 35

---

[72] Act 487 of 7 June 2006.

[73] It is regulated in Act No. 487 of 7 June 2006 on the citizenship test; cf. the citizenship test order of November 2006.

questions are based on a text book.[74] The book can be bought or viewed (free of charge) on the Ministry's homepage. Furthermore, it is possible to listen to the text by downloading an MP3 file. In addition, supplementary literature for preparation purposes may be downloaded from the Ministry's web page.

The citizenship test is held twice a year: in June and December. Applicants enrol for the test by appearing personally at a language school. A fee of 636 DKR (about 85 euros) is payable to the test organiser when enrolling.

3.9.3 *Development of the Test*

Until June 2008, 35 out of the 40 questions were selected from a question bank of 200 questions (in Danish). The question bank was made public on the homepage of the Ministry of Integration, where the applicants could read both the 200 questions and the corresponding correct answers. Once enrolled for the test, the applicants had 60 minutes to answer the 40 questions, 28 of which had to be answered correctly.

Based on this arrangement, where the applicant could learn all the answers to the questions in the test bank by heart, about 97% of those taking the test were successful. Many applicants considered the citizenship test a 'piece of cake' and, as a whole, it gave rise to criticism; see section 3.9.4 below.

The Danish People's Party demanded a revision of the citizenship test, but the Conservatives refused to introduce further restrictions on applicants for naturalisation.[75] However, also in this respect, the Metock judgement of 25 July 2008 by the European Court of Justice (ECJ) (cf. section 3.5.2 above), changed the situation.[76] Thus, through the agreement among the Liberals, the Conservatives and the Danish People's Party, the citizenship test was changed with effect from 10 November 2008.[77] Now, questions and answers can no longer be found on the home page of the Ministry of Integration; only sample questions are accessible. In addition, 32 out of the 40 questions (instead of 28) must be answered correctly in order to pass the test and candidates have only 45 minutes (instead of an hour) to finish the test.

---

[74] *Danmark for og nu – læremateriale om historie, kultur og samfundsforhold til indfødsretsprøve* (Denmark past and present – study material for the citizenship test on history, culture and society). Danish Ministry of Refugee, Immigration and Integration Affairs 2007.

[75] *Berlingske Tidende*, 13 May 2008; Tom Behnke, the chairman of the parliamentary Standing Committee on Nationality added, that even if it were possible to pass the test by rote learning, the applicants would know more than many Danes and, under any circumstances, it was too early to make amendments.

[76] Case C 127/08.

[77] See Circular No. 61 of 22 September 2008 on naturalisation.

3.9.4 *The Citizenship Test and the Textbook*

The citizenship test questions are asked within subject areas chosen from the 2007 textbook: *Danmark før og nu* (Denmark past and present) containing teaching material on history, culture and society. The book is prepared by the Ministry of Integration in cooperation with the Danish House of History (a privately-owned consulting company) with the aid of four experts from different universities, etc.[78]

The first chapter of the book gives an overview of Denmark's history from the beginning of the Viking Age (750) until now (Denmark in the Global society); furthermore, it includes thematic references for Danish geography, population and language, immigration to Denmark, the royal house, the flag, the national community (Greenland, the Faroe Islands), Christianisation, belief and the church in Denmark, norms and national holidays, youth culture, the Danish folk high school movement, schooling and education, family and family life, sport, the Culture Canon 2006, literature, art, music, architecture, film, science and media. Other chapters deal with Danish democracy, the Danish welfare system and Denmark and the surrounding world.

The citizenship tests held until now have contained questions of a primarily communitarian and republican character – fairly evenly divided. Among the 'communitarian questions', a number concerned the names of important persons and events, while others have dealt with historical and geographical issues. Among the 'republican questions', some concerned useful knowledge for the applicants – although this is often knowledge that persons in given situations would acquire.

3.9.5 *The Target Group*

All applicants for naturalisation have to pass the citizenship test, including persons with a Danish school-leaving examination (9th or 10th grade or grammar school equivalent). Thus, the citizenship test differs from the language requirement that accepts Danish school-leaving examinations as proof of the demanded skills; otherwise, the field of application is the same – including the (few) possibilities for exceptions.

[78] *Danmark for og nu – læremateriale om historie, kultur og samfundsforhold til indfødsretsprøve* (Denmark past and present – study material for the citizenship test on history, culture and society). Danish Ministry of Refugee, Immigration and Integration Affairs 2007.

3.9.6 *Public and Political Debate*

Before December 2008, when the citizenship test questions and the correct answers to the questions were published on the home page of the Ministry of Integration, it was widely held among foreigners who had taken the citizenship test that it was very easy to pass and therefore needless. Still, some participants were more positive than others. In general, those without a Danish education were more positive than those with Danish schooling.

A small survey conducted among language schools showed that many participants were irritated at having to 'waste their time on a test they considered unnecessary and very easy to pass' (most of them passed the test within 10 minutes).[79] A language school teacher stated that the students found the test meaningless, except for the fact that they had to pay in order 'to be able to file an application for Danish nationality'. Another teacher said that, especially in connection with the two first tests, most of the participants expressed anger/disappointment/humiliation because they were submitted to such a test.

Immigrant descendants in particular wondered why they had to take the citizenship test – many had a Danish education and/or work experience and had done well in Denmark for a long time. They considered it highly unfair that they were compelled to take a test concerning their knowledge of Denmark in order to be allowed to apply for Danish citizenship. In their opinion, if such tests had to be conducted, anyone with a Danish school background should be exempted.

Some participants without a Danish school background appreciated the idea that, in order to acquire Danish citizenship, a foreigner should be able to substantiate his or her knowledge of Denmark and Danish society, but they disliked a test form that did not check their knowledge of Denmark, but only their ability to learn by heart. Some had tested their Danish colleges at work and realised that they were unable to answer many of the questions. Other participants were unable to understand that naturalisation requirements had been strengthened all along and that they, as law-abiding, self-supporting and integrated human beings could not, as such, be accepted as Danish citizens. Some said that they felt powerless and became negative towards the Danish system.

The Danish People's Party was highly critical of the test conditions and the (Liberal) Minister of Integration tended to agree but, as already mentioned,

---

[79] Conducted by the author in spring 2008.

the third party to the agreement, the Conservatives, was against changing the test requirements. The spokesman for the Conservatives stated in May 2008 that the test was not imposed in order to exclude applicants from acquiring citizenship. Besides, it is not possible to question the test conditions as early as one year after introduction of the test; perhaps within the next couple of years, but not with a view to making the test more difficult.[80] However, in September 2008, after the Metock judgment, cf. 3.5.2 above, the Conservatives also accepted, under the 'Metock agreement', changing the test conditions.

New criticism arose once the new test rules had been published in November 2008, especially when it turned out that they entered into force on 10 November 2008 and applied to applicants who had already registered for the December 2008 test before the registration deadline, 5 November 2008, relying on the old conditions.[81] As a result, a number of registered persons withdrew their registration and, among those who took the test on 10 December 2008, the majority failed. Several headmasters from the language schools argued that the test was to be declared invalid and that participants ought to have their registration fees refunded.[82]

Experts in history, political science and other branches of science also criticised the test (among the critical experts was one of the authors of the textbook 'Denmark past and present'). For instance, most experts agreed that none of the three multiple choice answers to question 10 provided a correct answer. Asked, 'When did the word 'Danmark' appear for the first time?', candidates could put a cross against A: at 'Solvognen' around 1300 B.C.; B: at 'Jellingestenen' in Jutland around 955; or C: in the first Danish history book by Saxo around 1200. According to the answer book, the correct answer was B; but, according to the experts – and the textbook – the correct answer was not '955', but '890' or 'at the end of the 900s'.[83]

The expert criticism was supported by the opposition in Parliament and the media followed up with interviews. A news agency, Ritzau, had asked the language schools whether they knew of any participants who had failed to give the correct answer to question 10 and who had only 'one wrong answer

[80] www.berlingske.dk/article/20080514/danmark/705140053/.

[81] The transitional rules were criticised both for being introduced with retroactive effect for those who had already enrolled for the December test in 2008 and for divesting tests taken before December 2008 of their effect if an application for naturalisation is filed after 1 July 2009. Applicants who cannot apply before that date due to the residence requirement will have to re-take the test (and pay again for it).

[82] Politiken og TV 2 Nyhederne 15 December 2008.

[83] Politiken 18 December 2008.

too many to pass' (9 instead of 8 wrong answers). There were 89 such participants, including a 19-year-old medical student who had matriculated with a mark of 9.5 (according to the 7-point scale).[84] After checking, the Minister for Integration let these participants pass the test.

Six other questions and possible answers were criticised as being misleading or at least imprecise or ambiguous (questions concerning the composition of the Danish population in the Viking Age, the reformation, the secession of Norway to Sweden, the governing of Denmark during the German occupation, the Danish language's affinity and Danish wage negotiations). However, the criticisms of these questions did not impress the Minister.[85]

3.9.7 *Statistics*

As already mentioned, before December 2008, around 97% of all participants passed the citizenship test. However, in December 2008, out of 5,636 enrolled, 4,684 remained registered for the test and 1,103 passed (including the 89 re-evaluated participants). Thus, the pass rate in December 2008 was 23.5%.

By the test of 17 June 2009, only 2,809 foreigners had registered for the citizenship test at the 44 language centres across the country; 2,566 remained registered and among them 1,081 passed the test. Thus, in June 2009 the pass rate was 42,1% compared to the rate for December 2008, undoubtedly this had to do with the fact that this time the participants had time to prepare themselves by reading the textbook and/or taking lessons, which some private schools have offered for around 3000 DKR or more (around 400 euros) and some NGOs have offered for free.[86] The pass rate for the different language centres varied, and although there is no simple explanation for the differences, it is worth noting that at a language centre with a pass rate of 56.8%, half of the students had participated in a preparatory course and, of them, 55% passed; at another language centre, 12 students had participated in a preparatory course and all of them passed the test.[87]

---

[84] Politiken 18 December 2008.

[85] See hhp://nyhederne.tv2.dk/politik/article.php/id-19443724.html.

[86] Voluntary advisors from the Danish Refugee Council have related that, following such assistance, participants feel much better prepared – and better integrated. They confirmed that this would not have been the case without assistance.

[87] Information from Lærdansk Århus, laerdansk.dk/aarhus.

3.9.8 *To sum up*

The test system causes concerns for a number of reasons: giving brief answers to complex questions seems to be difficult, the textbook uses explanations and concepts not easily understood by all participants (without instruction) and multiple-choice questions invite learning by rote that is easily forgotten. Furthermore, the extensive target group poses a particular problem, especially as regards second-generation 'immigrants' with Danish schooling; this may have counterproductive effects as it signals the exclusion of persons who generally have found themselves included. Frequent restrictions and unfair transitional rules tend to lead in the same direction.

3.10 *Conclusion*

Integration has become a political hot potato in Denmark, which has experienced a shift in migration and integration since the late 1990s. A key element in immigrant integration programmes since 1998 has been a Danish language course. Learning the language of the host country undoubtedly contributes to giving immigrants the opportunity to be participating and contributing citizens, on an equal footing with other citizens. As for Danish language education, Denmark has done well in providing a range of learning facilities with three years of free education and possibilities for an extension in certain situations. Moreover, the Minister for Integration has a keen eye for improvements regarding language education for adult immigrants.

However, in the new millennium, a development has been underway, suggesting that long term migrants' socio-political membership of Danish society is no longer to be taken for granted. Membership has become conditional and the conditions have gradually been strengthened, while the trend towards law enforcement and a sanctions-based approach have steadily developed. Although integration is still seen as a two-way process, with integration contracts specifying which offers immigrants are to be given, the emphasis has shifted; as a starting point, the immigrant now takes most of the responsibility to integrate and to demonstrate motivation and goodwill.

The nature of some of the politics reflects the view that immigrants may not be willing to integrate into the Danish economy and society. As stated by the OECD, under conditions in which immigrant issues are sensitive, it is also unclear what message is implicitly being communicated to the domestic population through compulsory measures: that immigrants are being treated the same way as ethnic Danes or that, if left to themselves, they will not choose to integrate. Since the message is ambiguous, it risks confirming if not encouraging certain unfavourable attitudes.[88]

In the Integration Act of 1998, immigrants were offered an integration programme comprising, among other things, a free language course adapted to their needs, depending on their previous schooling. The rationale behind the arrangement could be said to be liberal-republican in character, since the purpose was to provide for immigrants as active participants in Danish society with an understanding of Danish values and norms. Failure to complete an introductory programme was not sanctioned; what was needed for issue of a permanent residence permit was only a certification of active participation in the programme (including a language course).

However, in the new millennium, the duty to participate has been emphasised. Language courses and introductory programme activities have become mandatory and sanction-oriented: the right to acquire a permanent residence permit and entitlement to social benefits may be lost in cases of failure to comply with the conditions – likewise the prospects of being granted family reunification and Danish citizenship.

As regards permanent residence and citizenship, participation or passing an examination no longer serve as qualification; a certain level (B1 and B2 respectively) is required. Moreover, Danish values are not just to be 'understood' by foreigners; they must be 'recognised'. Thus, the shift in the general discourse has been in a more communitarian direction.

This is clearly reflected in the perception of the acquisition of citizenship. Today, the majority in Parliament claims that Danish citizenship is something that should be earned. The possibility of the acquisition of citizenship is no longer perceived as a means of integration. Acquisition of citizenship presumes that the applicant 'is already integrated into Danish society' (see section 3.8.5 above).

Some of the problems this policy raises have been discussed, but others can still be added. As mentioned in the introduction to this book, the concept of integration is a derivative concept. Integration in a particular society presupposes a vision of this society. The assumption here seems to be that Denmark is a society in which citizens are active participants in elections, association activities, school boards, etc. It is a small step to ask whether this perception represents an image of highly educated, middle class persons or average Danish citizens (Guild, Groenendijk & Carrera 2009). The

[88] See *The labour market integration of immigrants in Denmark*; DELSA/ELSA(2006)7/REV1.

conclusion which immediately suggests itself is that future citizens have to do better than the average Danish citizen in order to be become member of the Danish citizenry.

In defence of the high naturalisation requirements, it is alleged that citizens who do not master the Danish language at level D3E (CEFR B2) are incapable of making political judgments. This is definitely going too far. For more than 150 years, the ability to speak and understand Danish has been sufficient. Besides, citizenship is of importance on other grounds. It is common knowledge that citizenship is valued for ideal reasons[89] and citizenship still means the right to have rights, in so far as a secure residence status, international protection, access to certain public positions and (in EU Member States) Union citizenship rights, in particular free movement rights, etc., are dependent on citizenship.

EU law has, it could be said, made the possibility of the acquisition of citizenship even more important. Union citizens have more rights than third-country nationals. They are not subjected to integration conditions – including language requirements – but can avail themselves of various education offers.[90] The difference between the two immigrant groups raises questions of both fairness and appreciation – and questions that are difficult to answer in terms of *necessity*.

Test requirements of fluency in the Danish language and knowledge of Danish history at a very high level and, almost without exception as regards naturalisation, fees and the lack of education (other than costly private education) in order to pass naturalisation and immigration tests appear to be instruments for selecting migrants. As such, they give rise to serious human rights concerns. Excluding those with poor education and those on a low income can hardly be reconciled with human rights non-discrimination principles. Furthermore, such action seems to disregard the human rights perspective of nationality. Denmark has ratified the European Convention on Nationality (1997), according to which state parties shall base their nationality legislation on the principle that, 'Everyone has the right to a nationality' (Article 4 a). The Convention's Article 6 (3) maintains that each state party shall provide in its internal law for the possibility of naturalising persons who are lawfully and habitually resident on its territory. In establishing its conditions for naturalisation, the state is assumed to provide reasonable conditions, especially with regard to integration (cf. the explanatory report to the

[89] The right to naturalise was also recognised in the late 1800s, before women gained voting rights, see Ersbøll 2008: 613.

[90] See also Elspeth Guild, Kees Groenendijk & Sergio Carrera 2009.

Convention). It is highly questionable whether strict naturalisation criteria that preclude certain groups of immigrants from being naturalised are in conformity with the ECN.

Such a policy may even impede the integration process. In a liberal democratic society, a liberal integration policy should be pursued.

We know about the consequences of being on trial and demanded the impossible of the famous Danish author H. C. Andersen's fairy tale *The Ugly Duckling* – which foreigners also have to be familiar with, since it is mentioned in the textbook 'Denmark past and present' that has to be read and remembered in order to pass the naturalisation test. The 'ugly duckling' is a young swan born in a duck-yard and an outsider from the very beginning. It flies over the fence and lands near a hut where an old woman lives with her cat and hen. The woman takes the duckling for a duck and it is 'admitted on trial' in order to see whether it can lay eggs. 'Lay eggs, or purr', is the message from the hen to the duckling, which can do neither of these things. When we read the fairy tale about the ugly duckling that becomes the most beautiful swan, we normally take the side of the duckling.[91]

Bibliography

Danish Ministry of Refugee, Immigration and Integration Affairs (the Ministry of Integration), *Aktiviteten hos udbydere af danskuddannelse for voksne udlændinge m.fl. i 2006* (Activity among suppliers of Danish courses for adult aliens and others in 2006), report of February 2009.

Danish Ministry of Refugee, Immigration and Integration Affairs (the Ministry of Integration), *Danmark før og nu – læremateriale om historie, kultur og samfundsforhold til indfødsretsprøve* (Denmark past and present – study material for the citizenship test on history, culture and society), udarbejdet af Ministeriet for Flygtninge, Indvandrere og Integration i samarbejde med Det Historiske Hus; bistand fra Professor Knud V. Jespersen, Syddansk Universitet, institutleder, professor Finn Hauberg Mortensen, Københavns Universitet, souschef, lektor Ove Outzen, CVU Sønderjylland, professor Michael H. Jensen, Aarhus Universitet, April 2007.

Ersbøll, E., Nationality Law in Denmark, Finland and Sweden, in: Randall Hansen and Patrick Weil (eds), *Towards a European Nationality*, New York: Palgrave 2001.

Ersbøll, E., Denmark, in: R. Bauböck, E. Ersbøll, K. Groenendijk & H. Waldrauch (eds.), *Acquisition and Loss of Nationality; Volume 2: Country Analyses*, Amsterdam: Amsterdam University Press 2006, pp. 105–148.

Ersbøll, E., *Dansk indfødsret i international tog historisk perspektiv*, Copenhagen: Jurist- og Økonomforbundets Forlag 2008.

[91] http://classiclit.about.com/library/bl.etexts/hcanderson/bl-hcanderson-ugly.htm.

Fleischer, T., Tidsubegrænset opholdstilladelse – nu kun med engelsk, *SprogcenterNyt* nr. 5, November 2006.

Guild, E., K. Groenendijk & S. Carrera, Understanding the Contest of Community: illiberal practices in the EU, in: E. Guild, C. Groenendijk & S. Carrera (eds.): *Illiberal Liberal States; Immigration, Citizenship and Integration in the EU*, Aldershot: Ashgate 2009.

Holm, L., *Folketinget og Udlændingepolitikken – diskurser om naturaliserede, indvandrere og flygtninge 1973–2002*, AMID, Aalborg Universitet 2007.

Joppke, C., Beyond National Models: Civic Integration Policies for Immigrants in Western Europe, *Western European Politics*, 2007, 30(1), pp. 1–22.

Jørgensen, L., *Hvad sagde vi!...om "De andre", Den udlændingepolitiske debat i Folketinget 1961–1999*, Ph.D. thesis, 2006.

Pedersen, P. J. & N. Smith, *International Migration and Migration Policy in Denmark*, Working Paper 01–05, 2001.

Rasmussen, H. K. (2007), *Den danske stamme, en befolkningshistorie*, Copenhagen: Politikens Forlag 2007.

Rerup, L. & N.F. Christiansen, *Denmark – History*, 6.17 and 6.18, 2005, www.um.dk.

Vedsted-Hansen, J., Tidsbegrænsning og forlængelse af opholdstilladelser, i Lone B Christensen et al. (eds.): *Udlændingeret*, Copenhagen: Jurist- og Økonomforbundets Forlag 2006, p. 531 ff.

Chapter 4

Integration Measures in France: An Evolving Process between Integration and Migration Issues

*Yves Pascouau**

Traditionally, the integration of third-country nationals has not really been a major political issue in France. Since the adoption, just after the Second World War, of an ordinance governing the entry and residence of foreigners,[1] which took into account the management of migration flows and the integration of third-country nationals, the migration side of the policy took over from integration issues.[2] This position could nevertheless be explained by French culture regarding integration. In fact, for some time, France has refused to set up a real integration policy considering, on the one hand, that such a policy would stigmatise foreigners and, on the other hand, that it

* PHD Researcher European Studies Institute, Université Libre de Bruxelles (Brussels, Belgium) and the Centre de Documentation et de Recherches Européennes, Université de Pau et des Pays de l'Adour (Pau, France). This article was written within the framework of an ARC project financed by the *Communauté française de Belgique.*

[1] *Ordonnance du 2 novembre 1945 sur l'entrée et le séjour des étrangers en France.* On that issue, see Julien-Laferrière 2000.

[2] See Neraudau & Kadouci 2008: esp p. 140: 'Il est vrai que si l'immigration est l'objet d'un débat public permanent et souvent passionné, celui-ci tend à se polariser sur certains des aspects du dossier et semble parfois ignorer les autres. Ainsi, le problème de l'opportunité et des modalités de la maîtrise des flux est-il au centre des préoccupations, comme en témoigne le contenu des interventions du législateur depuis les lendemains de la seconde guerre mondiale: depuis 1974, l'ordonnance de 1945 aura été modifiée à trente-trois reprises et tout dernièrement à l'occasion du vote de la loi du 26 novembre 2003. On ne saurait dire, en revanche, que les voies et moyens de l'accueil et de l'intégration des immigrants aient bénéficié d'une attention comparable', Rapport de la Cour des comptes *L'accueil des immigrants et l'intégration des populations issues de l'immigration*, Paris: Les Editions du Journal Officiel 2004, esp. pp. 9–10.

Van Oers, Ersbøll and Kostakopoulou, A Re-definition of Belonging?, pp. 153–183.
©2010 Koninklijke Brill NV. ISBN 978 90 04 17506 8. Printed in the Netherlands.

had succeeded in integrating foreigners in the past without such a policy.[3] Nonetheless, the changes affecting society and, more particularly since 1973 and the oil crisis, have undermined some integration factors. In this context, in addition to the decision to stop immigration for work purposes, a decree adopted in 1977 restricted family reunification to family members who agreed not to engage in employment.[4] Although this decree was cancelled by the French Council of State, it clearly demonstrates that immigration worries took over from integration issues.

Since the 1980s, integration issues have become more salient in France due to the transformation of the perception of migration flows. In fact, the idea of temporary migration for work purposes was overtaken by family migration, which had to be considered a lasting phenomenon. In that context, integration issues emerged as a key question and were formally institutionalised in 1989 with the creation of the *Haut Conseil à l'intégration* and the appointment of a secretary of State dedicated to this issue. In the field, several civil movements and rioting, occurring mainly in the 1990s, shed light on the lack of integration policy in France, mainly within French cities suburbs. These movements involved principally French citizens of the second generation. In fact, integration concerns were pointed out by French citizens, highlighting their difficulties in becoming fully integrated into society, and demonstrated the lasting phenomenon of migration for family reunification. This movement was clearly anchored in the public debate[5] and required an answer. As a consequence, the theme of integration started to be dealt with within immigration laws in 2003, around the concept of 'Republican Integration' and the word 'integration' appeared in the title of immigration laws adopted in 2006[6] and 2007.[7] From an institutional point of view, the political sensitivity of migration issues and the political will to give them an important place within

---

[3] Buffet, F.-N., *Rapport sur le projet de loi relatif à l'immigration et l'intégration*, Rapport n° 372, 13 May 2006, Sénat, 286 p., esp. 24.

[4] On this text, see Julien-Laferrière 2000: 26–27.

[5] This movement was summarised by a Member of Parliament who stated, in 2006, 'Il ne se passe pas une semaine sans que l'intégration ne soit, sous une forme ou sous une autre, au centre de l'actualité dans notre pays, et que la France ne s'interroge sur l'échec supposé de son modèle d'intégration', Mariani, T., *Rapport d'information sur les politiques d'intégration des migrants dans l'Union européenne*, Rapport n° 3502, Assemblée nationale, 6 December 2006b, 150 p., esp. 11.

[6] Loi n° 2006-911 du 24 juillet 2006 relative à l'immigration et à l'intégration, NOR: INTX 0600037, *Journal Officiel de la République française*, 25 juillet 2006 [this can be changed on each occasion, including the date].

[7] Loi n° 2007-1631 du 20 novembre 2007 relative à la maîtrise de l'immigration, à l'intégration et à l'asile, NOR: IMIX0756368L, *Journal Officiel de la République française*, 21 novembre 2007.

the governmental framework led to the creation of a Ministry responsible for immigration, integration, national identity and co-development.[8] Finally, meanwhile, the development of a European asylum and migration policy also required some reflexion on integration issues.

From a legal point of view, the question of integration appeared primarily within the framework of the acquisition of nationality. Hence, and according to the French Law adopted in 1945, an applicant for French nationality had to prove his assimilation into French society. In this regard, sufficient knowledge of the French language was considered a clue to such assimilation. Two laws adopted in 2003 and 2006 reinforced this condition and introduced into the Civil Code the criterion that sufficient knowledge of French language must be demonstrated as a condition for acquiring French nationality.[9] The link between integration issues and Aliens law appeared more recently, specifically during the 2000s. This movement started with the creation of an Integration Contract in 2003, implying a voluntary commitment by the foreigner to attend language lessons and training regarding French institutions, which became compulsory in 2006. It was followed by a law adopted in 2007, which required third-country nationals wishing to reunite with their families to fulfil integration requirements in their country of origin and to enter into an integration contract for the family, after entry to the territory, if children were involved in family reunification. Perceived as a two-sided movement implying action by the host society[10] as well as action by the migrant,[11] French integration policy has increasingly become a

---

[8] Décret n° 2007-999 du 31 mai 2007 relatif aux attributions du ministre de l'immigration, de l'intégration, de l'identité nationale et du codéveloppement, NOR: IMIX0755108D, *Journal Officiel de la République française*, 1er juin 2007.

[9] On this issue, see particularly, Fornerod 2008.

[10] 'L'intégration ne dépend pas que des efforts des seuls migrants: elle concerne tout autant la société d'accueil et les conditions qu'elle réserve aux nouveaux arrivants et à leurs descendants', Secrétariat général du Comité interministériel de contrôle de l'immigration, Rapport au Parlement, *Les orientations de la politique de l'immigration*, December 2007, esp. p. 119.

[11] 'L'intégration étant définie comme une logique de droits et de devoirs réciproques, il était cohérent d'établir un lien entre les efforts de l'arrivant pour réussir son parcours dans la société qui l'accueille et le statut que celle-ci lui apporte sur le plan du droit au séjour', Mariani, T., *Rapport sur le projet de loi relatif à la maîtrise de l'immigration et au séjour des étrangers en France*, Rapport n° 949, 1ère partie, 13 June 2003, Assemblée nationale, 92 p., esp. 22–23.

one-way process within which the migrant is asked to carry out most of the integration obligations.[12]

Hence, since 2003, the rules relating to integration of third-country nationals in France have changed repeatedly. This movement was initially geared towards the nature of integration measures, the scope of which has constantly expanded while their effects have constantly intensified (4.1). A new phenomenon, also taking place in neighbouring Member States, has had the effect of transforming the perspective of integration measures as they now have to be fulfilled in the country of origin in the case of family reunification (4.2). This illustrates an ongoing trend to institute compulsory integration measures and to shift the borders either in terms of the content of integration requirements or in terms of their geographical coverage. Besides the aim of enhancing the integration process of third-country nationals into French society, this ever-increasing trend for introducing integration measures within the scope of Aliens law also raised the question of whether these rules serve an integration purpose. In other words, are integration measures geared towards an integration purpose or do they serve as a tool for the management of migration flows?

4.1 *The Evolving Nature of Integration Measures*

The starting point of the movement involving integration measures can be regarded as the setting up of the concept of 'republican integration' (*intégration républicaine*) in a Law adopted in 2003. Since then, integration issues have consistently been taken into consideration in migration laws. What is interesting in this context is the ever-evolving nature of integration measures each time migration legislation is amended. In fact, such attention has had

12 'L'intégration des populations étrangères s'établissant sur le territoire national est un objectif majeur, qui a fait l'objet d'une attention particulière ces dernières années. En effet, une immigration socialement acceptée est indissociable d'une capacité d'intégration suffisante. Or, toute politique efficace en la matière doit, d'une part, imposer un parcours d'intégration aux personnes étrangères qui s'installent durablement sur notre territoire (c'est l'objet notamment du contrat d'accueil et d'intégration – CAI) et, d'autre part, conditionner résolument l'installation durable sur le territoire à l'intégration effective. Telles sont justement les orientations prises par la France depuis 2003', Diard, E., *Avis présenté au nom de la Commission des lois constitutionnelles, de la législation et de l'administration générale de la République sur le projet de loi de finance pour 2009, Tome IV 'Immigration, asile et intégration'*, Rapport n° 1203, 16 October 2008, Assemblée nationale, esp. p. 49.

the effect of widening the scope of integration measures (4.1.1) as well as strengthening the effects of integration measures (4.1.2).

4.1.1 *Widening the Scope of Integration Measures*

The concept of republican integration initially appeared within the context of long-term residence application, without being clearly formalised (4.1.1.1). It has since been outlined in detail through the creation of an integration contract, which became applicable to every person applying for a residence permit for one year (4.1.1.2). The final step in this evolution was reached with the creation of an integration contract for the family in cases of family reunification (4.1.1.3).

4.1.1.1 *The concept of republican integration applicable to long-term residence applications*

The idea of an integration duty involving third-country nationals was inserted into French aliens Law in 2003[13] under the concept of 'The republican integration of foreigners into French society'.[14] Republican integration was to be fulfilled by third-country nationals applying for the issue of a residence card.[15] This measure was incorporated into Article 8 of Law no. 2003-1119, which stated that, in any case foreseen by the law, the issue of the residence card is conditional upon republican integration of the foreigner into French society. This integration was to be assessed in terms of sufficient knowledge of the French language and the principles that govern the French Republic. This assessment was to be performed by a representative of the State – namely the *Préfet* and, in Paris, the *Préfet de police* – who could ask for advice on this point from the mayor of the town where the third-country national filed his application.

Article 21 of Law no. 2003-1119 defined the people affected by the issue of a residence card. This card could be requested by any third-country national who could prove lawful residence on French territory for at least five years. The residence card could also be delivered to the spouse and minor children

---

[13] See Article 8 of Law no. 2003-1119 (Loi n° 2003-1119 du 26 novembre 2003 relative à la maîtrise de l'immigration, au séjour des étrangers en France et à la nationalité), NOR: INTX 0300040L, *Journal Officiel de la République française*, 27 novembre 2003.

[14] For an overview of the French republican integration concept, see in particular Carrera 2009: 291–303.

[15] It must be stressed that a residence card is a residence permit issued under specific circumstances. Broadly speaking, the applicant for this card is a long-term resident. The beneficiary of the card may also be a refugee. This residence card is also delivered under other circumstances defined by the Law. See, in particular, Articles L 314-8 to L 314-12 of the current Aliens Code.

of a third-country national in possession of a residence card and authorised to stay in France on the basis of family reunification and to any third-country national who is the father or mother of a French child who has resided in France for at least two years on the basis of a temporary residence card. In those cases, and in accordance with Article 21 of the Law, the decision to grant the residence card was conditional upon the fulfilment of republican integration into French society by a foreigner aged over 18 years old.

The content of the conditions to be fulfilled were very imprecise since the law did not give any clear definition of what was encompassed by the concept of republican integration. A circular adopted by the Minister of the Interior nevertheless gave some indications to the administrative authorities in charge of implementing the law. Hence, republican integration could be assessed and therefore considered achieved on the basis of clues such as schooling, learning of the language, vocational training and participation in associative life or following an integration contract.[16] What is interesting here is that the law did not give any legal basis for the already (informally) existing integration contract. Recognising the integration contract in this regard would have achieved two aims. Firstly, this could have had the effect of circumventing the scope of the obligations to be satisfied in order to achieve republican integration. Secondly, it would have fulfilled the wishes of the French Republic President, expressed one year earlier, to set up such an integration contract.[17]

---

[16] '(...), la circulaire du ministre de l'intérieur n° NOR/INT/D/04/00006/C du 20 janvier 2004 relative à l'application de la loi n° 2003-1119 du 26 novembre 2003 indique aux préfets qu'il leur revient, dans le cadre de leur large pouvoir d'appréciation, de s'assurer du respect de la condition d'intégration. Elle doit s'apprécier sur la base d'un faisceau d'indices parmi lesquels l'apprentissage de la langue française, la connaissance et le respect des principes qui régissent la République française, la scolarisation des enfants, le suivi d'une formation professionnelle ainsi que la participation à la vie sociale locale. Cette même circulaire ajoutait que *la signature du contrat d'accueil et d'intégration sera également à terme un élément à prendre en compte pour l'appréciation de cette condition*', Buffet, F.-N., *Rapport sur le projet de loi relatif à l'immigration et l'intégration*, Rapport n° 372, 13 May 2006, Sénat, 286 p., sp. 69. See also Mariani 2003: 23.

[17] Speech given in Troyes on 14 October 2002 by the French President: '[...] l'égalité des chances suppose de donner une nouvelle vigueur à notre modèle d'intégration. Derrière ce mot d'intégration, les réalités sont multiples. Il y a la nécessité d'accueillir dans de bonnes conditions les nouveaux arrivants, ceux qui rejoignent notre pays légalement et qu'il faut aider à mieux s'insérer dans notre société. Je souhaite ainsi, qu'à l'instar de ce qui existe chez certains de nos voisins, chaque nouvel arrivant s'engage dans un véritable contrat d'intégration comprenant notamment la possibilité d'accéder à des formations et à un apprentissage rapide de notre langue', in: J.-P. Courtois, *Rapport sur le projet de loi relatif*

The reasons for such a situation could nonetheless be found elsewhere. It is worth noting that the roots of the introduction of the integration concept for an application for a residence card are to be found in the long-term residence directive.[18] While transposing the directive, the French authorities decided to extend the period required before application for a residence card, from three to five years, and to introduce integration measures that had never been required before within the context of migration law.

4.1.1.2 *The creation of an integration contract applicable to any residence permit application*

As explained above, an integration contract had already been implemented in France at the time Law no. 2003-1119 was adopted. Established by the government in July 2003, this contract was considered at the time a genuine charter of republican values aimed at foreigners willing to settle in France.[19] As a 'contract', it also implied a double commitment: the duty of the State to provide the necessary tools and the duty of the foreigner to comply with the obligations enshrined in the contract. Since the exercise had been successful in France, it was decided in 2005 to give a legal basis to the integration contract in a law dedicated to social cohesion.[20] This Law inserted a new chapter into the Code of Social and Family Affairs. It also merged the administrative structures regarding the reception of newcomers and created a single administration – ANAEM[21] – dedicated to those issues under the responsibility of the Minister of Social Affairs. The integration contract could therefore be implemented almost throughout the country to cover third-country nationals

à la maîtrise de l'immigration et au séjour des étrangers en France, Rapport n° 1, 1 October 2003, Sénat, 297 p., sp. 13.

18 Council Directive 2003/109/EC of 25 November 2003 concerning the status of third-country nationals who are long-term residents, *OJ* L 16/44, 23.01.2004.

19 Souvet, L. & V. Letard, *Rapport sur le projet de loi de programmation pour la cohésion sociale*, Rapport n° 32, 20 October 2004, Sénat, 413 p, sp. 47.

20 Loi n° 2005-32 du 18 janvier 2005 de programmation pour la cohésion sociale, NOR: SOCX0400145L, *Journal Officiel de la République française*, 19 January 2005.

21 *Agence nationale de l'accueil des étrangers et des migrations*. In March 2009, a decree changed the name of the ANAEM. It is now called OFII (*Office Français de l'Immigration et de l'Intégration*). Since the article was written before this modification, the name ANAEM has been maintained.

Décret n° 2009-331 du 25 mars 2009 substituant la dénomination 'Office français de l'immigration et de l'intégration' à la dénomination 'Agence nationale de l'accueil des étrangers et des migrations'.

willing to commit themselves voluntarily by signing it.[22] In 2005, and according to the statistics available, the integration contract was signed by 92.6 % of third-country nationals arriving in France.[23]

A milestone was reached in July 2006 when Parliament adopted new legislation on immigration.[24] This text has had several effects in the field of integration. Firstly, integration issues were directly linked to migration issues, since the integration contract was inserted in the *Code de l'entrée et du séjour des étrangers et du droit d'asile* (hereinafter referred to as the Aliens Code). This shift from the Social and Family Affairs Code to the Aliens Code demonstrated the will to assign this tool to the scope of migration issues and therefore to transfer part of the overall scheme to the responsibility of the Minister of Interior. Secondly, a new Article L 311-9 was introduced into the Aliens Code, with two major impacts on the integration contract. The integration contract became compulsory and applicable to any foreigner admitted to France for the first time and wishing to reside there on a long-term basis. According to this provision, the foreigners concerned have to prepare for their republican integration into French society and thus to sign the integration contract.

This provision also gives the list of persons exempted from this requirement to enter into the contact. This concerns foreigners who have been educated at a French secondary-level school abroad for at least 3 years, foreigners who meet the conditions for the acquisition of French nationality and foreigners who did not sign such a contract when they were admitted to France for the first time.[25] For these foreigners, the contract retained its voluntary nature. A regulation adopted in December 2006, inserting Articles R 311-19 to R 311-30 into the Aliens Code, exempted other people from the requirement to sign the contract, i.e. citizens of the European Union and nationals from countries party to the European Economic Area agreement and/or Switzerland. A decree adopted in October 2008 extends the scope of those exempted

---

22 In spring 2006 the integration contract was proposed in 82 French *départements* and it was projected to reach all 91 *départements* by July 2006.

23 See Mariani, T., *Rapport sur le projet de loi relatif à l'immigration et l'intégration*, Rapport n° 3058, 26 April 2006, Assemblée nationale, 434 p., esp. 62.

24 Loi n° 2006-911 du 24 juillet 2006 relative à l'immigration et à l'intégration, NOR: INTX 0600037L, *Journal Officiel de la République française*, 25 juillet 2006.

25 The law does not explicitly exempt people suffering from mental or physical disabilities. In practice, therefore, the person would have to ask the administrative authority for an exemption.

from the duty to sign the integration contract to include foreigners who have taken a course of higher education in France for at least one year.[26]

Apart from those who are exempt and, broadly speaking, third-country nationals who fulfil the conditions for the award of a residence permit as listed in Article R 311-19 of the Aliens Code, have to subscribe to the integration contract.[27] It should be noted that recognised refugees are also subjected to this commitment.

Notwithstanding the positive effect in terms of integration, specifically regarding learning the language of the host society, what is at stake here is the widespread effect on persons concerned by the integration contract. This tool serves either for the assessment of republican integration for foreigners entitled to apply for long-term residence status on the basis of a *carte de résident* or concerns any newcomer applying for a temporary residence permit. As such, the integration contract very quickly became the key tool of the integration policy emerging in France.

4.1.1.3 *The creation of an integration contract for the family in cases of family reunification*

This widespread effect was enhanced in a law adopted in November 2007 on the basis of a proposal by the newly established Minister of Immigration, Integration, National Identity and Co-development, who proposed creating

---

[26] Décret n° 2008-1115 du 30 octobre 2008 relatif à la préparation de l'intégration en France des étrangers souhaitant s'y installer durablement, *Journal Officiel de la République française*, 1er novembre 2008, article 2.

[27] Article L 311-19 'I.-Le contrat d'accueil et d'intégration prévu à l'article L. 311-9 est souscrit par l'étranger mentionné au premier alinéa de cet article, sous réserve qu'il ne soit pas ressortissant d'un Etat membre de l'Union européenne, d'un Etat partie à l'accord sur l'Espace économique européen ou de la Confédération suisse et qu'il remplisse les conditions requises pour l'obtention:

a) D'une carte de séjour temporaire portant la mention ' cientifique' (...);
b) D'une carte de séjour temporaire portant la mention 'profession artistique et culturelle' (...);
c) D'une carte de séjour temporaire autorisant l'exercice d'une activité professionnelle (...), à l'exception des cartes portant les mentions 'travailleur saisonnier', 'travailleur temporaire' ou 'salarié en mission';
d) D'une carte de séjour temporaire délivrée en application de l'article L. 313-11, à l'exception des étrangers mentionnés aux 3° et 11° de cet article, ou des articles L. 313-13, L. 313-14 et L. 316-1;
e) (alinéa supprimé);
f) D'une carte de résident délivrée en application des dispositions des articles L. 314-8, L. 314-9 et L. 314-11, lorsque l'étranger n'a pas signé le contrat d'accueil et d'intégration à un autre titre.'

a new integration contract for the family.[28] Entitled the 'Law related to the management of immigration, integration and asylum', the text introduces into the Aliens Code a new Article L 311-9-1. This provision creates an integration contract for the family within the framework of family reunification. More precisely, it states that a foreigner admitted to France and, if appropriate this person's spouse, if one or more children have benefited from the family reunification procedure, prepare for the republican integration of the family into French society. To this end, they and the State mutually enter into a welcome and integration contract for the family. On the basis of this contract, they commit to attending a one-day training session relating to the rights and duties of parents in France and to respecting education obligations. A decree adopted in October 2008 implements this provision of the Aliens Code by inserting a new sub-section into the regulatory part of the Aliens Code, entitled 'Provisions related to the welcome and integration contract for the Family'.[29]

Whereas the obligations that have to be fulfilled regarding this new integration contract are still fairly relaxed, since they rely mainly on attendance of a training session, some concepts nevertheless need to be pointed out. Firstly, this contract constitutes a new tool that contributes again to widening the scope of the integration policy, showing that integration is now clearly part of immigration policy. Secondly, the motives advanced for the creation of such a contract are somewhat dubious. According to a parliamentary report, integration into a new society is a difficult process for the parents but also, consequently, for the children who are disoriented by this new sociological, social and urban environment. The report adds that, in France, the rules governing the nuclear society are not easy to understand and are the result of legal and historical evolutions. To that end, it is legitimate to impose on the parents a specific tool that will help them to respond to specific difficulties they will face. Taking these motives into consideration and notwithstanding the goodwill of this project, one can hardly imagine that a one-day training session on parents' rights and duties might reach such a goal and therefore constitute a central element of the whole integration process.

[28] Loi n° 2007-1631 du 20 novembre 2007 relative à la maîtrise de l'immigration, à l'intégration et à l'asile, NOR: IMIX0756368L, *Journal Officiel de la République française*, 21 novembre 2007.

[29] Décret n° 2008-1115 du 30 octobre 2008 relatif à la préparation de l'intégration en France des étrangers souhaitant s'y installer durablement, *Journal Officiel de la République française*, 1er novembre 2008.

Setting up new tools to improve integration into society is undoubtedly a move in the right direction, providing these tools are efficient. To that end, it is necessary to assess the content and effects of such a contract.

4.1.2 *Strengthening the Content and the Effects of Integration Measures*

The integration contract constitutes a major tool and could be considered the concrete element of the broader concept of republican integration. Obtaining an insight into integration measures firstly requires identification of the content of the integration contract (4.1.2.1) and, secondly, determination of its effects regarding third-country nationals who are obliged to enter into the contract (4.1.2.2).

4.1.2.1 *The content of the integration contract*

As mentioned earlier, integration measures were introduced into French legislation under the concept of republican integration. The latter could be considered broad enough to encompass various criteria that could be taken into account when implementing this notion. Law no. 2003-1119, introducing the notion of republican integration, has framed the concept, stating that it should be assessed in particular on the basis of sufficient knowledge of the French language and the principles of the French Republic. Language knowledge has always been regarded as a crucial element in integration and, in that context, education is considered to play an important role. In that sense, the reference to language was self-evident. The notion of the principles of the French Republic was more difficult to describe since it could encompass many criteria, conditioned by different interpretations.

The content of republican integration was in fact mostly determined by the creation of the integration contract. The latter comprises two types of training, civic and linguistic, and an information session. Article L 311-9 of the Aliens Code states that the foreigner, when signing the contract, commits to attending a civic training course, introducing French institutions and the values of the French Republic. The latter can be considered part of the principles of the French Republic and comprise, for instance, the principles of equality between men and women and secularism.[30] Foreigners are also invited, if so assessed, to attend language courses. Finally, an information session on daily life in France is also offered to newcomers involved in the

[30] The principle of secularism derives from the shift between the State and religious society. In that sense, the State does not have any religious power and churches do not have any political power.

process. While the law provided the main elements of the integration contract, a decree adopted in December 2006 detailed its content.

Concerning the civic training, Article R 311-22 of Aliens Code defines its content. This instruction comprises an introduction to French institutions and French Republican values, more particularly in terms of equality between men and women, secularism, the Rule of Law, fundamental liberties, the security of persons and goods and the exercise of citizenship that provides compulsory and free access to education. This training lasts 6 hours and usually takes place in the main town of the sub-region (*département*). It is translated into the main languages of origin, if necessary with the help of an interpreter. Attendance of this day of civic training ends with the issue of a nominal certificate by the offices of the administrative authority dealing with integration issues, the ANAEM.

If we consider that knowledge of the French political and institutional framework is part of successful integration into society, language courses constitute the central focus of the process. Article L 311-9 forms the basis for the importance of this learning session, as this is the only part of the integration contract that culminates in a qualification or diploma recognised by the State. The linguistic content of the contract is defined by Article R 311-23 of the Aliens Code. It is organised on the basis of two steps. The first takes place during the first interview with the foreigner by the offices of the ANAEM. The latter evaluate the level of knowledge of written and oral French in order to decide if the person concerned has to take the linguistic training course. A bylaw adopted in January 2007 defines the evaluation criteria.[31] Third-country nationals are invited to take two tests, comprising an oral test[32] lasting 10 minutes and a written test[33] lasting 5 minutes. These 15

[31] Arrêté du 19 janvier 2007 relatif aux formations prescrites aux étrangers signataires du contrat d'accueil et d'intégration et à l'appréciation du niveau de connaissances en français prévues aux articles R. 311-22 à R. 311-25 du décret n° 2006-1791 du 23 décembre 2006 relatif au contrat d'accueil et d'intégration et au contrôle des connaissances en français d'un étranger souhaitant s'installer durablement en France et modifiant le code de l'entrée et du séjour et du droit d'asile (partie réglementaire), *Journal Officiel de la République française*, 30 janvier 2007.

[32] Compréhension orale: comprendre une annonce publique; comprendre une indication simple; comprendre des instructions simples; comprendre une information chiffrée, comprendre l'heure.

Production orale: comprendre les questions posées; donner sa date de naissance, un prix…; exprimer un besoin ou demander un rendez-vous; indiquer la nature d'un problème de santé

[33] Compréhension écrite: identifier la signalétique; comprendre des instructions simples; comprendre des informations de base; comprendre des informations chiffrées; reconnaître la nature et la fonction d'écrits simples.

minutes of testing are graded up to a maximum of 100 and correspond to a level A1.1. of the Common European Framework of Reference.[34] If the result is more than 50, the foreigner is exempted from the linguistic training and receives a ministerial certificate attesting that he has sufficient command of the French language as regards article L 311-9 of the Aliens Code.

The second step concerns foreigners who failed the test. In that case, the administrative authorities assess the length of the training needed, which cannot last more than 400 hours. The knowledge acquired during the linguistic training is assessed on the basis of a test which, if successful, leads to the issue of a diploma called the *diplôme initial de langue française*.[35] A bylaw adopted in December 2006 defines the tests that have to be fulfilled in order to acquire this diploma.[36] It must be noted that this test is longer than the one organised for the initial evaluation of the level of French language, as it last 75 minutes, including 35 minutes of testing for oral comprehension and expression and 40 minutes for the written tests. It must be emphasised that the requirements in the oral tests seem to be different because, for instance, an interview with the jury is organised. This leads to the idea that the French authorities believe that the linguistic training will ensure a higher level of knowledge than the level required for entry to the territory. In any case, the test is harder after the linguistic training.

Finally, an information session completes this process. It is regulated by Article R 311-25 of the Aliens Code. The session must impart knowledge concerning practical life in France, access to public services and, more particularly, access to employment, housing, health care, childhood, schooling

---

Production écrite: recopier une adresse, un numéro de téléphone; noter un numéro, un prix, une date; compléter un formulaire; laisser un message simple.

34 For an overview of the levels of language proficiency in the Council of Europe's Common Framework of Reference, please see Annex 1. Level A 1.1 does not exist in the European Common Framework of Reference. Nevertheless, parliamentary reports use this denomination in order to demonstrate that the level of language knowledge required in France is lower than the level A 1, instituted by the Common European Framework. See more precisely 'La compréhension des langues est classée, au plan européen, sur une échelle allant de A1 jusqu'à C. Or un niveau A1-1, encore plus bas que le plus bas niveau possible, a été créé pour le CAI', Mariani T., *Rapport sur le projet de loi relatif à la maîtrise de l'immigration, à l'intégration et à l'asile*, Rapport n° 160, 12 September 2007, Assemblée nationale, 263 p., esp. 54.

35 Décret n° 2006-1626 du 19 décembre 2006 relatif au diplôme initial de langue française et modifiant le livre III du code de l'éducation (partie réglementaire), *Journal Officiel de la République française*, 20 décembre 2006.

36 Arrêté du 20 décembre 2006 fixant le contenu des épreuves conduisant à la délivrance du diplôme initial de langue française, *Journal Officiel de la République française*, 30 décembre 2006.

and education choices as well as associative life. A bylaw adopted in January 2007 emphasises that this session lasts between one and six hours and attendance is rewarded by a certificate.[37]

When looking at integration measures established by French regulation, it appears that they do not constitute a huge obstacle. They are firstly based on two short compulsory training sessions, certified by the award of a certificate of attendance. The linguistic training does not imply a very high level of commitment, since it is equivalent to level A 1.1, i.e. lower than the first level A. 1 of the Council of Europe. Consequently, in practice, the figures demonstrate that only 25% of newcomers fail the test and are required to attend to the linguistic training.[38] In fact, the vast majority of persons involved in the integration contract are able to master or have a sufficient knowledge of French. This is mainly due to their origins, since more than 40% come from the Maghreb and another 20% from Cameroon, Congo, the Ivory Coast, Mali and Senegal.[39] These figures remained more or less identical in 2007.[40] Fur-

[37] Arrêté du 19 janvier 2007 relatif aux formations prescrites aux étrangers signataires du contrat d'accueil et d'intégration et à l'appréciation du niveau de connaissances en français prévues aux articles R. 311-22 à R. 311-25 du décret n° 2006-1791 du 23 décembre 2006 relatif au contrat d'accueil et d'intégration et au contrôle des connaissances en français d'un étranger souhaitant s'installer durablement en France et modifiant le code de l'entrée et du séjour et du droit d'asile (partie réglementaire), *Journal Officiel de la République française*, 30 janvier 2007.

[38] 'Les signataires du contrat, dans leur grande majorité, sont cependant francophones ou ont une connaissance du français jugée suffisante pour se voir délivrer une attestation ministérielle de compétences linguistiques (AMCL) lors de leur passage sur la plate-forme d'accueil de l'ANAEM. En définitive, environ un quart d'entre eux ont été invités en 2006 comme en 2005 à suivre une formation linguistique destinée à leur permettre d'acquérir un premier niveau de compétence linguistique', Secrétariat général du Comité interministériel de contrôle de l'immigration, *Rapport au Parlement. Les orientations de la politique de l'immigration*, December 2007, 228 p., esp. 107.

[39] 'L'analyse de l'origine géographique des signataires du CAI (voir tableau n° IV-4) révèle que, si le nombre de nationalités représentées est toujours aussi important (plus de 150), les plus nombreux sont, en 2006, pour 42,3 % originaires du Maghreb dont 21,3 % d'Algérie, 14,5 % du Maroc et 6,4 % de Tunisie, puis de Turquie (6,1 %). Les personnes venant d'Afrique subsaharienne, et notamment du Cameroun, du Congo, de Côte d'Ivoire, du Mali et du Sénégal, représentent 20,4 % du total des signataires contre 16 % en 2005; les personnes originaires de Russie et de l'ex-URSS forment 5,4 % du total, et les Chinois 3,3 %, en progression sensible'. Secrétariat général du Comité interministériel de contrôle de l'immigration, *Rapport au Parlement. Les orientations de la politique de l'immigration*, December 2007, 228 p., esp. 106.

[40] 'L'analyse de l'origine géographique des signataires du CAI (cf. tableau no III-3) révèle que, si plus de 150 nationalités sont représentées, les plus nombreux sont, en 2007, pour 43,1 % originaires du Maghreb dont 20,8 % d'Algérie, 15,5 % du Maroc et 6,8 % de Tunisie, puis

thermore, all sessions are free for newcomers. Notwithstanding the modifications introduced by the Law adopted in 2006, which have made the contract compulsory and have made the involvement of the foreigner more difficult regarding Article L 314-2 of the Aliens Code, the obligations that have to be fulfilled by third-country nationals must be put into perspective.

An identical assessment can be made regarding the integration contract for the Family. Article L 311-19-1 only requires that family members follow a training course and respect compulsory school attendance by children. Decree no. 2008–1115 indicates that the training the foreigners have to follow mainly deals with parental authority, equality between men and women, the protection of children and the principles covering school education in France.[41]

4.1.2.2 *The effects of the integration contract*

The compulsory nature of integration contracts implies that measures should be adopted in case the persons concerned do not fulfil the obligations set forth in the contract. The effects differ between the integration contract and the integration contract for the family within the framework of family reunification.

Integration contract

Article L 311-9 of the Aliens Code states that failure to respect the obligations set forth in the contract, if this is deliberate on the part of the applicant, can be taken into account when renewing the residence permit for the first time. This provision identifies the effects the integration measures play at the time the residence permit is first renewed. Apart from this element, the legislation does not disclose precisely what the consequences are in cases where the obligations are not fulfilled regarding renewal of the residence document.

Decree no. 2006-1971 has clarified the situation by inserting into the regulatory part of the Aliens Code a section dedicated to provisions relating

de Turquie (6,3 %). Les personnes venant d'Afrique subsaharienne, et notamment du Cameroun, du Congo, de Côte d'Ivoire, du Mali et du Sénégal représentent 14,8 % des signataires; les personnes originaires de Russie et des pays issus de l'ex-URSS forment 4,4 % du total, et les Chinois, en progression sensible, 3,2 %', Secrétariat général du Comité interministériel de contrôle de l'immigration, *Rapport au Parlement. Les orientations de la politique de l'immigration*, December 2008, 326 p., esp. 155.

[41] Décret n° 2008-1115 du 30 octobre 2008 relatif à la préparation de l'intégration en France des étrangers souhaitant s'y installer durablement, *Journal Officiel de la République française*, 1er novembre 2008, article 6.

to integration into French society.[42] Two situations must be distinguished. Firstly, when the residence permit is renewed, Article R 311-27 of the Aliens Code stipulates that the integration contract can be extended. The extension is a right if the linguistic training is duly followed at the end of the first year of the contract. The integration contract may also be extended if the linguistic training has been postponed for legitimate reasons. In that case, the fact that the foreigner has been unable, for legitimate reasons, to attend or finish the linguistic training within the allotted time frame, i.e., the one-year period of the integration contract, may not lead to non-renewal of the residence permit. In other words, the 'goodwill' of the third-country national in the integration process applies for the extension of the contract and may not constitute grounds for refusing to renew the residence permit. Secondly, according to Article R 311-28 of the Aliens Code, the integration contract may be terminated by the *Préfet* following a proposal from the ANAEM if the foreigner fails or ceases to participate in required training without legitimate reason. In that case, the *Préfet* notifies the person concerned of the intention to terminate the contract and allows him to submit observations within one month. The notification from the administrative authority shall indicate the motives for the termination of the contract and the consequences of such termination regarding the first renewal of the residence card. This situation takes into account all types of compulsory training imposed by the integration contract. We can therefore consider that the failure to attend the civic and/or training sessions, without giving legitimate reasons, may constitute grounds for the administrative authority to refuse to renew the residence permit. To summarise, if the third-country national does not meet or ceases to meet the obligations imposed by the integration contract, without legitimate reason, the administrative authority may, on this basis, refuse to renew the residence permit. On the other hand, if the foreigner has legitimate reasons that prevent him from completing the language course within the one-year period of the integration contract, and if the residence permit is renewed, the contract is extended. This means that the ongoing commitment by the foreigner may not constitute grounds for refusing to renew the residence permit.

Taken together, these provisions are based on the commitment of the third-country national to fulfil his obligations, in line with the legislative

[42] Décret n° 2006-1791 du 23 décembre 2006 relatif au contrat d'accueil et d'intégration et au contrôle des connaissances en français d'un étranger souhaitant durablement s'installer en France et modifiant le code de l'entrée et du séjour des étrangers et du droit d'asile (partie réglementaire), *Journal Officiel de la République française*, 31 décembre 2006.

provision which states that the third-country national promises to follow civic and linguistic training.[43] On the other hand, whereas the legislation stipulates that failure to respect the integration contract has to be assessed in terms of the 'characterised will' (*la volonté characterisée*) of the foreigner, the regulation bases the assessment on different grounds, since inability to attend the sessions must be justified by 'legitimate reasons'. This difference of wording could create a shift in the burden of proof because the applicant has to provide proof of such reasons, which is not the case when the administration has to assess the 'characterised will of the applicant'. In any event, the fact that the 'legitimate reasons' are not defined by the regulation leaves the administration and the judge much room for discretion and may lead to divergent interpretations. In practice, 'legitimate' reasons may be considered acceptable if the third-country national lives far from any language training centre and cannot organise his work schedule to attend to the sessions[44] or if he suffers from physical or mental disease. Would it be the same for the

---

[43] Article L 311-9 CESEDA, second indent, 'A cette fin, il conclut avec l'Etat un contrat d'accueil et d'intégration, traduit dans une langue qu'il comprend, par lequel il *s'oblige* à suivre une formation civique et, lorsque le besoin en est établi, linguistique'.

[44] This situation was highlighted during the discussions that accompanied the bill of law regarding the notion of the blatant failure to respect the contract's obligations. See, in particular, 'Le rapporteur a, en conséquence, présenté un amendement prévoyant que, lors du premier renouvellement de la carte de séjour, il pourra être tenu compte du non-respect manifeste par l'étranger des stipulations du contrat d'accueil et d'intégration. M. Serge Blisko a dénoncé l'hypocrisie de ce dispositif en soulignant que le non-respect des stipulations du contrat par l'étranger pourra résulter, non pas d'une mauvaise volonté de celui-ci, mais de difficultés matérielles insurmontables telles que l'éloignement des centres de formation ou encore l'inadaptation des plages horaires d'ouverture proposées. Il a regretté que les réalités humaines et les difficultés sociales rencontrées par de nombreux étrangers résidant en France soient ainsi méconnues et souligné qu'il peut être particulièrement difficile de parvenir à enseigner la langue française à des personnes étant illettrées dans leur propre langue. Il a enfin considéré que l'expression se référant au 'non-respect manifeste' était imprécise et qu'elle pourrait donner lieu à des interprétations contestables par l'administration préfectorale.

M. Étienne Pinte s'est interrogé sur les conséquences susceptibles d'être tirées par l'administration du défaut d'assiduité de l'étranger ayant conclu un contrat d'accueil et d'intégration. M. Jean-Christophe Lagarde a observé que de nombreuses inégalités existaient d'ores et déjà sur le territoire national en matière d'examen des demandes d'octroi des titres de séjour et de délivrance de ceux-ci. Il a estimé que la référence au non-respect manifeste de ses obligations par l'étranger constituait un critère pertinent d'évaluation de sa motivation, mais que l'introduction d'un tel dispositif risquait de conduire au développement d'un contentieux administratif massif. Soulignant à son tour le caractère imprécis et arbitraire du critère du non-respect manifeste des obligations, M. Bernard Roman a émis la crainte que les préfectures l'apprécient, non pas en fonction d'éléments objectifs liés à la personnalité

spouse of a third-country national living far from any training centre and taking care of children? Whereas these examples look quite simple, everyday situations may be more complex and lead to divergent interpretations between authorities or judges.

As mentioned in a report published in December 2008, it is still too early to assess the impact of these rules on the renewal of the residence permit. Two reasons can explain this situation. On the one hand, the integration contract in its compulsory form was launched in January 2007 and could be extended for one year. Therefore, it is difficult to evaluate the level of failure and to analyse the proportion of and reasons for decisions to refuse to renew the permit. On the other hand, monitoring mechanisms are lacking and need to be established.[45]

In conclusion, the effects of non-fulfilment of the integration contract are assessed on the basis of the commitment by the foreigner to fulfil the obligations set forth in the contract. If he can prove otherwise, it should be borne in mind that the refusal to renew the residence permit may not be based on failure to have fully completed the integration process.[46] On the contrary, fulfilment of the integration obligations may constitute an important element

---

de l'étranger, mais en fonction des objectifs quantitatifs d'immigration fixés par la loi dans chaque département.

Après que le président Philippe Houillon eut souligné le caractère perfectible de l'expression de 'non-respect manifeste' par l'étranger de ses obligations, le rapporteur a reconnu que les modalités pratiques de mise en œuvre des formations pourraient soulever des difficultés pour des étrangers désireux de s'y conformer mais exerçant, à titre d'exemple, une activité professionnelle incompatible avec les horaires d'ouverture proposés. Il a cependant indiqué que de nombreuses initiatives étaient d'ores et déjà engagées afin d'adapter les offres de formation à ces situations concrètes, notamment par l'intermédiaire de formations en soirée et proposées dans un nombre croissant de villes petites et moyennes. Il a ensuite expliqué que la référence au non-respect manifeste avait pour but de permettre à l'autorité administrative d'apprécier, et partant de s'assurer, de la volonté d'intégration de l'étranger en tenant compte d'éventuelles contraintes objectives par exemple liées à l'exercice d'une activité professionnelle. La Commission a *adopté* cet amendement', Mariani 2006a: 66–67.

45 Secrétariat général du Comité interministériel de contrôle de l'immigration, *Rapport au Parlement. Les orientations de la politique de l'immigration*, December 2008, 326 p., esp. 158.

46 As underlined by the report to the Parliament on the trends in immigration policy, 'L'échec du migrant à l'examen du DILF [Diplôme Initial de Langue Française] ne le prive pas *ipso facto* du droit de demeurer en France, mais est susceptible de constituer un élément d'appréciation défavorable de son intégration lors du renouvellement de son titre de séjour ou de l'établissement d'une première carte de résident', Secrétariat général du Comité interministériel de contrôle de l'immigration, *Rapport au Parlement. Les orientations de la politique de l'immigration*, December 2007, 228 p., esp. 107.

in granting a residence permit.[47] In any event, some uncertainties remain regarding the interpretation of the 'legitimate reasons'. Practice and court judgments will in future frame the interpretation and detail the effects of the contract vis-à-vis renewal of the residence permit.

The integration contract for the family within the framework of family reunification

The effects relating to failure to respect the integration contract for the family within the framework of family reunification are of different nature. As a reminder, this contract implies two commitments: the obligation to attend a training course on the rights and duties of parents and respect for compulsory school attendance by children. Monitoring of these commitments is under the responsibility of the ANAEM. It delivers a certificate of attendance on the training course and receives the certificate of registration for the children at an educational establishment. Article L 311-9-1 of the Aliens Code indicates that, when the provisions of the contract are not respected due to a characterised will of the foreigner or his/her spouse, the *Préfet*, informed by the ANAEM,[48] may ask the President of the sub-regional Assembly (*le Président du Conseil Général*) to enter into a 'parental liability contract' with the family. This contract reiterates the obligations the parents have to fulfil and sets forth any measures and social action to be taken to resolve the situation. If these obligations are still not respected, the President of the sub-regional Assembly may ask for suspension of payment of any social security benefits awarded for the children or take other legal action.[49] In that case, sanctions against the family will mainly be along economic lines. It must nevertheless

---

47 On this point, see, Administrative Court of Appeal of Nancy, 30 April 2008, M. X, no. 07NC01160, 'qu'au surplus, il ressort des témoignages produits et notamment de celui du directeur d'une entreprise d'insertion que M. X qui a suivi assidûment des cours de français, signé le 19 juin 2006 un contrat d'accueil et d'intégration, obtenu une attestation de formation civique et bénéficié de rapports très favorables dans les activités professionnelles exercées, manifeste une volonté réelle d'intégration à la société française'.

48 In accordance with Article R 311-30-15 of the Aliens Code.

49 Article L 222-4-1 du Code des affaires sociales et des familles, second indent, 'Lorsqu'il constate que les obligations incombant aux parents ou au représentant légal du mineur n'ont pas été respectées ou lorsque, sans motif légitime, le contrat n'a pu être signé de leur fait, le président du conseil général peut:

1° Demander au directeur de l'organisme débiteur des prestations familiales la suspension du versement de tout ou partie des prestations afférentes à l'enfant, en application de l'article L. 552-3 du code de la sécurité sociale;

2° Saisir le procureur de la République de faits susceptibles de constituer une infraction pénale;

be emphasised that article L 311-9-1 of the Aliens Code indicates that failure to respect the contract may be taken into consideration when renewing the residence permit. A bylaw adopted in December 2008 recalls in its Article 4 that the signatories to the contract are informed that the *Préfet* takes into account the signature and fulfilment of the contract when renewing the residence permit.[50]

In conclusion and notwithstanding the progressive modifications and strengthening of the integration contract through successive legislative amendments, it should be noted that the system of integration contracts remains quite flexible either in terms of content or in terms of effects. An evaluation of mid-term and long-term needs nevertheless to be conducted in order to assess to what extent this contract plays a role regarding the renewal of the residence permit and who the persons are who will be more affected by this situation.

The debate relating to integration measures was fostered with the adoption of a law in November 2007. Taking into account what was established in other Member States, the government has decided to institute a new regime of integration measures in cases of family reunification.

4.2 *The Establishment of Integration Measures in the Country of Origin*

After a clear trend towards enlarging the scope of integration measures and strengthening their effects, French policy has reached a new stage with the adoption of a third law, setting up compulsory integration measures for third-country nationals in their country of origin. The idea for such measures was launched at the end of the year 2006, mainly on the basis of an appraisal of a movement taking place in several Member States (4.2.1). The proposal was modified during the negotiations, for legal reasons, and culminated in the adoption of a law in November 2007, establishing integration measures that have to be fulfilled in the country of origin by third-country nationals applying for family reunification (4.2.2).

3° Saisir l'autorité judiciaire pour qu'il soit fait application, s'il y a lieu, des dispositions de l'article 375-9-1 du code civil'.

50 Arrêté du 1er décembre 2008 relatif au contrat d'accueil et d'intégration pour la famille mentionné aux articles R. 311-30-12 à R. 311-30-15 du code de l'entrée et du séjour des étrangères et du droit d'asile, NOR: IMIC0827548A, *Journal Officiel de la République française*, 11 décembre 2008.

4.2.1 *Framing the Project*

Taking into account the developments in neighbouring countries and particularly in the Netherlands, the French authorities started to frame the project and to set up its political objectives (4.2.1.1) while paying attention to legal limits that could not be exceeded (4.2.1.2).

4.2.1.1 *Political objectives*

In December 2006 Member of Parliament Thierry MARIANI issued an information report to the *Assemblée nationale* entitled, 'Migrant integration policies within the European Union' (Mariani 2006b). In this document, he described some policies developed in several Member States and came to the conclusion that a growing number of Member States tend to use integration measures as a condition for entering the territory. Identifying the rules adopted in the Netherlands and those forecast in Germany and Denmark, he demonstrated the will of these countries to start the integration process before entry to the territory. The aim of this movement is to make the integration process as effective as possible. He argued, regarding Germany, that the agreement given by the SPD and the CDU on this subject demonstrated that this question goes beyond political divisions and that a European consensus on this issue is growing. At the end of the information report, the Member of the French Parliament identified 10 proposals for successful integration in France. The first was dedicated to the establishment of integration tests abroad for family reunification applicants. This test would involve knowledge of the French language and the values of the French Republic, directly connected to the concept of republican integration.

Taking into account this widespread movement throughout certain European Member States, in March 2007 the Minister of the Interior, now French President Nicolas Sarkozy, announced the aim to establish integration tests, based on the Dutch example, in the country of origin for applicants for family reunification. This test would cover a basic command of the French language.[51] Elected President of the Republic in May 2007, he decided to create

---

[51] 'Je veux revenir, à cet égard, sur la question du regroupement familial. La réforme que nous avons mise en œuvre en France ne constitue, dans mon esprit, qu'une première étape. Nous avons défini les conditions que doit respecter l'étranger résidant en France et souhaitant y faire venir sa famille. Nous devrons, demain, définir les conditions pesant sur les candidats au regroupement familial, qui résident à l'étranger et désirent rejoindre leur conjoint dans notre pays.

Je souhaite que nous prenions exemple sur les Pays Bas, qui ont mis en place un 'test d'intégration' des candidats au regroupement familial, passé dans le pays d'origine.

a new Ministry of Immigration, Integration, National Identity and Co-development and to designate Brice Hortefeux minister in charge of these issues. The latter had the task of modifying once again the rules on family reunification and to insert the proposals announced by the President into the French Alien's Code.

A draft bill was presented in July 2007 under the emergency procedure. While its first provision was dedicated to the goal announced by President Sarkozy, the wording of the provision was slightly different, since the idea of establishing a test was replaced by an evaluation of language knowledge abroad that could lead, if considered adequate, to the issue of a visa for the purpose of family reunification. Notwithstanding integration concerns, the political objectives of the project were to be found elsewhere, more particularly in the desire to manage migration flows more effectively. The rapporteur of the *Assemblée nationale* on this draft bill was paving the way in this respect. He believed that, if failure to attend compulsory language courses within the framework of the integration contract could lead to a refusal to renew the residence permit, the efficiency of this mechanism was not totally warranted because of Article 8 of ECHR. In other words, even if the authorities are entitled to refuse to renew the residence permit due to failure to respect the integration contract, they are still obliged to renew the permit on the basis of the protection guaranteed by Article 8 ECHR. Hence, with the introduction of language courses in the country of origin, the national authorities will be given an efficient tool to monitor effective attendance of French lessons, otherwise the long-term visa will not be issued.[52] If the state-

L'Allemagne et le Danemark envisagent d'adopter un test similaire, ce qui marque une réelle convergence européenne.

J'y suis favorable, car l'intégration, pour être réussie, doit être préparée en amont. Elle doit commencer avant l'arrivée sur le territoire national, dès le pays d'origine.

Je souhaite donc que les candidats au regroupement familial soient soumis, dans nos consulats, à un 'test' démontrant leur connaissance sommaire de la langue française.

Avant de venir en France, ils doivent prouver leur volonté et leur capacité d'intégration, en apprenant notre langue et en parvenant à un niveau leur permettant de lire le français et de communiquer lors des actes de la vie courante', 3ème rencontre préfectorale et consulaire sur l'immigration, Intervention de M. Nicolas Sarkozy, Ministre d'Etat, Ministre de l'Intérieur et de l'Aménagement du Territoire à Marseille.

52 '…si l'absence d'assiduité aux formations dispensées dans le cadre du CAI peut donner lieu à des sanctions, notamment le non-renouvellement de la carte de séjour, votre rapporteur estime que la mise en œuvre effective de ces sanctions est très difficile, compte tenu notamment de l'article 8 de la convention européenne des droits de l'homme. Au contraire, dans le cadre de la formation linguistique préalable à l'étranger, l'autorité administrative disposera d'un outil très efficace pour s'assurer du suivi effectif des cours de français puisqu'en

ment was raising doubts about its legal compatibility with the right to family reunification enshrined in a Directive and recognised by the Court of Justice,[53] this would have provided some clues about the intentions that lay behind the integration measures project.

Still, what is more interesting in the draft bill is the absence of a real language test, which has been replaced by an evaluation of language knowledge. This modification of the initial purpose was the consequence of two legal limitations.

4.2.1.2 *Legal barriers*

Two legal obstacles, mentioned in the Parliamentary report on the Bill regarding the management of immigration, integration and asylum, advocated not imposing a language test before family reunification. The first obstacle was of a constitutional nature. Since family reunification is considered a constitutional right in France,[54] the introduction of a test would lead to a condition being imposed upon the exercise of the right. Hence, such a condition that is not based on public order grounds and follows constitutional objectives[55] would probably fall under the censure of the French *Conseil constitutionnel*.[56]

---

l'absence de présentation du justificatif d'assiduité, le visa long séjour nécessaire à l'entrée en France ne sera pas délivré', Mariani 2007: esp. p. 65.

[53] ECJ, 27 June 2006, *European Parliament v. Council of the European Union*, Case C-540/03.

[54] Tenth paragraph of the preamble to the 1946 Constitution, 'La Nation assure à l'individu et à la famille les conditions nécessaires à leur développement'.

[55] 'Considérant qu'il résulte de cette disposition [see above, in English] dixième alinéa du préambule de la Constitution de 1946] que les étrangers dont la résidence en France est stable et régulière ont, comme les nationaux, le droit de mener une vie familiale normale; que ce droit comporte en particulier la faculté pour ces étrangers de faire venir auprès d'eux leurs conjoints et leurs enfants mineurs sous réserve de restrictions tenant à la sauvegarde de l'ordre public et à la protection de la santé publique lesquelles revêtent le caractère d'objectifs de valeur constitutionnelle; qu'il incombe au législateur tout en assurant la conciliation de telles exigences, de respecter ce droit', Décision du Conseil constitutionnel, DC n° 93-325, 13 August 1993, paragraphe 70.

[56] See also, 'M. Serge Blisko a rappelé que la formation initiale reçue dans le pays d'origine serait complétée par une formation en France et qu'il était important de ne pas priver d'accès au territoire national un étranger qui n'aurait pas encore acquis un niveau totalement satisfaisant. Le souci du groupe Socialiste est d'éviter qu'un examen joue en la matière un quelconque rôle de couperet. Le rapporteur a indiqué que l'instauration d'un tel examen serait en tout état de cause contraire à la jurisprudence du Conseil constitutionnel qui a jugé que le droit au regroupement familial est un principe de nature constitutionnelle et ferait donc, à n'en pas douter l'objet d'une censure', Mariani 2007: esp. p. 75.

This would also have been the case if the language evaluation were subject to payment by the applicant.[57]

The second obstacle was derived from Article 7, paragraph 2, of the Directive on the right to family reunification. This provision deals with integration measures and does not open up the possibility of imposing integration conditions. This point of the Directive has been subject to an evaluation advocating such an interpretation. In fact, the wording of some directives, namely the Directive on long-term residents and the Directive on the right to family reunification, is different in terms of the integration requirements. Whereas the first enables Member States to impose 'integration conditions' for the award of long-term resident status, this is not the case for family reunification, which only makes possible the introduction of integration measures.[58] In other words, such measures should facilitate integration and not be adopted in order to pursue different aims.[59] It must be emphasised that the Commission's assessment of this issue is radically different from the position initially defended by Commissioner Frattini. In response to the Dutch government on the compatibility of integration conditions with the Directive, the Commissioner considered that the Directive provides the possibility for adopting integration conditions.[60] In the end, and on the basis of these legal assessments and uncertainties, the initial French project to introduce an integration test, i.e. integration conditions, was modified in order to set up a language evaluation, i.e., an integration measure.

---

[57] 'Se pose la question de la prise en charge financière du test, étant précisé que la Constitution ne permet pas d'imposer des conditions financières limitant l'exercice du droit à une vie familiale normale' (...) 'Votre rapporteur considère qu'il aurait été légitime de pouvoir demander une participation financière aux bénéficiaires de cette formation, sur le modèle de la pratique de l'ensemble de nos partenaires. Cette participation aurait été un gage de volonté d'intégration et aurait responsabilisé les personnes qui vont suivre une formation qui ne sera elle-même sanctionnée par aucune évaluation. Cependant, cette participation financière aurait pu être considérée comme une condition financière à l'exercice d'un droit constitutionnellement protégé, celui du regroupement familial', Mariani 2007: esp. pp. 56, 70.

[58] On this issue, see more particularly, Groenendijk 2004.

[59] Report from the Commission to the European Parliament and the Council on the application of Directive 2003/86/EC on the right to family reunification, COM(2008) 610 final, 8 October 2008, sp. 7–8.

[60] As noted in a French parliamentary report, 'Préalablement à l'adoption de la loi, le gouvernement néerlandais a interrogé la Commission européenne sur la compatibilité de cette condition d'intégration avec la directive du 26 novembre 2003 sur le regroupement familial. Par lettre du 14 juin 2005, le commissaire Frattini a répondu que la directive, notamment son article 7, autorisait les Etats-membres à exiger des mesures ou conditions d'intégration aux étrangers candidats au regroupement familial', Mariani 2007: esp. p. 66.

4.2.2 *Implementing the Project*

The law was adopted on 20 November 2007 and inserted a new Article L 411-8 into the Aliens Code.[61] While this law did evoke a huge public debate regarding the DNA tests that were established in order to prove family ties, the question of language evaluation in the country of origin was not debated at all. The Aliens Code states that the issue of the visa for the purpose of family reunification is conditional upon fulfilment of the required integration measures. This new provision therefore institutes an evaluation process in the country of origin for the purpose of family reunification (4.2.2.1), which may lead to the obligation to attend training sessions (4.2.2.2). The implementing decree contains exemptions from the obligation to attend the sessions (4.2.2.3). In the end, and if the other conditions for the exercise of the right to family reunification are met, the visa shall be delivered to the applicant.

4.2.2.1 *Evaluation of the knowledge level*

Article L 411-8 of the Aliens Code stipulates that, in order to allow his republican integration into the French society, a foreigner aged over 16 and under 65 who applies for family reunification, is subject in the country of origin to an evaluation of his level of language and knowledge of republican values. A decree adopted in October 2008 implements this legislative provision and inserts a new sub-section into the Aliens Code entitled, 'Provisions relating to preparation for integration in the country of origin'.[62]

The organisation of evaluations abroad falls under the responsibility of the ANAEM. While the ANAEM is to manage these operations in the countries where it has offices, specifically Algeria, Tunisia, Morocco, Turkey, Mali and Senegal, which together represent almost 70 % of total evaluations,[63] the decree indicates that these operations may be managed by other partners based on a convention signed with the ANAEM (hereinafter referred to as 'the appointed partner'). According to a parliamentary report, these partners may be represented by structures belonging to the French cultural network, such as Cultural Centres or the *Alliance française*, and ensure coverage for almost all regions of the world.[64]

---

[61] Loi n° 2007-1631 du 20 novembre 2007 relative à la maîtrise de l'immigration, à l'intégration et à l'asile, *Journal Officiel de la République française*, 21 novembre 2007.

[62] Décret n° 2008-1115 du 30 octobre 2008 relatif à la préparation de l'intégration en France des étrangers souhaitant s'y installer durablement, *Journal Officiel de la République française*, 1 November 2008.

[63] The rapporteur estimates that the ANAEM will be in charge of nearly 70% of the evaluations. Mariani 2006a: esp. p. 68.

[64] Mariani 2007: 34.

The ANAEM, or the appointed partner, proceeds with an evaluation of the knowledge during the visa application procedure. Article R 311-30-2 of the Aliens Code stipulates that the evaluation shall take place within 60 days of issue of the receipt attesting that the complete file for family reunification has been submitted by the sponsor to national authorities in France. The evaluation of the language level is similar to that presented within the framework of the integration contract in France. In other words, the applicant is invited to take an oral[65] and a written[66] test lasting 10 minutes and 5 minutes respectively. These 15 minutes of tests are graded up to a maximum of 100 and correspond to a level A1.1 of the Common European framework reference. According to Article R 311-30-2 of the Aliens Code, foreigners who have studied for at least 3 years at a French secondary school or at a francophone school abroad, or who have studied for at least one year at a higher education establishment in France, are exempted from the test. These exemptions are identical to those organised within the framework of the integration contract signed upon arrival in France. Revealing a slight difference, Article R 311-30-2 of the Aliens Code indicates that the exemption is granted at the request of the foreigner.

The evaluation of the knowledge of republican values is assessed on the basis of oral questions in a language the candidate claims to understand. These questions are formulated with reference to republican values foreseen in the civic integration session given within the framework of the integration contract i.e. equality between men and women, secularism, Rule of Law, fundamental liberties, the security of persons and goods and the exercise of citizenship that opens the way to compulsory and free access to education. A bylaw adopted in December 2008 organises the evaluation, which lasts 10

[65] Compréhension orale: comprendre une annonce publique; comprendre une indication simple; comprendre des instructions simples; comprendre une information chiffrée, comprendre l'heure.

Production orale: comprendre les questions posées; donner sa date de naissance, un prix…; exprimer un besoin ou demander un rendez-vous; indiquer la nature d'un problème de santé

[66] Compréhension écrite: identifier la signalétique; comprendre des instructions simples; comprendre des informations de base; comprendre des informations chiffrées; reconnaître la nature et la fonction d'écrits simples.

Production écrite: recopier une adresse, un numéro de téléphone; noter un numéro, un prix, une date; compléter un formulaire; laisser un message simple.

minutes.[67] The applicant has to answer 6 questions.[68] The evaluation is successful if the applicant correctly answers 5 questions.

Several observations should be outlined regarding this evaluation system. Firstly, the language evaluation is identical to the evaluation organised within the framework of the integration contract in order to assess the need to follow language training. Secondly, knowledge of republican values is also aligned with the content of the civic instruction organised as part of the integration contract. Finally, Article 1 of the bylaw adopted in December 2008 indicates that the level of knowledge of the French language and the values of the French Republic must be evaluated during an individual interview lasting not more than 20 minutes. Whereas this correctly represents the total extent of the oral examination, this statement seems to overlook the written evaluation. In any event, depending on the different stages, the evaluation should last 25 minutes and lead to different outcomes regarding the results.

4.2.2.2 *Consequences of the evaluations*

Several situations may result from the evaluation. First of all, if the foreigner passes both tests, the ANAEM, or the appointed partner, delivers a certificate attesting that the applicant satisfies the evaluation's obligation set forth in Article L 411-8 of the Aliens Code. Concerning the language requirement, this certificate exempts the beneficiaries from taking the language evaluation in France as well as from attending the language training.

When the evaluations show an insufficient level of knowledge of the language and/or republican values, the applicant needs to follow training in one or both domains, according to the results. These courses must begin no later than two months after notification of the results. The training relating to republican values lasts three hours.[69] It deals with the following topics: equality between men and women, the principle of secularism, respect for

---

[67] Arrêté du 1er décembre 2008 relatif à l'évaluation dans leur pays de résidence du niveau de connaissance, par les étrangers, de la langue française et des valeurs de la République et aux formations prescrites dans ces domaines conformément aux articles R. 311-30-1 à R. 311-30-11 du code de l'entrée et du séjour des étrangers et du droit d'asile, IMIC0827547A, *Journal Officiel de la République française*, 5 décembre 2008.

[68] The questions are kept secret. They deal with the following topics: liberty, equality, solidarity, secularism and any other open question.

[69] Arrêté du 1er décembre 2008 relatif à l'évaluation dans leur pays de résidence du niveau de connaissance, par les étrangers, de la langue française et des valeurs de la République et aux formations prescrites dans ces domaines conformément aux articles R. 311-30-1 à R. 311-30-11 du code de l'entrée et du séjour des étrangers et du droit d'asile, IMIC0827547A, *Journal Officiel de la République française*, 5 décembre 2008.

individual and collective rights, the security of goods and persons, as well as rules relating to children's education and school attendance.[70] Its content shall be determined by the Ministry of Immigration. If the foreigner fails the language evaluation, the ANAEM, or the appointed partner, specifies the number of hours he has to attend, depending on the results of the first evaluation. Article R 311-30-6 of the Aliens Code states that the length of the language training may not be less than 40 hours. Whereas this provision does not give any time limit for the training, it cannot last more than two months according to Article L 411-8 of the Aliens Code. At the end of the training course(s), the ANAEM, or the appointed partner, immediately delivers a certificate of attendance to the foreigner, which may also mention any absence during the training. The ANAEM, or the appointed partner, sends a copy of the certificate of attendance to the diplomatic or consular offices in charge of examining the visa application. These training courses are entirely covered by the French authorities, which means that the candidate pays no fees.

According to Article L 411-8 and the implementing Decree no. 2008-1115, a second evaluation, similar to the first,[71] is organised after the training course(s). This second evaluation has an impact on measures to be taken depending on the level of language knowledge. On the one hand, if the foreigner meets the language level required, he is exempt from taking the language evaluation or following linguistic training following arrival in France. According to the Decree, he may nevertheless request training following his arrival in France, in order to prepare for the initial diploma in the French language. In any event, satisfactory results in the language evaluation do not exempt the foreigner from signing the integration contract in France. They only exempt him from taking the language evaluation and from attending the language training once he has arrived in France. He is still obliged to sign the integration contract and to attend the classes relating to civic and daily life in France. On the other hand, if the foreigner does not meet the required level, the results enable the ANAEM, or the appointed partner, to

[70] Article R 311-30-5 CESEDA.

[71] Article R 311-30-8 CESEDA, reproduced in the Annex, we believe contains an error. It should not read, 'Article R 311-11-2', which does not exist in the Aliens Code at the moment, but 'Article R 311-30-2'. To foster this assessment, see also the last sentence of the Annex to the Arrêté du 1er décembre 2008 relatif à l'évaluation dans leur pays de résidence du niveau de connaissance, par les étrangers, de la langue française et des valeurs de la République et aux formations prescrites dans ces domaines conformément aux articles R. 311-30-1 à R. 311-30-11 du code de l'entrée et du séjour des étrangers et du droit d'asile, IMIC0827547A, *Journal Officiel de la République française*, 5 décembre 2008.

determine the characteristics of the linguistic training he will have to take in France within the framework of the integration contract.

To summarise, the training in the country of origin shall enable the foreigner to strengthen his level of language knowledge and to be exempt from the linguistic training offered following his arrival in France within the framework of the integration contract. Regarding knowledge of republican values, no such exemption is granted. This means that, notwithstanding the results of the evaluation organised abroad, the foreigner shall attend the civic training planned upon arrival in France within the framework of the integration contract.

4.2.2.3 *Exemptions*

Article L 411-8 envisages that an implementing decree shall determine the legitimate grounds that may exempt the applicant from attending the training. Article R 311-30-10 of the Aliens Code, introduced by Decree no. 2008-1115, determines two series of situations in which the applicant can apply to the consular or diplomatic office to be exempted from the training sessions.[72] This request may be granted if disruption of public order, war, natural or technological disasters in the country of residence make any move difficult or threaten the security of the foreigner.[73] An exemption may also be granted if attendance of the training places incompatible burdens on the applicant's physical or financial abilities, his professional duties or his security. This provision of the Decree leaves room for discretion to the diplomatic or consular authorities, as the exemption may be awarded to the applicant. Moreover, whereas these exemption criteria cover a wide range of situations, they also leave room for diverse interpretations from different authorities. For example, will illiterate people fall under the scope of these exemptions according to their limited capacities? How will natural disasters be evaluated? How will disruptions to public order be assessed in order to decide on an exemption? If the implementation of these rules gives answers to these questions, the adoption of a ministerial circular may also be called for, in order to circumvent the risk of divergent interpretations. It must however be emphasised that, regarding Article R 311-30-10 CESEDA, the exemption may be requested at any moment during the procedure, even after the beginning of the training.

[72] Article R 311-30-10 of the Aliens Code.

[73] There is no mention of refugees because, according to the law, they are only required to sign the integration contract after the issue of the residence card recognising them as refugees.

Nevertheless, an exemption awarded in the country of origin does not prevent the foreigner, upon arrival in France, from signing an integration contract and fulfilling the obligations enshrined in it.

4.3 *Conclusion*

Integration issues have acquired great significance in the past few years in French legislation. Whereas this movement constitutes the continuation of an ongoing process that has been taking place since the 1980s, the link between integration and migration has never been so tight. Firstly, from an institutional point of view, since the management of integration has become one of the competences of the Minister of Immigration. Secondly, whereas integration has traditionally been considered a question to be dealt with within the host country, the establishment of integration measures to be fulfilled in the country of origin reveals the dual nature of integration. On the one hand, it exposes a genuine concern for enhancing the capacity of third-country nationals to acquire the basic minimum for becoming more easily integrated. On the other hand, it demonstrates the will to link integration measures with the management of migration flows.

Concerning this last point, it may also be supposed that the purpose of integration measures might lie elsewhere. The requirement to fulfil integration measures abroad may act as a deterrent for certain categories of people. In practice, people coming from third countries are asked to respect our most advanced values. While such requirements do not constitute an obstacle to people coming from industrialised countries, this might not be the case for persons coming from countries where political, economical, cultural and religious values are different. This appears then to be an additional criterion or justification for controlling entry to the territory by certain categories of migrants.[74] While the French measures are still very basic for the time being and do not constitute an obstacle *per se*, nothing prevents these measures from being tightened up in the future. In that case, the balance between integration and migration control may be called into question. It must nevertheless be borne in mind that, within this framework, Directive 2003/86/EC on the right to family reunification acts as a restraint, since it does not allow the imposition of integration conditions.

---

[74] 'On nous dit que pour maintenir une société accueillante à la diversité, il faut filtrer les frontières car les candidats au séjour appartiennent à des cultures rétrogrades et antidémocratiques. En clair, c'est justifier le contrôle obsessionnel des frontières au nom de nos valeurs les plus progressistes', Michel Feher, *Libération*, 25 February 2009.

Bibliography

Buffet, F.-N., *Rapport sur le projet de loi relatif à l'immigration et l'intégration*, Rapport n° 372, 13 May 2006, Sénat

Carrera, S., *In Search of the Perfect Citizen? The Intersection between Integration, Immigration and Nationality in the EU.* Leiden: Martinus Nijhoff Publishers 2009

Cour des Comptes, *L'accueil des immigrants et l'intégration des populations issues de l'immigration*, Paris: Les Editions du Journal Officiel 2004

Courtois, J.-P., *Rapport sur le projet de loi relatif à la maîtrise de l'immigration et au séjour des étrangers en France*, Rapport n° 1, 1 October 2003, Sénat

Diard, E., *Avis présenté au nom de la Commission des lois constitutionnelles, de la législation et de l'administration générale de la République sur le projet de loi de finance pour 2009, Tome IV 'Immigration, asile et intégration'*, Rapport n° 1203, 16 October 2008, Assemblée nationale

Fornerod, A., La langue française en droit de la nationalité et en droit des étrangers, *R.F.D.A.*, November-December 2008, p. 1097–1109

Groenendijk, K., Legal Concepts of Integration in EU Migration Law, *European Journal of Migration and Law* 2004, pp. 111–126

Julien-Laferrière, F., *Droit des étrangers*, Paris: P.U.F. 2000, pp. 23–25.

Mariani, T., *Rapport sur le projet de loi relatif à la maîtrise de l'immigration et au séjour des étrangers en France*, Rapport n° 949, 1ère partie, 13 June 2003, Assemblée nationale

Mariani, T., *Rapport sur le projet de loi relatif à l'immigration et l'intégration*, Rapport n° 3058, 26 April 2006a, Assemblée nationale

Mariani, T., *Rapport sur les politiques d'intégration des migrants dans l'Union européenne*, Rapport n° 3502, 6 December 2006b, Assemblée nationale

Mariani, T. *Rapport sur le projet de loi relatif à la maîtrise de l'immigration, à l'intégration et à l'asile*, Rapport n° 160, 12 September 2007, Assemblée nationale

Neraudau, E. & N. Kadouci, L'intégration des étrangers en France, in: I. Blanquez Rodriguez, *Regiones, Union Europea e integracion de inmigrantes. Une perspectiva desde el Derecho comparado*, Atelier Libros Juridicos 2008, 172 p., pp. 139–170

Secrétariat général du Comité interministériel de contrôle de l'immigration, Rapport au Parlement, *Les orientations de la politique de l'immigration*, December 2007

Secrétariat général du Comité interministériel de contrôle de l'immigration, *Rapport au Parlement. Les orientations de la politique de l'immigration*, December 2008

Souvet, L. & V. Letard, *Rapport sur le projet de loi de programmation pour la cohésion sociale*, Rapport n° 32, 20 October 2004, Sénat

Chapter 5

Integration Tests in Germany. A Communitarian Approach?

*Ines Michalowski**

In the years between 2005 and 2008 Germany introduced three new integration tests: one for family migrants as a condition for reunification, one as a condition for permanent residence and one as a condition for citizenship. Germany is by no means the only EU Member State to have done this but, compared to the others, it has some experience in this field. As a study of the EU 15 Member States' conditions for access to permanent residence from the year 2000 actually showed, Germany was the first Member State to require language skills for the award of a permanent residence permit (Groenendijk, Guild & Barzilay 2001). Furthermore, Germany was the first EU Member State to introduce language tests in the country of origin as a precondition for immigration because, in 1997, language tests were made compulsory for ethnic German immigrants from Central and Eastern Europe.[1] Finally, Germany also was the first country to introduce language tests for family members in their country of origin, even though this regulation, which

* Senior researcher at the Social Science Research Center in Berlin (WZB).

[1] The so-called *Spätaussiedler* are the descendants of German emigrants who have maintained – sometimes for hundreds of years – German diasporas in Central and Eastern Europe. Upon arrival in Germany, they are quickly assigned German citizenship. The peak of this immigration was in the early 1990s, right after the end of the Soviet Union. In an attempt to bring down numbers, a German language test was introduced in 1997 (Süssmuth Commission, 2001: 181). This language test had a very special function since it was not supposed to facilitate integration upon arrival. The test does not even focus on German language as it is contemporarily spoken in Germany, but on dialects that are outmoded in today's Germany, but spoken and preserved in the diaspora families. Knowledge of this special form of dialect serves as a proof that the person requesting the status of ethnic German really is of 'German descent', a quality which otherwise is difficult to establish (Seveker, 2006).

Van Oers, Ersbøll and Kostakopoulou, A Re-definition of Belonging?, pp. 185–210.

entered into force in 2005, first applied only to the family members of ethnic Germans.

Therefore, it can be argued that the introduction of additional language and integration requirements for other groups of migrants and family members at large has not been as much of a revolution in Germany as it might have been in neighbouring countries. In Germany, the introduction of integration requirements has been a slow and incremental change brought about by administrative actors and logics rather than a paradigmatic change provoked by conservative political entrepreneurs, as suggested by the literature relating to other European Member States. At the same time, however, a minor revolution seems to have taken place in Germany too, since the new nationwide citizenship test explicitly shifted away from the communitarian approach of some of its regional predecessors and, instead, demonstrates a republican understanding of citizenship.

This contribution will begin by summarising why and under what circumstances the various German integration requirements have been introduced, before presenting their legal framework and, finally, their content in more detail. The few existing evaluations and statistics about the functioning of these integration requirements and tests will then be presented in order to discuss what the added value of these measures is (supposed to be), why they have been created and in accordance with which approach: the libertarian, liberal, republican or communitarian approach.

5.1 *Why and under what Circumstances were the Tests Introduced?*

Three major reasons frequently put forward in literature to explain the creation of (restrictive) integration tests are

1) the rising presence of populist right-wing political parties triggered the tightening up of requirements for naturalisation (De Hart & Van Oers 2006: 318, Joppke 2007: 15);
2) the liberalisation of the nationality law in the past fed the assumption that naturalisation had become too easy and the tests were introduced in order to bring numbers down (De Hart & Van Oers 2006: 318, Joppke 2007: 8);
3) the identity of a state was at stake and national heritage needed to be protected (Cesarani & Fulbrook 1996: 214).

A closer study of the German tests, however, shows that these arguments do not fully explain the situation in Germany: the tests were developed under a Social Democrat/Green federal coalition government and, later on, under a Social Democrat/Christian Democrat coalition government without the pressure from right-wing populist parties whose influence so far has been largely limited to a few states. The second argument given in the existing literature does not fully explain the German case either since the liberalisation of German nationality law did not lead to a permanent and sharp increase in numbers, and even provoked discussions about why the liberalisation failed. As for the third argument of national identity being at stake, it is difficult to prove its effect. However, it seems safe to say that the introduction or modification of citizenship tests is always related to the definition, affirmation or redefinition of national identity. Nonetheless, and in order to be more specific in explaining the German context, a couple of additional explanations will be discussed below.

The three different tests that were introduced in Germany before immigration, when applying for permanent residence and applying for naturalisation, emerged at three different moments in time. The starting point for all these developments in German immigration and integration policy is 1999, when the Social Democrats and the Greens, who had come to power the year before, decided to set up a new immigration scheme for highly skilled workers, the so-called German Green Card, which was followed in 2000 by a new nationality law that introduced a *ius soli* regulation. This same government set up a Commission for Immigration (*Süssmuth Commission*) which presented its report in July 2001 and suggested the creation of an integration programme for newcomers, largely modelled on the Dutch programme that had been introduced in 1998. Interestingly, this Süssmuth report rejected the use of sanctions and did not even mention the possible establishment of a link between (successful) participation in the integration programme and the attribution of a permanent residence permit. Instead, it largely drew upon the suggestions made by the former Commissioner for Foreigner Affairs (Marieluise Beck of the Green Party), who had suggested using government funding for language and social orientation courses and handing out a bundle of vouchers for such courses to every newly arrived immigrant. Thus, when the German integration programme was first discussed, even some traditionally very pro-migrant actors were in favour of it because it was seen as more public funds being made available for measures to help immigrants integrate. The Dutch programme introduced in 1998 that had served as a model actually focused on the same idea. The sanctions that were foreseen for migrants who did not participate in the programme were exclusively financial (as opposed to today's sanctions that are related, for instance, to a secure residence status or to immigration) and rarely applied. However, when the proposal for a new German law on immigration, integration and asylum was presented for the first time in November 2001 (the law did not enter into force until 2005) it contained sanctions such as linking successful participation in the integration programme to the award of a permanent residence permit even though in other respects it largely followed the recommendations of the Süssmuth Commission.

This emergence of a restrictive element in a measure that was conceived as a social policy can be explained by several elements. One is the *role of political entrepreneurs* and parties who obviously played a role in shaping the immigration reform and who were opposed to the more liberal ideas put forward by the Süssmuth Commission. One important political entrepreneur in terms of this German legislation was the fairly conservative Social Democratic former interior minister, Otto Schily, who was responsible for the new immigration act and who, in the aftermath of 9/11 had particularly strong security concerns which he translated into a more restrictive legislation.

Other factors also explain why the restrictive regulation appeared in the proposal as well as in the final law, although the Süssmuth Commission had clearly argued against it. In fact, Germany has a *legal tradition* in this field because in 1978 the residence regulation (*Verfestigungsregeln*) required 'basic' and subsequently 'sufficient' language skills for permanent residence. Therefore, when the 2005 Immigration Act stipulated that 'sufficient' language skills could be demonstrated by participation in a state-run integration programme and that, in addition to language skills, a basic knowledge of German society was also required, this was only a small change. Thus, in a country where the link between immigration control (including access to permanent residence) and the promotion of immigrant integration has long been established, it is no surprise that an increased government programme, involving up to 600 hours of language courses plus 30 hours of civic education, would not only raise expectations with regard to the achievements expected of participants; it also raised expectations concerning what immigrants are supposed to know when applying for permanent residence. In fact, the establishment of a state-run programme favoured the administration of an individual integration process and led to a formalisation of expected outcomes (Michalowski 2007).[2] Thus, one of the reasons Germany

[2] The anticipated relationship between (financial) input and (human capital) output, however, has not been established in an empirical or scientific way. In other words, the fact that 600 hours of language tuition in Germany should lead to level B1 of the Common European Reference Framework for Languages has not been established through research. It is rather the result of political objectives (i.e. the creation of a programme to help migrants lead a socially and economically independent life which would require minimum language skills at level B1 with budgetary restraints (allowing the financing of 600 hours). The Süssmuth

has introduced language and integration tests is that it has a legal tradition in this field and that the extension of the existing legal and administrative logic from one case to another has been easy. This argument also holds true for the introduction of integration requirements in the country of origin, since Germany introduced language tests for ethnic Germans from Eastern and Central Europe as early as 1997. In 2001, the Süssmuth Commission also suggested introducing language tests prior to immigration for the family members of these ethnic Germans, arguing that, once they arrived in Germany they would quickly acquire German citizenship. Although this regulation was applied to a very special group of migrants, the German government definitely had some experience when language requirements for potential family migrants were introduced in January 2008.

A third factor in why Germany introduced an increasing number of formalised integration tests is *exchange at the European level.* The Netherlands served as a model for the German state-run integration programme, as well as for introducing integration requirements for family migrants in the countries of origin. Together with Austria, during the negotiations Germany and the Netherlands pushed for the Directive on the right to family reunification (2003/86/EC) to provide the possibility that, 'Member States may require third country nationals to comply with integration measures, in accordance with national law' (Article 7.2). The Netherlands and Germany then profited from these negotiated changes to the Directive on family reunification, as well as from the regulations of the Directive on the rights of long-term residents (2003/109/EC), when they introduced integration requirements as a precondition for family migration and for permanent residence. Thus, the European venue has been used strategically as a way of introducing new (restrictive) policies at the national level (cf. Guiraudon 2000).

A fourth additional reason for the multiplication of integration tests that use immigration-related sanctions could be that the issue of immigrant integration has been moved from Social Affairs to Justice and Home Affairs. One example is the relocation of the Commissioner for Foreigner Affairs, who was moved from the Ministry for Social Affairs to the Chancellor's Office in 2005. Another example is the creation in 2003 of the Federal Agency for Migration and Refugees (BAMF), which has been placed under the auspices

---

Commission suggested these 600 hours of language training without giving even one reason why it should be 600 rather than 400 or 900 hours. Instead, it largely relied on the Dutch model. A year earlier, however, the Dutch *Rekenkamer* (court of auditors) had criticised the fact that there obviously was no scientific or empirical justification for the correlation between the number of hours and the fixed learning objective in the Netherlands (Rekenkamer, 2000: 31).

of the Ministry of the Interior. This *move towards law-and-order ministries* has taken place not only in Germany but also in a number of neighbouring countries, such as France and the Netherlands, as well as at the European level, where the social affairs ministers who were traditionally in charge of immigrant integration issues have been replaced by Justice and Home Affairs ministers for negotiations on the EU directives in the field of migration and integration.[3] These politicians, administrations and agencies that were already in charge of immigration control and were then charged with integration issues, quite naturally linked immigration with integration issues and also looked for more instruments of control than actors from the field of social affairs might have done (Carrera 2006).

Public debates, which are often mentioned as one of the reasons why integration requirements were introduced, played a rather unspecific and general role in the creation of German integration courses. Criticism levelled at previous German integration policies (or rather at the absence thereof) as well as the oppressive social reality of the 1990s, marked by xenophobic attacks on asylum-seekers, were the background for the reforms that the Social Democrats and the Greens launched after they had come to power. The reform itself provoked huge discussions which delayed its adoption for almost 4 years. These discussions, however, focused entirely on the immigration-related parts of the proposed bill, while the only issue related to the proposed integration programme was whether the states or the federal government should finance it. The programme itself did not provoke major public debates because those who had criticised the German government's previous official refusal to recognise that Germany was an immigration country and had to engage in the integration of its new citizens (Thränhardt 1996) appreciated that the government they had voted for finally took action on this issue. On the other hand, those voters in favour of a more restrictive policy welcomed the programme because it was supposed to ensure that all migrants settling in Germany would learn the language.

The introduction of language requirements in the country of origin did not directly depend on public debates either, since the way had been paved for the introduction of these measures long before[4] the grand coalition of Christian Democrats and Social Democrats tried to justify these measures by associating them with the prevention of forced marriages. It therefore

[3] For the change in competencies in the Netherlands and the accompanying new definition of integration, see Groenendijk 2004.

[4] Through the EU negotiations on the Directive on family reunification that took place in the early 2000s.

seems safe to say that the public debate about forced marriages has been used as a way of illustrating the 'cultural incompatibility' between some family migrants and German society (Ratia & Walter 2009), even though this was not the initial motivation for creating the tests. In fact, what was not said as explicitly in Germany as in France is that language tests for family migrants are an efficient way (at least until the courts intervene) to reduce largely unwanted family migration, deemed unskilled and harder to integrate. The justification the government tried to give by pointing to the prevention of forced marriages, however, did not prevent a public and political debate about the rights and wrongs of selecting more resourceful family migrants. One group of strong opponents were the migrant organisations that denounced the unequal treatment of family migrants from Turkey, who have to prove their language skills in the country of origin, compared to family migrants from the US and other visa-exempt countries who do not have to prove these skills

Finally, public debates did play an important role with respect to the federal naturalisation test, since previous tests that had been set up by some *Länder* have been strongly criticised. When the federal test was drawn up, policy-makers wanted to avoid similar criticism. Thus, the bad example set by Baden-Württemberg, which had formulated a test specifically addressed at Muslims, asking questions about their opinions and attitudes, was explicitly discontinued by the federal test. Instead, as will be discussed in more detail below, the Federal Government has opted for a test that asks about knowledge of and respect for common laws.

5.2 *The Existing Integration Requirements*

Since 2008, German law stipulates integration requirements for the immigration of certain family migrants, for access to permanent residence and for naturalisation.

a) *Before immigration*: Copied from the Dutch policy of 'starting integration in the country of origin' (*Wet Inburgering in het Buitenland*), Germany introduced a language requirement for potential family migrants in their country of origin. This legal change was introduced by the law of 19 August 2007[5] that implemented several European Directives, among them the

[5] Gesetz zur Umsetzung aufenthalts- und asylrechtlicher Richtlinien der Europäischen Union vom 19. August 2007 (*BGBL*. 2007, Teil I, Nr. 42).

Directive on the right to family reunification (2003/86/EC, Article 7(2)) and on the legal status of long-term residents (2003/109/EC, Article 5(2)), which regulate the conditions under which Member States '(...) may require third-country nationals to comply with integration measures, in accordance with national law'.[6]

Since the German integration test in the country of origin has been strongly 'inspired' by the Dutch test dating from March 2006, they have some similarities. First of all, the Dutch and German integration requirements are aimed at family migrants who, in both countries, have the reputation for being poorly skilled or even unskilled and therefore not adapted to the needs of the national labour market. A second similarity is not related to the target group but to the fact that both countries decided to introduce these integration requirements without offering state-financed courses in the immigrants' countries of origin. This shared decision against language courses in the country of origin is interesting because several alternative solutions have been tabled: first of all, Germany itself has a long tradition of offering German language courses to ethnic Germans in their countries of origin (Seveker 2006). Secondly, the second Dutch Balkenende government (Balkenende II) initially thought of proposing language and integration courses in preparation for the test, at least in the major countries of origin (Van de Bunt 2003).[7] Thirdly, the French have, in the law of November 2007 (*Hortefeux law*), decided to introduce French language courses and tests in the immigrants' countries of origin. The Netherlands and Germany, however, have decided not to offer special state-run language classes in the immigrants' countries of origin. This is why their integration tests in the countries of origin clearly are an instrument for the selection of (more highly) skilled migrants and only indirectly linked to the integration of immigrants in the receiving country.[8] The expectation is that immigrants will be selected who are sufficiently skilled and motivated to prepare for a language test without

[6] For the question whether integration tests can be defined as integration measures, see the debate between Kees Groenendijk (2006; 2007) and Karin de Vries (2006; 2007) in *Migrantenstudies*.

[7] Offering language and integration courses in only some countries of origin proved impossible because it would have resulted in unequal treatment of immigrants who do not come from one of the major countries of origin.

[8] The underlying assumption is that the integration of immigrants in the receiving society will improve if the migrants are more highly qualified. These tests do not focus on the integration of an individual but on the situation as a whole, including the kind of human capital entering the country. For an individual, this logic can imply that the integration of migrants in Germany is expected to improve if he or she is not admitted to the country.

the help of the future receiving country and who, therefore, can be expected to become proactive and independent citizens.

Despite the similarities between German and Dutch policies in this field, some differences also exist. First of all, differences are evident with respect to the level of language skills required. The Dutch test asks 30 out of 100 questions about Dutch society and life in the Netherlands, all of which (including the correct answers) are published in the respective study guide. The language skills that are necessary to answer the questions correspond to the level of 'A1 minus', a new level that the Dutch added to the Common European Reference Framework for Languages to designate language skills that are restricted to the knowledge of approximately 500 words and a very basic grammar.[9] The language and integration test is taken at a Dutch embassy or consulate and it is organised as a telephone call with a voice recognition computer program. Immigrants to Germany, however, do not take a test at a German embassy and they do not have to demonstrate knowledge of German society and life in Germany. Instead, they are asked to produce a language certificate at level A1 when applying for an immigration visa to Germany. This certificate can be acquired by passing a language test at the Goethe Institute or another officially certified institution in their country of origin. Candidates for family reunification can take a language class at the Goethe Institute in order to prepare for the certificate but the German state does not pay for these language courses.[10]

Both countries, the Netherlands and Germany, consider it generally possible to reach the required level of language skills (and civic education skills in the Netherlands) through self-study. In the Dutch case, this can even be a necessity because the Netherlands does not have an equivalent of the German Goethe Institute, offering German language courses in many countries around the world. This is why the German government only published a flyer listing the different possibilities for learning German besides attending language classes at the Goethe Institute, while the Netherlands prepared a full learning kit containing a book for learning Dutch, a film about the Netherlands and a book to prepare for the civic education test, based on the film. This learning kit can be bought from Dutch libraries and also via the internet (www.naarnederland.nl) for the price of € 65. A candidate for immigration

[9] The Common European Reference Framework for languages distinguishes 6 levels: A (A1+A2) Basic User, B (B1+B2) Independent User, C (C1+C2) Proficient User.

[10] It has to be added, though, that the general infrastructure of the Goethe Institute is tax-financed.

who has bought this kit should have most of what is needed to prepare for the Dutch test. This is less clear from the German flyer, which – besides the Goethe Institute language classes – mentions language courses broadcast by the *Deutsche Welle*, internet websites for learning German and even German vocabulary downloads for mobile phones.[11]

Finally, the prices for the tests differ: while the Dutch language and civic education test costs € 350 in every country in the world, taking the A1 certificate for German is priced differently depending on the country. In Bangkok, for example, it costs € 53 to take the test, while the Goethe Institute in Istanbul charges € 66.[12]

b) *Access to permanent residence*: The German *Zuwanderungsgesetz* that entered into force in January 2005 introduced, for the first time, so-called integration courses (*Integrationskurse*), which today consist of 600 to 900 hours of language tuition and 45 hours of civic education. These integration courses are compulsory for most newcomers from outside the EU and especially for family migrants. The law also stipulates that, among the migrants who are obliged to participate in an integration course, only those who participate successfully in the integration course may be awarded a permanent residence permit, which means that they achieved level B1 of the Common European Reference Framework for languages.[13] So far, this regulation has not been applied because migrants have to have stayed in Germany for at least 5 years before they can apply for permanent residence.

Since the evaluation of these new German integration courses was published in 2007, some changes were proposed and entered into force in January 2008. One of these changes was that the numbers of language course hours was increased from 600 to 900 hours for those who need more extensive training; another change was that the language test at the end of the integration programme became compulsory for every participant. In fact, the initial act from January 2005 only envisaged an optional test, which had led to major bias in the statistics since only participants who were able to pass a test at level B1 presented themselves for the exam, while the others stayed at home. Furthermore, a test has been introduced at the end of the civic education course and the number of hours dedicated to civic education

[11] Cf. www.konsularinfo.diplo.de/Vertretung/konsularinfo/de/BAMF-Ehegattennachzug,property=Daten.pdf, last visited on 3 March 2009.

[12] Prices and exchange rate as of January 2009.

[13] Verordnung über die Durchführung von Integrationskursen für Ausländer und Spätaussiedler (Integrationskursverordnung – IntV) of 13 December 2004, § 3(2).

has been raised from 30 hours initially to 45 hours. While the cost of the tests is entirely covered by the federal government, an immigrant who (is obliged to) participate(s) in an integration programme has to contribute € 1 per hour taught.

c) *Naturalisation*: In the year 2000 Germany introduced a new nationality law that, amid much publicity, introduced the principle of *ius soli* for foreign children born in Germany.[14] It also modified a couple of other elements of the German naturalisation procedure, one of them being that every office that accepts applications for naturalisation and awards citizenship certificates should be decorated with a portrait of the German federal president and with the German flag. Furthermore, the law of 2000 requires that the applicant for naturalisation sign a declaration of loyalty to the German Constitutional Law (*Bekenntnis zur freiheitlichen demokratischen Grundordnung, Loyalitätserklärung*). In this 1-page declaration, the applicant agrees to particular elements of the Constitutional Law, such as free and democratic elections, the rule of law, the right to parliamentary opposition, the right to change the government, the independence of the courts, the rejection of any form of despotism and the human rights set forth in the German Constitutional Law. The applicant also declares that he has never and does not currently pursue any activities contrary to liberal democratic principles.[15] Furthermore, the German nationality law of 2000 requires 'sufficient oral and written German language skills', which are defined in the directive implementing the law as level B1.

The law of 19 August 2007 then added that, starting in September 2008, candidates for naturalisation also have to prove their knowledge of the social and judicial order and of living conditions in Germany.[16] This means that candidates for naturalisation have to pass a citizenship test. The test costs € 25 and can be repeated several times. In order to pass the test, candidates have to give the correct answer to 17 out of 33 questions that are taken from a pool of 300 federal and 10 regional questions for each *Land*. All the questions, as well as the four multiple choice answers, are published. As preparation for the test, the law mentions that citizenship courses will be offered.

[14] Until then, German citizenship law was largely dominated by the *ius sanguinis* principle, showing openness to ethnic Germans from Eastern European diasporas rather than to migrant workers who had lived and worked in the countries for decades. Naturalisation rules were very comprehensive and demanding, which resulted in very low numbers. See Brubaker (1992) for an extensive analysis.

[15] The passage on the declaration of loyalty is a summary, not a literal translation.

[16] See § 10, par. 7 of the German nationality law (Staatsangehörigkeitsgesetz).

However, as of January 2009, such courses have only been set up in a couple of *Länder* because of very limited demand.[17]

The creation of these federal naturalisation tests may have raised the expectation of a fully standardised and similar naturalisation procedure throughout the country, especially since the ministerial circular for implementation of the new law explicitly called for the goal of preventing naturalisation from being easier in one town than in another.[18] Indeed, past (Dornis 2001) and present (Thränhardt 2008) research on naturalisation rates and procedures in Germany shows that there are large differences not only among the *Länder* but also within one and the same *Land*, depending on the municipalities. In 2006, for example, the naturalisation rate in Schleswig-Holstein was the highest in Germany, where it was 5.8 times higher than the rate in Brandenburg, which was the lowest in Germany (Thränhardt 2008: 19). The introduction of the nationwide integration test, however, does not prevent such disparities since the evaluation of other decisive criteria that comprise the so-called 'integration prognosis', such as the candidate's income or, as is the case in some cities, the candidate's partner's additional income, are still evaluated at local level.

5.3 *A Closer Look at the Content of German Integration Requirements*

Unlike the Netherlands, Germany has introduced integration requirements rather than integration tests. This means that applicants do not have to pass a test as part of the official procedure but that they have to prove existing skills, for example by submitting a language diploma. The naturalisation test is the only exception since it can be organised by an official administration. Very often, however, adult education centres (*Volkshochschulen*) have been made responsible for it. The integration requirements in Germany either concentrate solely on language or they consist of a combination of language and civic education knowledge (see table below).

---

[17] Hauke Friederichs, Deutscher in drei Minuten, *Die Zeit*, 6 November 2008, no. 46–10.

[18] See 'Vorläufige Anwendungshinweise des Bundesministeriums des Innern', of 19 October 2007, point 10.7.

Table 1: Integration requirements in Germany

	Language requirements	Civic education requirements
Integration test in the country of origin	A1	None
Integration course and test for newcomers in Germany	B1	Yes
Integration test upon naturalisation	B1	Yes, higher than at the end of the integration course

The *language requirements* in Germany are comparably high. This is true for all three tests. According to the Dutch and French legislation, potential family migrants only have to reach a level of language skills in the country of origin that is below level A1 of the Common European Reference Framework for Languages. According to German legislation, level A1 has to be attained. In addition, the level of language skills required for permanent residence and for naturalisation is higher in Germany (B1) than it is in the Netherlands (A2 for permanent residence and for naturalisation) or in France (below A1 for permanent residence and for naturalisation).[19]

The comparatively high German language requirements have been justified by the objective of making migrants independent actors in daily social interactions as well as in professional life. In fact, language users at level B1 are described by the Council of Europe as users who, 'can understand the main points of clear standard input on familiar matters regularly encountered in work, school, leisure, etc.. [...The users] [c]an describe experiences and events, dreams, hopes and ambitions and briefly give reasons and explanations for opinions and plans'. Compared to this, users at level A2, 'can understand sentences and frequently used expressions related to areas of most immediate relevance (e.g. very basic personal and family information, shopping, local geography, employment)', while users at level A1, 'can understand and use familiar everyday expressions and very basic phrases aimed at the satisfaction of needs of a concrete type. [...The user] [c]an introduce him/herself and others and can ask and answer questions about

[19] The French language requirements are surprisingly lenient since participants in the integration courses and candidates for naturalisation only have to acquire language skills at the level of the DILF Diploma. The DILF is below A1 level because of very limited requirements in written language skills. However, it should be borne in mind that most immigrants to France are already francophone upon arrival.

personal details such as where he/she lives, people he/she knows and things he/she has. Can interact in a simple way provided the other person talks slowly and clearly and is prepared to help.'

While the Council of Europe has undertaken this Europe-wide standardisation of language skills and thereby dramatically improved the comparability of language skills and requirements in the wider Europe, no common standards exist with regard to *civic education*. Instead, Member States set their own curricula and tests, thereby taking national specificities into account. The German Federal Agency for Migration and Refugees (BAMF) in charge of these issues has, with the help of external advisors, developed a curriculum for the integration course and the integration test and also developed the Federal naturalisation test. However, an important difference between the two tests – one for permanent residence and one for access to nationality – is that naturalisation is fully standardised and therefore the same in Munich as in Berlin. This is not the case for the civic education course (called *Orientierungskurs*) and the test that takes place at the end of this course. Thus, while the naturalisation test consists of 300 federal questions plus 10 extra questions for every state and the four possible answers to every question (all published), the BAMF only published a curriculum for the test at the end of the civic education course, which lists the subjects to be covered and the time that should be spent on each subject. It advises setting a written test of approximately 45 minutes, with 50% of the questions relating to politics in democracy, 30% on the individual and society and 20% on history and responsibility. The rest is left up to the teacher.

According to the curriculum, the *general objectives* of the German civic education course (called *Orientierungskurs*) are to increase participants' understanding of how the German state and government work, to foster a positive image of German democracy, to inform them about the rights and obligations of residents and citizens, to teach participants where to obtain more information, to enable migrants to participate in social life and to teach them intercultural competences. This implies affective learning targets (such as the positive evaluation of and agreement with the principles of democracy and freedom), cognitive learning targets (basic knowledge that refers to the everyday life experiences of the participants) as well as a general increase in competences (meaning that acquired knowledge is applied to a concrete situation). The stimulation of discussions among participants is the most important way in which the German civic education course is to reach these objectives.[20] Participants are asked to compare their experiences in their

[20] This corresponds to the didactics generally employed in German schools, in contrast to learning by heart, which is more prominent in French schools.

countries of origin to the new experiences acquired in Germany. By way of instruction for the teacher, the curriculum also stipulates that participants should learn about tolerance and the way democracy works in a pluralistic society rather than about 'cultural standards'. If participants are supposed to learn about rules, norms and behaviour in situations of everyday life, this is again rather through discussions with other members of the group and a comparison of their own behaviour with the behaviour they observe in Germany. Although the naturalisation test (*Einbürgerungstest*) works in a slightly different way, studying the 310 questions and the multiple choice answers is also expected to have a positive influence on the candidate's integration. For example, the Commissioner for Integration, Maria Böhmer (Christian Democrats), emphasised that preparing for the test and acquiring the knowledge it requires was a good basis for life and political participation in Germany.[21]

The *content* of the integration courses is threefold: the most important part deals with politics in democracy and makes up 19 of the 45 hours of civic education envisaged in the integration course for newcomers. During this unit, participants are supposed to learn about the political and administrative structure of Germany, about the role of the democratic institutions, the German voting system, the welfare state, as well as about the rights and duties of a citizen. The second subject (9 hours) is called 'history and responsibility'. Of course, it pays special attention to the German Nazi past and it stresses that the ideological principles that were inherent in the Nazi regime are incompatible with today's German Constitutional Law. The history unit also outlines the most important historical stages in the German Federal Republic and the German Democratic Republic. The major objective of this historical review is to provide a better understanding of today's life and living conditions in Germany. The final unit takes 13 hours and teaches the integration course participant about the individual and society, which is mainly a reflection on culture and cultural difference.

The naturalisation test does not follow this division into three major subjects although the external advisors who have developed the naturalisation test have relied on the existing curriculum for the civic education course in order to devise their own test questions. Interestingly, the naturalisation test concentrates wholly on the working of democracy, the political system, German history and geography and on existing legislation, while omitting questions about social norms. The very few questions related to German culture concern customs and traditions, such as putting up a Christmas tree at

[21] Maria Böhmer, press release no. 300 of 8/29/2008, 'Böhmer begrüßt Einführung der Einbürgerungstests'.

Christmas, hiding eggs at Easter and wearing costumes for Carnival. There are no questions about punctuality, keeping the environment clean or 'the culture of giving', which, according to the curriculum, are German characteristics (BAMF 2008a: 29). Questions about individual lifestyles, gender equality and homosexuality all relate to legal principles applicable in Germany, not to opinions and convictions. Thus, from this perspective the new German federal naturalisation test fulfils its promise of being 'a pure knowledge test' (*ein reiner Wissenstest*) and not following the poor example of the hotly debated questionnaire that was introduced in the *Land* of Baden-Württemberg in January 2006 (Van Oers 2006: 117). This Baden-Württemberg questionnaire was and still is supposed to check the convictions of applicants from 'Muslim countries' with regard to Muslim extremism and liberal democratic principles. In explicit dissociation from the practice in Baden-Württemberg, the new federal German naturalisation test that was introduced in September 2008 does not check convictions, but knowledge of legal facts.

In summary, it can be said that the standardisation of the German federal naturalisation test, in view of its full publication, has curbed any possible ambitions with regard to the cultural assimilation of immigrants. Instead, the test is a confirmation of the thesis that liberal democracies will eventually converge towards a liberal model of dealing with cultural differences (Joppke & Morawska, 2003), thus adopting what is understood in the US and France as a republican way of immigrant integration: emphasis is placed on the commitment that citizens share to a set of democratic rules, rather than their commitment to a religious or ethnic identity.

5.4 *Results of Existing Evaluations and Effectiveness of the Measures*

The introduction of new integration requirements, such as requirements for language skills, usually reduces the number of applications filed and received. As previously mentioned, Germany acquired some early experiences in this regard, when language skills were introduced as a requirement for ethnic Germans in 1997 and, subsequently, in 2005 when language skills were required of their family members. The Süssmuth Commission (2001: 181) stated that the language test introduced in 1997 has had 'an important filtering function' since only 63.9% of applicants for the status of ethnic German passed the language test in 1997 and this percentage actually declined to 47.7% in 2000. Consequently, the number of ethnic Germans and their family members emigrating to Germany has declined from 178,000 in 1996 to 103,000 in

1998 (BMI/ BAMF 2007: 52).[22] Later on, the introduction of the language test for family members considerably accelerated this reduction since numbers have declined further from 59,100 in 2004 to 7,750 in 2006 (BMI/BAMF, 2007: 52). The figures for 2005, the year of introduction of these language requirements, show that of the 1,468 family members of ethnic Germans who were invited to take the language test, only 871 attended and only 216 (i.e. 15% of the total and 25 % of those who took the test) passed the test.[23]

Given these past experiences, it is expected that the language test that will have to be taken by family members of foreign residents in Germany and of German citizens before being awarded an immigration visa will also significantly reduce the numbers. According to statistics that have been made public by the German parliament, 59% of the tests taken between January and August 2008 in the 15 major countries of origin were successful, while 41% were not. During the same period, the number of visas for family reunification issued worldwide dropped by 24%: while 18,716 visas were issued in the first half of 2007, this number fell to 14,229 in the first half of 2008 (Drucksache 16/10732, p. 22). These numbers show that the share of unsuccessful exams (40%) was higher than the actual decline in attributed visas (24%) which may lead to the expectation that, unless the unsuccessful tests are repeated quickly, the decline will become even more important.

So far, no comparable data exist with regard to access to permanent residence because the migrants who were the first to be subject to the new legislation in 2005 will only start applying for permanent residence 5 years afterwards, i.e. from 2010 onwards. In principle, the law that entered into force in January 2005 also stipulates that a refusal to participate in the integration course can ultimately lead to non-renewal of the temporary residence permit if the foreigner's residence in Germany is not under special protection. An evaluation of the Immigration Act showed that this sanction is not applied, partly because of insufficient cooperation between the language course providers and the aliens' administrations, and partly because the aliens' administrations find that the groups of migrants concerned were under special protection, because they were either refugees or family migrants. While some aliens' administrations decided to sanction foreigners

[22] It should be mentioned, however, that the number of ethnic Germans and their families coming to Germany has constantly decreased since reaching a peak of almost 400,000 at the beginning of the 1990s. This constant decrease is due to policies such as the introduction of language requirements, as well as due to decreasing potential.

[23] Press release by the Commissioner for ethnic Germans and national minorities of 10 February 2006, 'Spätaussiedlerzuzug auch im Januar 2006 weiter rückläufig.'

who refuse to participate in the integration course by only renewing their temporary residence permit for 6 instead of 12 months, most aliens' administrations seem to rely purely on financial sanctions, namely the reduction of welfare benefits (Rambøll 2006: 70–71).

While the law stipulates that simple participation in the integration course is taken into consideration for the renewal of the temporary residence permit, *successful* participation (defined as having reached level B1) is supposed to be taken into consideration for the issue of a permanent residence permit. As mentioned above, the first cases where this might become relevant cannot be expected to occur prior to 2010. However, the evaluation of the integration courses showed that, should this rule be applied to the letter, over half of participants may experience difficulties in obtaining a permanent residence permit. In fact, only between 38% and 53% of participants in the early years have managed to reach the B1 (Rambøll 2006: 34; 54–55) and these were mainly more highly qualified migrants (Rambøll 2006: 57). A precise evaluation of the numbers however has been difficult because the language test at the end of the integration course remained optional until January 2008. This means that self-selection has had a strong effect in the sense that 70.8% of all participants who took the test passed it, while only between 38.4% and 52.8% of all participants who finished the programme[24] reached level B1 (see Table 2).

Table 2: Participants in the German integration courses at different stages

Total	Characteristics	Participants achieving B1
322.311	Participants who were entitled to participate	9.6%
219.973	Participants who started the programme	14.1%
185.000	Participants who received at least 100 hours[25]	16.8%
80.700	Participants who finished the civic education course	38.4%
58.602	Participants who received 600 h. of language teaching	52.8%
43.809	Participants who took the final language test	70.8%
30.996	Participants who reached level B1	100%

Source: Rambøll 2006: 34; 54–55.

[24] In this case, it is still a question of definition as to whether the programme is completed after 600 hours of language teaching or after 600 hours of language teaching and 30 hours of civic education.

[25] In theory, 100 hours is the minimum requirement for a newcomer who is obliged to take part in the programme and this is why, in theory, people who have attended at least 100 hours might have finished the course.

Since the language test at the end of the integration course was made compulsory in January 2008, a new preliminary statistic has been published for the period between 1 January and 30 September 2008. It shows that a total of 53,077 participants passed a language test. Among them, 50% reached level B1 or higher, 11% reached level A2 and 39% failed to reach any level (BAMF 2008b: 14).[26] Thus, a large proportion of the participants (i.e. almost 40%) either has to study and retake the language test or will face difficulties when applying for permanent residence. In addition, it is unclear today what will happen to the 11% who only reached level A2, since it is explicitly mentioned in the law and the implementation directive that the integration course is only completed successfully if level B1 is reached. However, the introduction of a special A2 language certificate suggests that an administrative solution might be aimed at for this group.

The introduction of the federal naturalisation test seems too recent to draw any reliable conclusions about its effect. The introduction of the Dutch naturalisation test certainly has led to a decrease in the number of applications for naturalisation (Van Oers 2006) so that this can also be expected to take place in Germany. In fact, 4 months after the start of the German naturalisation test, a German newspaper[27] published the information that, according to the Federal Agency for Migration and Refugees (BAMF), 18,000 candidates for naturalisation had registered to take the test and that as many as 98.9% had passed it. Many other media published these numbers, most of them suggesting that the test was too easy since virtually everybody seemed to be able to pass it. Again, however, it seems judicious to compare the number of candidates who took the test to the number of naturalisations in the previous year. This comparison shows that if the number of 18,000 naturalisations for a quarter of a year is multiplied by four, only 72,000 naturalizations per year could be expected in Germany after the introduction of the new test. While numbers were already declining for the most part in recent years, there were still 113,030 naturalisations in Germany in 2007 (Statistisches Bundesamt 2009). Even though these are only extremely rough estimates, they help reappraise what it would mean if almost all the candidates for naturalisation who registered for the test passed it: those who were afraid of failing the test did not take it.

[26] In the statistics published by the Federal Agency, it is unclear what happened to a further 8035 participants who finished the integration course during the first 9 months but had not taken a language test.

[27] *Rheinische Post*, online: http://www.rp-online.de/public/article/panorama/deutschland/660718/ 989-Prozent-bestehen-den-Einbuergerungstest.html, 14 January 2009.

5.4.1 *Discussion of the Effectiveness of Integration Requirements in Germany*

So what can be said about the effectiveness of these integration requirements? Despite the fact that all of these requirements seem to have a 'filtering' function, the German government insists on presenting all of them as measures that promote the integration of immigrants. Very often, however, their effectiveness on the integration of these migrants is difficult to establish while the decline in numbers is a very tangible result.

In an answer to the parliament, the German government explicitly denies that the prevention of family reunification is one of the objectives of the *test for family members in their country of origin*. Language requirements that potential family migrants have to fulfil in their country of origin are rather, according to the government, supposed to promote the future social integration of migrants and to prevent forced marriages (Drucksache 16/10732, answers 16 + 21). At the same time, the government acknowledges that no statements can be made about the number of forced marriages that might have been prevented by this new legislation (Drucksache 16/9722, answers 6 + 7). In addition, the government evades another question about the efficiency of the test: members of parliament wondered about the use of acquiring language skills at level A1 in the country of origin if the immigrants, once in Germany, usually have to start language learning all over again since the language skills they acquired at relatively high cost in their country of origin are not sufficient to grant direct access to advanced-learners' language courses (Drucksache 16/10732, question and answer 15). In answering this question, the government referred to an earlier document in which it explains that it is not crucial whether the costs of learning the language are higher or lower abroad or in Germany. What is crucial, according to the government, is that participation in an integration course after arrival is not necessarily successful, while scanning for language skills before immigration guarantees an actual basic knowledge of the German language (Drucksache 16/7288, answer 23b).

In summary, the German government lists three reasons for the introduction of these tests in the country of origin, i.e.: to prevent forced marriages, to improve the social integration of migrants through better language skills (since this can obviously not be guaranteed by the state-run integration courses) and to select migrants who demonstrate a certain willingness to integrate by studying German in their country of origin (on this last point, see Drucksache 16/10732, answer 17).

How effective the tests in the country of origin really are when it comes to these three objectives is very difficult to say. As already mentioned, there is virtually no way to quantify the number of forced marriages that might not have taken place as a result of the test, nor does the government assume, as provocatively asked by some members of the German parliament, that the decline in visas awarded for family reunification can be placed on a level with the number of forced marriages prevented (Drucksache 16/10732, question 4b). Qualitative studies might examine whether or not the presumed reciprocity between the test and forced marriages has been at work in selected cases, but they cannot provide any quantification of the phenomenon. As to the question of whether the tests improve the social integration of family migrants after immigration, again statistics are lacking. A publication by the BAMF (2008b: 5) showed that between 1 January and 30 September 2008 only 313 individuals, i.e. 0.4% of all participants, took an intensive course of 400 instead of 600 hours of language tuition, but the vast majority still took between 600 and 900 hours. If starting to learn the language abroad has a significant impact, one would expect that the number of participants who only take 400 hours of language tuition once they have arrived in Germany would increase because these immigrants are already familiar with the introduction to the German language that is given during the first 200 hours. In other respects, no studies seem to be available that could, in a rather experimental fashion, compare migrants who have followed the state integration measures (including language tests in the country of origin) to migrants who have not done so. In fact, it is difficult to set up a control group that would allow for such comparisons (Svensson, Michalowski & Seveker 2008). Thus, while waiting for the other goals to become measurable instead of only symbolic, the third goal seems to be the only one that is fulfilled: the tests do select family migrants who have been willing and able to study German in their country of origin. Again, however, it can only be assumed that once these people arrive in Germany their motivation and goodwill actually do make a difference and genuinely lead to better integration outcomes than those of family migrants who have not taken the test.

When it comes to the effectiveness of the *integration courses in Germany* and the language and civic education tests, the government itself states that there is no guarantee that participation in such a course fosters integration (Drucksache 16/7288, answer 23b). In fact, the courses do not show overwhelming absolute[28] effectiveness, since 39% of all participants only reach

[28] Of course, it can be argued that the criteria applied in evaluating the effectiveness of the course are too broad and too high and therefore largely ignore the individual progress that may have been made, for example, by an illiterate person who only reached level A1. However, compared to the political objectives that were announced when the programmes were

level A1 or below. In addition, the evaluation also showed the significant influence of the migrant's initial qualification on his or her successful participation in the course (Rambøll 2006: 57). This means that poorly-skilled migrants, who were the initial target group of these state-run measures, very often fail to achieve the required language skills. For the time being, the effects that this may have on the attribution of permanent residence permits cannot be evaluated since the measure has not been in place long enough.

Finally, the effectiveness of the *naturalisation test* is difficult to evaluate for the same reason. At the time of writing of this contribution, it had only been in place for less than a year. Initial numbers, published in January 2009, however, provoked discussions about whether the test might have failed in its objective, which is that future citizens learn about the political system, history, geography and culture of Germany in order to achieve better (political) integration. When it became clear that 98% of those who had taken the test during the first 4 months of its existence had passed it, critics suggested that the test might be too easy (cf. above for a more balanced appreciation). Teachers of civic education who had seen very low demand for their preparatory classes, which remained largely empty, also doubted whether candidates for naturalisation who passed the test had 'really learned' something or 'just learned by heart'.[29] Even though the high success rate suggests that the test can be passed easily, one unintended effect of the test might be that the number of applications for naturalisation declines because potential candidates for naturalization do not feel ready for the test.

In summary, it can be said that one tangible result of these integration tests and requirements is often that the numbers decline. At the same time, it is difficult to know what effect these tests have on the very complex process of integration. They certainly are a contradiction of the previous understanding of a secure residence status as a contribution to, not a result of, integration (Groenendijk 2004).

5.5 *Discussion: Integration Requirements and Cultural Assimilation*

An important final question is whether the multiplication and formalisation of integration requirements that have taken place in Germany in recent years

set up (specifically, to make immigrants independent actors in daily social and professional interactions), the output of the programme remains limited.

[29] Pressemitteilung Sächsischer Volkshochschulverband e.V., 1 September 2008.

allow Germany to be held up as an example of a communitarian model of integration and citizenship (Kostakopoulou 2003; cf. also the introduction to this volume). I argue that this is not the case because each of the three integration requirements that have been analysed in this contribution reveals a logic of citizenship other than communitarian:

1) The integration tests in the country of origin are not selecting for culturally close ethnic groups but for qualified migrants and therefore have to be discussed in the light of the present concerns in European Member States regarding qualified migrants. The tests are highly debatable, not because they select by ethnic origin, but because they try to prevent persons with lower financial, social and intellectual resources from having a family life in Germany. This logic corresponds more to a libertarian or market-liberal approach than to a culture-communitarian approach.
2) The integration courses and tests that take place after immigration to Germany might be regarded as following an assimilatory and communitarian approach because migrants are trained to function in German society. However, the curricula for the civic education course (*Orientierungskurs*) and for the test at the end of this course explicitly favour discussions about how a democratic society deals with pluralism rather than teaching cultural norms. In addition, the initial objective of the integration course is to help poorly-skilled migrants with an inadequate knowledge of the German language and society to improve their skills so that their risk of unemployment and social exclusion is diminished. So again, the libertarian seems to be more adequate than the communitarian model. In fact, Rogers Brubaker (2003) coined this welfare-state related integration policy as a form of 'economic assimilation.'
3) Finally, the naturalisation test is an example that Germany is moving away from a communitarian understanding of citizenship towards a more republican model. In fact, it was made explicit that the previous example from Baden-Württemberg, which clearly demonstrated a communitarian approach, should not be followed by the federal test. This is why the federal test does not ask what the candidate thinks is morally right or wrong, but asks what is allowed and forbidden under German law. Similar moves towards a more republican approach can be observed in the German Islamic Conference (*Deutsche Islamkonferenz*) and have also been shown to be the result of the long back-and-forth exchange between the legislature and the judiciary in the fight over headscarves in German schools (Henkes & Kneip, 2008).

Finally, we might ask[30] what carries more weight in the assessment of integration requirements: the restrictive effect they have on family reunification and on access to permanent residence and nationality, or the incremental move away from an ethnic and cultural definition of citizenship towards a liberal and republican definition? Or, to put it bluntly: does it make any difference if a migrant is excluded on liberal and republican grounds rather than on cultural and ethnic grounds? The answer probably is that for the individual migrant it does not make a difference if he or she is not naturalised or allowed into the country on the grounds of being a Turkish Muslim or for being an 'uneducated immigrant'. It can also be argued that the introduction of such requirements does not demonstrate a new political and public culture of openness, which was claimed when the new German citizenship law was introduced. This also confirms Rogers Brubaker who, in his comparison of citizenship and nationhood in France and Germany, argues that there is more to a non-ethnic, republican model of citizenship than nationality legislation. Brubaker writes that, '(…) liberalized naturalization rules alone will do little to further the civic incorporation of immigrants. Immigrants as well as Germans continue to associate the legal fact of naturalization with the social and cultural fact of assimilation, yet neither German political culture in general nor the specific social, political, and cultural context of the postwar immigration is favourable to assimilation. Add to this the fact that dual citizenship is permitted only in exceptional cases, and it seems likely that naturalization rates will remain quite low, and that the citizenship status and chances of immigrants in France and Germany will continue to diverge' (1992: 184–185).

However, besides the backlash of a restrictive definition of who can be part of the nation, the current trend towards a more (market-)liberal and republican rather than ethnic and cultural citizenship regime is certainly more of a step towards the re-definition of belonging than integration requirements from the 1980s, as the avowal (*Bekenntnis*) to the German 'Kulturkreis'. This article has shown that integration requirements formulated in Germany over the past few years have opened the path towards a new, more political and meritocratic understanding of citizenship. At the moment, such a re-definition of citizenship is impeded by at least two factors: firstly, a meritocratic understanding of citizenship is applicable to family migrants whose selection based on qualifications is problematic from a legal and human rights perspective. Secondly, if citizenship in Germany were to become more meri-

[30] I thank Dora Kostakopoulou for doing so and I would also like to thank the other two editors of this book for their very helpful suggestions of how to improve this contribution.

tocratic, this would also have to imply the abandonment of the existing glass ceilings that currently impede the advancement of immigrants and new citizens in Germany.

Bibliography

BAMF (Bundesamt für Migration und Flüchtlinge), *Curriculum für einen bundesweiten Orientierungskurs*, Nuremberg 2008a, see www.bamf.de.

BAMF, *Bericht zur Integrationskursgeschäftsstatistik für den Zeitraum vom 01.01.2008 bis 30.09.2008*, 2008b.

Brubaker, R., *Citizenship and Nationhood in France and Germany*, Cambridge 1992.

Brubaker, R., The Return of Assimilation? Changing Perspectives on Immigration and its Sequels in France, Germany, and the United States, in: C. Joppke & E. Morawska (eds.), *Toward Assimilation and Citizenship: Immigrants in Liberal Nation-States*, Houndmills/Basingstoke 2003, pp. 39–58.

Bunt, H. van de, *Inburgering in het land van herkomst*, Tweede Kamer, 27083 No. 36, 2003.

Carrera, S., *A Comparison of Integration Programmes in the EU. Trends and Weaknesses*, Challenge Papers, No. 1, 2006.

Cesarani, D. & M. Fulbrook, Conclusion, in: D. Cesarani & M. Fulbrook (eds.), *Citizenship, Nationality and Migration in Europe*, London: Routledge 1996, pp. 209–217.

De Hart, B. & R. van Oers, 'European Trends in Nationality Law'. In: R. Bauböck, E. Ersbøll, K. Groenendijk & H. Waldrauch (eds.), *Acquisition and Loss of Nationality, Policies and Trends in 15 European Countries. Volume I: comparative Analyses*, Amsterdam: Amsterdam University Press 2006, pp. 317–357.

Dornis, C., Einbürgerung in Deutschland. Die Verwaltungspraxis der verschiedenen Regionen im Vergleich, in: Dietrich Thränhardt (ed.), *Integrationspolitik in föderalistischen Systemen*, Münster/London 2001.

Groenendijk, K., E. Guild & R. Barzilay, *Le statut juridique des ressortissants de pays tiers résidents de longue durée dans un Etat membre de l'Union européenne*, Report for the European Commission 2000.

Groenendijk, K., Legal Concepts of Integration in EU Migration Law, *European Journal of Migration and Law*, no. 6(2), 2004, pp. 111–126.

Groenendijk, K., Nieuw inburgeringsrecht strijdig met Gemeenschapsrecht, *Migrantenrecht*, no. 10, 2006, pp. 366–368.

Groenendijk, K., Inburgeren in het buitenland: de Gezinsherenigingsrichtlijn biedt meer bescherming dan artikel 8 EVRM, *Migrantenrecht*, no. 3, 2007, pp. 111–113.

Guiraudon, V., European Integration and Migration Policy: Vertical Policy-making as Venue Shopping, *Journal of Common Market Studies* 38/2, 2000, pp. 249–69.

Henkes, C. & S. Kneip, *Parliament, courts and unintended laicism – the outcome of the German debate about teachers wearing headscarves*, Paper presented at the conference 'Die Verfassung der Demokratie', University of Osnabrück, 21–23 November 2008.

Joppke, C. & E. Morawska, Integrating immigrants in liberal nation-states: policies and practices, in: C. Joppke & E. Morawska (eds.), *Toward assimilation and citizenship. Immigrants in liberal nation-states*, Basingstoke 2003, pp. 1–36.

Joppke, C., Beyond national models: civic integration policies for immigrants in Western Europe, *West European Politics*, 30, 2007, pp. 1–22.

Kostakopoulou, D., Why Naturalization, *Perspectives on European Politics and Society*, Leiden: Brill 2003, pp. 85–115.

Michalowski, I., *Integration als Staatsprogramm. Deutschland, Frankreich und die Niederlande im Vergleich*, Münster 2007.

Mohr, K., Stratifizierte Rechte und soziale Exklusion von Migranten im Wohlfahrtsstaat, *Zeitschrift für Soziologie*, 34(5) 2005, pp. 383–398.

Oers, R. van, *De naturalisatietoets geslaagd? Een onderzoek naar de totstandkoming en effecten van de naturalisatietoets*, Nijmegen: WLP 2006.

Rambøll Management, *Evaluation der Integrationskurse nach dem Zuwanderungsgesetz. Abschlussbericht und Gutachten über Verbesserungspotenziale bei der Umsetzung der Integrationskurse*, Berlin 2006.

Ratia, E. & A. Walter, *International exploration on forced marriages. A study on legal initiatives, policy and public discussions in Belgium, France, Germany, Great Britain and Switzerland*, draft, Nijmegen, January 2009.

Rekenkamer, *Inburgering en taalonderwijs allochtonen*, Tweede Kamer 1999–2000, 27275, no. 1–2, 2000.

Seveker, M., Sprachpraxis und Sprachangebote in der russlanddeutschen Minderheitensituation: die Siedlung Gljaden' in der westsibirischen Altairegion, in: A. Walter, M. Menz & S. De Carlo (eds.), *Grenzen der Gesellschaft? Migration und sozialstruktureller Wandel in der Zuwanderungsregion Europa*, IMIS Schriften 14, Osnabrück 2006, pp. 219–239.

Süssmuth Kommission (Unabhängige Kommission Zuwanderung), *Zuwanderung gestalten, Integration fördern*, Berlin, 4 July 2001.

Svensson, J., I. Michalowski & M. Seveker, Ervaringen met de indicatormethodiek in een vergelijkende evaluatie van lokaal inburgeringsbeleid, *Migrantenstudies*, 24(4) 2008, pp. 22–39.

Thränhardt, D., Germany - An undeclared immigration country, in: Thränhardt, Dietrich (eds.) (1996), *Europe. A new immigration continent*, Münster: Lit Verlag 1996, pp. 198–223.

Thränhardt, D., *Einbürgerung. Rahmenbedingungen, Motive und Perspektiven des Erwerbs der deutschen Staatsangehörigkeit*, Gutachten für die Friedrich-Ebert-Stiftung Bonn 2008.

Vries, K. de, Het nieuwe Nederlandse inburgeringsstelsel, *Migrantenrecht*, no. 8, 2006, pp. 272–282.

Vries, K. de, Inburgeringseisen en gemeenschapsrecht. Een reactie, *Migrantenrecht*, no. 3, 2007, pp. 109–110.

Chapter 6

Ethnic Citizenship – Can it be Obtained and Tested?

*Judit Tóth**

6.1 *Introduction*

Although Hungary has considered itself to be a country of transit rather than a target country for migrants, without a (well) established integration policy (Hajduk 2008), the testing system at the level of migrants, or fragments of it, have appeared in the legislation of contemporary Hungary. While the foreign population living here is below 2%[1] of the total and its majority is derived from the ethnic Hungarian communities in adjacent states,[2] the testing provisions contain an embarrassing proportion of civic and ethnic citizenship components.

What are the legally defined criteria for the integration of migrants and how are these supported and tested in practice? Taking into account the rules in force and available statistics, an *inconsistent picture of migration policy and law* can be discerned for the following groups of migrants in Hungary: (a) internationally protected persons (applicants and migrants in possession of a recognised status) who have to cope with Hungarian legislation in combination with a minimal support system and a penalty for reduced integration efforts; (b) residence and settlement permit-holders, including EEA nationals, family members and third-country nationals through direct and indirect

* Associate Professor of Law, Department of Constitutional Law, University of Szeged.

[1] In the period 1993–2008, this rate has grown from 1.19 to 1.74%. In absolute terms this means 123–175,000 migrants annually. *Demographic Yearbook 2007*, Budapest: Central Statistical Office 2008, p. 88.

[2] The ethnic origins of migrants are not statistically gathered, but, in 2007, 65% of settled migrants and 86% of naturalised persons held the citizenship of Romania, Ukraine, Serbia, Slovakia or Croatia. *Demographic Yearbook 2007*, p. 93.

Van Oers, Ersbøll and Kostakopoulou, A Re-definition of Belonging?, pp. 211–240.
 ISBN 978 90 04 17506 8. Printed in the Netherlands.

integrative provisions in new laws; and (c) applicants for naturalisation through the constitutional examination and procedural requirements. This article is an initial attempt to describe *immigration legislation and practice as reflected in the measurability of migrants' integration in a kin-state that is basically applied to a kin-minority.*

6.2 *Acquisition of Citizenship*

The Constitution contains a few *guarantee* provisions relating to Hungarian citizenship,[3] while the other rules pertaining to acquisition and loss of citizenship are contained in a law adopted by a two-thirds voting majority.[4] This represents the obligation to reach *consensus on the notion and principle of this legal instrument between the ruling and opposing parties.* On the one hand, it ensures stability and continuity of legislation, but, on the other hand, it makes regulations difficult to amend, even if this were urgent. Strangely enough, there is no such mandatory restriction relating to entering into international commitments concerning nationality law.

The Hungarian Nationality Act[5] in force is the fourth nationality law since 1879. It defines seven legal titles of acquisition of Hungarian nationality with different requirements. Of those, the test of the integration level of applicants is relevant only in the naturalisation process, while the other modes of acquisition only presuppose the existence of (advanced) integration of the person concerned. From this point of view, we can identify two groups of acquisition modes, depending on the requested imminent integration or formally obtained integration of individuals.

(a) In the first group, we include the acquisition of citizenship *by birth* (the child of a Hungarian citizen based on *ius sanguinis*, regardless of the place of birth); acquisition with *presumption* (the child of a stateless immigrant in possession of a permanent residence permit or an abandoned child of unknown parents shall be considered a Hungarian national unless or

[3] Act XX of 1949 on the Constitution of the Hungarian Republic, as it was thoroughly reformed by Act XXXI of 1989, establishing the rule of law, including an Article on Hungarian citizenship. Art. 69(1) of the Constitution forbids any arbitrary deprivation of Hungarian citizenship.

[4] Art. 69(4) of the Constitution requires this voting majority to pass the Hungarian nationality law, including its amendments.

[5] Act LV of 15 June 1993, entered into force 1 October 1993.

until this presumption is rebutted. There is no time limit for rebuttal); by *declaration* (the Hungarian nationality of exiled nationals who were deprived of their nationality between 1945 and 1989 shall be restored upon request by a declaration addressed to the President of the State. The acquisition of nationality is also possible by declaration in cases where an applicant was born in Hungary but has not acquired nationality by birth and is being brought up in Hungary); by *family law facts (*presumptive paternity ensures nationality by law for a child born out of wedlock if a parent declares paternity or if a judgment recognises paternity/maternity, or if the parents subsequently marry); by *restitution* (upon request, the restitution of citizenship is ensured if the applicant cannot obtain a new citizenship within one year of his/her renunciation of Hungarian citizenship); and by *re-naturalisation* (its requirements include possession of a permanent residence permit by the prior national whose nationality has ceased, a clean criminal record and no current criminal proceedings, proven means of stable livelihood and residence in Hungary, and the assurance that the applicant's naturalisation does not violate Hungarian national interests).

(b) *In the second group, we find the different types of preferential and non-*preferential naturalisation. In non-preferential, basic cases, the applicant must meet all of the following requirements: permanent residence in Hungary for eight years while in possession of a permanent residence permit or an EEA nationals' registration card, a clean criminal record and no current criminal proceedings, proven means of stable livelihood and residence in Hungary, the naturalisation must not violate the national interest of the state and the applicant has to pass *an examination on the basic constitutional issues, which must be taken in the Hungarian language.*

Preferential naturalisation requires a shorter continuous period of residence before application. The permanent residence requirement is reduced to five years if the applicant was born on Hungarian territory, established residence in Hungary before reaching the age of majority, or is stateless. The permanent residence requirement is reduced to three years if the applicant has been married to a Hungarian citizen for three years, if he or she has a minor child who is a Hungarian citizen, or if he or she has been adopted by a Hungarian citizen or is a recognised refugee. If the applicant's ancestors were Hungarian nationals and he or she declares himself or herself an ethnic Hungarian, there is no waiting period for an applicant in possession of a permanent residence permit. However, in this case the longer naturalisation procedure (at least 18 months) diminishes this advantage. The permanent residence requirement can be waived in cases where naturalisation is extended to a minor child submitting the application together with his or her parents, or the minor applicant has been adopted by a Hungarian national, or the applicant's naturalisation is based on the overriding interests of the state. In order to acquire Hungarian citizenship, applicants for preferential naturalisation also have to pass the examination on the basic constitutional issues. Exemption from this requirement can be considered as a benefit provided for certain applicants.

By granting easier access to Hungarian nationality to ethnic Hungarians (preferential naturalisation) and former nationals (re-naturalisation), Hungarian citizenship law holds a strong ethnic component. This ethnic component is confirmed by the content of the citizenship examination, which requires a high level of Hungarian language skills.

Table 1 demonstrates the dominant role of naturalisation and re-naturalisation in the nationality law procedure. However, millions of emigrants and their descendants around the world submit applications for ascertaining their citizenship, which draws our attention to 'dormant citizenship',[6] which may be activated without any integration test or genuine link to the country requirement. To this may be added that the pure fact of leaving Hungary cannot terminate Hungarian citizenship. Owing to *ius sanguinis* and 'endless citizenship', there are unknown numbers of second, third, fourth etc. generation emigrated citizens. Statistics show that the number of applicants for naturalisation, re-naturalisation and for nationality certification fluctuates mainly in line with amendments to the Act.[7]

[6] Due to strong emigration waves from Hungary (Hungarian Kingdom) since the 1880s, millions of Hungarian citizens have left the country and established diasporas all over the world. Emigrants and their descendants have preserved their Hungarian nationality due to *jus sanguinis* and, with exception of some periods in the history, mere emigration has not been a legal basis for loss of nationality ('endless nationality'). However, numerous emigrants are not aware of their own Hungarian citizenship. This dormant citizenship is legally controlled in a procedure and a certificate holder can obtain a passport and enjoy free movement as a Hungarian national.

[7] Act LV of 1993 amended in 2001, 2003, 2005, 2006, 2007 and 2008.

Table 1: Applications for Hungarian nationality[8]

Applications for acquisition of nationality	2002	2003	2004	2005	2006	2007	2008
For naturalisation and re-naturalisation together	4,453	4,916	5,761	3,898	9,127	5,437	4,143
Submitted declaration	212	151	144	136	104	85	68
Ascertainment of citizenship[9]	4,401	4,803	5,984	5,482	4,121	4,276	4,958
For restitution	1	1	1	0	0	0	0
Total	9,067	9,871	11,890	9,516	13,352	9,798	9,169

Table 2: Number of naturalisations

(Re)Naturalisation proceedings	2002	2003	2004	2005	2006	2007	2008
Persons naturalised and re-naturalised in a given year	3,890	5,579	5,667	9,981	6,564	9,398	8,132
Rejected applicants	468	502	502	482	424	552	628

Table 2 indicates the actual number of naturalised persons.

Refusals of naturalisation are not justified and not open to recourse. This is a severe obstacle to further research into the actual basis for the preconditions for the integration. Consequently, the testing method can be neither evaluated nor developed. For this reason, the integration requirement is barely transparent in practice. As Table 2 shows, it is relevant for 5–8% of applicants for naturalisation whose claim is rejected yearly. Without deeper information, this low rate of rejection indicates that many potential applicants are excluded from submission or that only the 'guaranteed' applicants are applying for naturalisation. In fact, the group of persons for re-naturalisation can be neglected: they are exempted from the requirement to pass the examination and it is hardly likely that their applications will be refused.

[8] Compilation of tables is based on OIN data, www.bmbah.hu/statistics (25 February 2009). An application may cover more applicants because it contains a minor's application (below age 14) together with the parents'.

[9] Office for Immigration and Nationality (OIN) is exclusively entitled to issue a certificate which attests to whether the applicant (a) is a Hungarian national, (b) was a Hungarian national but nationality ceased for a given reason and at a fixed time, or (c) has never been a Hungarian national. This certificate is necessary to obtain a passport for nationals living abroad or returning to Hungary.

6.2.1 *Examination of applicants*

The Hungarian Nationality Act of 1993 introduced the *examination of constitutional issues* that has to be taken in the Hungarian language by applicants for naturalisation.[10] The executive rules governing the Act[11] regulate procedural issues, including the topics of the oral and written tests and the examination competence of county administrative offices. Although this idea or requirement was an entirely new concept in naturalisation in 1993, the Explanatory Report to the Bill gives this short reasoning for its introduction:

> The obligation to take the examination in fundamental historical and constitutional knowledge based on the language competence of applicant for naturalisation is known in international practice. It is a legitimate expectation that applicants of majority age should be in possession of this knowledge by passing an examination demonstrating their attachment to Hungary.[12]

In 1993, following the growth in migration pressure, all political parties supported some restrictions on the acquisition of Hungarian nationality, including the examination requirement. However, the liberals and socialists urged regulation (in the Act or in the executive decree) on the substance of the examination and procedural rules.[13] For instance,

> It is crucial to define which body is entitled to evaluate the examination and how the examination shall be taken, because these conditions shall not be so difficult that ordinary people are unable to give answers.[14]

On behalf of the Government, the state secretary summarised the response to the criticism:

> Despite the discussion on the name and substance of the examination, the Government intends to keep the original proposal in the Bill because the examination on constitutional basics taken in the Hungarian language would best serve our aim through the introduction of this novelty. However, the government accepts the proposal from opponents, specifically that the examination also be

[10] Act LV of 1993, amended, maintaining the examination system and ensuring further exemptions.

[11] Government Decree no. 125 of September 22 1993. It has been altered numerous times.

[12] Explanatory Report to the Bill made by the Government (Ministry of the Interior), to Art 4. Parliamentary Diary (www.mkogy.hu).

[13] Laszló Mészáros (Free Democratic Alliance), Pál Vastagh (Hungarian Socialist Party), 2 March 1993, Parliamentary Diary (www.mkogy.hu).

[14] Istvan Szigehty (Free Democratic Alliance), 6 April 1993, Parliamentary Diary (www .mkogy.hu).

required of ethnic Hungarian applicants, thus they would have to demonstrate their knowledge of Hungary and our constitutional system.[15]

In the absence of past experiences, the examination is based on two pillars: the linguistic ability of the applicant and his or her knowledge of the constitutional, cultural and historical heritage of Hungarians. The former fits in well with the other provisions of the nationality law, since a possible ethnic component requires a *strong command of the Hungarian language, as follows:*

(a) An oral and written test on constitutional basics must be taken in Hungarian at any national/metropolitan administrative office (there are 20 around the country). County administrative offices regularly organise examinations before a board of lawyers, administrators and teachers, nominated by the office director. The Government Decree defines the format of application to take the examination, the major components of the examination procedure (subjects in the oral part and the written test, how members of the examination body are appointed, what protocol relates to procedure) and its certificate. Each county administrative office has its in-house rules on the management and procedure of the examination. In Eger, for example, the Examination Rules cover 21 pages and contain details about lists of questions, preparation time and answering time, criteria for successful oral and written part of the examination, frequency of examination – at least four times per annum – time frame for the correction of tests, failure, repetition of examination, absence from the examination, and the fee for a partially/wholly repeated examination. In Budapest or in Szolnok, on the other hand, many of these issues are not regulated, while the examination questions, and the fees for the preparatory course or consultation are slightly different. However, this diversity has been neither unified nor evaluated by the Office for Immigration and Nationality (OIN).

(b) Naturalisation proceedings are conducted in Hungarian (completed questionnaire, CV hand-written by the applicant and his or her personal hearing is also conducted in Hungarian). There is no provision for an applicable mediating language or interpreter. However, the local clerk or registrar is generally not able to speak a foreign language at as high a level as the majority of society, so linguistic pressure is exerted.

(c) All documents (e.g. birth, marital status, occupation) must be attached in an authentic translation into Hungarian.

(d) The naturalisation oath must be taken solemnly in Hungarian before the Mayor of the location in which the naturalised person has settled.

(e) The name of the naturalised person may be changed at his or her request (e.g. to the name of a Hungarian ancestor or a translated name).

(f) The name of the birthplace of the naturalised person is also indicated, at his or her request, in the Hungarian official version in the registry, if applicable.

[15] Dr. Fabian Józsa (State Secretary, Ministry of the Interior), 1 June 1993, Parliamentary Diary (www.mkogy.hu).

As is evident, the *standardisation of the language requirement* takes place mainly through procedural provisions regarding naturalisation, rather than through a formally determined language competence or level of grammatical skills.

Some types of *support are available to applicants* to help them pass the examination:

a) The examination must be taken at the *county administrative office near the habitual residence of the applicant.* However, applicants recognising the diversity in the in-house rules may, in practice, obtain temporary residence in the territory where the examination set by the county administrative offices is easier.[16] This tacit praxis may support certain applicants.
b) There is *no legal consequence for failing the examination.* It can be repeated endlessly, provided fees are paid; the residence status and social, employment or other allowances remain unaffected. If the applicant has missed the examination, he or she can submit a further application for the next examination period without repercussion.
c) The *examination fee* is fixed (€ 20).
d) *The issues (subjects) and method of the examination* are publicly defined in the Appendix to the Government Decree.
e) *Preparatory courses* are organised by some county administrative offices for a fee,[17] through personal consultations or civil organisations. For instance, the Hungarian Association for Migrants deals with cultural, lexical and linguistic obstacles, especially among refugees, by providing free preparatory courses. However, the preparatory course is optional for both applicants and the national offices.
f) A unified *textbook for examination preparation* has been available since 2006.

The new, cheap textbook for the citizenship examination in Constitutional Basics[18] has 120 pages and covers the following topics: (i) Hungary in Europe,

[16] Interview with Dr. Mária Ugróczky, former head of the Nationality Law Directorate, OIN (10 April 2009).

[17] For instance, it costs € 16 in the Public Administration Office, Pest County (December 2008). Statistics on preparatory courses are not available.

[18] Ugróczky, M., *Alkotmányos alapismeretek. Segédanyag az alkotmányos alapismeretek vizsgára készülő nem magyar állampolgárok számára* [Constitutional handbook. Textbook for non-national applicants for naturalisation], BM Duna Palota és Kiadó 2006. It costs € 6.

a brief history from establishment of the state in the 10th century to the constitutional reform of 1989; (ii) national symbols and holidays; (iii) outstanding personalities and authors in fine art, literature, music and science in Hungary, including the historical monuments and eras of artistic style; (iv) basic institutions in the constitutional system (structure of public authorities, legislation, courts, public administration, political parties, trade unions); (v) fundamental rights and commitments (e.g. taxation, military service); (vi) Hungarian nationality, naturalisation, statelessness and dual citizenship. The Appendix contains the full text of the national anthem, the EU anthem, pictures of the flag, a map of Hungary, the Parliament, crown and some kings and state leaders. The almost pocket-sized book is based on the knowledge of a moderately well educated person with good linguistic competence. It is a mixture in substance of culture, geography, history, the constitutional system of the state and fluency in Hungarian as a whole. However, this textbook does not succeed in passing on common democratic values or in giving information which is useful for the everyday life of immigrants. Thus, the examination based on this textbook is able to screen out the missing linguistic competence and applicants below the information level of a 14-year-old teenager who has completed public school in Hungary. As the *Introduction* to the textbook says, the threshold is the knowledge of pupils attending the final year of elementary school. In other words, there are dual preconditions for a successful candidate: a lexical knowledge that can be collected within a maximum of 14 years for a person of general intellectual ability and total fluency in Hungarian. I am afraid that it is only in the case where an applicant has lived in Hungary for a total of 14 years that he or she will be able to pass the examination, unless the applicant has an excellent intellectual and linguistic talent, which will open up the possibility to reach these dual peaks sooner.

The *success rate for the examination* is 60–70% according to an estimate by the OIN (there are no national statistics). This relatively high rate may conceal two major obstacles for non-native applicants and/or those not educated in Hungary. Firstly, from the very start of naturalisation proceedings a high level of knowledge of Hungarian is required; no alternative or supported means of communication are available. This is a major burden on non-Hungarian speaking (non-ethnic) applicants. In the absence of free language courses for settled migrants and owing to the limited supply of language lessons for refugees (in the past, about 300 hours), the language condition is the most severe difficulty for applicants. Furthermore, the examination based on lexical, legal and abstract information on Hungarian culture, society and state is a nightmare for less well-educated or non-European applicants. For instance, some comprehensive questions have to be answered, such as,

> Can you determine the centuries of the beginning and end of the Roman and Gothic styles, the Renaissance, Classicism and Art Nouveau? What were the most important consequences and damage caused by WWI in Hungary? What are the major tasks of the UN and the Council of Europe? Can you list at least six prominent writers or poets from the history of Hungarian literature in 20th century?

I put some of these questions to Hungarian nationals and students – and they failed.

It is important to study the mutual effects of the examination on the cultural, economic and community integration of applicants and whether or not the presumption of migrants' existing cultural proximity (from adjacent states) can be maintained in the future.

There are some *exemptions to the constitutional examination in the naturalisation procedure*:

a) for applicants below the age of majority and over 65;
b) for applicants who are unable to sit the examination for health reasons (e.g. suffering from mental disease, chronic or severe illnesses that impede his/her communication or mobility);
c) for applicants who attended public (elementary) or secondary school where the subjects were taught in Hungarian, regardless of whether this was in Hungary or in other states in which Hungarian public education is available (e.g. in kin-minority communities in adjacent states, see table 3).

According to the practice of OIN,[19] proof of Hungarian courses is acceptable for an exemption to the examination if (i) the certificate is issued in Hungary, or (ii) any foreign document is officially translated into Hungarian and contains a clear reference to the language of the (partial) education/examination of the holder, especially in Hungarian literature and history, or the school/college issues an appropriate certificate for the language of the (partial) education/examination of the applicant in Hungarian (or in a local language that must also be officially translated into Hungarian), and (iii) it

[19] There is an interactive question and answer sub-page (FORUM) on the homepage of the OIN. By reading frequent questions from the applicants and answers from the OIN unit leaders, the most problematic points of nationality law can be determined. However, other registered clients may also share reactions, criticism, experiences with the OIN or opinions with readers (under cover names). www.bmbah.hu/reply. Accordingly, in practice numerous questions are raised if the applicant is in possession of a foreign school or professional document without any reference to the language of the full or partial curriculum.

demonstrates the successful completion of minimally compulsory schooling (e.g. eight years at elementary school).

Exceptions may be made ex officio in cases based on age and proof of Hungarian curricula, but mental or physical disability must be demonstrated by medical documentation, although this would increase the discretionary power of the OIN.

6.2.2 *Debates on the Examination*

The introduction of the examination on constitutional basics has been neither discussed nor evaluated in a comprehensive way since 1993. Public dialogue has been limited, involving only OIN clients, some MPs and journals.

The issues of the constitutional examination were defined in 15 topics in the Appendix to the Government Decree that was later reduced to nine topics. The *substance* of the constitutional basics was available in different locally prepared printed materials or textbook chapters between 1993–2005, so a common textbook was ordered by the Ministry of Justice and Law Enforcement. As the textbook was published, the list of topics in the Appendix to the Government Decree became wider without any echoes of why the original material of the constitutional structure and state symbols were gradually extended to literature, art, science and national history. This thematic enlargement was an internal decision by the competent ministry and the amendment of the Appendix was passed as a technical requirement rather than an important instrument of reception policy.

The fee for the examination was fixed in 1993–2001 at 50% of the legal minimum monthly salary. Following complaints from the press and some MPs – not directly from the applicants – the power to grant a fee reduction or exemption was given to the leader of the national administrative office.[20] His discretionary power is based on equality at the request of the applicant in the naturalisation procedure and the Code of Public Administration Process (1957) had to be implemented, taking into account individual conditions. It may represent a controversial migration and kin-minority policy. On the one hand, means of subsistence are required of an immigrant (Tóth 1995), but ethnic Hungarians, as the most typical applicants for naturalisation from poorer adjacent states, would be exempt from the reasonable examination fee. The fee was fixed at HUF 28,000 (approx. € 120) in 2003, maintaining the possibility of reduction or exemption upon request.[21] Finally, under political

---

[20] Government Decree no. 103 of 21 June 2001 entered into force on 1 July 2001.

[21] Government Decree no. 128 of 19 August 2003, entered into force on 1 September 2003.

pressure from a failed referendum (5 December 2004) on *ex lege* acquisition for ethnic Hungarians living in an adjacent state (dual citizenship), the examination fee was reduced for all to € 20 without a deeper analysis of the real management cost of the examination or the financial threshold for applicants. [22]

Between 1993 and 2001, only minors were exempt from taking the constitutional examination. Further reasons related to mental and physical conditions were tacitly applied without formal exemption (e.g. an applicant suffering from dementia was only formally examined) because the regulation was incomplete. The main reason for public debate was the exception made for immigrant students studying for a certificate in Hungary. Naturally, they have strong linguistic skills in Hungarian and are familiar with daily life, are settled and have family here. This amendment, together with the exemption on health grounds and legal incapacity, was adopted by the parliament smoothly in 2001.[23] The other widely supported modification, the reduction of the examination fees, was clearly linked to kin-minority policy in addition to political pressure to make up for the frustration with the failed referendum on dual citizenship (5 December 2004). A new exemption to the constitutional examination was introduced in 2006, when it was decided that the examination was not required for '*persons who graduated in the Hungarian language from a school or educational institution or institute of higher education*'[24] (Article 4/A b). This means that naturalisation was further facilitated for ethnic Hungarians. As mentioned above, its interpretation is not clear: this exemption ignores how constitutional basics may educate applicants in democratic and constitutional values or citizens' awareness; it is, therefore, based on the supposed cultural-linguistic proximity of migrants, specifically ethnic Hungarians. However, kin-minorities have faced all the problems of diaspora life in adjacent states for decades, losing their own cultural and political identities in school curricula. From the perspective of the possible definition of integration, we have to refer to the explanation of preferential naturalisation for family relationships: '*Preferences relate firstly to close family relationships under which stronger ties to the country and closer integration into society would be assumed.*'[25] Thus schooling, birth and family ties are the major defining factors for social and cultural integration and the examina-

[22] Government Decree No. 119 of 28 June 2005, entered into force on 1 January 2006. For more detailed information on the referendum, see below.

[23] Act XXXII of 2001, entered into force on 1 July 2001.

[24] Act XLVI of 2005, entered into force on 1 January 2006.

[25] Explanatory Report to the Bill prepared by the Government (Ministry of the Interior), to Art. 4. Parliamentary Diary (www.mkogy.hu).

tion (including its preparation and implementation) can at most be a supplementary instrument for integration as well as its measurement.

While the national regulation of the examination procedure is fragmented, some components are determined. In the wake of a corruption case,[26] by-laws on the examination process had to be accepted by each county administrative office and the official format of documents was also determined in 2001.[27] The certification of the examination is issued by the county administrative office, and the protocol based on the examination process was regularised. Furthermore, the examination certificate was described as a *'security document'*, requiring common data and updating conditions in order to avoid abuse, falsification or abusive actions against these documents, in the same way as other documents relating to nationality, marital status or the identity of individuals.[28]

These amendments reveal an ambivalent policy: on the one hand, self-subsistence is required of applicants for naturalisation – as for all migrants – thus a fixed fee cannot be considered a major burden unless the documents relating to self-subsistence are manifestly false. On the other hand, exemptions from the examination have become so widespread that many question the function of the test of a migrant's integration level and basic knowledge of common values, unless it means covert discrimination against non-ethnic applicants.

On 5 December 2004, a *referendum* was held on whether Hungarian citizenship should be offered through preferential naturalisation to ethnic Hungarians living outside the borders of the Hungarian state. The referendum raised the option of the removal of all residency requirements from the pre-conditions for obtaining Hungarian (second) citizenship upon request at consular offices (Tóth 2007). In brief, *dual citizenship* inspired a polarised and harsh debate in contemporary Hungary (Kovács 2005, Halász 2005), but the possible role of the constitutional examination or other integration test was not mentioned at all. However, the rejected legislative proposal strongly contributed to *nation building* and the existing diaspora policy through various compensatory measures in the legislation, such as amendments to

---

[26] Officials of the Ministry of Justice and of the Parliament falsified or obtained false certifications for the constitutional examination for a bribe in 1995–2000. The criminal justice proceedings had limited publicity but legislative lessons were quickly drawn.

[27] Government Decree no. 103 of 21 June 2001, entered into force on 1 July 2001.

[28] Government Decree no. 182 of 5 November 2003, modifying the Government Decree no. 86 of 14 June 1996 concerning security documents and their treatment and protection. The modification entered into force on 5 December 2003.

the Nationality Act and the Government Decree including exemption from examination (Tóth 2000a, Tóth 2000b).

6.2.3 *Statistics*

There is no answer to the simple question of how many foreigners take the examination every year. Tables 3 and 4 show the limited number of applicants taking the examination. Although the tables refer to the citizenship of applicants, not their national minority origin, other surveys prove that a ratio of at least two-thirds ethnic Hungarians to migrants is calculated (Tóth, P. 1995, Tóth, P. 1997). This means that applicants coming from the three major source countries (Romania, Serbia-Montenegro and Ukraine), representing a total of 75–85% of all applications, make up a larger part of examination candidates than candidates from other European countries, non-European countries and stateless candidates together. This rate can be explained by the fact that public education is available in Hungarian in these three countries, where Hungarian is a minority language. Consequently, a great majority of applicants from Romania, Serbia-Montenegro and Ukraine are generally exempt from the obligation to pass the examination.

In parallel, Table 4 presents legal evidence of a high rate of preferential cases in naturalisation. We can see a significant part of kin-minority applicants with reference to strong preference for naturalisation (63–78% of all naturalisation cases). Consequently, the rate of examination candidates without exemption and who were not brought up in Hungary is 'marginal, I cannot give the rate'.[29]

Table 3: Nationality of applicants for naturalisation and re-naturalisation together

Applicants by original nationality in %	2002	2003	2004	2005	2006	2007	2008
Romania	61.20	60.30	63.62	67.80	66.00	67.80	60.63
Serbia-Montenegro	16.70	15.10	12.68	11.00	9.30	10.00	11.66
Ukraine	10.60	14.40	14.28	12.30	11.90	12.20	14.87
Others from Europe	5.60	3.90	4.96	4.30	6.40	4.40	2.59
Non-Europeans	4.80	5.30	3.44	3.00	5.70	5.10	6.69
Stateless	1.10	1.00	1.02	0.70	0.70	0.50	0.47

[29] Interview with the director of the Nationality Directorate, OIN (27 February 2009).

Table 4: Distribution of naturalisation decisions

Types of legal title	Application 2002	%	Application 2007	%	Application 2008	%
No preference (basic decision) (Article 4 § (1) Nationality Act)	244	6.27	186	2.71	206	3.39
Weak preference (applicant was born in Hungary) (Article 4 § (4) a)	3	0.0	90	1.31	70	1.15
Weak preference (applicant immigrated as minor to Hungary) (Article 4 § (4) b)	2	0.0	136	1.98	136	2.24
Medium preference (applicant's spouse is Hungarian national) (Article 4 § (2) a)	325	8.35	402	5.87	380	6.26
Medium preference (applicant's minor child is Hungarian national) (Article 4 § (2) b)	49	1.25	123	1.79	118	1.94
Medium preference (applicant is a recognised refugee) (Article 4 § (2) d)	17	0.4	43	0.62	22	0.36
Strong preference (applicant is a minor) (Article 4 § (5))	9	0.2	27	0.39	11	0.18
Strong preference (applicant is a minor adopted by a national) (Article 4 § (6))	30	0.7	4	0.05	7	0.11
Strong preference (applicant is an ethnic Hungarian) (4 § (3))	2,447	62.9	5,158	75.33	4,713	77.66
Re-naturalisation (Article 5)	764	19.6	676	9.87	403	6.64
Total	3,890	100.0	6,845	100.0	6,066	100.0

According to the available statistics from the OIN,[30] we can see that there is a difference between the numbers of applications and of persons in question, since the applications of under-age minors are attached to their parents' application. Following years of naturalisation proceedings, the trend in the absorption capacity or attractive power of Hungarian nationality can be detected in retrospect. The annual 6–10,000 applicants for naturalisation

30 www.bmbah.hu/statistics and www.irm.hu.

and 4–10,000 naturalised persons proves the stability of inclusion. However, the rejection rate is also stable, at about 10%, and figures for successful and other examination candidates are not aggregated annually. Thus, we can conclude that without statistics and a regular evaluation of examination results or respondents, the overall test for integration has not been interpreted. Moreover, the (supposedly) low rate of examination failure perhaps indicates that only candidates with a high chance of passing the examination actually submit applications for naturalisation. Consequently, the linguistic and cultural test can be considered an awkward procedural or alienating measure, rather than an integrative instrument for non-exempt (non-native, non-ethnic) applicants. The examination matches ethnic/native (kin-minority) Hungarians' linguistic competence, so its main purpose is to educate the non-exempt ethnic applicants in how to become better informed citizens. In this context, non-natives are virtually considered atypical applicants.

6.3 *Required (Pre)integration of Refugees*

Parliament adopted a new *Asylum Act* that entered into force on 1 January 2008. It entitles the Government to determine the form and conditions for material allowances, community services for subsistence and 'pre-integration care as well as support' for *applicants for international protection, recognised refugees, and temporarily or subsidiary protected migrants.*[31] Accordingly, certain allowances can be considered contributions to the integration of applicants on merit (after the pre-screening phase) and migrants in a protected status (recognised persons) if they are below the threshold for the minimum monthly income (almost all of them).[32] While applicants for international protection are in a position *to opt to participate in language and integration programmes*, the status of recognition implies a restriction on non-participation. How can we prove this? Applicants for international protection during the proceedings are entitled

a) to request a public transport travelling allowance in order to participate in an outsourced (integration) programme managed by an NGO (based on the discretionary power of the refugee authority);
b) to participate in a preparatory linguistic course for those over the age of five years in order to make a good start at elementary school. However,

[31] Art. 32 (1)–(2), (9) and Art. 93 (1)c of Act LXXX of 2007 regarding Asylum.
[32] Government Decree no. 301 of 9 November 2007 on executive rules to the Asylum Act.

its form and frequency are not regulated and there is no penalty for not attending;

c) to request cover for schooling and vocational training and participation in them (including accommodation, textbooks and travel expenses) up to the age of 18. This is not directly related to special but rather to general cultural and social integration, but nationals have no subjective right to similar benefits.

Unlike the option for applicants for international protection, recognised persons (with refugee, subsidiary or temporary protection status) have to participate in suggested programmes because there is a *formal connection between language training and integration courses* and *subsistence support*. This relationship is established in the following provisions:

a) During school-age years (6–18), attendance at a public education establishment is a precondition for the subsistence allowance.
b) Participation is compulsory in a 520-hour Hungarian *language course* managed by the refugee authority, with regular attendance and progressive examinations. In order to obtain the subsistence allowance within 24 months of recognition, exceptions apply: (i) if the person is over 60 or (ii) if the person is unable to study the Hungarian language for health reasons (e.g. trauma, dementia), documented by an appropriate physician.
c) The subsistence allowance after recognition is available for 25–48 months if he or she is of working age and in good health and continuously *co-operates with the employment service*, including looking for work, *participation in re-training or vocational training courses* for at least one year, or community service of at least three months.
d) Optional participation in a catch-up Hungarian *language course* is managed by a refugee authority for schoolchildren up to age 18.
e) A public transport travelling allowance is available in order to enable the applicant to participate in a Hungarian language course managed by the refugee authority or in an outsourced integration programme managed by an NGO or to look for work.
f) The applicant can request cover for a preparatory linguistic course in order to enter higher education (including accommodation costs) but further contributions to higher education costs (e.g. textbooks) depend on enrolment and regular study on the preparatory course.
g) Optional participation in an *integration programme* (to improve linguistic, cultural, social or employment knowledge) is managed by the refugee authority, the local community or NGOs; its practice has not been developed.

Neither the substance of these courses nor their impact on genuine integration progress are known; legislation is not based on impact assessment or an evaluation of spontaneous or supported integration programmes. The small population of refugees and their support may seem to be an experiment.[33] The support system has been very poor and rigid, suggesting that a majority of protected persons treat the country as a transit area and have no real desire to integrate into this society.[34] However, the low rate of recognised refugees may also explain this non-receptive regime.[35] Thus, the Directive on reception conditions, in particular the reduction or withdrawal of reception conditions in cases of 'bad behaviour',[36] or examples from other Member States would contribute to maintaining rigidity (Nicholson 2006), with a combination of '*enforcing the support system*'. In other words, the 'narrow integrationist approach, comprising mainly language and training measures, in many cases emphasises the need for immigrants to adapt'.[37]

For protected persons, *study of the Hungarian language is a precondition for subsistence support*. This is a completely new approach in migration rules without clarification of whether its support component is a priority for integrating protected migrants into Hungarian society or for frightening (potential) refugees by means of a restriction. If the latter rationale of this provision is based on how to make refugee conditions in this country less attractive, then this will lead to a continuation of Hungary as a transit country with a rigid integration policy.

---

[33] The number of protection seekers yearly has been 2–4,000 persons and the recognised status of all kinds of protection has been below 1,000 in Hungary since 2004. Source: www.bmbah.hu/statistics.

[34] There are figures for protected migrants in Hungary as stock data e.g. on 31 December 2007. The Demographic Yearbook and OIN statistics keep data on decisions regarding recognition for the calendar year. For this reason, the myth of transit migration cannot be denied.

[35] For instance, the recognition rate in 2002–2007 was 5.6% on average. *Demographic Yearbook 2007*, Budapest: Central Statistical Office 2008, p. 167.

[36] Council Directive 2003/09 setting forth minimum standards for the reception of applicants for asylum in Member States (*OJ* 2003 L 31/18). Art. 16 allows this, for instance if the asylum seeker abandons the place of residence determined by the relevant authority.

[37] Joint report on social inclusion summarising the results of the examination of the National Action Plans for Social Inclusion (2003–2005) COM (2003), 773, p. 95.

6.4 *Covert Integration of other Third-Country Nationals*

Following the transposition of migration-related directives,[38] prior alien law was replaced by *two separate acts on the rights to free movement and residence (of EEA nationals and their family members) and conditions for the entry and residence of third-country nationals* in early 2007, entering into force on 1 July 2007.[39] Accordingly, the further legislative signs of the supposed or procedurally *tested integration of migrants* are based on social, economic, cultural and family integration. However, these umbrella terms are neither clearly defined nor illustrated using examples ('in particular') regarding how its extent can be measured or evaluated in terms of authorisation, as is common in other organic laws.[40]

a) Third-country nationals are, for an unlimited number of times, entitled to entry and residence in Hungary for longer than three months and up to five years if they are in possession of a *national visa or residence permit* on the basis of an international treaty if they want to reside in Hungary for the specific purpose of *national (ethnic) integration*.[41] Specifically, this relates to an applicant (in practice a kin-minority or his or her family member) who intends to master the Hungarian language, to strengthen his or her own cultural and ethnic identity, to participate in non-institutional study or training, or to maintain family ties – outside family reunification. This residence permit can be extended for a further

---

[38] Council Directive 2003/86 on the right to family reunification (*OJ* 2003 L 251/12), Council Directive 2003/109 concerning the status of third-country nationals who are long-term residents (*OJ* 2004 L 16/44), Council Directive 2005/71 on a specific procedure for admitting third-country nationals for the purposes of scientific research (*OJ* 2005 L 289/15), Council Directive 2004/114/EC on the conditions of admission of third-country nationals for the purposes of studies, pupil exchange, unremunerated training or voluntary service (*OJ* 2004 L 375/12) and Directive 2004/38/EC of the European Parliament and of the Council on the right of citizens of the Union and their family members to move and reside freely within the territory of the Member States, amending Regulation (EEC) 1612/68 and repealing Directives 64/221/EEC, 68/360/ EEC, 72/194/EEC, 73/148/EEC, 75/34/EEC, 75/35/EEC, 90/364/EEC, 90/365/EEC and 93/96/EC (*OJ* L 158/30).

[39] Act I of 5 January 2007 on entry and residence rights of persons being entitled to free movement and right to residence and Act II of 5 January 2007 on the entry and residence of third-country nationals.

[40] Entry, residence and departure from the country shall be regulated by qualified majority voting (two-thirds majority) by the Parliament (Art. 69 of the Constitution).

[41] Art. 14(1)c, (2)b, Art. 27 of Act II of 2007.

five years and is clearly based on the *ethnic preference policy* without a formal test of integration level.

b) The *national (non-EC) settlement permit* can be issued to a third-country national on the basis of living in a family community for at least two years or alone for three years continuously, or to a third-country national who has ever held Hungarian citizenship or whose ancestor has (held) Hungarian citizenship. This residence permit is also issued taking into account 'individual conditions, for family ties' at the discretion of the Minister of Justice and Law Enforcement.[42] Although it does not entitle the holder to move freely within the Union, its award requires fewer preconditions than the long-term migrant status (EC settlement) authorisation (Directive 2003/109/EC), such as five years' prior residence in Hungary.

c) The expulsion of a third-country national must be based on an assessment of the consequences of a decision regarding family members and the person in question, taking into account the length of residence in Hungary, and '*his attachment to Hungary and the country of origin*'.[43] We have to add that a third-country national's residence and subsistence threshold conditions are not defined more clearly than to say they must be 'proper' and that they must be documented in terms of legality and authenticity.[44] However, family life for a national (non-EC) settlement authorisation is defined as: '*living together under the same roof in a household*'. The reference to 'proper subsistence' is missing, if 'the [breadwinner] is of working age but through his own fault is regularly in need of social assistance and support'.[45]

To sum up, the provisions for the residence and the migration of third-country nationals, including visa and long-term residence permit (settlement permit) *authorisation, indirectly require a minimum level of social, economic and cultural integration.* Cultural proximity as a guarantee of a high level of cultural and social integration is assumed if a kin-minority applicant is migrating, but it practically excludes non-native applicants. Due to the absence of provisions for measuring the level of integration achieved and of requirements concerning how to prove it in general, only the individual

[42] Art. 35(1)d, 36 (2) of Act II of 2007.

[43] Art. 45(1) of Act II of 2007.

[44] For instance, Sections 29 and 64 of Government Decree no. 114 of 24 May 2007 regarding executive rules to Act II of 2007.

[45] Section 103 (4) and 105 (1)b of Government Decree no. 114 of 24 May 2007 regarding executive rules to Act II of 2007.

evaluation of a migrant's personal circumstances is applicable in visa, residence or expulsion decisions. Moreover, optional or compulsory services (programmes, language courses) are not established or implemented for long-term migrants or their family members.

6.5 *Free Movement for Supposedly Integrated Persons*

Following the implementation of Directive 2004/38 EC on the right of EU citizens and their family members to move and reside freely in the territory of the Member States, the Act I of 2007 on entry and residence rights of persons being entitled to free movement and right to residence changed completely the legal approach to EEA and EU citizens and their family members. Due to the legal status of EU citizens and family members, the personal scope of about 50 different laws were amended with reference to *'persons being entitled to free movement and right to residence'*.[46] However, this right and freedom can be limited for certain reasons.

[46] Art 1.(1) The Republic of Hungary shall ensure the right of free movement and residence in accordance with the provisions of this Act:
a) with the exception of Hungarian citizens, to nationals of any Member State of the European Union and States who are parties to the Agreement on the European Economic Area, and to persons enjoying the same treatment as nationals of States who are parties to the Agreement on the European Economic Area by virtue of an agreement between the European Community and its Member States and a State that is not a party to the Agreement on the European Economic Area with respect to the right of free movement and residence (hereinafter referred to as 'EEA nationals');
b) to the family member of an EEA national who does not have Hungarian citizenship, accompanying or joining the EEA national (hereinafter referred to as 'family members of EEA nationals');
c) to the family member of a Hungarian citizen who does not have Hungarian citizenship, accompanying or joining the Hungarian citizen (hereinafter referred to as 'family members of Hungarian citizens'); and
d) to any persons accompanying or joining an EEA national or a Hungarian citizen, who:
da) are dependants or members of the household of a Hungarian citizen for a period of at least one year, or who require the personal care of a Hungarian citizen due to serious health grounds;
db) had been dependants or members of the household of an EEA national in the country from which they are arriving, for a period of at least one year, or who require the personal care of an EEA national due to serious health grounds,
and whose entry and residence has been authorized by the authority on grounds of family reunification.
(3) This Act shall not apply to persons to whom the Hungarian refugee authority has granted asylum, or placed under any subsidiary form of protection or under temporary protection schemes.

The '*unreasonable burden*' (as a regularly returning exclusive precondition) means that an EU[47] as well as an EEA national does not have at least the minimum lawful old age pension per month per capita in the family (approx. € 120) – as the general threshold for social benefit – or has obtained for at least three months (continuously or in parts within a calendar year).[48]

- regular social allowance,
- regular age benefit, or
- nursing benefit on the grounds of Act III of 1993 on Social Administration and Social Benefits

Any decision regarding removal of an EEA national or his or her family member who is a third-country national shall also consider – on the basis of proportionality and necessity of expulsion – family circumstances, economic environment, length of residence in Hungary and '*level of social and cultural integration of the person concerned in Hungary*', as well as '*his close or weak ties to the country of origin*'.[49] The EEA national's residence, subsistence and family ties can be simply demonstrated ('by a proper authentic document'). Authority shall evaluate the prior length of residence in the country, length of provided social benefits and reasons for the material shortage of the family or the persons concerned (e.g. timely shortage or standard need).

It can be seen that only the financial conditions of EU and EEA nationals and family members can be objectively assessed, while cultural and social ties are empty terms without explanation, with the exception of length of residence as an automatic prominent factor of integration. We can conclude that EU citizens and EEA nationals together with family members are 'supposedly integrated' and this presumption is rebutted if there is a financial shortage in the family.

On the other side, this conclusion is coloured by another component of financial burden. Namely, all non-nationals (EU citizens, EEA nationals, family members and third-country nationals) entering the territory of the country have to prove as a minimal source 1,000 HUF (€ 4) for residence *per entry*[50] and not per capita per day. It is obviously anachronistic but today is hardly in harmony with the 'social burden rule'. But due to kin-minori-

[47] Directive 2004/38/EC of the European Parliament and of the Council.

[48] Sections 21 and 35 of Government Decree no. 113 of 24 May 2007 regarding executive rules to Act I of 2007.

[49] As required by Art. 44 of Act I of 2007. By country of origin, the state of the migrant's citizenship is implied.

[50] Section 25 of Decree of the Minister of Justice and Law Enforcement No. 25 of 31 May 2007 implementing the Act I of 2007 and Government Decree No. 113 of 24 May 2007.

ties living across the (EU) borders, this amount has not been increased for years.

6.6 *Half-hearted Policy*

While 4% of the EU population come from third countries, in Hungary the percentage of foreigners is below 2%. Moreover, most migrants come from the adjacent regions in cultural proximity to the Central European environment. In this context, the cultural diversity, ethnic distance or 'otherness' is based on homogeny of local communities rather than on international migration. It is precisely this homogeneity of population that may explain the low acceptance of migrants in Hungary. This may be demonstrated by the recent index of migrants' integration policy (MIPEX) on the grounds of the immigrants' chances of finding employment, family reunification, settlement/long-term residence, participation in local political life, antidiscrimination regulations and naturalisation (conditions for the acquisition of citizenship, security of status and tolerance of dual nationality).[51] The aggregated supportive index in the EU25 identifies two main groups of states:

a) Rigid integration countries, where scores are below 50%. This proportion was *48%* in Hungary and this rigid group covers new Member States.[52]
b) More accepting countries, over 50%, including only one new democracy.[53]

Taking into account the nationality law supportive index, Hungary also belongs among the less integrative group of receiving states, if we divide the EU Member States into two major groups, as follows:

a) less accepting countries, where the rate is below 50%, including Hungary at 36%;[54] and

---

[51] Jan Niessen, Thomas Huddleston & Laura Citron in cooperation with Andrew Geddes & Dirk Jacobs, *Migrant Integration Policy Index*, British Council & MPG, September 2007.

[52] Aggregated MIPEX 2007: Latvia 30%, Cyprus, Austria 39%, Greece, Slovakia 40%, Malta 41%, Denmark, Poland 44%, Lithuania 45%, Estonia 46%, Czech Republic 48%.

[53] Aggregated MIPEX 2007: Ireland, Germany 53%, France, Slovenia 55%, Spain 61%, UK 63%, Italy 65%, Finland 67%, The Netherlands 68%, Belgium 69%, Portugal 79%, Sweden 88%.

[54] Nationality law MIPEX 2007: Austria 22%, Greece, Latvia 25%, Estonia 26%, Malta 29%, Denmark, Italy 33%, Cyprus 36%, Germany, Lithuania 38%, Slovakia 40%, Spain, Slovenia 41%, Finland 44%, Luxembourg and Poland 45%.

b) more accepting countries, at over 50%.[55]

This less receptive policy manifests itself in the reluctant transposition of the Directive on the right of citizens of the Union and their family members to move and reside freely within the territory of the Member States.[56] Regardless of the fact that '*the overall transposition of Directive 2004/38/EC is rather disappointing, not one Member State has transposed the Directive effectively and correctly in its entirety.*'[57] Hungary has failed to correctly transpose Article 3(2) on the rights of other family members, since it makes the right of residence conditional upon the third-country family member entering the country lawfully. Furthermore, Article 7(3), which provides for the retention of the status of worker, is not correctly transposed, mostly due to the fact that the law provides for the retention of the right of residence, but not of the status of worker, which is a wider concept. In the transposition of the right of permanent residence under Article 16, Hungary makes this right incorrectly conditional upon conditions related to the right of residence.[58] At first sight, this is based on the issue of the integration test, but these shortcomings may prove a rigid migration and integration policy in Hungary.

The Ministry of Justice and Law Enforcement is working on an Act for the Integration of Migrants, as has been announced in numerous forums in recent years. Its preparation and the debate on its principles can be found among the project priorities in the national plan, supported by the European Integration Fund. The most targeted issue is *how to incorporate the task of the integration of migrants into the competences and responsibilities of each ministerial organisation and state agency.* There is no solution yet.

What are the potential components of this migrant-absorbing and integration policy that is 'halfway to best practice'?

6.7 *Who are we?*

Due to Hungary's century-long dependence and its weak sense of statehood, the newly obtained sovereignty makes the fragmented national identity vis-

[55] Nationality law MIPEX 2007: Czech Republic 50%, Netherlands 51%, France 54%, Ireland, UK 62%, Portugal 69%, Belgium and Sweden 71%.

[56] Directive 2004/38/EC of the European Parliament and of the Council of 29 April 2004.

[57] Report from the Commission to the European Parliament and the Council, COM (2008) 840/3.

[58] Report from the Commission to the European Parliament and the Council, COM (2008) 840/3.

ible (Tóth & Sik 2003). It is not only public debates on kin-minority policy, dual citizenship, referendum on EU and NATO accession or workshop discussion on the Bill on Integration that prove this, but also severe shortages in public education.

Public education is decentralised: nursery, elementary and secondary schools are run by the 3,200 local governments. As a result of social and economic transition, there is a deep crisis in the transmission of values in the schooling system, while dysfunction in institutional operation and finance places a severe burden on local communities. While the public education costs as a share of the Gross Domestic Product (GDP) are growing (5.9% in 2004) the amount of money applicable is below the average in older Member States (EU15). Although compulsory schooling lasts 12 years (6–18 years old), the rate of students at higher elementary and secondary school (ISCED[59] 3–4) is decreasing, youngsters are disappearing from school to a greater extent than in the EU15 (Kenyeres 2007). This means that fewer students and more teachers consume more public money while the pedagogical efficiency of teaching declines (see the PISA monitoring results).[60] The Hungarian public education system, which segregates poor and Roma students, starts foreign language teaching after the age of 10. Furthermore, the salaries of teachers are low (0.52–0.72% of GDP per capita in 2004), with no motivation for an inclusive, integrative and tolerant form of education (Szilágyi 2004). The conclusion can, hence, be drawn that cultural diversity cannot be absorbed by attending public school.

The high speed of European integration, overlapping with the transition in the economy and social values means a crisis of identity at national level, which has inspired a policy of ethnic preference, including the nationality law (Mavi 2007). The creation of a political community or efforts to build constitutional patriotism have to battle with the inconsistencies of the anti-discrimination and equal treatment policy that is related to the commitment to diversity and respect for otherness in Europe (Shaw & Wiener 1999: 6). While Article 151 of the Treaty provides a new legal basis for a common cultural policy, Member States block all Union attempts at 'protecting' public education as an important shaper of national identity. It takes about four

[59] The International Standard Classification of Education (ISCED) was designed by UNESCO in the early 1970s to serve, 'as an instrument suitable for assembling, compiling and presenting statistics of education both within individual countries and internationally.' See more details of definitions at www.unesco.org/education/information/nfsunesco/doc/isced_1997.html (1 March 2009).

[60] OECD Programme for International Student Assessment (PISA), results for 2005 (see www. oecd.org/pages/0,3417,en).

decades to establish equality in the social and economic rights of settled migrants, but the same results in the field of political, cultural and other fundamental rights would require even longer, in particular with regard to linguistic rights.[61] Moreover, a common legal status for Euroregions is lacking, as are consistent rules on cross-border cooperation (CBC) imposed by the common law competences of local communities, authorities and municipalities. Thus, the initiatives (such as the European Grouping on Territorial Cooperation through Directive 1082/2006/EC) and numerous cross-border cooperation programmes cannot develop the eastern periphery of the Union (Hegedüs 2007).

These controversies may explain the short-term and harsh reaction of acceding kin-state states to ethnic policy, including preferential naturalisation and dual citizenship in Hungary.[62] This nation-building policy is in competition with the European integration process and may provoke tension between the kin-state and country of residence of the kin-minority,[63] in particular through the unilateral legal solutions adopted (such as status law rules, kin-minority legislation, modification of nationality law) (Osamu 2006), instead of bilateral or multilateral commitments regarding cooperation.

In brief, the nation state, regional and local communities and civilian organisations together have to implement all the instruments, such as CBC, European Neighbourhood Policy and EU (cultural) policy to form an identity-building model(s), opting for the utilitarian, spontaneous, institutional or cultural versions (Egry 2007). In this process, the Hungarian experiences

[61] European Commission, *Third Annual Report on Migration and Integration*, 12 September 2007; Craufurd Smith 2004.

[62] The Law on Bulgarian citizenship (1998) requires six conditions for the acquisition of citizenship: majority age (18), permanent residence status for at least five years, clean criminal record, having income or work in Bulgaria, fluency in the Bulgarian language and release or prospective release from present citizenship. Applicants of Bulgarian origin are exempted from all but two requirements: minimum age and clean criminal record and their procedure takes about three months (12 months for others) – since this amendment was adopted in 2001. The number of applicants grew steadily in the period 2001–2006, while the number for granted citizenship was fairly stable and low (rejection rate was 75% of applications) but 90–99% of them were ethnic Bulgarian (Tchorbadjiyska 2007).

[63] For instance, there are 800,000 applicants from Moldova for Romanian nationality but this huge number would require a lengthy procedure. An amendment to the Nationality Law was proposed by the state president while Moldova seriously debated this high number of applications: the total population of Moldova is 4.4. million and 2% of them were declared a Romanian minority in the last census. Rostás Szabolcs www.kronika.ro Cluj-Napoca (10/02/2008).

with nationality and migration law – with its failures and debates – would provide lessons.

6.8 *Conclusions*

Acts regarding entry to, residence in and departure from the country have to be passed by a qualified majority in the Parliament, and this constitutional requirement has been respected since 1990. Thus, political consensus on ethnic preferences has been continuous even in recent transposition rules relating to the Directives on migration. However, ambivalent legislation – whether it defines genuine support for facilitated integration or only sets up the formal test requirements for being (supposedly) integrated – can also be observed in Hungary. Compulsory participation in integration courses and cooperation with employment offices as a precondition for obtaining the status of protected persons are new components of the reluctant regulation of migration to produce a manifestly communitarian model in this connection.

Reception and integration policy has been rigid in comparison to other Member States, and also according to the Migration Policy Index, focusing on six major aspects of migration rules. Hungarian policy is based on a spontaneous individual integration of migrants without active support or community services. The recently adopted acts of 2007 go further, because obtaining benefits for refugees and maintaining residence (not removal) are attached to a certain level of integration, but without effective and applicable community social and integration services. The communitarian model has also been developed entirely through ethnic-based naturalisation. In this logic, the acquisition of nationality is the end point, not the means to the integration process.

These components of migration policy have deep roots in kin-state and kin-minority relations that make integration policy formally superfluous. Although many aspects of the migration Directives have been transposed into the national legislation, ethnic citizenship precedes civic citizenship. This communitarian model of citizenship includes tests covering language, ties to the country and culture, while the majority of immigrants have come – so far – on the basis of ethnic proximity from the adjacent regions. So why care about non-Hungarian foreigners? As already mentioned, while only 4% of the EU population comes from third countries, this rate is even lower in Hungary. In this context, cultural diversity, ethnic distance or otherness is based much more on heterogeneous local communities than on international migration. Precisely this homogeneity of the population may explain the low acceptance of migrants.

In the legislation, schooling, birth and family ties are the major contributors to social and cultural integration and the examination (including its preparation and implementation) can be at most a supplementary instrument for integration as well as its measurement. Alongside the stable numbers of applicants for naturalisation each year, growing numbers of migrants have been exempted from the examination since 1993. Recently, this has meant that theoretically a maximum of 25% of applicants (non-Europeans, stateless persons and non-ethnic Hungarians from adjacent and more distant European states) must take the examination. In the absence of data on how many persons participate in preparatory courses or consultations, how many have to take the examination because they are not exempt and what the examination pass rate is, any evaluation of the overall testing method and its impact mechanism is one-sided, based on legislation and some indirect information. It seems to me that the constitutional examination is a screening method rather than an instrument for facilitated, supported integration. The constitutional examination may control the level of applications for citizenship instead of disseminating information or education about citizenship and political community values. On the other hand, the efficiency or impact of the examination on inclusion and integration cannot be easily determined in the absence of (regular) evaluation.

To sum up, Hungarian nationality is partly a form of civic citizenship following successful examination of basic constitutional issues, taken by the applicants. It may provide an education for non-native migrants in how to become active, democratic members of the community. On the other hand, nationality is partly a form of ethnic membership, taking ethnic preferences into account in the procedure as well as substantial linguistic and cultural proximity. Moreover, statistics prove how preferences dominate naturalisation cases. For these reasons, Hungary applies an assimilative-input model: successful applicants have to be ready-made Hungarians. The introduction of the examination of constitutional basics has been neither discussed nor evaluated in a comprehensive way since 1993. The Ministry of Justice and Law Enforcement is working on an Integration Act, perhaps beyond the existing (not overly supportive) rules. Cultural diversity cannot be absorbed in the decentralised, segregated public school system in Hungary. The fast-track European integration process, together with dramatic transitions in the economy and in the social and values system would inspire a policy of ethnic preferences in order to protect national identity, including the nationality law in Hungary. Cultural and ethnic proximity has continued to form the basis for reception and integration policy. As a result, the nationality law has merely followed this basically ethnic and less citizenship-dominant form of nationality. Why and how would we want to test ethnicity using a constitutional examination?

Bibliography

Central Statistical Office, Demographic Yearbook 2007, Budapest, 2008.

Craufurd Smith, R. (ed.), *Culture and European Union Law*, Oxford University Press 2004.

Egry G., Alkotmány „miniszerzödés, európai identitás, *Európai Tükör* 2007/9: 3–13.

Hajduk, A., (ed), *Chance or threat? Immigration to Hungary*, Open Society Institute and DEMOS, October 2008, Budapest.

Halász, I., Dual Citizenship as an Instrument of the Hungarian Policy Towards the Nation?, *Regio*, 8, 2005, pp. 73–86.

Hegedüs D., Új elemek, új lehetüöségek a határokon átnyúló együttműködés európai szabályozásában. Az Európai Területi Együttmüködési Csoportosulás a magyar nemzetpolitika szempontjából, *Európai Tükör* 3, 2007, pp. 86–93.

Kenyeres L., Közoktatás az Európai Unióban, *Európai Tükör*, 2, 2007, pp. 115–125.

Kovács, M., The Politics of Non-resident Dual Citizenship in Hungary, *Regio*, 8, 2005, pp. 50–72.

Mavi V., Az európai uniós alkotmányozási folyamat tudományos és módszertani szerepéröl, értékeléséröl, *Jogtudományi Közlöny*, 12, 2007, pp. 568–573.

Migrant Integration Policy Index: Jan Niessen, Thomas Huddleston and Laura Citron in cooperation with Andrew Geddes and Dirk Jacobs. British Council & MPG, September 2007.

Nicholson, F., Challenges to Forging a Common European Asylum System in Line with International Obligations, in R. Peers (ed.), *EU Immigration and Asylum Law: Text and Commentary*, Leiden: Martinus Nijhoff Publishers 2006, pp. 505–537.

Osamu I. (ed.), *Beyond Sovereignty: From Status Law to Transnational Citizenship?*, Slavic Research Centre, Hokkaido University, Sapporo, 2006.

Shaw, Jo and Wiener, A., *The paradox of the European polity*, working paper, JeanMonnetprogram.org/papers/99/991001.

Szilágyi, G., *Megbukott az iskola?*, Osiris, Budapest, 2004.

Tchorbadjiyska, A., Bulgarian Experiences with Visa Policy in the Accession Process: A Story of Visa Lists, Citizenship and Limitations on Citizens' Rights, *Regio*, 10, 2007, pp. 88–105.

Tóth, J., Who are the Desirable Immigrants in Hungary under the Newly Adopted Laws?, in: M. Fullerton, E. Sik & J. Tóth (eds.), *Refugees and Migrants: Hungary at a Crossroads – Yearbook of the Research Group on International Migration, the Institute for Political Science of the Hungarian Academy of Sciences*, Budapest, 1995, pp. 57–68.

Tóth, J., Diaspora in Legal Regulations: 1989–1999, in: I. Kiss & C. McGovern (eds.), *New Diasporas in Hungary, Russia and Ukraine: Legal Regulations and Current Politics*, Budapest: Open Society Institute/COLPI 2000a, pp. 42–95.

Tóth, J., Diaspora Politics: Programs and Prospects, in: I. Kiss & C. McGovern (eds.), *New Diasporas in Hungary, Russia and Ukraine: Legal Regulations and Current Politics*, Budapest: Open Society Institute/COLPI 2000b, pp. 96–141.

Tóth, J., Is it possible to regulate citizenship by referendum?, *Minorities Research* 9, 2007, pp. 88–121.

Tóth, J. & E. Sik, Joining an EU identity. Integration of Hungary or the Hungarians?, in: W. Spohn & A. Triandafyllidou (eds.), *Europeanisation, National Identities and Migration. Changes in Boundary Constructions between Western and Eastern Europe*, London: Routledge 2003, pp. 223–244.

Tóth, P. P., *Haza csak egy van? Menekülök, bevándorlók, új állampolgárok Magyarországon. 1988–1994.* Püski Kiadó 1997.

Tóth, P. P., Refugees, immigrants and new citizens in Hungary. 1988–1992, in: E. Sik (ed.), *Refugees and Migrants*, Hungarian Academy of Sciences, 1995, pp. 69–82.
Ugróczky M., Alkotmányos alapismeretek. Segédanyag az alkotmányos alapismeretek vizsgára készülö nem magyar állampolgárok számára. BM Duna Palota és Kiadó, 2006.

Chapter 7

Latvian Integration Policy: Lost in Translation

*Kristine Kruma**

7.1 *Introduction*

Migration and citizenship attribution are sensitive issues in the Baltic States which, after a period of Soviet occupation in 1940, restored their independence and citizen body in 1991. During the Soviet occupation, a large group of immigrants from former Soviet republics arrived in Latvia, encouraged by the so-called Russification policy. The latter sought to instil Soviet values and ideals and made Russian an official language alongside Latvian. A dual-stream education system existed; namely, Latvian and Russian. Russian was part of the curricula of Latvian schools. In addition, the media were controlled by Moscow and aimed at indoctrination and the imposition of Soviet values.

When Latvia regained its independence, politicians contemplated two options. Latvia could opt for a state succession model, thereby becoming a new state. This would have led to the adoption of a new constitution and laws, including those defining 'the Latvian people', that is, the citizens of Latvia. Another option was to claim that Soviet occupation was illegal and that Latvia had never been part of the USSR *de jure*. This option was based on the principle of state continuity, i.e. the continuity or identity of states as legal entities under international law, and required the articulation of a set of claims in accordance with the applicable international law rules or procedures when referring to statehood (Ziemele 2005: 118). Latvia opted for the latter option; it argued that the Soviet occupation was illegal and that illegal occupation could not legalise Latvian loss of statehood (*ex inuria ius non oritur*).

---

* LL.D.cand Lund University, Sweden; Lecturer at Riga Graduate School of Law.

Van Oers, Ersbøll and Kostakopoulou, A Re-definition of Belonging?, pp. 241–269.

Latvia's preferred option of claiming state continuity was accepted by the international community.[1]

State continuity meant that fundamental laws and the Constitution of the pre-occupation period had to be revived. According to the principle of State continuity, decision-makers renewed the Citizenship law of 1919, as amended in 1927, and reconstituted the body of citizens on the basis of the *ius sanguinis* principle. This meant that only those who were citizens at the time of occupation and their descendants were recognised as Latvian citizens (Kruma 2007: 63–64, Thiele 1999:12). It was claimed that the automatic conferral of Soviet nationality on the population of Latvia as a consequence of the annexation in 1940 was unlawful under international law provided Latvia was presumed to exist (Ziemele 2001: 233). Accordingly, politicians argued that only a restored body of citizens would be entitled to elect a Parliament which would then be entrusted with drafting a new citizenship law. This approach led to the situation where the status of Soviet-era immigrants became undetermined.[2]

Committed to preserving state continuity, Latvia had to respect international law requirements including obligations to reduce statelessness and to integrate 'non-Latvians'. To solve the problem of statelessness, Latvia introduced the status of non-citizens. Former Soviet citizens who did not qualify for Latvian citizenship because they or their predecessors were not Latvian citizens or residents of Latvia in 1940 could apply for the special status of non-citizen. This status was intended to be temporary since it was envisaged that non-citizens would naturalise or eventually apply for citizenship of another State.

The transition from Soviet republic to an independent state made citizenship and integration policy highly-sensitive issues. As the subsequent discussion shows, Latvian integration policy has been characterised by relative successes and failures. Below I will discuss the experience of Latvian integration policy by focusing on citizenship, language and education reforms. The

[1] See collection of documents of recognition in *Dokumenti par Latvijas valsts starptautisko atzišanu, neatkaribas atjaunošanu un diplomatiskajiem sakariem, 1918–1998*, Latvijas arhivistu biedriba, LR Arlietu ministrija, Latvijas valsts veētures arhivs, NORDIK, 1999.

[2] The Law on the Entry and Residence of Foreigners and Stateless Persons did not enter into force until 2 July 1992. It imposed conditions for visas and residence permits. Until that date, governmental instructions were in force which prohibited the permanent registration of persons arriving between 4 May 1990 and 2 July 1992. The 1992 Law was not applied in a uniform manner and in certain cases even retroactively. Therefore, the status and residence rights of Soviet-era settlers were confusing at the time.

article departs from the context in which the basic principles of integration were defined, i.e. that of republican and communitarian democracy. Republican democracy is primarily concerned with political participation and legitimacy (Blatter 2008: 13). Most approaches to communitarian democracy overlap with republican approaches since they are opposed to liberal individualism. For communitarians it is the national society/polity that should provide orientation and identity for the individual (Blatter 2008: 16). Loyalty to the State, community and nation has specific significance in this regard. It can be argued that by overcoming the consequences of occupation and becoming a member of the EU, the Latvian model has faced significant challenges.

Since the European Union needs new supranational values to succeed it is challenging the traditional republican model which needs to adapt to a more liberal model of democracy. This has been the driving factor behind economic integration and, with the adoption of common immigration policies, it has also become part of integration policies. While, during the pre-accession process, Europe was active in liberalising Baltic integration policies, it is less enthusiastic nowadays when implementing integration guidelines under the Hague Programme.[3] This article will show the significance of EU intervention and tasks for the future of common European integration policies by taking into account the relevance of Latvian successes and failures in this context.

7.2 *Context and Challenges for Latvian Integration Policies*

By 1991, when the Republic of Latvia regained its independence, the titular nation had almost become a minority, representing only 52% of the population, with Russians and other non-Latvian nationalities comprising 48% of the population. This made Latvians feel insecure about their State and identity. By comparison, in 1935 Latvians comprised 75.5% of the total population. In the light of the state continuity thesis, strict citizenship policies based on *ius sanguinis* resulted in the exclusion of 28.2% of the total population from Latvian citizenship in 1993.[4] This approach caused psychological problems for many people who did not qualify for Latvian citizenship. They argued

[3] *Integration Handbook for policy-makers and practitioners*, Directorate-General for Justice, Freedom and Security, November 2004.

[4] For a more detailed account of Latvian citizenship policy, see Kruma 2007.

that, during the process of the restoration of independence, everyone was promised that they would be entitled to Latvian citizenship and that was the reason they supported the process.

The Western allies required Latvia to adopt a new citizenship law which would accommodate the requirements of international law and would lead to the integration of society. Lengthy discussions were held on the new citizenship law and, after the first version was turned down by the President, the new law was adopted on 22 July 1994 (Kruma 2007: 65). The Citizenship Law introduced the 'window system', which provided for gradual naturalisation of different age groups. For instance, a person who was 45 years old could not apply for citizenship until 2000, while a person who was 20 could apply in 1996. The reason for this approach was fear that considerable numbers of Soviet-era settlers would opt for citizenship. This was seen as an obstacle to smooth naturalisation as well as a threat to Latvian democracy. The newly naturalised were not perceived as loyal to the State by citizens and were seen as a threat to national statehood. As a reaction to these perceptions, many Soviet-era settlers chose either to opt for Russian or other citizenship or to apply for the status of non-citizen.

In an attempt to strike a balance between the State continuity thesis and the obligation to avoid statelessness, Latvia introduced the special status of 'non-citizen' in 1995 (Law on the Status of Former Soviet Citizens who are not Citizens of Latvia or any Other State, Official Gazette no. 63, 25 April 1995). Former Soviet citizens and their children could register for this status if they were not citizens of another State and resided in Latvia. Their status envisaged that they should be more than permanent residents, but not yet citizens. The Constitutional Court of Latvia has defined the status of non-citizen in the following way:

> The status of non-citizens is not and cannot be considered a mode of Latvian citizenship. However, the rights given to non-citizens, and the international obligations which Latvia has undertaken in relation to these persons, mean that a legal link between non-citizens and Latvia is recognised to a certain extent and, on that basis, mutual obligations and rights have emerged. This is derived from Article 98 of the Satversme, which states among other things that anyone who holds a Latvian passport has the right to State protection and the right to return freely to Latvia (Latvian Constitutional Court Case no. 2004–15–0106, *Official Gazette* no. 40, 9 March 2005).

Non-citizens hold a special passport and enjoy diplomatic protection and rights similar to those of citizens, with the exception of the right to vote and to hold certain positions. As already mentioned, this status was not intended to be permanent. It was considered a temporary regulation until all non-citizens have been naturalised or opt for another citizenship. Latvia has consistently defended its position that non-citizens cannot be qualified as stateless persons and this view has been accepted by international human rights monitoring bodies (Ziemele, Kruma 2003).[5] For instance, the Human Rights Committee and the Committee on the Elimination of Racial Discrimination have accepted that non-citizens are not stateless persons. At the same time, they have emphasised the need to encourage the naturalisation of those persons and their integration. Therefore, they have indirectly suggested that non-citizen status cannot become permanent and that all possible differences in treatment between citizens and non-citizens should be eliminated.[6]

During the period 1991–2007, the ethnic composition of the population of Latvia did not experience further significant changes since the number of Latvians increased by only under 10%. The latest data available are included in the table below.

Table 1: The population of Latvia as of 01.07.2008

	Citizens	Non-citizens	Foreigners or stateless individuals	Total	%
Latvians	1.340,824	1,667	1,162	1.343,653	59.1
Russians	367,181	240,784	26,194	634,159	27.9
Byelorussians	31,207	49,085	2,734	83,036	3.7
Ukrainians	17,670	34,635	4,687	56,992	2.5
Poles	40,428	12,432	859	53,719	2.4
Lithuanians	18,388	9,943	2,272	30,603	1.4
Estonians	1,492	558	448	2,498	0.1
Other (incl. undeclared or unknown	41,528	16,060	9,369	66,957	2.9
Total	1.858,718	365,164	47,725	2.271,617	100

Source: Office of Citizenship and Migration Affairs, http://www.pmlp.gov.lv/lv/documents/statistika/IRD/ISVN_Latvija_pec_TTB_VPD.pdf, 5 January 2008.

[5] See, for instance, Concluding Observations of the Human Rights Committee: Latvia, 3 October 1995. CCPR/C/79/Add.53; A/50/40, paras. 334–361. www.unhchr.ch. Concluding observations of the Committee on the Elimination of Racial Discrimination: Latvia, 12 April 2001. CERD/C/304/Add.79. www.unhchr.ch.

[6] See Consideration of Reports Submitted by State Parties Under Article 9 of the Convention. Concluding observations of the Committee on the Elimination of Racial Discrimination, 55th Session 2–27 August 1999, CERD/C/304/Add.79 12 April 2001, paras 12–14, and 63rd Session, 4–22 August, CERD/C/63/CO/7 10 December 2003, paras 12–13. Consideration of Reports Submitted by State Parties under Article 40 of the Covenant, Human Rights Committee, 79th Session, CCPR/CO/79/LVA, 1 December 2003, paras 16–18.

As the table above shows, the most sizeable ethnic minority groups in Latvia are Russians, Byelorussians, Ukrainians and Poles. Those belonging to the group of former Soviet nationals have traditionally tended to identify themselves with post-Soviet or Russian culture and are typically slower to accept the new legal framework and the integration conditions imposed by Latvia. Therefore, Latvia had to integrate large numbers of people not holding Latvian citizenship immediately after regaining its independence. A number of laws in the fields of citizenship, education and language had to be re-drafted to accommodate claims to continuity and modern-day realities. This was in addition to the transformation of the whole institutional and legal framework to correspond to the requirements of democratic governance and the rule of law.

After regaining its independence, Latvia defined its foreign policy priorities as being to join the Western democratic community and to become a member of the Council of Europe as well as, most importantly, the EU and NATO. International organisations and individual member states of these organisations used this proclamation of foreign policy goals to impose political criteria on membership and to require Latvia to take active measures to integrate society and encourage naturalisation (Kruma 2004: 33–53). This could be seen as pressure on Latvia to depart from its traditional republican model of democracy in favour of a more inclusive, liberal model that would accommodate, at least partially, the claims of people who arrived in Latvia during Soviet occupation.

7.2.1 *The Influence of the European Union*

During the pre-accession process the EU applied so called 'human rights conditionality' as a foreign policy instrument. The entire pre-accession process was based on an Association agreement, including a Human Rights clause, as well as the Accession Partnership, based on so-called Copenhagen criteria adopted by the European Council in 1993 (Kruma 2004: 36–37). The first Copenhagen criterion requested States, for instance, to ensure respect for human rights and the protection of minorities (Bulletin of the EC, 6/1993, 113). During the accession process, the European Commission drafted annual Regular Reports. It has regularly taken a close look at non-discrimination issues in relation to non-citizens. The report on Latvia in 1998 notes that, 'a number of areas were underlined in the Commission's Opinion in which non-citizens were treated differently from citizens', and acknowledges that some progress has been made. The major issues raised concerned the abolition of professional restrictions on non-citizens wishing to practice certain professions (Kruma 2004: 47).

In order to meet the requirements imposed by different international actors, Latvia not only drafted the most sensitive laws in accordance with Western experts' advice, but also embarked on a number of measures that comprise the national Programme, 'The Integration of the Society in Latvia', adopted in 2001 (hereafter referred to as 'the Programme'). In order to ensure the effective implementation of the Programme, the Parliament established the Fund for the Integration of Society in 2001. The Fund allocates money to different projects submitted by NGOs, minorities, schools, media and the like. The funding is allocated from the State budget, EU funds and individual donors, such as the Norwegian government financial instrument (Sakss 2004: 23). In 2002 the Special Assignment Secretariat for the Integration of Society was established as part of the Government. The Secretariat has become the main institution with the competence in integration issues. In addition, about 20 local governments have units dealing with integration. Therefore, being under international pressure, Latvia has continuously kept the integration issue on its internal agenda.

7.2.2 *Russia's Influence*

Apart from these internal challenges to integration and pressure from the West, an important external challenge also exists which differentiates Latvia from other states, that is the impact of the Russian Federation's policy of support for ethnic Russians resident abroad (the 'Compatriots Policy'; other designations often used by state authorities of the Russian Federation include: 'Russian Compatriots', 'Russian Diasporas' or 'Russian speakers') on the social and ethnic integration process in Latvia. Many Russians felt snubbed by the loss of their former privileges when Latvia regained its independence. They perceived this as the humiliation of a great nation. This support for 'compatriots' has been strengthened over the years and has acquired different and much more meaningful content recently, especially in view of developments in Georgia, Moldova and Ukraine. Since 1992, the Russian Federation has attempted to influence the policy of Latvia with regard to the so-called 'Russian-speakers' issue in different ways.

Russia has used three major tools to reinforce its policies: international organisations, NGOs and Kremlin-controlled mass media. As Nils Muižnieks notes, Russia has incessantly attempted to place 'issues involving Russian Compatriots' on the agendas of all the major regional and international organisations.[7]

[7] In 1992 Russia pressured the UN Secretary General to send a fact-finding mission to Latvia to 'investigate alleged discriminatory practices against minorities'. The mission's report

In doing so, Russian officials routinely dramatise the situation of their countrymen in Latvia (Muižnieks 2006b: 121–122). According to the Foreign policy concept of the Russian Federation (11 July 2008), the Russian strategic goal is:

> to contribute to the consolidation of the organisations of compatriots so as to ensure more efficient protection by them of their rights in their countries of residence and to preserve the ethnic and cultural identity of the Russian diaspora and its links with its historic motherland, to consistently create conditions to assist with the voluntary resettlement in the Russian Federation of those compatriots who make such a choice.

These policies fuel tensions because Russia, in promoting the consolidation of compatriots and manipulating their status, destroys the policies of integration and causes the sense of belonging to be divided between Russia as lobbyist and Latvia as host of a particular community.

7.2.3 *Integration Programme*

Taking into account these complexities, Latvia had to develop a sophisticated Programme to accommodate Latvian commitment to a republican democracy, based on continued Latvian statehood and the claims of Soviet-era settlers which were supported by Russia. However, the Programme was unfocused and aspired to be a panacea for all potential problems, which in some cases were attributable not to society but to politicians and civil servants themselves, i.e. social and regional differences, corruption, alienation and low standards of living. The main emphasis was placed on overcoming the consequences of a totalitarian past and the development of a democratic civic society. The 'red line' throughout the Programme is securing the irreversibility of independence. On a number of occasions, the authors stressed that Latvia is a unitary, national state where the right of self-determination of the people is respected. Integration should not support the formation of a dual-community State.

---

noted 'anxiety' among minorities 'about their future status', 'rather than any gross violation of human rights'. Subsequently, the Russian Federation raised the issue of the treatment of Russian in various UN bodies virtually every year through letters, *notes verbales*, draft resolutions and speeches. Russia has been active in the CSCE/OSCE, drawing attention to compatriots in Latvia. Russia was increasingly critical in 2000 and especially in 2001. The Council of Europe and its Parliamentary assembly has been an important forum for Russia to attack Latvia. Russia regularly joins the politically sensitive cases against Latvia in the European Court of Human Rights as a third party. In 1999 the Russian Foreign Ministry appealed to the European Council to reconsider Latvia's invitation to negotiate EU membership (Muižnieks 2006c: 123).

Much attention has been devoted to explaining the term 'integration'. This was necessary because, at that time, Latvians still felt threatened and were generally opinionated about Soviet-era settlers while Russian-speakers considered the Programme a step towards their assimilation. The Programme stressed that integration does not jeopardise Latvian identity. It was also stated that, 'Life in Latvia requires additional effort from minorities. They should not only know the national language and participate in the life of the state and society, but also master their own native language.'[8]

The Programme placed the Latvian language ('knowledge of Latvian by non-Latvians as a chief indicator of integration'), history ('objective understanding of the past') and naturalisation at the centre of the integration policy (naturalisation is an important part of integration). The basic approach of the Programme is described as follows:

> An integrated civil society is one where all residents of Latvia are active participants in social life, where non-Latvians have a good command of the Latvian language, have overcome alienation from Latvian values and culture, and are taking an active part in striving for common goals with the rest of the society.

It can be concluded that Latvia was committed not only to state continuity but also to the principles common to republican and communitarian democracy. Latvian integration policy places identity and loyalty at the centre of developing a Latvian nation and citizenship policy and Latvian language are seen as means of strengthening national identity and loyalty. The following sections will discuss the success and failure of such an approach.

7.3 *Main Issues of Integration*

The main issues of integration historically have been those associated with citizenship attribution, language policy and education policy. These will be outlined in the historical perspective by taking into account the provisions of the Integration Programme.

7.3.1 *Naturalisation and the Issue of Non-citizens*

Although Latvia chose a strict citizenship policy, fearing the numbers of Soviet-era settlers, empirical data show that the number of naturalised persons

[8] National Programme, 'Sabiedribas integracija Latvija' [The Integration of Society in Latvia], Riga, 2001, pp. 8–11. Available at http://www.np.gov.lv/index.php?lv=fjas_lv&saite=integracija.htm, 15 July 2007.

remained low. Different international organisations have voiced their concerns regarding the slow pace of naturalisation. In 1998 Latvia adopted further amendments, thereby liberalising the Law on Citizenship. The amendments abolished the 'window system' and granted citizenship to children born in Latvia after 21 August 1991 to stateless persons or non-citizens. However, non-citizens still constitute 16% of the total population (see Table 1 above and Table 3 below).

The facilitation of naturalisation has continuously been on the political agenda with varying degrees of importance. While it was more of a priority during the period before accession to the EU, since 2004 it has become marginalised. The overall problem has been correctly formulated by the authors of the Integration Programme, in stating that:

> For many non-citizens who came to Latvia from Russia, Ukraine, Byelorussia and other countries, making of sense of belonging to the Latvian State involves quite a difficult choice. They have to find an answer to many vitally important questions: about their future place of residence, loyalty, future of their children, etc. The Soviet lifestyle has left strong and invincible imprint, especially in the minds of elderly people. [...] The modern world has become alien to them, since they have not found their place in it.[9]

Therefore, the integration process aimed at consolidating civil society, founded on shared basic values that were well-known to Latvian citizens but alien to those who arrived during Soviet times. It is doubtful whether the objectives set forth in the Programme could be achieved by simply encouraging the naturalisation process.

Naturalisation tests covering both language and history, introduced after the adoption of the Citizenship Law, have been simplified over the years and opinion polls suggest that they are no longer seen as a major obstacle for people who want to become naturalised citizens. Those who are naturalised say that the exams turned out to be easier than they expected.

Exams are generally supported by both citizens and non-citizens.[10] This might be seen as a result of the activities of the Naturalisation Board in organising special seminars in which the candidates can test their knowledge.

---

[9] *Ibid.*

[10] In the survey conducted in 2008, 92% of citizens and 62% of non-citizens supported language exams. By comparison, the numbers for 1997 and 2000 were 83% and 85% of citizens and 54% and 56% of non-citizens respectively. The knowledge exam is supported by 44% of citizens and 12% of non-citizens. In 1997 and 2000 the numbers were 56% and 67% of citizens, while 34% and 41% of non-citizens supported the exam. The view that all exams have to be abolished is supported by 31% of non-citizens and 7% of citizens. The public opinion survey, 'Kvantitativs un Kvalitativs Petijums par Sabiedribas Integracijas un Pilsonibas

Table 2: Views on the difficulty of naturalisation exams compared to the level expected by 'new citizens'

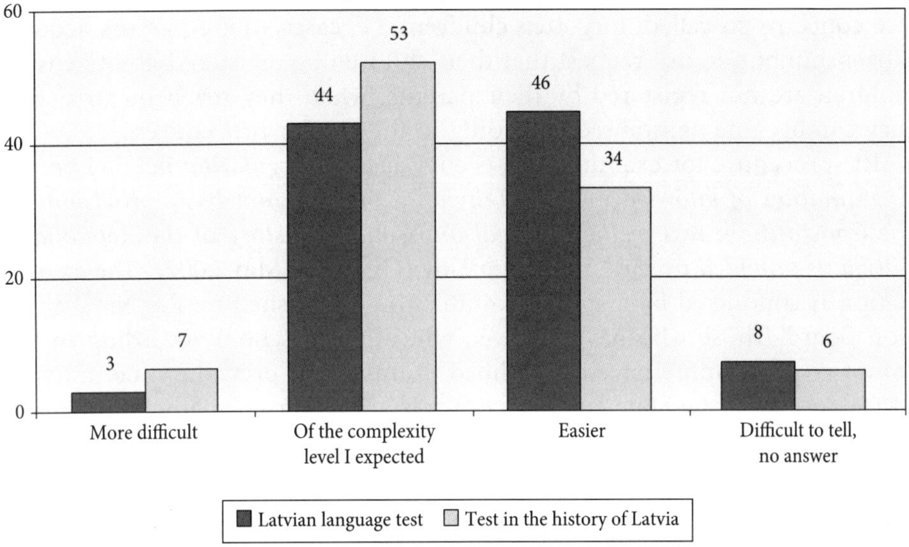

Source: Baltic Institute of Social Sciences, available at http://www.biss.soc.lv/downloads/resources/jaunpilsoni/jaunpilsoni2001.pdf, 17 January 2008.

According to *Regulation no. 234 on the State Duty for the Submission of Applications for Naturalisation* (OG no. 97, 22 June 2001 with amendments up to 2008) the State fee for naturalisation is 20 LVL (EUR 28). The fee of 3 LVL (EUR 4.3) is set for the poor and unemployed, family members from families including three or more minor children, pensioners, severely and moderately disabled persons[11] and persons attending state-accredited education establishments. Persons exempted from fees are the politically repressed (victims of Soviet repression), the very severely disabled, orphans and children who are not cared for by parents, as well as those persons who are registered in social care facilities.

The general procedure for naturalisation, including the list of documents to be submitted, is set forth in *Regulation no. 34 on the Procedure for the Acceptance and Review of Naturalisation Applications* (OG No. 32/33, 4 February 1999, with amendments up to 2006). The Regulation provides that

Aktualajiem Aspektiem' (2008), SIA 'AC Konsultacijas', is available at http://www.politika.lv/index.php?id=16923, 1 December 2008, pp. 15–16.

[11] The system in Latvia stipulates that disabled persons are grouped into three categories: very severely disabled persons, severely disabled persons and moderately disabled persons. The category for each person is established by the Commission that evaluates to what extent a person has lost his or her ability to work.

persons who become naturalised can request the granting of citizenship to their children aged under 15 by filling in the form. The problem in practice concerns so-called 'forgotten children', i.e. cases where parents acquire citizenship but do not request that their children be registered as citizens. If children are not registered by their parents, when they reach majority age they can become naturalised according to the regular procedures.

The procedure for examinations is envisaged in *Regulation no. 353 on the Examination of knowledge of the Latvian Language and basic provisions of the Constitution, text of the national anthem and history of the Republic of Latvia as provided by the Citizenship Law* (OG of 29 May 2007). The examination is conducted by a special commission established by the Naturalisation Board. Those who have received education at school according to the minority programme have a simplified examination procedure, i.e. transfer of the results of the State language exam is automatic. For others, the exam takes place within 2 months once all the documents have been received by the Naturalisation Board. If a person does not sit the exam, the next exam can take place no earlier than 6 months later but, in the event of a second or third attempt – no less than three months later.

Language exams take place in two parts. During the exam, the applicant's ability to listen and understand, to read, write and communicate on everyday topics is examined. No books, vocabularies or other supporting materials are allowed. The reading, listening and writing part takes 90 minutes. The second part – the interview – takes up to 15 minutes. Applicants over 65 years old are obliged to take only the second part. Exemptions from both the language and knowledge exams are granted to the very severely disabled, severely disabled persons with progressive mental illness and disabled persons who are deaf or deaf and dumb. Regulation no. 353 sets forth in great detail the specific groups of severely and moderately disabled persons who, because of their illness, cannot take either the written or oral part of the exams. For instance, deaf persons are exempt from the interview, the blind are exempt from written exams and so on. Other disabled persons not mentioned in the Regulation can be exempted from the exam following a decision by the Head of the Naturalisation Board. The reason for the detailed Regulation regarding the exemption of disabled persons is the heated political debates on the subject. Right-wing politicians in particular supported a restrictive exemption policy.

The examination of knowledge takes place in Latvian in writing or orally, as the applicant wishes. Supporting materials are not allowed. If an applicant chooses an oral exam she/he shall demonstrate knowledge of the national anthem and answer a number of questions. The time allocated for preparing an answer is 30 minutes and answering itself takes 15 minutes. The answers are recorded. If answers are provided in writing, the test must be completed. In this case, knowledge of the national anthem is demonstrated either orally or in writing. The time allocated for written answers is 45 minutes.

Sample language and knowledge exams are available on the internet.[12] The questions appear to be simple. For instance, the language exam in reading part consists of four parts. The first task contains a simple statement and multiple choice answers requiring identification of the correct explanation of the statement.[13] The following parts contain two simple texts and applicants are required to mark correct statements based on the texts. The fourth part includes short advertisements and the applicant is required to identify which adverts might interest persons whose profile is described in brief. The knowledge exam contains questions, including multiple choice, on who is Latvia's president, when Latvia declared independence, which country has a land border with Latvia, what is meant by freedom of expression, when referendums can be held, etc.

During the period when naturalisation sky-rocketed, i.e. in 2004 (see Table 3), about 64.3% of non-citizens interviewed responded positively to the question of whether they wanted to acquire nationality, only 19,3% indicated that they had not thought about it (Stalidzane 2004: 13). According to studies, the main motives for naturalisation are the following: the fact that the person lives in Latvia, the sense of belonging to the State, the need to increase safety, citizenship is better for children, it makes travelling easier, there are no professional restrictions and no limits on purchasing land. Latvian accession to the EU has also been mentioned as important. The indicators for loyalty among new citizens are also relatively high. Thus, 75% of new citizens would be ready to defend Latvia while about 20% still support joining the Commonwealth of Independent States.[14]

Upon accession to the EU, the question of granting EU citizenship to non-citizens was raised by left-wing political parties, such as For Human Rights in United Latvia (FHRUL). However, it was never seriously debated in ruling coalitions. Two important considerations may explain the latter: firstly, the discussion would inevitably lead to the rejection of EU membership in a referendum on joining the EU. Secondly, EU citizenship significantly reduces interest in naturalisation.

---

[12] See http://www.np.gov.lv/index.php?id=503&top=0, 5 January 2008.

[13] Applicants are required to answer multiple choice questions concerning the meanings of the phrases 'For staff only!', 'The road is slippery', 'The Post office is closed at weekends'.

[14] Baltic Institute of Social Sciences http://www.biss.soc.lv/downloads/resources/jaunpilsoni/jaunpilsoni2001.pdf, 8 January 2008.

7.3.2 *Latvian Language as Single State Language*

The Latvian language was considered a basis for building a civil society and defining a shared system of values. It has been commonly assumed that the language is 'threatened' because of Soviet Russification policies. Therefore, the Integration Programme provided for a set of actions to be taken, including compulsory teaching at schools. Although the Programme noted that Latvia respects '…the rights of ethnic minorities to cultivate and preserve their language and culture as the basis of their ethnic identity', it did not address the use of these languages and did not specify measures for their protection. This has been one of the most debated issues in Latvia and the reason behind Latvia's hesitation to ratify the Framework Convention on the Protection of Minorities.[15]

The basis for Latvian language policy is the State Language Law (1999) and the Constitution which, since 1998, has contained an Article declaring Latvian the only official language. The drafting of the Language Law was cumbersome since it took place just after the referendum on liberalisation of the Citizenship Law and right-wing political parties were making every effort to appeal to national voters. International experts from OSCE, EU and the Council of Europe were involved.

The Law includes general provisions for the use of Latvian in the public and private sectors. In addition to the Law, regulations also provide for language requirements for different professions in the public and private sectors. In the private sector, it remains the responsibility of employers to ensure adequate knowledge of the language by employees. If language inspectors establish that a person does not have sufficient knowledge to practise a certain profession, both the employee and the employer are fined. However, as a result of international law jurisprudence,[16] Latvia had to abolish the system allowing for verification of the knowledge of persons standing as candidates for elections and who already held a certificate of language proficiency.

[15] Latvia signed the Convention in 1995 but ratified it only in 2005. Upon ratification of the Convention, Latvia made declarations concerning the application of Article 10, paragraph 2 and Article 11, paragraph 3. Both provisions are related to the use of minority languages in areas inhabited by persons belonging to national minorities either traditionally or in substantial numbers. The Latvian declarations state that Latvia will apply the provisions of the Convention without prejudice to the Constitution and legislative acts governing the use of the national language effective upon accession.

[16] *Podkolzina v. Latvia*, Application no. 46726/99, Judgment by the European Court of Human Rights of 9 July 2002, Communication no. 884/1999, *Ignatane v. Latvia*, Concluding Observations of the Human Rights Committee of 31 July 2001, CCPR/C/72/D/884/1999.

The carrot/stick approach has improved language skills among Russian speakers. Russian-speakers willing to be employed in Latvia in various positions had to learn Latvian. However, practical use and further development of skills is lacking in areas inhabited by non-Latvians. Statistics and sociological surveys show that the number of Latvian speakers has been slowly increasing. Over the period from 1989 to 2000, the number of those familiar with Latvian increased by almost 20% (Djackova 2004: 15). As a result of strict language policies, awareness of the need to know Latvian has also increased. The younger generation has better language skills, the middle-aged and older generations have poorer skills (Djackova 2004: 17).

As for the methods of learning Latvian, most people in all the age groups learned Latvian at school (55%). A predominant role in learning the language has also been played by communication with colleagues at work or fellow students (23%) and informal or social communication (19%). Only about 17% of those interviewed have taken Latvian language courses and 10% learned Latvian through self- education (Djackova 2004: 22).

The learning of Latvian has been extensively supported by national institutions and international donors. The major donors were the UNDP, EU, OSCE, the USA, Sweden and Norway. The European Union has been particularly active as well. For instance, the National Agency for Latvian Language Training (NALLT) was financed in large part by both EU and NATO Member states (total amount approximately EUR 10 million) and the EU PHARE Programme (total allocation during 1996–2002, EUR 5 million) (Lerhis & Kudors 2008: 18). Language courses were provided for both candidates for naturalisation and the general public, mainly the unemployed and job-seekers. The main institutions involved in these processes were the National Programme for Latvian Language Training, the Naturalisation Board and the Fund for the Integration of Society. Although the donations have been impressive and courses well attended, the overall numbers are not significant. For instance, the courses within the National Programme during the period 1996–2002 were attended by 50,000 people (12% of those whose native language is not Latvian) (Djackova 2004: 46, 49, 54).

The emphasis on the Latvian language has led to the mushrooming of institutions with overlapping competencies, such as the State Language Centre, the National Programme for Latvian Language Training, the President's State Language Committee and the State Language Agency. However, the practical results in promoting the use of Latvian still remain dependent rather on State language inspection than on a willingness to speak Latvian or to accept it as a 'shared value'.

Uniform information space is challenged by the globalisation process and modern technologies (satellite television, the internet, etc.), where the

Russian language information environment in Latvia has become largely self-sufficient and, in terms of size, has long outgrown the corresponding information environment in the Latvian language. It also seems that the influence of the Russian mass media has been overlooked over the years. A network of Russian mass media is being employed to discredit Latvia systematically by covering events in the Baltics in line with the Kremlin's interpretation (Lerhis, Kudors 2008: 57).[17] In June 2007 President Putin signed a decree establishing the governmental NGO *Russkiy Mir Foundation*, for the purpose of 'promoting the Russian language as Russia's national heritage and a significant aspect of Russian and world culture, and supporting Russian language teaching programmes abroad.'

Therefore it can be concluded that the status of Latvian as the single official language has been strengthened over the years and the general level of knowledge has increased. However, the problem remains that it is still not practised on a daily basis in many sectors. In addition Russian information space decreases the motivation for those who are not native speakers to practise Latvian.

7.3.3 *Education Reform*

Since Latvia regained its independence, the education system in Latvia has undergone constant changes. As already noted above, until the mid-1990s, two different school systems – Russian and Latvian – existed in Latvia, each with its own curriculum. When the new Language Law came into force, requiring knowledge of Latvian for different posts, it was acknowledged that the education system has to be adjusted so that all graduates have equal opportunities on the labour market.

Since 1996, only one subject had been taught in Latvian at elementary school level, two subjects in primary school but, at secondary school, three subjects were taught in Latvian in Russian schools. In 1999 bilingual education was introduced in primary schools, when each educational institution providing education in the Russian language chose one of the four ethnic minority primary education models developed by the Ministry of Education

[17] This network covers the Russian State Federal television channels *Rossija* and *Pervij kanal* (the former ORT) to the 'export versions', *RTR-Planeta* and *Pervij Baltijskij kanal*, which provide broad coverage of the activities of pro-Moscow forces in Latvia. The announcements and proclamations of the Ministry of Foreign Affairs of the Russian Federation and other Russian State institutions are published via the official news agencies, *ITAR-TASS* and *Interfax*, and routinely reprinted in Latvia by Russian-language newspapers, *Chas* and *Vesti Segodnya*.

and Science. The bilingual curriculum had to be implemented in all national minority primary schools by the academic year 2002–2003. Policy-makers believed that if the Latvian language was taught only as a subject area, students would never start speaking Latvian. They stressed that the Latvian language is the basis for Latvian statehood (Klava, Šupule & Zepa 2004: 25).

After long political debates and public involvement, further changes were introduced in the Education Law of February 2004. The new system envisaged that 40% of the study time instruction should be in the minority language and 60% (or 5 subjects) in Latvian. This increase was phased, starting with 10th grade in 2004 and followed by 11th grade in 2005 and 12th grade in 2006.[18] Primary schools had to continue with the bilingual curriculum. Out of 1009 general education schools, only 149 had to implement the gradual transfer to 60% of teaching in Latvian in 2004 (Kristovska & Visocka 2004: 35). In order to carry out the reform, substantial funds were allocated by the National Programme of Latvian Language Training and the Foundation for the Integration of Society.[19]

The representatives of minority schools, students and their parents expressed dissatisfaction with the course of the reform and demanded its repeal (Dedze, Heyneman, Austers & Lune 2004: 12). Headmasters argued that neither are teachers ready for reform nor are there sufficient teaching materials. About 46% of student parents were against the reform and only 26% supported it; 24% expressed limited support (Kristovska & Visocka 2004: 40). Numerous demonstrations took place. A special organisation – the Headquarters for the Protection of Russian Schools – was established, although not registered, and it even made threats of violence if the reform continued.

Despite initial difficulties, certain positive tendencies emerged. It has been observed that, since the reform, the percentage of graduates entering higher education establishments has increased. Previously, more non-Latvians ended up in vocational training (Kristovska & Visocka 2004: 43). Moreover, increasing numbers of non-Latvians choose to acquire an education in Latvian schools. According to the Ministry of Foreign Affairs, in the academic

---

[18] Children in Latvia start school at age 7, in grade 1. Compulsory education continues for 9 years, ending in grade 9, at age 16. The option is available to continue into the final three grades (10–12) from ages 16 to 18/19. The same institution provides both primary and secondary education.

[19] The National Programme of Latvian Language Training has spent almost €6.5 million. The Society Integration Foundation financed 18 projects worth approx. €50,000 from the State budget in 2003, 9 projects worth EUR 40,000 in 2004 and 5 projects worth €7,000 in 2005.

year 2006–2007 about 73.5% of first-graders began their studies in Latvian schools.[20]

Despite these positive tendencies, several problems which might have affected the general success of the integration policy have to be mentioned. Firstly, during the planning of the reform, the opinions of minority representatives and teachers were neglected. This was predominantly an elite-driven process. Secondly, inadequate communication took place with society in general and the willingness to find a compromise solution acceptable to all was lacking. Policy-makers have often demonstrated that education reform is complete at the moment the decision is made and no further monitoring is required. Thirdly, the overall objectives of the reform were not explained. The policy-makers declared that the aim of the reform was the integration of society and increased competitiveness of minority school graduates on the labour market. However, the minority representatives remained convinced that the reform had a hidden agenda, which will eventually lead to assimilation (Dedze et al. 2004: 13). This approach has led to conflict, the marginalisation of minority groups and general scepticism about integration.

7.4 *Current Discussions on Integration*

Since joining the EU and NATO, no further criteria have to be fulfilled and Latvian policy-makers are relaxed in their attitude towards integration. The possible negative effects of the lack of monitoring mechanisms after enlargement were mentioned by minority rights experts (Packer 1999). The feeling of self-sufficiency of being a Member State of major organisations tends to overshadow local integration problems. However, the problems have not disappeared. They can be summarised as follows. Firstly, naturalisation data show that the process has almost stopped. Secondly, the long-term citizenship policy is unclear. Thirdly, there is no reasoned position concerning the arrival of new immigrants.

7.4.1 *Stagnating Naturalisation Numbers*

Firstly, the naturalisation statistics are pessimistic. The number of applications for naturalisation is steadily decreasing.

---

[20] Ministry of Foreign Affairs of the Republic of Latvia. Minority Education in Latvia 27 July 2007. Available at http://www.mfa.gov.lv/en/policy/4641/4642/4643/?print=on, 18 January 2008.

Table 3: Number of people acquiring citizenship by naturalisation

Year	Persons applying for naturalisation	Naturalised persons
1995	4,543	984
1996	2,627	3,016
1997	3,075	2,992
1998	5,608	4,439
1999	15,183	12,427
2000	10,692	14,900
2001	8,672	10,637
2002	8,370	9,844
2003	11,268	10,049
2004	21,297	16,064
2005	19,807	19,736
2006	10,581	16,439
2007	3,308	6,826
2008 (October)	2,271	2,622
Total	127,302	130,408

Source: Naturalisation Board, www.np.gov.lv, 20 December 2008

In 2004, the Minister for Integration, together with the Minister for Children and Family Affairs, conducted an information campaign, sending information to the parents of children who were eligible to become citizens as a result of the 1998 amendments to the Citizenship Law, i.e. children born after 21 August 1991 to parents who are stateless or non-citizens. They can be registered as citizens if the parents submit an application on their behalf. As a result of the campaign, an increase in the number of applications occurred, i.e. the number of applications received during 2004 was equal to the numbers received from 1998–2004. A total of 13,740 children have been naturalised, together with their parents, while 7728 children acquired citizenship pursuant to amendments to the Citizenship Law in 1998, allowing parents to submit an application to naturalise their children.[21] Experts have suggested replacing the current system with the automatic registration as nationals of children born to parents who are stateless or non-citizens.

According to estimates by the Naturalisation Board, about 130,000 people will remain non-citizens for the rest of their lives (National News Agency LETA: 1 February 2005). Recent opinion polls suggest that only 24% are planning to apply for citizenship while 48% admit that they will not apply.

[21] See statistics of the Naturalisation Board, available at http://www.np.gov.lv/lv/faili_lv/lpp1_latv.pdf, 2 March 2009.

In general, there is lack of interest in applying for Latvian citizenship because non-citizens feel comfortable on an everyday basis and the prestige of Latvian citizenship is low. Thus, only 44% of respondents consider Latvian citizenship as prestigious. In comparison with 2000 the changes are insignificant.[22] In most cases, non-citizens mention that they lack the motivation to acquire citizenship (44% of those unwilling acquire citizenship). Others mention the lack of time (29%), insufficient knowledge of the language (37%), insufficient knowledge of history (24%). This is worrisome because simplified exams, different courses and language policy have not yielded adequate results.

Other surveys reflect similar concerns. For instance, a survey conducted in schools among teachers and students concludes that non-citizens are unwilling to naturalise because they associate the process of naturalisation with assimilation. Students often perceive Latvia as a territory that is ethnically populated by Latvians. Accordingly, they do not see Latvia as a democratic society, held together on the basis of the fundamental principles of the Constitution. In this respect, they find it difficult to identify the benefits and significance of citizenship (National News Agency LETA, 19 November 2008).

The pass-rates for the naturalisation exams are also declining. During 2004 and 2005, when naturalisation reached its peak, the percentage of those who failed the knowledge test was 3.7% and 4.8% respectively, but by 2007 and 2008 those figures had already reached 10.4% and 17.8%. The results for the language exam are similar. During 2004 and 2005, the percentage of those failing was 10% and 16% respectively then, for 2007 and 2008, the failures amount to 21% and almost 28%.

Some of the answers suggest that non-citizens feel marginalised. Those who are not planning to apply for citizenship have responded that they see naturalisation as humiliation (21%) and participation in elections is not important (21%). They do not feel that they belong to Latvia (17%).[23] At the same time, 86% of non-citizens want their children to be Latvian citizens.[24] This suggests that non-citizens see their future in Latvia rather than in any other state.

Certain non-citizens are willing to maintain closer ties with Russia. They mention that loss of the status will be an obstacle for travel to Russia (10%). On 18 June 2008 Russia adopted a decision to facilitate the procedure for

---

[22] Public opinion survey, 'Kvantitativs un Kvalitativs Petijums par Sabiedribas Integracijas un Pilsonibas Aktualajiem Aspektiem' (2008), SIA 'AC Konsultacijas', available at http://www.politika.lv/ index.php?id=16923, 1 December, 2008, p. 20.

[23] *Ibid.*, p. 21.

[24] *Ibid.*, p. 22.

the entry of non-citizens from Latvia and Estonia to Russia. The President of Russia, Dmitry Medvedev, has signed a decree that establishes the procedure for entering Russia for former Soviet citizens currently living in Latvia, who have not obtained another country's citizenship. These persons will be allowed to travel to Russia without a visa and will only need to provide a valid travel document – a non-citizen passport in the case of Latvia. The same applies to the minor children of those persons (Russian national news agency RIA NOVOSTI, 18 June 2008). In the opinion of politicians, Russia creates obstacles to Latvian attempts to encourage naturalisation by making the status of non-citizen more attractive. Moreover, they have visa-free travel within the EU on the basis of Regulation 1932/2006/EC.

In general, it can be argued that naturalisation numbers dropped because those who were willing to acquire Latvian citizenship did so by 2004 or 2005. However, the high number of non-citizens is not satisfactory and Latvia will have to persuade people to naturalise, all the more so in view of the ever-expanding Compatriot policies pursued by Russia.

7.4.2 *Long-term Citizenship Policy*

Secondly, a number of issues remain unresolved in relation to citizenship policy. Firstly, there is an idea to liberalise the policy of dual citizenship. The strict policy of dual citizenship has been criticised by Latvians who migrated to other EU Member States after enlargement. Estimates are that about 86,000 Latvian citizens left Latvia and numbers are steadily growing (Indans, Kruma 2007: 165). Moreover, Latvia has Europe's lowest birth rates and depopulation continues. The Latvian government has established a working group that is due to formulate proposals for regulation. However, no tentative results have emerged so far. Other proposals are related to national security considerations in cases involving terrorists and persons working in the security services of other states. However, these proposals have not been specific enough and the debate remains general.

7.4.3 *The Position of New Immigrants*

In relation to the third issue, that is the integration of new migrants, the government's policies are controversial. Although particular decisions on the liberalisation of procedures to attract foreign workers have been adopted, the overall approach remains unclear. Both Latvians and non-Latvians are conservative regarding an open immigration policy. The experts explain this as a legacy from Soviet times, a feeling of insecurity about identity and a fear of competition leading to unemployment. According to surveys, around 32% of Latvians and 39% of non-Latvians consider that an increase in immigration will exacerbate ethnic tensions among representatives of different nationalities: Latvian feelings are mainly associated with historic experiences, while non-Latvians, especially non citizens (30%) fear losing their jobs and becoming socially alienated (Indans 2004: 34).

The lack of interest in addressing the problem of the integration of third-country nationals can be explained by the low numbers of immigrants arriving so far. The Latvian labour market remains relatively closed to foreign workers from outside the EU and it is unattractive to workers from the EU. The main reasons for low interest are low salaries, difficulties with integration and learning the language. According to data from the Office of Citizenship and Migration Affairs (OCMA), the number of residence permits increased slowly – from 3074 temporary residence permits in 1995 to 9317 in 2006 and from 612 permanent residence permits in 1995 to 10,267 in 2006. Moreover, most permanent residence holders are former non-citizens who have become Russian citizens. The numbers of foreign nationals arriving for work are about 1000–2000 annually, most of them coming from Russia and Ukraine.[25]

At the same time, Latvia has been liberal in transposing the relevant EU Directives, i.e. Directive 2003/109/EC on long-term resident status and Directive 2003/86/EC on the right to family reunification. The only discussions which caused controversies were related to non-citizens and their access to the status of long-term resident.

On 22 June 2006 Parliament adopted the *Law on EC Long-Term Resident Status*.[26] The only integration requirement for acquisition of the status that is included in the Law is knowledge of the Latvian language. The reasons for introducing it were the references to strict policies by some EU Member

[25] Russian citizens hold 21,777 of permanent residence permits while the closest number of Lithuanian citizens account for only 1,773 permits. Most job offers from employers were submitted for Ukrainian nationals – 961 (in 2006–275), Moldavians – 847 (in 2006–296), Uzbekistanis – 343 (in 2006–100), Byelorussians – 226 (in 2006 – 91), Russians 198 (in 2006–131) and Armenians – 90 (in 2006–45). See National News Agency LETA, 24 January 2008.

[26] OG no.107 07.07.2006. The Law had already been adopted on 25 May 2006. However, the President refused to sign the law because non-citizens were not singled out as a specific group. According to the Law, they will have to prove continuous and legal residence in Latvia as well as passing the language test. See *Prezidente liek parskaūt EK pastaviga iedzivotaja statusa likumu* [President requests review of EC long-term resident status law] www.apollo.lv, 31 May 2006. After repeated consideration, the Parliament adopted the law without amendments proposed by the President and left-wing parties. See *Saeima nemaina likumu par Eiropas Kopienas pastaviga iedzivotaja statusu Latvija* [Parliament does not change the Law on EC long-term resident status in Latvia], www.apollo.lv, 22 June 2006.

States as well as the Latvian language policy. The specific requirements of proficiency in Latvian are set by the Cabinet of Ministers Regulations. No further amendments were made in related laws. In this very context, Latvian policy can be considered liberal.

In order to qualify for a permanent residence permit, a foreigner shall demonstrate proficiency in Latvian corresponding to level 1B in accordance with the Regulations.[27] Level 1B requires basic knowledge of the Latvian language. State fees to be paid for the examination are LVL 10 (EUR 14). In addition, the Regulation provides that a certificate of primary or secondary education attesting that the centralised exam in the Latvian language, level E, is adequate to prove proficiency in Latvian at the required lowest (B) level.[28] A certificate demonstrating a knowledge of Latvian at the respective level issued in another country will be considered valid. A foreigner taking the exam shall submit valid travel documents and a check for payment of the state fees. The institutions involved in evaluating the adequacy of language proficiency are the OCMA and the Centre for the Content of Education and Examinations. The exam consists of both written and oral parts. Therefore, while the overall approach to immigration is strict and society is generally hesitant in accepting new immigrants, Latvia has not used tools, as the other EU Member States have, to adopt stringent immigration requirements in terms of integration exams and other conditions.

These confusing policies can be explained by the fragmented institutional setup for managing immigration and integration affairs. As with language policy, too many institutions are involved, but with limited co-ordination.

[27] On 4 April 2006 the Cabinet of Ministers adopted Regulation no. 252 on the necessary level of knowledge of the official language and the procedure for verification of the command of language proficiency, as well as verification procedures for the documents attesting national language proficiency for foreigners who are entitled to apply for a permanent residence permit (OG no. 57, 7 April 2006 with amendments, to Regulation no. 995, 12 December 2006, OG no. 200, 15 December 2006). Regulation of the Cabinet of Ministers no. 252 and no. 296 on the necessary knowledge of Latvian for the performance of professional duties. (See also Regulation no. 109 on state fees for the examination of proficiency in the national language for foreigners and the procedure for payment of state fees, 13 February 2007, OG no. 28, 16 February 2007).

[28] The Latvian system is compared to grades A-F at school, where A is the highest level (III B) and F is the lowest (I A). It is divided into three categories, each of which has its A and B levels (IA, IB, IIA, II B, IIIA, IIIB). Level I B can be compared to level A 2 of the Common Framework of Reference of the Council of Europe. For further details, see the home page of the Centre for Curriculum Development and Examinations, http://isec.gov.lv/valval/index.shtml, 26 February 2009. For an overview of the levels of language proficiency in the Common Framework of Reference, please see annex 1.

Since the adoption of the Integration Programme, special units have been created within both the Ministry of Justice and the Ministry of Education and Science, which were later concentrated into the Special Assignment Secretariat for the Integration of Society. At the same time, the problems of non-citizens concerned the competences of the Ministry of the Interior and the Ministry of Welfare. The Secretariat could not resolve the problems occurring in spheres outside its competence and its performance had its ups and downs. The Secretariat played an important role during the education reform and co-ordinated the campaign inviting non-citizen parents to register their children as Latvian citizens, as well as during the ratification of the Framework Convention on the Protection of National Minorities.

However, in recent years the Secretariat has prioritised other issues, unrelated to naturalisation and integration. The documents and policies have been weak and vague. On 30 November 2007 the Secretariat released a document entitled, 'Main Trends in the Policy of the Integration of Society 2008–2018'. The document was too general to make any assumptions about priorities or plans for action. During 2008 the Secretariat acknowledged that it is incapable of drafting a programme and sub-contracted a private PR agency to do the job.

At the beginning of 2009 the Secretariat was merged with the Ministry for Children and Family Affairs, which might lead to the further marginalisation of integration issues on Latvia's political agenda. Moreover, it has been decided that, for different initiatives in the sphere of integration, only EUR 360,000 will be allocated during 2009 (National News Agency LETA, 22 January 2009). As a positive sign, the decision by the President to renew the work of the Consultative Minority Council should be mentioned. However, taking into account the marginal role of the Council during the Presidency of Guntis Ulmanis, the practical results of this decision are cautiously anticipated.

7.4.4 *Obstacles to the Integration of Society*

Latvia in general still preserves certain characteristics of a parochial society. Participation in public life by both citizens and non-citizens is low.[29] This has allowed policy-makers to implement integration policy as a 'one-direction' process, where only those belonging to minority groups are obliged to

---

[29] In an opinion poll, only 12% of respondents admitted that they have participated in demonstrations and 11% in NGOs. Public opinion survey, 'Kvantitativs un Kvalitativs Petijums par Sabiedribas Integracijas un Pilsonibas Aktualajiem Aspektiem' (2008), SIA 'AC Konsultacijas', available at http://www.politika.lv/index.php?id=16923, 1 December, 2008, p. 31.

integrate, while the State remains passive. Nils Muižnieks has argued that, since 2001, Latvia has not moved any closer to achieving the objectives of the Integration Programme, i.e. the consolidation of personal values and the promotion of the sense of belonging to Latvia (Muižnieks 2006a: 5).

In a recent public opinion poll, people responded that the main dividing factor in society is related to social and financial issues (47%). In second place is the factor closely linked to integration, i.e. language (35%). Language determines the information space in Latvia. Therefore, it is not surprising that a large group of people see divisions in different dialogues in the information space. For instance, pronouncements from left-wing and right-wing parties (31%), the mass media (18%) and foreign propaganda (17%) are often mentioned as dividing factors.[30] Similarly, other studies mention different perceptions of history, the conservative and pro-Latvian political elite, a divided mass media and the inefficient institutional setup (Apine, Boldane, Dribins, Gaugere, Šnitnikovs, & Vebers 2006).

Media experts conducted a two-year monitoring operation of the mass media, speeches by MPs and legislative initiatives. Their conclusion is that there a consistent division exists between the Latvian and Russian information space. While Latvians portray themselves as a threatened nation which has endured much suffering, Russians stress insult and discrimination (Golubeva, Rožukalne, Kažoka, Curika, Arnesta, Herca, Buševa, Jermaks & Merdana 2008, Rožukalne 2008). Another study on the different perceptions of history in schools showed that only 5% of Russian-speaking students agree that Latvia was occupied. At the same time, 62% of Latvian-speakers agree with this statement. Only 2% of Russian speakers want to study Latvian history and 11% of them would prefer to study Russia's history. Similar divided results were also given concerning the responsibility of Russia for the occupation, the general attitude towards 'Soviet times' and the like (National News Agency LETA, 6 February 2009). These results are worrisome, since the information space remains divided. History in turn forms the basis for understanding Latvian statehood and the continuity thesis. Serious division in the younger generation leads to the conclusion that N. Muižnieks was right in his critique of Latvian integration policy.

The central problem of integration in Latvia has been combining the idea of the national state based on elements of republican and communitarian democracy with a multi-cultural society not necessarily sharing the same values as the titular nation. Latvians want a unitary, national state with one official language, inhabited by citizens who share the same identity and values.

[30] Public opinion survey, p. 30.

Non-citizens see it mostly as a territory in which they reside and that grants them certain rights. They feel self-sufficient by living in their own information space without much motivation to become involved in political affairs of the state.

7.5 *Conclusion*

Latvia has become 'lost in translating' the model of a republican democracy as it existed in 1920s into the more liberal model required for society as it now exists in Latvia. When drafting the integration programme, Latvia disregarded the fact that birth and death rates were the lowest among EU Member States. The elite-driven one-direction process has led to the situation where some non-citizens feel marginalised and the risk of long-term political alienation is present. The public information space sustained by Russia has facilitated these negative processes.

Currently, Europe is developing its approaches to integration and has already faced initial difficulties in defining the term and its scope. For instance, some question who should be the targets of integration – immigrants or ethnic minorities and, if immigrants, should they be regarded as one group.[31] These discussions do not seem relevant since the consequences of failing to implement integration policy will be felt irrespective of strict definitions and groupings.

The Latvian lesson allows us to draw several conclusions. Firstly, an effective and permanent integration policy is required, which should be adjusted to address the needs of society at a specific time. As noted in the Integration Handbook, integration is a two-way process, in which close partnerships exist between different levels of government and non-governmental actors.[32] What is missing, however, is the need not only to ensure economic, socio-cultural and civic needs, but also to re-think the possibilities of political participation.

Nowadays, integration policy has to be based on values which go beyond national confines and are rooted in trans-national and multi-cultural contexts. This means that conservative democracies have to liberalise. Globalisation poses another challenge to the success of the integration policy. According

---

[31] *Integration Handbook for policy-makers and practitioners*, Directorate-General for Justice, Freedom and Security, November 2004, p. 8.

[32] *Ibid.*, p. 9.

to Latvian experience, integration becomes even more difficult if it requires changes in value perceptions, adaptation to the processes of global communication, the mass media and propaganda from non-democratic regimes. Although education and integration policies can provide a counter-balance, the ethnic, cultural and patriotic sense of belonging as well as cross-border information exchange should be taken more seriously by decision-makers.

The role of the EU in these processes should be stronger. Latvian experience shows that, owing to various internal political factors, states are unwilling to compromise their internal political agendas for economic and modern-day realities without external pressure. Collective goals encourage trade-offs between benefits and costs within a community in order to produce some overall benefit for the community as a whole (Dworkin 1977: 91). The goals of the EU include sustainable development of economic activities, the promotion of values and the well-being of its people. This requires the EU to define its approach not only by sharing good practices, but also by carefully analysing failures. Although integration is still predominantly a national question, the EU should aim to find ways to intervene and to inject European values into national policies. In order to achieve the goals of the EU, Europe has to think about a more open and attractive market by integrating firstly those who are second-generation immigrants and, secondly, those target groups Europe is willing to attract. The EU has to be made aware that to preserve its role on the global market it has to adjust and to compete for people on the global market. Its Member States, although unwilling to admit it, are no longer in a position to impose their strict republican rules on the global community of individuals striving for better living conditions.

Bibliography

Apine, I., I. Boldane, L. Dribins, K. Gaugere, A. Šnitnikovs, & E. Vebers, *Pretestiba sabiedribas integracijai: celoni un parvarešanas iespejas (etnicitates, valsts un pilsoniskas sabiedribas mijiedarbibas analize)*, Latvijas universitates Filozofijas un sociologijas instituts, LU agentura 2006, available at http://www.politika.lv/index.php?id=11551, 2 February 2008.

Blatter, J.K., *Dual Citizenship and Democracy*, Working Paper Series 'Global Governance and Democracy', Faculty of Humanities and Social Sciences Institute of Political Science, Universität Luzern, WP 01, 2008, available at http://www.unilu. ch/eng/workingpapers_287648 .aspx, 29 December 2008.

Dedze, I., S. Heyneman, I. Austers & E. Lune, *Education Reforms in Latvia: Underpinning Integration and Prosperity. Annual Report on Education. 2003/2004*. Riga: Providus Centre for Public Policy 2004.

Djackova, S., *Latvian language proficiency and the integration of society*, 2008, available at http://www.politika.lv/print.php?id=3989, 2 February 2008.

Dworkin, R., *Taking Rights Seriously*, London: Duckworth 1977.
Golubeva, M., A. Rožukalne, I. Kažoka, L. Curika, I. Arnesta, M. Herca, T. Buševa, M. Jermaks & L. Merdana, *Izaicinajumi pilsoniskajai lidzdalibai, 2008, gada gala zinojums*, Sabiedriskas politikas centrs Providus, Open Society Institute 2008, available at http://www.politika.lv/index.php?id=17059, 6 February 2009.
Indans, I., *Effects of the Immigration on Ethnic Relations in Latvia*, Riga: Institute of International Affairs and Fr. Ebert Foundation 2004.
Indans I. & K. Kruma, Vienoti daudzveidiba: imigracija un integracija (United in Diversity: Immigration and Integration), in: *Savejie un Svešie. Sabiedribas Radikalizacijas Tendences Latvija, Eiropa un Pasaule (Belonging and Remaining Outside. Tendencies of Radicalization of Society: Latvia, Europe and the World)*, Zinatniski petnieciskie raksti 6(16), Zinatne 2007, pp. 149–176.
Kalvaitis, R., Citizenship and national identity in the Baltic States, *Boston University International Law Journal*, 16, 1998, pp. 231–271.
Kļava, E., I. Šupule & B. Zepa, Dual-Stream Schools – Assessment of an Example of Bilingual Education, in: I. Dedze, S. Heyneman, I. Austers & E. Lune (eds.), *Education Reforms in Latvia: Underpinning Integration and Prosperity. Annual Report on Education. 2003/2004*, Riga: Providus Centre for Public Policy 2004, pp. 22–34.
Kristovska, I. & A. Visocka, Minority Schools and the Education Reform of 2004, in: I. Dedze, S. Heyneman, I. Austers & E. Lune (eds.), *Education Reforms in Latvia: Underpinning Integration and Prosperity. Annual Report on Education 2003/2004*, Riga: Providus Centre for Public Policy 2004, pp. 34–45.
Kruma, K., 'Stocktaking of EU Pre-Accession Monitoring Process, Citizenship Issues and Non-Citizens in Estonia and Latvia: a Litmus Test for European Union Human Rights Policy', *Baltic Yearbook of International Law*, Vol. 4, 2004, pp. 33–53.
Kruma, K., Chapter 2: Checks and balances in Latvian nationality policies: National agendas and international frameworks, in R. Bauböck, B. Perchinig & W. Sievers, (eds), *Citizenship Policies in the New Europe*, IMISCOE Research, Amsterdam: Amsterdam University Press 2007, pp. 63–88.
Lerhis, A. & A. Kudors, *Outside Influence on the Ethnic Integration Process in Latvia*, 2nd ed., Centre for East European Political Studies 2008.
Muižnieks, N. (ed.), *Latvian-Russian Relations: Domestic and International Dimensions*, Riga: LU Apgads and Baltijas Socialo zinatnu instituts, Integracijas prakse un perspektivas, Riga: BSZI 2006, available at http://www.politika.lv/index.php?f =1069, 12 June 2008.
Muižnieks, N., Russian Foreign Policy Towards 'Compatriots' in Latvia, in: Muižnieks, N. (ed.), *Latvian-Russian Relations: Domestic and International Dimensions*, Riga: LU Apgads and Baltijas Socialo zinatnu instituts, Integracijas prakse un perspektivas, Riga: BSZI 2006, available at http://www.politika.lv/index.php?f =1069, 12 June 2008, pp. 119–130.
Packer, J., 'Report from the EU Human Rights Forum, 30.11–01.12.1999', quoted after E.G. Heidbreder, & L. Carrasco, *Assessing the Assessment. A Review on the Application Criterion Minority Protection by the European Commission*, Working Paper No. 2003/W/4, Maastricht: European Institute of Public Administration 2003, p. 23.
Rožukalne, A., *Sarunas ar spogulattelu*, available at public policy portal http://www. politika.lv/index.php?id=17047, 28 January 2009.
Sakss, N., Minutes of Seminar, 'Integration of Society – experience and problems', Dikli 18–19 March, 2004, available at http://www.np.gov.lv/lv/faili_lv/Sabiedribas_integracija_protokols.pdf, 5 January 2009.

Stalidzane, I. (2004), Minutes of Seminar, 'Integration of Society – experience and problems', Dikli 18–19 March 2004, available at http://www.np.gov.lv/lv/faili_lv/ Seminars-protokols1 .doc, 4 February, 2008

Thiele, C., *The Criterion of Citizenship for Minorities: The Example of Estonia*, ECMI Working Paper 5, 1999.

Ziemele, I., *State Continuity and Nationality in the Baltic States: International and Constitutional Law Issues*, Cambridge: Cambridge Faculty of Law 1998.

Ziemele, I., State Continuity, Human Rights and Nationality in the Baltic States, in: T. Jundzis (ed.) *The Baltic States at Historical Crossroads*, 2nd ed., Riga: Academy of Sciences of Latvia 2001.

Ziemele, I. & K. Kruma, Eiropas Savienibas pilsoniba un Latvijas nepilsoni, *Latvijas Vestnesis, Jurista Vards*, No. 33, 2003.

Ziemele, I., *State Continuity and Nationality: The Baltic States and Russia. Past, Present and Future as Defined by International Law*, Leiden: Martinus Nijhoff Publishers 2005.

Chapter 8

Language and Integration Requirements in Belgium: Discordances Between the Flemish Policy of 'Inburgering' and the Federal Legislators' View(s) on the Integration of Newcomers and Migrants

*Marie-Claire Foblets & Zeynep Yanasmayan**

8.1 *Introduction*

Citizenship, a long-neglected term, has made an astonishing return to the political agenda of European States. At a time when its demise had been predicted by some (Soysal 1994; Sassen 1996), national citizenship has risen from the ashes and has now assumed a renewed role in the social cohesion of society. Most significantly, it has come to be seen as *the* most appropriate response to the challenge of cultural and ethnic diversity in European States. The frequency of amendments made to nationality legislations in recent decades clearly reveals the importance of this mechanism.[1]

A State's policy of inclusion (or integration) is closely correlated with its configuration of citizenship (Geddes 2003: 23). The nexus between these issues has usually been perceived as a spectrum from assimilation to multiculturalism, with two countries at the two extremes, France and Great Britain respectively. Assimilation by definition implies a process of becoming the 'same', hence absorption of immigrants into the host society's culture.[2]

* Marie-Claire Foblets is Professor of Law and Anthropology at the Universities of Leuven (Louvain), Brussels and Antwerp. Zeynep Yanasmayan is a PhD candidate at the Faculty of Social Sciences of the Catholic University of Leuven (KUL).

[1] See, for instance, Bauböck, Ersbøll, Groenendijk & Waldrauch 2006b for a genealogy of nationality legislations in the EU-15.

[2] Brubaker (2003) distinguishes between transitive and intransitive meanings of assimilation. For him, only the former entails forced adaptation and a uniform end result. See further Brubaker, 2003: 21.

Van Oers, Ersbøll and Kostakopoulou, A Re-definition of Belonging?, pp. 271–305.

It not only relies on an idealised homogenous society prior to immigration, but it also promotes a utopian end result where individuals become undistinguishable. Multiculturalism, on the other hand, takes the recognition of 'difference' as its departure point. 'Multicultural politics' is more than a simple acknowledgement of cultural diversity; rather it is an attempt to address the real inequalities that prevail despite the principle of formal equality. Evidently, these are typological models representing the two extremes; in practice it is barely possible to observe them in their pure forms in the current Nation State configuration. Hence, Joppke & Morawska distinguish between *de facto* and official multiculturalism, where the former stands for the mere recognition of cultural diversity that is regarded as occurring in most liberal European States and the latter a State engagement to maintain this (Joppke & Morawska 2003: 10). Nevertheless, over time it has become practically impossible to categorise States' policies under one heading since even the most traditional States are borrowing concepts from others. Within this context, Koopmans *et al.* have offered one of the most elaborate typologies of citizenship, based on the juxtaposition of two axes: ethnic/territorial and cultural monist/pluralist. Not only has this typology added another dimension to the well-known categorisation, but it also allows for moves among the axes because it conceives of citizenship not in the static categories of typological models, but as a conceptual space (Koopmans, Statham, Giugni & Passy 2005: 9).

Conceiving of citizenship as a conceptual space is very useful when looking at some broader patterns of change and points of convergence in a contemporary setting. Joppke, for instance, in analysing the move on the part of most liberal States toward introducing civic integration courses and tests for newcomers, concludes that convergence is evident with respect to the general direction, although some variation in implementation may be present (Joppke 2007: 1). It is true that the so-called 'civic integration' measures have become a widely-known phenomenon throughout Europe and Belgium has also participated in this broader trend. Since 2004, Flanders has required 'its' newcomers to follow a citizenship trajectory and to attend integration courses. The aim of this paper is to identify the position of Belgium in the delicate and overwhelming debate regarding civic integration.[3] We argue that, despite the adoption of similar integration policies, Belgium stands out as a particular example that may provide new insights into the debate.

The first section of this chapter starts with an overview of the federal system in Belgium. It is important to clarify the features of the system in order

---

[3] See below, Section IV.

to pinpoint competences concerning issues of immigration and integration. Then, the policies and instruments at federal and regional levels respectively are presented. The second section kicks off the discussion of the Flemish policy of mandatory civic integration, known as *inburgering.*[4] While the first sub-section introduces the documents and the main elements of the policy, the second sub-section explains the political and public debate prior to their adoption. The last sub-section draws attention to the problems in and effects of the implementation of *inburgering*. Lastly, the final section seeks to display how the Belgian federal system, which has its limitations, can at the same time shed new light on our understanding of integration policy.

8.2 *The Belgian Case*

Belgium is a federal State made up of three regions (the Flemish Region, the Brussels-Capital Region and the Walloon Region), and three linguistic communities (the Flemish Community, the French-speaking Community and the German-speaking Community). A very complex system of power sharing exists between the different levels of governance. To put it very simply, the federal government is in charge of affairs that concern all residents of Belgium (e.g. defence and justice), the communities have competence for matters more directly relating to the people they comprise (e.g. education, health and culture) and, finally, the regions have power over territorial or spatial (Loobuyck & Jacobs 2006: 113) issues. Against this background, it is important to ask where the competences lie on issues concerning immigration and integration.

Since Belgium does not have a single government body dealing with every issue, related topics are distributed among different levels according to their scope. Territorial admission is considered an issue of mutual concern, independent of one's linguistic or cultural background. Hence, entry onto Belgian soil is mainly regulated at the federal level[5] and, to some extent, by international regulations.[6] While no provision of the Belgian Constitution

---

[4] We prefer to keep the word in the original language since it implies more than integration; a literal translation would be something like 'making a citizen' or 'becoming a citizen'.

[5] The Act of 15 December 1980 on access to the territory, residence, establishment and expulsion of foreigners and the royal implementing decree of 8 October 1981, hereafter referred to as the Foreigners' Law.

[6] See, for EU-wide measures: the 1985 Agreement between the governments of the States of the Benelux Economic Union, the Federal Republic of Germany and the French Republic on the gradual abolition of checks at their common borders and the 1990 Convention

assigns power to control immigration to the communities or to the regions, it is explicitly stated that the power to make laws with respect to nationality and naturalisation rests with the federal legislator (Articles 8 and 9, respectively) (De Vries 2007: 5). When it comes to the integration of immigrants, the responsible bodies are the communities, since this is a matter pertaining to personal affairs. Nevertheless, since 1994, integration policy has been somewhat regionalised, which implies that integration is now administered through the regions, with the Flemish Region deciding on behalf of the Flemish Community and the French-speaking Community delegating its competence to the Walloon and the Brussels-Capital Regions (Gsir 2006: 1). Therefore, it is crucial to look at the policies one-by-one and region-by-region in order to gain a more accurate picture of the integration policy pursued in Belgium.

8.2.1 *Federal Institutions and Instruments*

8.2.1.1 *Advisory bodies*

Similarly to other Western European countries that have experienced substantial labour migration, Belgium failed to admit its status as an immigration country for a long time (Loobuyck & Jacobs 2006: 107). Hence, it was not until the late 1980s that an attempt to develop an integration policy was launched by the federal State. Indeed, it was only after the rise of the extreme right and, more particularly, of the *Vlaams Blok* (an anti-immigrant, Flemish nationalist party) that a consultative body was deemed necessary[7] (Cornil 1998: 131). The government has therefore established the Royal Commissariat for Migration Policy[8] which was given the role of issuing policy recommendations to the public authorities. Initially designed as a transitory body – with a mandate of four years – the Commissariat has since been transformed into a permanent body with a broader mission. It has also been renamed the Centre for Equal Opportunities and Opposition to Racism.[9]

implementing the Schengen Agreement of 14 June 1985 between the governments of the States of the Benelux Economic Union, the Federal Republic of Germany and the French Republic on the gradual abolition of checks at their common borders. See also the 1951 UN Convention relating to the Status of Refugees.

7 Blommaert criticises the establishment of the Royal Commissariat in response to the rise of extreme right. He states that such action holds the immigrant population – and their assumed inability to integrate – responsible for the success of *Vlaams Blok* (2006: 212).

8 *Le Commissariat Royal à la politique des immigrés.*

9 The official translation of '*Le Centre de l'Egalité des chances et de la lutte contre le Racisme*'.

Over a period of four years, the Commissariat has prepared many reports and proposals but, most significantly, it has attempted to offer a definition of the term 'integration' within the Belgian context. Accordingly, integration occurs in line with three guiding principles:

- Assimilation, where public order demands it;[10]
- Consistent promotion of the best possible 'fit', according to guiding principles that support the culture of the host country and that are related to 'modernity', 'emancipation' and 'true pluralism', as understood by a modern Western State;
- Unambiguous respect for cultural diversity as providing mutual enrichment in all other areas (Bousetta & Bernes 2007: 46, Loobuyck & Jacobs 2006: 108).

This broad definition has, however, not been transformed into legislation, which has hindered a uniform application of the principles. In the following chapters we will see how the Flemish and French-speaking communities have emphasised different dimensions of this definition and have embraced two different trajectories to integration.

The successor to the Royal Commissariat, the Centre for Equal Opportunities and Opposition to Racism, has adopted more of a mediating role between the public authorities and the immigrant populations (Bousetta & Bernes 2007: 47). Like its predecessor, through its recommendations it has sought to push through reforms which would improve the situation of foreigners in Belgium. It has also focused more on developing an anti-racist policy and has established complaints offices in the provinces for the victims of racism[11] (Cornil 1998: 133).

Evidently, the Centre's recommendations have proved to be of pivotal importance because they have led to changes in many instances, such as influencing some of the amendments made to the Nationality Code (Cornil 1998: 133). Despite this normative influence, it remains a consultative body without explicit decision-making power. This power remains with the federal government. Among the main competences that directly or indirectly affect the integration of immigrants, it entails anti-discrimination legislation,

---

[10] Public order refers to the general rules that apply to everybody regardless of national, religious or linguistic divisions, since they are assumed to reflect the basic values of society, such as gender equality, human dignity and the right to a fair trial.

[11] With the new anti-discrimination legislation in 2003 as part of the requirement for transposition of the EU Directives, the Centre has also assumed the role of 'watchdog' over the new legislation (Bousetta and Bernes 2007: 48).

anti-racism and equal opportunities measures and nationality legislation. Since our focus for the purpose of this chapter is on compulsory integration measures, we will only elaborate upon the Nationality Code of Belgium. Although integration policy is an exclusive competence for the Communities, it is intrinsically linked to citizenship policy, which, in the case of Belgium and as mentioned above, remains a federal competence.

Citizenship legislation is associated with the integration of immigrants in two major ways. Firstly, it tells us about the self-conceptualisation of a community, i.e. whether and how an immigrant can become a member of that community. Secondly, it is the *main* instrument that guarantees access to full political rights and therefore to the achievement of a significant level of political integration. Later, we will see how this second feature of nationality law has shaped political debates in Belgium.

8.2.1.2 *Successive amendments of the Nationality Code*

It is scarcely possible to elaborate on every mode of acquisition and loss of nationality within the scope of this chapter. Hence, we are only going to focus on aspects relevant to the integration of immigrants. Within this context, if we take easy (or easier) access to the acquisition of nationality as a sign of willingness on the part of host societies to integrate their immigrants, then some policies seem more favourable than others. Examples of such easier access are the extensive use of the principle of *ius soli*, the acceptance of dual nationality, a short residence requirement and the absence of integration criteria.

Belgian nationality law dates from the 28 June 1984; nevertheless, it has so far been updated several times (1991, 1995, 1998, 2000 and 2006) (Foblets & Loones 2006: 71). We will expand on the Act of 1 March 2000, which generated innovative changes as well as a number of criticisms. More recently, the Belgian government adopted new amendments with the law of 27 December 2006 with a view to addressing the criticisms that have been voiced by lawyers and academics.[12]

Belgian legislation at present allows a resident to apply for naturalisation after three years of residence – two years for refugees.[13] This residence requirement is the shortest period in any EU15 country (Waldrauch 2006: 37).

---

[12] Such as the provision for the loss of nationality in cases of false documentation or the extension of the deadline for the public prosecutor to four months.

[13] Article 19 of the Nationality Code.

A more striking procedure in Belgium enables foreigners who have resided[14] in Belgium for seven years to acquire Belgian nationality by simple declaration:[15] foreigners who meet this seven-year residence condition do not need an approval decision from the Belgian authorities. The procedure does not leave any room for discretion. It is sufficient for the public prosecutor to issue a positive recommendation on an individual declaration. The opinion has to be issued within four months[16] of receipt of a declaration; failure to do so is considered a positive recommendation. A negative opinion can only be issued when an impediment exists 'based on important facts pertaining to the individual applicant' and when the basic conditions of the procedure are not met (Foblets & Loones 2006: 74). Not surprisingly, the declaration constitutes the method most frequently used by foreigners acquiring Belgian nationality (De Hart & Van Oers 2006: 329). As for dual nationality, it can be said that it is a widely accepted practice among foreigners in Belgium, since none of the modes of nationality acquisition (declaration, option and naturalisation) requires the renunciation of previous citizenship.

Curiously, at a time when integration tests seem to be very fashionable and are proliferating[17] across Europe, the Belgian Act of 1 March 2000 abolished the provision relating to proof of 'the willingness to integrate' from the legislation. In the 1990s, in practice this provision mainly implied sufficient knowledge of one of the three languages of Belgium (De Hart & Van Oers 2006: 325). Nevertheless, as a result of its vagueness, it has been applied very arbitrarily (Favell & Martiniello 1999: 15) and has led to contradictory decisions (Foblets 2000: 226; Louis 2000: 98). With its removal from the text, the 'willingness to integrate' is now considered proven by the mere fact of applying for naturalisation and residence is emphasised as the most important criterion on which integration is based (De Hart & Van Oers 2006: 325).

Apart from legislative measures, Belgium has also taken serious steps towards eliminating procedures that can be a deterrent to naturalisation. For instance, the amendments to the Nationality Law of 2000 have also removed the fees that were normally requested as part of the naturalisation procedure (Foblets 2006: 224). In the light of these developments, it can be argued that the Act of 1 March 2000 has made Belgium a country with one of the most

[14] At the time of declaration, the foreigner must be in possession of a permanent residence permit.

[15] Article 12 bis of the Nationality Code.

[16] The period foreseen increased to four months with the amendments of 27 December 2006; it used to be one month in the text of the Act of 1 March 2000.

[17] E.g. Denmark, the Netherlands, Germany and the United Kingdom. See Joppke (2007) for an elaboration of the argument.

liberal legislations in Europe (De Hart & Van Oers 2006; Loobuyck & Jacobs 2006; Foblets 2006; Foblets & Loones 2006).

The ongoing liberalisation of nationality legislation since 1984 indicates that the Belgian federal authorities conceive of naturalisation as a means of integration, rather than as the end result of a successful integration process, which clearly contrasts with the dominant philosophy in many other European countries.[18] These amendments are made against a background of an optimistic vision of a society, where foreigners applying for naturalisation are considered willing to contribute to the well-being of the society (Foblets & Loones 2006: 78). Nevertheless, idealism alone falls short of offering a full explanation for the frequent amendments made to the Nationality Code. Belgium operates within a particular system of power politics that does not necessarily result in a unitary actor. Hence, we should look at the political dynamics behind the adoption of such measures facilitating nationality acquisition.

8.2.1.3 *The political dynamics behind citizenship policies: 'ethnos' vs. 'demos'*

According to Gsir, the debate on integration in Belgium revolves around two axes: citizenship and nationality (Gsir 2006: 5). More than a purely semantic difference, in the Belgian context, citizenship is dissociated from nationality and stands for the attribution of political rights to foreign residents. Thus, the Act of 1 March 2000 is usually perceived as the victory of nationality over citizenship since it emerged from a political compromise that aimed to prevent attempts to extend voting rights to immigrants (Louis 2000: 94). Belgium has long been reluctant to grant political rights to its foreign residents and has usually preferred to use nationality as an essential instrument to stimulate integration and political participation (Loobuyck & Jacobs 2006: 109). In 1998, prior to the eventual adoption of the 2000 amendments, the debate about extending political rights to non-EU residents was high on the political agenda due to a constitutional change that granted these rights to EU nationals. Article 8 of the Constitution has also opened up the possibility of a further extension to non-EU residents (Foblets 2006: 229). The Flemish liberals – who formed the ruling party at that time – were very sensitive[19]

---

[18] See the previous note for countries which require fulfilment of an integration condition prior to naturalisation.

[19] The reasons for this sensitivity are very closely related to the particular historical experience of the Flemish in the Belgian State. Since the establishment of the federal State in 1993, the Flemish have been very keen to preserve their political power. The enfranchisement of non-EU residents has been perceived as a threat, especially in the Brussels context, because most of the non-EU residents are French-speaking rather than Dutch-speaking. Hence, it was

to the enfranchisement of non-nationals and were reluctant to make use of this possibility. Hence, they opted for amending the nationality legislation in order to overcome the deadlock (Foblets 2006: 229, Louis 2000: 94). The question of voting rights was finally settled in 2004 by the attribution of municipal voting rights to all foreigners who have a residence record of five years.

However, the precipitation of amendments to the nationality law without a proper inquiry into their feasibility and coherence has been very much criticised by lawyers. They have drawn attention to the inability of the public prosecutor to issue an opinion within a month, especially considering that they began receiving five times more applications after the simplified procedure had been implemented –, the incompatibility with other legislative instruments such as the Foreigners' Law[20] and the lack of measures regarding the loss of nationality, particularly in cases of fraud, deceit or false statements (Foblets 2006; Louis 2000). Foblets elsewhere explains the shortcomings of the nationality law through the attempt by legislators to bring together its multiple roles (Foblets 2006: 232). According to Foblets, since 1984 the Belgian legislator has relied on the Nationality Code to fulfil three different tasks: nationality as a facilitator of the integration of foreigners into society, nationality as the guarantor of parliamentary democracy, opening up the citizen's participation at all levels, and nationality as the guardian of the laws on immigration (Foblets & Loones 2006:79).[21]

The rush to enact the amendments leads one to observe a different agenda behind the scenes. The apparently uniform vision at the federal level has masked important divergences between Flemish and French-speaking communities with regard to nationality law (Jacobs & Rea 2006: 11). The majority of Flemish politicians wanted to maintain a number of more 'subjective' criteria (such as the degree of cultural integration or loyalty to the receiving society) and language-related criteria, whereas the majority of French-speaking politicians preferred to retain only the 'objective' criteria, such as the length of legal residence on the territory (Jacobs & Rea 2006: 11). According

assumed that this would lead to a weakening of the electoral position of Flemish politicians in Brussels. In addition, the Flemish parties also feared a white backlash and an increase in strength of the extreme right (Loobuyck and Jacobs 2006: 109). Favell and Martiniello further argue that the Flemish political parties were hostile to the concept of voting rights due to the fact that 'the introduction of large numbers of minority voters into the system would encourage some Francophones to challenge the special status of the Flemish in the city; that is, ask why they should have any special status *at all*' (1999: 13).

[20] See footnote 5 above.

[21] See Foblets & Loones 2006, for an elaboration of the argument.

to these two authors, the discussions undeniably reflect a more general pattern on the part of the Communities. 'The argumentative frame for the Flemish is fed by references to the *ethnos* (a cultural vision of the nation) while the Francophones tend to privilege the *demos* (a political vision of the nation)' (Jacobs & Rea 2006: 11). These conceptualisations obviously have an effect on their policies of integration, which will be discussed in the following sections.

8.2.2 *Wallonia*

The Walloon policy of integration is widely influenced by the French-speaking community's perspective. As stated above, the French-speaking community's self-definition is conceived more in politico-civic terms than in ethno-cultural terms. Hence, the discourse and policy regarding immigrants are devoid of ethnic references. Along similar lines to the French Republican model, the Walloon Region places the emphasis on individual integration. This also explains why the granting of political rights to non-nationals has not encountered the controversy it aroused in Flanders.

The use of terms such as '*allochtoon*'[22] – which is firmly established in the northern part of the country – is categorically rejected in Wallonia. Accordingly, policies usually address social exclusion in general without singling out a targeted group. 'Integration policy is embedded within indirect schemes (priority action zones, zones of positive discrimination, etc.), which use social and demographic criteria to pinpoint areas of attention' (Jacobs & Rea 2006: 12). In 1998, furthermore, the French-speaking community adopted the Decree on Positive Discrimination which principally deals with socio-economically disadvantaged schools (Gsir 2006: 9).

The policy towards immigration has been given a new twist with the Decree of 4 July 1996 on the integration of foreigners and citizens of foreign origin.[23] The Decree provided the Walloon Region with the legal instrument to support its integration policy. It has promoted the establishment of seven regional integration centres (Liège, Charleroi, Namur, Mons, Verviers, Tubize and La Louvière). Unlike the reception centres in Flanders,[24] these centres perform a supporting task and aim to develop integration activities in a wide range of areas with the co-operation of local authorities and associations. The Decree has also created the Walloon Consultative Council for

---

[22] A person with at least one parent or one grandparent born in a foreign country.

[23] *Le décret du gouvernement wallon relatif à l'intégration des personnes étrangères ou d'origine étrangère*, 4 July 1996.

[24] See section III.1 below.

the Integration of Foreigners and of Persons of Foreign Origin, which gives advice to immigrants about access to social, cultural, economical, legal and political rights (Carrera 2005: 13). Reception programmes also exist in Wallonia that consist of French language courses and civic instruction. However, these are by no means mandatory so we will not expand on them in this chapter.

Despite the recent steps specifically targeting immigrants, Wallonia has a less articulated and less selective integration policy than Flanders. Bousetta & Bernes (2007) note that the factors that triggered a more pro-active policy in Flanders have not taken place in Wallonia: 'This latter region has not had to deal with the electoral success of the extreme right nor has it faced violent unrest on the part of the youth of ethnic minority origin, as did the Brussels Region' (Bousetta & Bernes 2007: 49). Evidently, this policy of indifference is also affected by the particularities of Walloon history, which considers immigrants an intrinsic part of regional identity (Jacobs & Rea 2006: 13). Hence, cultural and religious diversities are not only disregarded but they are also considered to have been smoothly accommodated over time (Jacobs & Rea 2006: 13). We will see how this is remarkably different from the situation in Flanders.[25]

8.2.3 *Brussels-Capital*

Brussels is at the very crossroads of the Flemish and French-speaking Communities' political interests, as well as representing the 'headquarters' of the European Union. It therefore forms an intriguing case for the integration of immigrants. On the one hand, the repercussions of two separate understandings of integration result in a non-unitary and inconsistent policy in the region. On the other hand, this very inconsistency provides new channels and opportunities for the expression of immigrants' voices.

The Brussels-Capital Region, which is geographically an enclave within the Flemish Region, has been an officially bilingual area since 1989, in which the two Communities have jurisdiction. As a consequence, its integration policy is dominated by two different organisations: the COCOF-French Community Commission (*Commission comunautaire française*) and the VGC-Flemish Community Commission (*Vlaamse Gemeenschapscommissie*).

[25] Nevertheless, one should bear in mind that the composition of the immigrant community in Wallonia is also significantly different from that in Flanders. A majority of the immigrants is from south-eastern European countries whereas, in Flanders, they are mainly of Turkish or Moroccan origin.

The VGC's policy in Brussels parallels the policy in Flanders. The recognition of ethnic minorities and their cultural 'differences' as such has led to the development of a targeted approach, which does not seek to eliminate these differences. Therefore, the VGC has had a clear preference for subsidising migrant organisations tending towards a cultural function. Moreover, in co-operation with *Le Foyer* reception centre, the VGC fosters a policy based on three pillars; emancipation, reception and securing the minimum needs of illegal residents (Gsir 2006: 11). With the recent changes in Flemish policy that will be discussed in the third section of this chapter, the VGC also began to promote Dutch language classes (Gsir 2006: 11). Flowing from this new policy, the funding for migrant organisations has begun to require the use of the Dutch language, at least at the executive level, with a view to creating 'Flemish' migrant organisations (Bousetta, Gsir & Jacobs 2005: 13).

In Brussels, the basic inspiration for setting up an integration policy by the French-speaking community between 1993 and 2003 came from a policy document on the 'integration and cohabitation of local communities' (Jacobs & Rea 2006: 13). This policy mostly sought to address the problems of disadvantaged neighbourhoods and to improve inter-community relations (Gsir 2006: 11). In 2004, a decree on social cohesion was adopted, which paved the way for the COCOF to develop policies regarding the reception of newcomers and the teaching of French. Jacobs & Rea criticise the Decree for its reluctance to refer explicitly to terms such as 'foreigners' and 'people of foreign origin' and to acknowledge the relevance of ethno-cultural differences (Jacobs & Rea 2006: 13). Unlike the VGC's policy, the COCOF's approach implies major difficulties for migrant organisations seeking subsidies and profiling themselves as 'immigrant' or 'ethnic' (Jacobs 2004: 289).

Overall, it can be said that the Brussels context offers an intricate landscape of authorities that strive to develop their own approach by combining elements from all of the available models (Gsir, Martiniello, Meireman & Wets 2005: 11). Although an obvious discrepancy exists in the perception of ethnic diversity between the two Communities, it should also be pointed out that, 'the difference is very much interconnected with strategies used by the political establishment of both linguistic groups as contenders in the political field of Brussels' (Jacobs 2004: 291). Indeed, it would not be an overstatement to claim that the practice of funding migrant organisations is part of the strategic endeavours of the Flemish authorities to increase their sphere of influence in the Brussels-Capital Region[26] (Bousetta, Gsir & Jacobs 2005: 13).

---

[26] Again, the contention is very closely linked to Belgian history. Brussels has always been at issue due to the diverging social and ideological representations of the city. Territorially a

These attempts are raising doubts within the French-speaking community regarding the intentions of the Flemish. The Francophones 'rely on their dominant position within Brussels and the status of French as lingua franca leading to (automatic) immigrant incorporation' (Jacobs 2004: 291).

Hence, in the Brussels context, the immigrant groups were given the opportunity to acquire very strong bargaining power to elicit special cultural funding especially *vis-à-vis* the Flemish community, which is more eager to promote its contacts among immigrants (Favell & Martiniello 1999: 16). These groups can 'strategically opt for different forms of collective mobilisation – stressing either ethnic identity or neutral forms of social insertion'[27] (Jacobs 2004: 292).

8.2.4 *Flanders*

The integration policy of Flanders is constantly evolving. In this sub-section we will only provide the general philosophy that shapes the Flemish approach to integration. The next chapter will offer a detailed analysis of the fairly recent policy of *inburgering*.

Following the developments at federal level, but also largely inspired by the work of the Royal Commissariat,[28] the Flemish government adopted its first policy note on migrant policy in 1989. Acknowledging the permanent presence of immigrants in Flanders, the note was geared towards achieving a 'multicultural society with intercultural exchange' (Loobuyck & Jacobs 2006: 110). With a view to creating such a society, the Flemish authorities have, from the beginning, embraced a practice of supporting migrant organisations (Jacobs 2004: 285).

During the 1990s, not only was the scope of migrant policy broadened, but a more co-ordinated and integrated policy has also since succeeded in

---

part of the Flemish region, the Flemish tend to see it as their capital, hence the presence of all the Flemish governmental institutions in Brussels. Nevertheless, the city is largely inhabited by the French-speaking community, which does not necessarily associate itself with the Walloon region but is still keen to keep Brussels a French-speaking zone. The problem has already spread to the suburbs of Brussels, which are geographically in the Flemish region and therefore monolingual. However, since a considerable number of French-speaking people live in this zone, they have been granted the right to receive public services in French in certain municipalities (*les communes à facilités*). The unilateral decision to suspend these rights has been at the heart of the governmental crisis that Belgium has experienced very recently.

[27] For an analysis of how these alternative channels of interest representation might hinder access to mainstream political forms and institutions, see Favell and Martiniello (1999).

[28] Cf. supra, section II.1.1.

putting down roots. With the strategic plan for ethno-cultural minorities in 1996, the Flemish Parliament established that every ministry and administration had to take into account minorities when making decisions in their own field of competence and that measures specifically targeting minorities should be restricted to temporary use (Loobuyck & Jacobs 2006: 110). As already mentioned when discussing the Brussels-Capital Region, the new Flemish minority policy was composed of three pillars. Firstly, it contains a policy of emancipation aimed at full social participation by legally settled citizens of foreign origin and of travelling groups.[29] Secondly, it includes a policy for the integration of newcomers and, lastly, a policy regarding illegal residents in order to satisfy their minimum needs with regard to healthcare, welfare and education has been put in place (Loobuyck & Jacobs 2006: 110).

The new policy has been formalised by the Ethno-cultural Minorities Decree of 1998. The Decree more clearly identified the actors involved and distinguished an *integratiesector*. The latter constitutes a striking contrast with Wallonia since it specifically and directly targets minorities. It provides funds for integration-specific policies and interest representation by the groups themselves. Therefore, 'although the Flemish government seeks to have an inclusive policy according to which diversity should be automatically taken into account in other policy fields, there is still ample room for "categorical policy" which is specially (in fact exclusively) oriented towards foreign-origin groups' (Jacobs & Rea 2006: 12).

The Decree distinguishes five target groups: (1) '*allochtoon*' citizens, (2) recognised refugees, (3) travelling groups, (4) non-Dutch-speaking newcomers and (5) illegal residents. Overall, these groups are referred to as 'ethno-cultural minorities' (*etnisch culturele minderheden*) (Jacobs 2004: 286).

The Flemish minority policy, with its emphasis on ethnic minority groups instead of an individual-oriented approach, is very much inspired by Dutch policy of the early 1990s (Jacobs & Rea 2006; Loobuyck & Jacobs 2006). The support given to the ethnic migrant organisations can also be considered an extension of this influence. It has notable parallels with the idea of emancipation in the Netherlands, which fosters different institutional arrangements as a means of preserving group identity (Entzinger 2003: 64). Nevertheless, the policies of the two polities have one major difference; in Flanders no official recognition is given to particular ethnic communities.[30]

---

[29] E.g. groups who are not settled, such as the Roma, and not travellers, such as tourists.

[30] Jacobs argues that this often takes place in practice (2004: 286). A more comprehensive comparison of Dutch and Flemish policies on *inburgering* will be provided in the last section of this paper.

In March 2004, the Flemish government updated the previous strategic plan and adopted an ambitious programme that aims to promote the co-existence in diversity of *all* citizens (Loobuyck & Jacobs 2006: 110, emphasis added). The purpose of the authors of the document is to achieve a more inclusive policy that would engage all of society rather than a selection of target groups only. Moreover, the Flemish policy has increasingly stressed the reception of newcomers, which was on the agenda from the beginning but was not emphasised previously. This concern has resulted in the adoption of citizenship trajectories (*inburgeringtrajecten*) for newcomers. The next section expands on these trajectories as part of the policy of *inburgering.*

8.3 *Flanders and Inburgering*

8.3.1 *A Review of Official Inburgering Policy*

The politics of *inburgering* was first regulated by the Decree of 28 February 2003 and its implementing decision of 2004. In the mean time, both have been updated; the former by the Decree of 14 July 2006[31] and the latter by its implementing decision of 15 December 2006. In addition to the legislation, the Ministry of Integration, which has also been recently established,[32] issues an annual report which entails a yearly programming of policy goals.

Before analysing the legislation on this matter, we should clarify the term '*inburgering*'. *Inburgering* implies a process of becoming a citizen which is not necessarily denoted by the term 'integration'.[33] The Decree defines *inburgering* as an interactive process that implies rights and duties both for the newcomers and for the Flemish government. The *inburgering* policy strives to create a society based on the values of shared citizenship and of active participation.[34] This new emphasis on active participation departs from the previous 'multicultural' policies, which were more inclined toward the recognition of ethnic minorities. The concept of *inburgering* is innovative in that it accentuates the commonalities on basic grounds, such as knowledge of Dutch language, while respecting diversity and different backgrounds.

[31] Actually, the Decree was once again amended on 1 February 2008 in order to make it compatible with the changes regarding asylum applications that were made to the Foreigners' Law. It has also streamlined the provisions.

[32] Established in 2003 and since led by Marino Keulen (Minister for Home Affairs, Urban Policy, Housing and Civic Integration).

[33] The French translation, '*citoyennisation*', remains more faithful to the literal meaning.

[34] Article 2 § 1 of the Decree.

'The individuality and cultural identity of each citizen needs to be respected, within a set of prevailing norms and values that are to remain the cornerstones of the democratic society' (Gsir et al. 2005: 10). On the one hand, the adoption of *inburgering* as a concept reveals a change of focus in integration policy from groups to individuals. On the other hand, the Flemish government is very keen to affirm that it is not urging the assimilation of newcomers. Another shift is discernable in the wording of the policy: 'diversity' policy seems to have replaced 'minorities' policy. The so-called diversity policy is therefore also mentioned in the annual reports of the Ministry. It is expected to be made official in spring 2009 with the modification of the Minorities' Decree.[35] The government issued a first policy note in February 2008 and is now in the process of developing a document based on the reactions to this first note (Beleidsbrief inburgering 2008: 14).

Since *inburgering* is viewed as a process of becoming citizen, its implementation requires a policy of assistance to newcomers during this period by offering citizenship trajectories (*inburgeringtrajecten*). The citizenship trajectories are composed of two complementary parts. Although the first route might be mandatory for certain groups of people, the second route is never obligatory because it goes beyond the acquisition of basic knowledge of society and of the language. It should be noted that the second part of the trajectory does not specifically target immigrants; it is available to everyone eligible for this route. It consists of one-to-one guidance in relation to the future career of the newcomer. This second route is only available upon completion of the first route and it seeks to help immigrants to fully participate in Belgian society, especially with regard to accessing to the labour market.[36]

The first part of the *inburgeringtraject* is particularly emphasised by Flemish policy-makers because the intention is to involve a wider range of people as a result of its compulsory nature. It includes three different programmes: language courses (Dutch as a second language NT2), civic orientation and vocational guidance. These courses aim to provide an opportunity for the newcomers to learn about and to become familiar with their new social environment.

Identifying the target group of the *inburgering* policy is a rather difficult task because not only has it been broadened by the Decree of 2006, but it is also constantly evolving. The Decree of 2003 initially only targeted newcom-

---

[35] *Decreet van 28 april 1998 inzake het Vlaamse beleid ten aanzien van etnisch-culturele minderheden* (Decree of 28 April 1998 regarding Flemish policy towards ethno-cultural minorities).

[36] Article 4 of the Decree.

ers arriving in Belgium for permanent residence. Hence, foreigners who met two basic conditions were considered covered by the scope of the policy: 1) being registered in a Flemish or Brussels municipality recently and for the first time; 2) having reached the age of majority. The target group also excluded foreigners involved in family reunification with Belgian nationals.

In 2004 the new government took the view that the target group definition was very limited in the 2003 Decree and thus substantially amended it in 2006. A major extension has been to bring established immigrants of non-EU origin, including Belgian nationals born outside Belgium (known as '*oudkomers*'), within the scope of the Decree.[37] Accordingly, non-EU family members joining Belgian nationals need to attend the integration courses. This has been of paramount importance for the new government since it has been observed that a majority of non-EU nationals arriving in Belgium through the family reunification channel have actually joined naturalised Belgian nationals (Foblets, Vanheule & Loones 2004).

Ultimately, the target group of the Decree of 2006 as a whole consists of adult foreigners staying in Belgium for non-temporary purposes and adult Belgian nationals who were born outside Belgium and who have at least one parent born outside Belgium.[38] This evidently leads to a much more diversified list of persons, ranging from asylum-seekers who submitted their asylum applications over four months ago to Belgian nationals who are receiving social security assistance.

The target group of the *inburgering* policy (2006) is not only comprehensive but it also entails multi-layered implications. The compulsory character of the trajectory varies with the categories of newcomers who fall within the scope of the Decree. All those within the target group have the right to participate in the citizenship trajectories; nevertheless, a number of them are required to do so. Therefore, the first group of compulsory participants is composed of foreigners who have been registered in Belgium for less than twelve months, religious ministers and recognised refugees[39] who have been registered as such for less than twelve months. On top of this, in order to qualify for a compulsory course, the foreigner has to reside in Flanders; those living in the Brussels-Capital Region are by necessity exempt from the obligation since the Flemish government cannot impose its policy outside Flanders.

---

[37] If Belgium were to sign the European Convention on Nationality, this distinction might breach the Convention's Article 5 § 2, which forbids discrimination between nationals whether they are nationals by birth or have acquired nationality subsequently.

[38] Article 3 § 1 of the Decree.

[39] This difference between recognised refugees and other newcomers was abolished in the 2008 amendment of the Foreigners' Law.

The Decree of 2006 provides for the extension of compulsory participants to include *oudkomers* – including Belgian citizens – who are receiving social security benefits (unemployment benefit) or social assistance (CPAS). These measures have not yet been implemented but, with the creation of the necessary structures, they are likely to be implemented in the near future.[40]

Alongside the compulsory participants, the voluntary participants are further divided into priority and non-priority groups. Priority refers to the first categories to be served if demand exceeds the availability of the courses. The rationale is that priority is being granted to the categories that are likely to be compulsory in the future. Hence, for the moment, the *oudkomers* who receive social security benefits or social assistance are in the priority group. Moreover, resident immigrants with school-age children are among the priority participants. Nevertheless, their transition to the compulsory category has proved difficult because it is hard for the authorities to identify them. Priority is also given to immigrants who are renting or on a list to rent community housing in the Flemish Region and to family members of EU nationals (not Belgians) who have the right of free movement. Lastly, a non-priority group of voluntary participants is allowed to attend courses, space permitting.

A number of immigrant categories are exempt from the obligation to follow an integration programme. Since the EU Directive (2004/38) on free movement forbids any impediment being imposed on the residence of EU and EEA nationals and their family members, they are exempt from this obligation.[41] In addition, persons who have a serious illness or a mental or physical disability, those over the age of 65, those who can prove their integration using certain certificates or diplomas are also exempt.[42] Lastly, labour migrants – with the exception of religious ministers – and their families are categorised as exemptions because they are assumed to have come for a limited period of time.[43]

Two other groups are also partly exempt and therefore do not have to follow the entire programme. Immigrants who have already fulfilled integration requirements in another EU Member State in order to obtain long-term resident status (in accordance with Article 5 of Directive 2003/109/EC) are only required to attend Dutch language classes.[44] Secondly, asylum-seekers

[40] Information gathered from interviews at the Ministry of Integration.

[41] The Directive is solely applicable to EU nationals who move to another EU State. Therefore, Belgian nationals are not covered by it.

[42] Article 5 § 2 of the Decree.

[43] Information gathered from interviews at the Ministry of Integration.

[44] Article 5 § 6 of the Decree.

who are authorised to stay on the territory while their application is under investigation have to follow the civic orientation part of the trajectory.[45]

In order to follow an integration programme, both newcomers and *oudkomers* have to go to the reception centre (*onthaalbureau*) of their province once they have registered in a Flemish municipality. In total, there are eight reception centres, five in each province (Antwerp, Limburg, East Flanders, Flemish Brabant and West Flanders) and three in the major cities of Antwerp, Ghent and Brussels. There, newcomers sign a 'contract of civic integration' concerning their individual programme. After an initial assessment at the reception centres, immigrants are directed to the responsible bodies for different aspects of the programme. Usually, the programme begins within three months of the newcomer's application to the reception centre and overall the training should not last more than one year.

Huizen van het Nederlands (Houses of Dutch) are in charge of evaluating the level of Dutch knowledge of the participants and then assigning them to the education centres. Various institutions offer language classes, such as centres for basic education, for adult education and the university language centres. The total number of hours comprising the education varies between 120 and 240, depending on the education level of the applicant (Timmerman, Geets & Van der Heyden 2006: 317).

Vocational guidance, which focuses on access to the labour market and lasts approximately 20 hours, is provided by the Flemish Employment Service, the VDAB (*Vlaamse Dienst voor Arbeidsbemiddeling en Beroepsopleiding*) (Timmerman, Geets & Van Der Heyden 2006: 317). Recently, a careers advisory task, which is still at the pilot stage, has been added to the duties of the *onthaalbureau* (Beleidsbrief inburgering 2008: 7).

The civic orientation course is offered by the *onthaalbureau* and covers a wide range of topics relating to Flemish society, such as the State structure, education, mobility and health.[46] The courses are given in the native language of a group of immigrants from the same country of origin. The detailed content of the curriculum was initially determined by the *onthaalbureaus*. Indeed, the lack of a centralised curriculum, combined with the absence of classes in Dutch, has rendered the training highly dependent on the discretion of the 'teacher'. To avoid this, a commission of seven people – academics and experts from different backgrounds – has been created by the Flemish government. The Commission was charged with suggesting a list of values and principles that are deemed the constituent pillars of Belgian/Flemish society. In 2006 it issued its opinion, which focused on five key

[45] Article 5 § 7 of the Decree.
[46] Information taken from the website of the Ministry of Integration, www.inburgering.be.

issues: liberty, equality, respect, citizenship and solidarity. Based on these values pinpointed by the Commission, the government has published a course book and related materials, such as DVDs, for the civic orientation courses. According to the last annual report, as of 1 January 2009 the *onthaalbureaus* were expected to work with this package of course books for participants, teacher's guide, website and supporting short films for the lessons (Beleidsbrief inburgering 2008: 22).

The obligation of the immigrants is in principle limited to attendance at the courses. They need to attend 80% of the courses (Beleidsbrief inburgering 2007: 6). However, more flexible measures apply to those who are active on the labour market, to illiterates and to persons with a low level of education (De Vries 2007: 9). In cases of failure to comply, immigrants can be fined between 50 and 5000 euros.[47] A fine can also be imposed if the person refuses to cooperate with his integration programme or to sign an integration contract. Moreover, failure to complete the integration programme might impede an application for unemployment benefit and/or social housing at a later stage.[48] Upon completion of the civic integration contract, the *onthaalbureau* awards an attestation to participants. There is no official examination or test that assesses the skills learned on the trajectory. However, the amended Decree mentions the possibility of introducing such a test. In that case, in addition to participation, achievement of a certain level would be expected and required. The Flemish government agreed earlier in 2008 to introduce an examination for civic orientation but not yet for language, an issue which also falls within the competence of the Ministry of Education and thus needs its approval. However, lately it seems that the idea of an examination has been put on hold. The University of Antwerp has started developing a test that is expected to be ready by the end of 2009, but it is conceived as a means of checking whether people need the civic orientation courses and not as a means of assessing their knowledge.[49]

8.3.2 *The Public and Political Debate*

The political autonomy of the Communities in the field of integration has not only enabled them to develop policies in line with their history and local sensitivities, but also to circumvent controversies that might have arisen

---

[47] Article 25 § 2 of the Decree. The 2008 amendment converted the pecuniary fines into administrative fines.

[48] Information taken from interviews at the Ministry of Integration adds legal basis for this measure.

[49] Information taken from interviews at the Minorities Centre of Flanders.

due to the distinct approaches of the two communities. Flanders has mostly emphasised the significance of language and the preservation of ethnic and cultural identity (Loobuyck & Jacobs 2006: 118). Hambye & Lucchini point out that 'The dominant ideology in Flanders asserts the primary importance of language in belonging to a community and the fact of knowing Dutch as one of the conditions for effective integration of citizens' (Hambye & Lucchini 2005: 2).

Therefore, the formulation of the policy of *inburgering* has not met with substantial opposition and the Decree in general has undergone a fairly smooth adoption process.[50] Two arguments prevailed and justified the need for a policy of *inburgering*. First of all, the previous policy of integration (run by the *integratiesector*) has been discredited over time because it is believed that the subsidies available were used inefficiently. The general preference of minorities for using the funds for their own organisations has significantly impeded the development of more inclusive policies (Timmerman, Geets & Van Der Heyden 2006: 315). Moreover, the paternalistic behaviour on the part of the sector and its composition of mainly *autochthoon*[51] Belgians have alienated it from the minorities. This disappointment has also coincided with a change of mentality in Flanders. Integration, previously considered the duty of the government, has now come to be seen as a mutual responsibility. A culture-relativist approach has made way for an intercultural approach that is geared towards mainstream organisations with a view to making them more inclusive. The second factor, which is also related to the assumed failure of the *integratiesector*, is that there appeared to be no visible improvement in successive generations in terms of successful participation in the labour market or command of the Dutch language within the immigrant groups. Hence, the government decided to design a pro-active and comprehensive policy, which aimed to overcome the pitfalls of the previous policy through its mandatory nature.[52]

This is not to say that the *inburgering* policy has not been the subject of any discussion. The first controversy occurred over the name of the policy. As previously mentioned, the reception of newcomers has been on the agenda ever since the adoption of the minorities' policy. Nevertheless, over time the policy experienced a shift in name from 'reception' to *inburgering*. Alongside this came a shift in mentality from welcoming newcomers to teaching them

[50] Information taken from interviews at the Ministry of Integration.

[51] Native Belgians who do not have a parent born in another country for at least three generations.

[52] Information taken from interviews at the Ministry of Integration.

'our' values.[53] This change has been criticised by the reception centres that were not at ease with the harsh sound of the new policy.[54] The compulsory nature of the trajectories has further aroused controversy and divided right-wing and socialist politicians into two camps (Michalowski 2004: 11). While liberals and conservatives were in favour of obligations and sanctions, socialist politicians argued that an obligation is only fair when sufficient tuition is available and waiting lists for classes have been eliminated (Loobuyck & Jacobs 2006: 112). On the other hand, Loobuyck and Jacobs assert that these discussions were misplaced. Instead of legitimising the policy in terms of the qualification and emancipation of women, they concentrated on assimilation and obligations (Loobuyck & Jacobs 2006: 112). Timmerman, Geets & Van der Heyden subscribed to this justification on the grounds of emancipation by disclosing that most of the newcomers are in favour of an obligation since it constitutes a way out of their closed community and of escaping the totalitarian power of their spouses (2006: 306).

While the compulsory nature of the *inburgering* policy was widely debated prior to the adoption of the Decree of 28 February 2003, it no longer constituted a contentious topic for the amended Decree of 14 July 2006. Since the amended Decree's most innovative feature is the enlargement of the target group, this has drawn more attention than any other issue. For the reasons explained above the new government has decided that established non-EU immigrants and naturalised Belgian nationals – the so-called *oudkomers* category – also need to participate in the courses. This has proved hard to include in a policy document because it is rather tricky to announce to these groups that they are now required to attend a class after many years of residence.[55] The liberals also put forward the idea that the *oudkomers* – mainly established residents dependent on social assistance – could stop taking the courses once they begin working. They argued that by being active on the labour market, immigrants contribute to society and thus no longer constitute a burden on the welfare system.[56] However, faced with opposition from other parties, they accepted a compromise solution: *oudkomers* who are active on the labour market can benefit from more flexible hours, such as evening classes, but the attendance requirement remains unchanged.

---

53 Information taken from interviews at the Minorities Centre of Flanders.

54 *Ibid.*

55 Information taken from interviews at the Ministry of Integration.

56 *Ibid.*

8.3.3 *Implementation and its Measurable Effects*

From the initial implementation of the *inburgering* policy, the Flemish government has been very keen on observing its outcomes and modifying the policy accordingly. With this aim in mind, it regularly commissioned independent studies to shed light on the implementation of the *inburgering* policy. The first (and currently the latest) reports were published in 2007[57] and offer an overall evaluation of the policy. These reports provide very detailed information with regard to the practicalities of implementation, such as the difference in quality among language centres, and make concrete recommendations. Nevertheless, their scope is limited to this material monitoring; it does not expand on the measurable effects on society. Therefore, it has been difficult to claim at this stage that the courses indeed helped newcomers in their job-hunting or in developing social relationships with the rest of the population. The Flemish government recently issued a call for projects that would specifically address this aspect; the results are expected to be known by the end 2009. Without going into too much detail, in this section we aim to pinpoint a couple of relevant issues drawn from the data available in the reports and through interviews conducted at the Ministry of Integration and the Minorities Centre of Flanders.[58]

8.3.3.1 *The number of newcomers in Flanders*

We start with some figures: in 2004 5,590 newcomers went to an *onthaalbureau* in Flanders; this number rises to 11,528 in 2005 and to 12,703 in 2006 (Lambert, De Cuyper, Geets, Struyven, Timmerman, Van Den Eede & Wets 2007: 8). Nevertheless, this does not constitute the aggregate number of the newcomers, since the same study shows that only 38.1% of new arrivals actually went to an *onthaalbureau* (*Ibid.*: 7). It is hard to say why all the registered newcomers did not turn up because the registrars in the municipalities do not distinguish between people who have a right to follow the programme and those who are obliged to do so. Therefore, the low number may be due to the reluctance of the newcomers to follow an integration trajectory or they may simply not be within the target group of the *inburgering* policy. Looking at the ratio of people who sign an integration contract to those who ultimately obtain an attestation is much more revealing for our purposes.

---

57 See http://binnenland.vlaanderen.be/inburgering/onderzoek.htm for the reports in their entirety.

58 The authors are grateful to expert informants who helped us in updating and clarifying the ramifications of the policy: (in alphabetical order) Mirjam Amar, Badra Djait, Gerlinde Doyen, Marc Haertjens and Eric Somers.

Of this group, 41.7% finish the trajectory successfully within an average of seven months – considerably shorter than the one-year period foreseen by the *onthaalbureaus*. In general, the participants reported they were satisfied with the courses; however, the satisfaction level seems to be negatively correlated with the education level. That is to say, the lower the education of the participants, the more satisfied they were with the programme and the more they wished it lasted longer (Lambert *et al.* 2007: 21). In our view, this finding points to the need for a more tailored approach when it comes to determining the target group. Whereas the highly educated should preferably be exposed to a more sophisticated programme that would be responsive to their demands, the less well-educated may be given the opportunity to follow courses for a longer period of time.

8.3.3.2 *The social characteristics of the immigrants*

The aforementioned report also allows us to profile the potential target group. Accordingly, men and women are equally represented within this group which is largely composed of young people. Two-thirds of the newcomers are under 35 years old, while the average age is 33. The report also points out that with age it becomes harder to set out on the trajectory (*Ibid.*: 7). As for marital status, two-thirds (66%) are registered as married or in a long-term relationship/partnership. Lastly, when it comes to nationality, traditional migrant groups (Moroccans and Turks) remain highly represented among newcomers, but Eastern Europeans and residents from countries of Sub-Saharan Africa are also increasing in number.

8.3.3.3 *Enforcement and sanctions*

Although sanctions have been previously dealt with under the heading III.1, it should be mentioned here that a recent change in the fine system has been introduced by the government, based on the output of the evaluation study.[59] It has been observed that newcomers were informed of the fact that the sanctions were not being properly applied (Beleidsbrief inburgering 2008: 21). In order to overcome this error, the government has decided to pursue a double-faceted policy, which consists of investing in the improvement of the quality of the offer on the one hand, and introducing administrative pecuniary fines on the other hand (Beleidsbrief inburgering 2008: 21). The difference in the latter system from the previous system is that the authorities no longer need to go through the judicial system to impose a fine on a newcomer. Another

[59] http://binnenland.vlaanderen.be/inburgering/onderzoek/pdf/Het%20Vlaamse%20Inburgeringsbeleid%20geevalueerd_synthese.pdf, site accessed 20 January 2009.

problem encountered in terms of enforcement of the policy has been the lack of recognition of the attestation granted by the *onthaalbureau.* It has been noted by the Flemish authorities that the attestations were not familiar to employers and were therefore not appreciated as expected. A final complication that has been observed is the existence of a group of participants who simply appear unable to learn the language, no matter how long they take courses. For the moment, no flexibility is offered to this group of people who lack the necessary linguistic skills, although the Flemish government envisages offering them a medical exemption and granting them the attestation on this basis.

8.4 *Peculiarities of Belgium*

Citizenship tests (as they are known) and courses are a rapidly expanding phenomenon all over Europe.[60] It would be an overstatement to argue that consensus or complete agreement exists on the necessity for such measures, since different national approaches have always been apparent. These differences can be explained against the background of the national context in each country – and that context varies. Nevertheless, we should not turn a blind eye to the proliferation of integration tests and courses that are spreading through policy emulation. Although nation-states are still keen on staying 'national' and maintaining their discretion in the regulation of their internal affairs, they no longer refrain from 'copying' the solutions experimented with by neighbouring states facing similar problems. In Europe, the Dutch civic integration policy pioneered the process and quickly became a model for Europe (Joppke 2007: 9). The question we are interested in here is showing that Belgium has managed to develop its own *inburgering* policy, even though the terminology has been borrowed from the Dutch policy. Our argument is that, despite the evident influence of the Dutch model on its European counterparts, Belgian policy is singled out not least because of its complex federal system. The delicate equilibrium upon which the Belgian system depends generates different opportunities and insights for the development of integration policies. We are aware that this might be shaky ground, since the system is constantly being reshaped[61] and the opportunities

[60] See note 17 above.

[61] The institutional reforms regarding the competences of different layers of governance – which have provided the basis of the federal system – are always high on the Belgian public agenda. For the new government, the re-distribution of power constitutes one of the

of today might turn out to be deficiencies or might very simply cease to exist in the future. However, our contention is that the Belgian system, which is usually perceived as extremely limiting, does shed new light on matters of integration.

8.4.1 *A Hybrid Approach: Mixing Multiculturalism and Civic Integration in Flanders*

The renewed emphasis on citizenship implies a critical point in the understanding of integration in Europe. The principle of civic integration, in which newcomers are asked to adopt a shared standard of language and values, certainly resonates closely with the traditional 'philosophy' of republican assimilation (Joppke 2007: 9). Therefore, it is surprising that *inburgering* has become so swiftly ingrained in the Netherlands, which used to be the most markedly multicultural state. The same is true for Flanders. So, has Flanders completely abandoned the practices that are the legacy of multicultural politics? We are tempted to argue that this is not the case. First of all, the policy of *inburgering* is officially accompanied by a diversity policy, which is a re-christened minorities' policy. The most recent annual reports by the Flemish government allude to the aim of a more efficient and more effective diversity policy, which will be achieved by modifying the Ethnocultural Minorities Decree mentioned earlier (Beleidsbrief inburgering 2007: 5; Beleidsbrief inburgering 2008: 14). Certainly, it remains to be seen how the new decree will define diversity and which values will be stressed. In the annual reports, the focus is on shared citizenship and on the responsibility on the part of individuals for harmonious co-existence (Beleidsbrief inburgering 2007: 26). Nevertheless, the mere existence of this policy reveals the willingness to maintain a multicultural or rather a hybrid policy, in the sense that the presence of ethnic and cultural differences is kept on the agenda and is assumed to require targeted policies. Among other things, diversity policy allocates funds to projects touching upon a wide range of issues concerning immigrants. Priority is given to projects with concrete and measurable results, which aim to mainstream diversity (Beleidsbrief inburgering 2007: 26). Lastly, in practice, although they are expected to stress their 'intercultural' aspects more than they used to in the past, migrant organisations still receive funding.[62]

---

important topics that need to be addressed. See '*L'accord de gouvernement*', downloadable from http://www.premier.be/ fr/accord-de-gouvernement-0.

[62] *Ibid.*

Drawing attention to the common practice of consultation with immigrant organisations, Jacobs also concludes that the idea of multiculturalism in Flanders has not been deeply discredited (Jacobs 2004: 289). For him, the financing of the mosques[63] and the granting of holidays on religious festivities for Jews and Muslims in the Flemish education system can be cited as examples of the persistence of multicultural policies (Jacobs & Rea 2006: 13). He explains this rather hybrid approach using two major reasons; the changing political landscape of Flanders and the intertwining of integration issues with multinational politics, especially in Brussels-Capital Region context (Jacobs & Rea 2006: 13). Since the latter is elaborated in sub-section II.3, suffice it to say here that the recognition and promotion of ethno-cultural diversity is very much perceived as a means of safeguarding the influence of the Flemish community – and thus of the Dutch language – in the Belgian capital. The transformation of the Flemish political landscape is closely linked with the emergence of 'new politics'. While traditional political axes, in particular the right-left divide, began to fade, they have been replaced by new dividing lines. According to Jacobs, in the Flemish political arena, two new fracture lines appeared: materialist/post-materialist and ethnocentrist/multiculturalist (2004: 293). Hence, issues pertaining to these divides started to determine voting behaviour to a large extent. This has led the political parties to (re)position themselves in a way that makes them take sides with respect to these issues. Within this context, the *Vlaams Belang* emerged – formerly known as *Vlaams Blok* – a Flemish nationalist party that takes a strong anti-immigrant and xenophobic stance. A fairly specific aspect of the Flemish political scene since the 1980s is the so-called *cordon sanitaire*, which is an agreement among all other Flemish political parties with a view to leaving the *Vlaams Belang* out of any government coalition. Hence, democratic forces 'have continuously remained in power and have kept defending the stress on recognition of diversity' (*Ibid.*: 294). As said before, this is evidently a very delicate equilibrium; however, in retrospect, the strategy has proved successful. In the last five years, *Vlaams Belang* has lost some of its appeal and made space for new contestants in the political arena, such as LDD (*Lijst de Decker*) and NV-A (nationalist Flemish party, split from *Volksunie*). Therefore, it may be unlikely that *Vlaams Belang* will ever again achieve an electoral success that would allow it to impose itself on the other parties.

---

[63] Although one should note that, at the time of writing, Wallonia had more recognised mosques than Flanders has.

8.4.2 *Discordance between Flemish Inburgering and the Belgian Nationality Code*

The 'peculiarities' of Belgium are best revealed through a comparison of its integration policy with those states making use of similar instruments. The Netherlands once again stands out as a benchmark in that sense. In other European states, compulsory integration courses usually go hand in hand with the obligation to take an integration test for naturalisation. However, in Belgium this link between integration and citizenship has been gradually broken; most recently, with the removal of the condition of the 'willingness to integrate' in the Nationality Act of 1 March 2000, no legitimate grounds exist for assessing one's integration when granting citizenship. Hence, at the federal level, residence is deemed a sufficient condition for becoming a citizen and the mere fact of applying for citizenship is considered proof of integration. As explained in detail in section II.1, these amendments stem from a combination of factors: reluctance on the part of legislators to grant political rights to non-EU residents, the instrumentalisation of nationality law as a means of integrating immigrants and, last but not least, from the idealistic vision of belonging to a society.

By way of reaction to these prior amendments, which attribute Belgian citizenship more easily to foreigners, the Flemish government has reinforced its *inburgering* policy. *Inburgering* policy in its amended version operates regardless of nationality: the fact of being Belgian does not exempt one from the obligation to integrate.[64] Still, it is hard to distinguish integration and citizenship policies analytically, which are however institutionally separate in Belgium. Inevitably, this situation creates discordances both in practice and in theory. *Inburgering* policy promotes the idea that foreigners can only achieve full membership in society providing they learn the language and the basic values of the society, which clearly are not what are sought as criteria at the federal level. Loobuyck & Jacobs contend that, apart from the philosophy behind the nationality law and the political compromise within which

[64] The fact of being a foreigner does not necessarily imply such a duty either. The exemption for labour migrants and the obligation for citizens dependent on social assistance are clearly evidence that the underlying logic is economic, rather than anything else. This also resonates closely with Joppke's claim that, 'civic integration is the equivalent on the part of immigrants to the 'workfare' policies that the general population is subjected to in the context of shrinking welfare States, seeking to make people both self-sufficient and autonomous by illiberal means'. Hence, for him, the repressive measures taken by European States do not stem from racist or nationalist appeals, but from liberalism itself – the Foucault-inspired reading of liberalism based on power and discipline, rather than a Rawlsian liberalism based on equality, individual rights and neutrality (2007: 15–16).

it emerged in the first place, the lack of language tests at federal level is also due to the fact that no agreement exists between the Francophones and the Flemish concerning the geographical areas – in particular on the periphery of Brussels – in which knowledge of which of the national languages is deemed necessary (Loobuyck & Jacobs 2006: 10). Once again, the disagreement in the multinational political arena between the two Communities is imported into multicultural politics, whereby the conflicts over the 'spheres of influence' generate more favourable provisions for those immigrants who are willing to naturalise. This is not intended as a judgement on the requirement of integration tests in cases of the acquisition of nationality, but rather as a means of demonstrating that, based on previously defined criteria, the absence of tests is inevitably favourable to naturalisation. The introduction of citizenship tests after all rests upon the meaning embedded in a society's concept of nationality.[65]

Since the issue of the enfranchisement of foreign residents has been settled,[66] there now seems to be consensus between the Flemish political parties that the nationality law needs to be revised (Loobuyck & Jacobs 2006: 10). However, it seems for the moment fairly impossible to link the outcomes of the two policies because the Walloon region does not have a policy of *inburgering* and, since French-speaking political parties oppose the idea of compulsory integration – particularly the Socialist Party – it is not likely to have such a policy in the near future. The failure of subsequent federal governments to stay in power for a full term has so far prevented any substantial change being made to the nationality law. At the time of writing this chapter, the government that came to power in December 2008 included in the *accord de gouvernement* the removed provision of the proof of 'willingness to integrate',[67] according to which willingness could be proven by, for instance, an attestation from a competent local authority. However, all migration and asylum matters in the *accord de gouvernement* have been blocked politically since 14 October 2008, despite the new prime minister's negotiation and consultation efforts.[68] If they were to be unblocked, the provision concerning proof of 'willingness to integrate' could be reintroduced. Nevertheless,

[65] For instance, the most recent amendments to the Belgian Nationality Code have also been criticised on the grounds that they transformed nationality into a mere confirmation of residence. It is assumed that it no longer reflects a consistent view of belonging to a State, a nation and a community at large (Foblets and Loones, 2006: 91).

[66] See the discussion in section II.1.3.

[67] See page 37 of *'L'accord de gouvernement'*, downloadable from http://www.premier.be/fr/accord-de-gouvernement-0.

[68] Information taken from interviews at the Minorities Centre of Flanders.

the text of the *accord de gouvernement* is rather vague as to the content of the provision – whether it would merely be a language criterion or a broader condition. In either case, it seems very unlikely (not to mention legally complicated) that Flanders would be allowed to apply its *inburgering* policy as a condition for acquiring nationality.

8.4.3 *Flemish Policy of Inburgering in the Light of the Dutch Example*

If citizenship and integration policies are two corners of a triangle in policy-making concerning the participation of immigrants in life in society at large, then territorial admission constitutes the third corner. Again, with the Netherlands leading the process, more and more states (such as Germany and France) have made the issue of a long-term residence permit conditional upon completion of an integration test, course or contract. Hence, two previously distinct fields – migration control and immigrant integration – are conflated and the integration domain is potentially subordinated to the demands of migration control (Joppke 2007: 8). In some countries, these measures are further required before arrival in the host country. In the Netherlands and Germany, would-be immigrants are asked to take a test in order to obtain a visa. Joppke defines the integration measures abroad as, 'the perfect tool of preventing unwanted immigration' (*Ibid.*)

Following Joppke, we can state that combining the previously separate policy areas seems to cast a shadow on the purported aim of the integration courses. Hence, their credibility can be questioned owing to the presence of sanctions preventing entry into the territory. In Belgium, territorial admission is a federal competence, therefore it is by no means linked to the successful fulfilment of integration requirements. Loobuyck & Jacobs argue that a valid case can be made for placing the policies of integration and admission at the same level of governance because they are in a dialectical relationship with each other (Loobuyck & Jacobs 2006: 116). Although this argument opens the way for a regionalisation of territorial admission policies, the authors conclude that in the face of increasing Europeanisation, regionalisation is neither likely nor efficient. Having established this, we return to possible sanctions of the *inburgering* policy. Failure to integrate in Flanders, which is not assessed by a test but by mere attendance of the courses, might ultimately have an impact on social rights. Although obstructing access to social housing and social assistance is critical for one's welfare, the system in Belgium does not endanger immigrants' legal security. Putting immigrants in the potentially vulnerable situation where their legal residence might be withdrawn cannot promote the development of anticipated bonds. In this case, Belgium's peculiar institutional situation provides a credible foundation, more inclined to embrace immigrants with a certain knowledge of its society and hopefully, in the end, to foster social allegiances.

Moreover, although it is possible that tests might be introduced in Flanders, this is being considered solely as a complementary measure. This mentality also differs widely from the Netherlands, where attendance at the courses is not of central importance; only the results count (Joppke 2007: 7). In Flanders, the courses themselves are conceived as a vital part of the training because attendance allows immigrants to familiarise themselves with a multicultural environment. Therefore, not only what is taught in the classes, but also what is experienced by attending the courses is seen as part of the learning process. Time will tell whether Flanders is only following a few years behind the Netherlands or whether this is really a peculiarity of Belgium. However, putting the introduction of the tests on hold seems to suggest that Flanders is willing to devise its own approach and remain different.

> Whilst the consociational elements of Belgian politics perpetuate a situation of permanent 'crisis' and potential gridlock between the two rival linguistic communities, it also ensures that progress is only made at the mutual benefit of both parties and is never zero-sum. Therefore there is an accent on internalising solution-finding within the elite institutions, so that technical and consensual compromises can be found (Favell & Martiniello 1999: 9–10).

Particularly when it comes to integration policies, we find the two conventionally competing philosophies within Belgium itself; hence, the compromises reached on these policies definitely shed new light on how to reconcile these two opposing views.

8.5 *Concluding Remarks*

National citizenship has recently acquired renewed importance with the introduction of civic integration courses and tests throughout Europe. Compulsory participation in integration programmes has become a regular part of immigration and national citizenship legislation and, in most States, it constitutes a precondition for a secure legal status. Hence, one can speak of a shift from conceiving of citizenship as a means of promoting integration to a reward bestowed at the end of a successful integration process. Carrera argues that through these tests, 'traditional stereotypes of how to be 'national' are taken as the model to evaluate if the immigrant is well-integrated' (Carrera 2005: 1).

These measures are supposedly geared towards ensuring that foreigners in the country have the necessary knowledge and skills to pursue an autonomous and harmonious life in the host society. Nevertheless, in many instances, they are used as a tool of immigration policy that seeks to control entry to the territory of unwanted immigration. However, it would be misleading to assume by looking at the general pattern that each and every policy of civic integration is identical. Much room for manoeuvre is still available within the given policy area, depending on national sensitivities. Therefore, the content, the target group and the implementation of these integration programmes are of pivotal importance in evaluating whether they actually serve their purported aim.

In this contribution, we have tried to cover some of the main aspects pertaining to both the *inburgering* policy and to immigrants in general. Throughout this chapter, in addition to explaining the Flemish compulsory integration policy and its ramifications, we have also aimed to draw attention to the coexistence of different policies under the same 'Belgian' roof. Hence, our claim is that the dynamics shaping the Belgian political system in a very particular way also generate 'peculiarities' regarding the policy of integration. These dynamics permeate Belgium, causing it to pursue a double-edged policy of integration, which is both multicultural and assimilationist at the same time. They also provide for a decoupling of the policies of citizenship and of integration, which seem to offer more credibility to both, while their conflation only leads to restrictiveness.

Bibliography

Bauböck, R. *et al.*, *Acquisition and Loss of Nationality, Volume I: Comparative Analysis; Policies and Trends in 15 European Countries*, Amsterdam: Amsterdam University Press 2006a.

Bauböck, R. *et al.*, *Acquisition and Loss of Nationality, Volume II: Country Analyses*, Amsterdam: Amsterdam University Press 2006b.

Blommaert, J., Le Discours Politique Relative aux Minorités, in: B. Khader, M. Martiniello, A. Rea, C. Timmerman (eds.), *Penser l'immigration et l'intègration autrement*, Brussels: Bruylant 2006.

Brubaker, R., The return of assimilation? Changing perspectives on immigration and its sequels in France, Germany, and the United States, in: C. Joppke & E. Morawska (eds.), *Toward Assimilation and Citizenship: Immigrants in Liberal Nation-States*, New York: Palgrave Macmillan 2003.

Cornil, J., Une politique publique de lutte contre le racisme: Le cas de la Belgique, in: A. Rea (ed.), *Immigration et Racisme en Europe*, Paris: Editions Complexes 1998.

De Hart, B. & R. van Oers, European Trends in Nationality Law, in: R. Bauböck *et al.* (eds.), *Acquisition and Loss of Nationality, Volume I: Comparative Analysis; Policies and Trends in 15 European Countries*, Amsterdam: Amsterdam University Press 2006.

De Vries, K.M., *A comparative legal study of integration requirements in the Netherlands, Belgium, the United States and Canada*, Paper presented in the CEPS Training School, Brussels, 23–24 November 2007.

Entzinger, H., The Rise and Fall of Multiculturalism: The Case of the Netherlands, in: C. Joppke & E. Morawska (eds.), *Toward Assimilation and Citizenship: Immigrants in Liberal Nation-States*, New York: Palgrave Macmillan 2003.

Foblets, M.C., D. Vanheule, & S. Loones, Inburgering in Vlaanderen: enkele vragen bij de afbakening van de doelgroep en de verplichting tot inburgering onder het inburgeringsdecreet, *Tijdschrift voor vreemdelingenrecht*, 1, 2004, pp. 5–23.

Foblets, M.C., Les changements de la loi sur la nationalité Belge, in : B. Khader, M. Martiniello, A. Rea, C. Timmerman (eds.), *Penser l'immigration et l'intègration autrement*, Brussels: Bruylant 2006.

Foblets, M.C. & S. Loones, Belgium, in: R. Bauböck *et al.* (eds.), *Acquisition and Loss of Nationality, Volume II: Country Analyses*, Amsterdam: Amsterdam University Press 2006.

Hansen, R. & P. Weil, *Towards a European Nationality: Citizenship, Immigration and Nationality Law in the EU*, New York: Palgrave 2001.

Jacobs, D., Alive and Kicking? Multiculturalism in Flanders, *International Journal on Multicultural Societies* (IJMS), 6(2) 2004, pp. 280–299.

Jacobs, D. & A. Rea, *The end of national models? Integration courses and citizenship trajectories in Europe*, paper prepared for the EUSA conference, Montreal, 17–19 May 2007.

Jacobs, D. & A. Rea, Construction et importation des classements ethniques. Allochtones et immigrés aux Pays-Bas et en Belgique, *Revue Européenne des Migrations Internationales*, 21(2) 2005, pp. 35–59.

Jacobs, D. & A. Rea, Construction and Import of Ethnic Categorisations: 'Allochthones' in the Netherlands and Belgium, 2006, accessible on http://www.feem.it/ Feem/Pub/Publica tions/WPapers/default.htm.

Joppke, C. & E. Morawska, *Towards Assimilation and Citizenship: Immigrants in Liberal Nation-States*, Basingstoke: Palgrave Macmillan 2003.

Joppke, C., Beyond National Models: Civic integration policies for immigrants in Western Europe, *West European Politics* 30(1) 2007, pp. 1–22.

Koopmans, R., P. Statham, M. Giugni & F. Passy, *Contested Citizenship: Immigration and Cultural Diversity in Europe*, Minneapolis/London: University of Minnesota Press 2005.

Loobuyck, P. & D. Jacobs, The Flemish immigration society: Political challenges on different levels, in: L. d'Haenens, M. Hooghe, D. Vanheule, H. Gezduci (eds.), *New Citizens, New Policies? Developments in Diversity Policy in Canada and Flanders*, Ghent: Academia Press 2006.

Michalowski, I., *An overview on Introduction Programmes for Immigrants in Seven European Member States*, Amsterdam: Adviescommissie voor Vreemdelingenzaken 2004.

Oers, R. van, *Justifying Citizenship Tests in the Netherlands and the UK*, Paper presented in the CEPS Training School, 23–24 November 2007.

Sassen, S., *Losing control? Sovereignty in an age of globalization*, New York: Columbia University Press 1996.

Soysal, Y.N., *Limits of Citizenship: Migrants and Postnational Membership in Europe*, Chicago: University of Chicago Press 1994.

Timmerman, C., J. Geets & K. Van Der Heyden, Les Nouveaux Arrivants en Flandre, in : B. Khader, M. Martiniello, A. Rea, C. Timmerman (eds.), *Penser l'immigration et l'intègration autrement*, Brussels: Bruylant 2006.

Waldrauch, H., Methodology for Comparing Acquisition and Loss of Nationality, in: R. Bauböck et al. (eds.), *Acquisition and Loss of Nationality, Volume II: Country Analyses*, Amsterdam: Amsterdam University Press 2006.

Electronic Sources

Bousetta, H., L.A. Bernes, *Muslims in the EU: Cities Report, Belgium*, Open Society Institute, EU Monitoring and Advocacy Program 2007, downloadable from http://www.eumap.org/topics/minority/reports/eumuslims/background_ reports/download/belgium/belgium.pdf.

Bousetta, H., S. Gsir, & D. Jacobs, *Active Civic Participation of Immigrants in Belgium*, Country Report prepared for the European research project POLITIS, Oldenburg 2005, www.uni-oldenburg.de/politis-europe.

Carrera, S., A Typology of Different Integration Programmes in the EU, Briefing Paper: Order Form No. Ip/C/Libe/Of/2005–167, 2005, http://www.libertysecurity.org/article1192.html.

Carrera, S., A Comparison of Integration Programmes in the EU: Trends and Weaknesses, *Challenge Papers*, No. 1/March 2006, Brussels: Centre for European Policy Studies, downloadable from http://shop.ceps.eu/BookDetail2.php?item_id= 1310&.

Delruelle, E., R. Torfs, Rapport Final de la Commission du Dialogue Interculturel, 2005, downloadable from http://www.diversiteit.be/NR/rdonlyres/4BF1128D-1AED-4863–B2A5–38E57087F19D/0/rapportdialogue.pdf.

Favell, A. & M. Martiniello, *Multi-national, multi-cultural and multi-levelled Brussels: National and ethnic politics in the 'Capital of Europe', paper proposed for Transnational Communities* online working paper series, WPTC-99–04, 1999, http://www. transcomm.ox.ac.uk.

Gsir, S., *Belgique : intégration et cohésion sociale: Quelle intégration ? Welche Integration?*, Exposé dans le cadre de la journée nationale de la Commission fédérale des Etrangers (CFE), Bienne, 16 November 2006, downloadable from http://www.eka-cfe.ch/d/Doku/themen/gsir.pdf

Gsir, S., M. Martiniello, K. Meireman & J. Wets, Belgium, in: J. Niessen, Y. Schibel & C. Thompson (eds.), *Current Immigration Debates in Europe: A Publication of the European Migration Dialogue*, 2005, downloadable from http://www.migpolgroup.com/ multiattachments/2959/DocumentName/EMD_Belgium_2005.pdf.

Hambye, P. & S. Lucchini, *Sociolinguistic Diversity and Shared Resources: A Critical Look at Linguistic Integration Policies in Belgium*, 2005, downloadable from http://www6. gencat.net/llengcat/noves/hm05primavera-estiu/docs/a_hambye.pdf.

Lambert, M., P. De Cuyper, J. Geets, L. Struyven, C. Timmerman, S. van den Eede & J. Wets, *Het Vlaamse Inburgeringsbeleid geëvalueerd*, 2007, downloadable from http://binnenland.vlaanderen.be/inburgering/onderzoek/pdf/Het%20Vlaamse%20Inburgeringsbeleid%20geevalueerd_synthese.pdf.

Le Texier, E., Du modèle républicain à des modèles culturalistes hybrides : les cas belges et français, in: Les Politiques d'intégration en Europe : le 'contrat d'intégration' en question, *In Varietate Concordia*, 15 April 2006, downloadable from http://gbf.typepad.com/concordia/2006/04/index.html/.

Leman, J. & C.L. Pang, *Immigrants and Cultural Diversities in Belgium*, downloadable from http://www.emz-berlin.de/projekte_e/pj32_1pdf/IntPol_Belgium.pdf.

Louis, B., *La loi du 1er mars 2000 révolutionne 'par défaut' l'acquisition de la nationalité belge*, 2000, downloadable from http://www.ulb.ac.be/socio/germe/documentsenligne/2lou00.pdf.

Martiniello, M. & A. Rea, *Belgium's Immigration Policy Brings Renewal and Challenges*, 2003, downloadable from http://www.migrationinformation.org/Profiles/display.cfm?ID=164.
MPG and the British Council, *European Civic Citizenship and Inclusion Index*, 2005, down loadable from http://www.migpolgroup.com/.
MPG and the British Council, *MIPEX Migration Integration Policy Index*, 2007, browseable on http://www.integrationindex.eu.
Sénat français, *La Formation des Étrangers à la Langue du Pays d'accueil*, Les Documents de Travail du Sénat, Série Législation Comparée, no. LC 150, September 2005.
ECRE, Caritas, *Introduction programmes and language courses: Recommendations for the integration of refugees and migrants in Europe*, Report of NGO Network of Integration Focal Points 2006.
www.inburgering.be.

Official Documents

Beleidsnota inburgering 2004–2009.
Beleidsbrief inburgering 2005–2006.
Beleidsbrief inburgering 2006–2007.
Beleidsbrief Inburgering 2007–2008.
The Civic Integration Decree of the Flemish Government of 28 February 2003 and its implementing decision of 2004 (*Inburgeringsdecreet* of 2003).
The amended Decree of 14 July 2006 and its implementing decision of 15 December 2006 on the Flemish civic integration policy.
The Minorities' Decree of 1998 (*migrantenbeleid*).
The Decree of 4 July 1996 on the integration of foreigners and citizens of foreign origin of the Walloon Government.
Nationality Code of Belgium, 1984 (last amended in 2000 and 2006).

Chapter 9

Mapping the redefinition of belonging in Europe

Ricky van Oers, Eva Ersbøll and Dora Kostakopoulou

Language and civic orientation tests are key features of the policy agendas of many European Union Member States and the European Union. Although the modalities of integration tests and courses vary among the Member States, their introduction and the accompanying official discourses confirm the changing relationship between legal status, integration and political belonging. Political belonging has been redefined and made conditional upon newcomers' commitment to the host country and acceptance of its values. Between 2002 and 2008, Austria, Denmark, France, Germany, the Netherlands and the UK introduced a 'knowledge of society' test as a condition for naturalisation. Additionally, in certain Member States, the informal language test that accompanied naturalisation has recently been replaced by a formalised test, devised and organised by language institutions.

The contributors to this volume have examined the introduction and implications of civic integration programmes in nine Western and Eastern European countries. The discussion has shown that while in the past the integration of newcomers was the main goal of multifarious processes of socio-political incorporation, in the new millennium it has been closely aligned with migration policy imperatives. Accordingly, integration tests are not simply citizenship tests, that is, requirements attached to gaining formal political inclusion into the citizenry, but are also migration tests. The latter are administered both internally, in the countries of destination, as well as externally, in the countries of origin.

Integration requirements as a condition for immigration have been introduced in France, Germany and the Netherlands since 2006 (see Table 1 below). In Denmark, an immigration test will come into effect in 2010 and will be taken in Denmark. Austria is also expected to introduce a pre-entry requirement for spouses. The UK has considered the introduction of such a requirement, too. In all countries, the requirements only apply to applicants for family reunification, who are generally assumed to be poorly skilled or

Van Oers, Ersbøll and Kostakopoulou, A Re-definition of Belonging?, pp. 307–331.

even unskilled and therefore not adapted to the needs of national labour markets.[1] Family migration from certain countries therefore appears to be regarded as largely unwanted.

Table 1: Integration requirements before immigration

	Integration requirement?	Language Requirement Content[2]	Leading to test?	Possibilities for preparation	Consequences of not complying with requirements
Austria	No, but introduction has been announced.	X	X	X	X
Belgium	No.	X	X	X	X
Denmark	Yes, test expected to be introduced in 2010.	Knowledge of Danish language level A1 minus of the CEF and knowledge of society (higher level).	Yes, oral test that will cost €400. Test to be taken in Denmark.	Free preparatory package prepared by Government. Questions on knowledge of society accessible via question bank of 100 questions. Preparation for language test is immigrant's own responsibility.	Residence permit for family reunification will not be granted.
France	Yes, since 2007.	An evaluation of knowledge of French language (level below level A1 CEF) and republican values (oral evaluation in language	In cases where applicant had to follow language training in country of origin on the basis of the first evaluation, a second evaluation will follow. If successful, the spouse will not have to attend linguistic training in France. If the level is not met, the spouse will have to attend linguistic training in France.	French Government provides French language courses in countries of origin.	In cases of insufficient knowledge of language after the second evaluation, the authorities will determine the characteristics of the French language training the foreigner will have to take in France within the framework of the integration contract.

[1] In Denmark the requirement also has to be fulfilled by religious preachers.

[2] For an overview of the levels of language proficiency in the Council of Europe's Common Framework of Reference, please see annex 1.

Table 1 (*cont.*)

	Integration requirement?	Language Requirement Content	Leading to test?	Possibilities for preparation	Consequences of not complying with requirements
		of applicant) for all applicants for family reunification. If the level of knowledge is considered insufficient, the applicant has to attend language courses in the country of origin. If the evaluation demonstrates sufficient knowledge of French language, no language formation to be followed in the country of origin or in France.			
Germany	Yes, since 2007.	Yes; level A1 of the CEF.	Yes; language skills need to be proven by test certificate from Goethe Institute or other certified institution. According to case law of German administrative courts, proof of knowledge is, however, not limited to submitting a certificate from the Goethe Institute. The requirement of such specific proof cannot be derived from the Act.[3]	Goethe Institutes present in most countries of the world.	Visa for family reunification not granted.
Hungary	No.	X	X	X	X
Latvia	No.	X	X	X	X

[3] Oberverwaltungsgericht Berlin-Brandenburg, judgment of 28 April 2009 (OVG 2 B 6.08).

Table 1 (*cont.*)

	Integration requirement?	Language Requirement Content[4]	Leading to test?	Possibilities for preparation	Consequences of not complying with requirements
Netherlands	Yes; since 15 March 2006.	Yes; knowledge of language at level A1 minus; knowledge of Dutch society and life in the Netherlands.	Yes; test costs €350. Government offers no possibilities for preparation.	Self-study with learning kit.	Visa for family reunification not granted.
UK	No, introduction has been considered but postponed.	X	X	X	X

The Netherlands was the first country to introduce a pre-entry integration requirement in 2006. Together with Austria and Germany, this country lobbied for the introduction of a clause in the Family Reunification Directive, opening up the possibility for Member States to "require third-country nationals to comply with integration measures, in accordance with national law" (Article 7(2) Directive 2003/86/EC). The Dutch policy on pre-departure integration served to a certain extent as a model in Denmark, Germany and France.[5] In this respect, one can find similarities among national policies, which are not confined to the target group, as well as important differences. Even though in the French parliamentary debates reference was made to the Dutch policy, Table 1 shows that the French integration abroad requirements differ significantly from the Dutch (and German) requirements. Whereas the French Government provides language courses in the countries of origin, the Netherlands and Germany place the emphasis on the individuals' own initiative, rather than the provision of state-financed courses. As Michalowski rightly observes in Chapter 5 of this volume, this shows that immigration tests in the Netherlands and Germany, "clearly are an instrument for the selection of (more highly) skilled migrants and only indirectly linked to the integration of immigrants in the receiving country." This observation may not apply to the Danish case, since applicants for family reunification will

[4] See above p. 308, n. 2.

[5] One could, however, also argue that Germany extended its language tests in the country of origin which were addressed to ethnic Germans (1997) to the family members of these ethnic Germans (2005) and then to all family migrants (2007).

be granted a temporary visa to take the test in Denmark, since it is explicitly presumed not to limit the number of family reunifications.

In Denmark and Germany, as is the case in the Netherlands, migrants have to pass a test in order to fulfil the integration requirement. Again, this situation differs from the French case, where applicants for family reunification are only subjected to a language *evaluation*. If the evaluation shows that their knowledge of the French language is inadequate (below level A1 minus), migrants will have to follow extra language courses, the duration of which may not exceed two months. If their knowledge of republican values is deemed to be insufficient, three hours of extra training must be undertaken. Once the courses have been completed, the visa for family reunification will be granted. Conversely, in Germany and the Netherlands a visa will only be granted if the candidates have passed the required tests. As already stated above, applicants for family reunification in Denmark will be granted a visa in order to take the test there. After passing the test, a residence permit will be granted.

The costs of compliance with language and civic orientation tests are not uniform across the Member States examined in this book. In France, the language evaluation is free of charge. In Denmark, Germany and the Netherlands candidates have to pay for the test. While the price of the German test varies from country to country and does not exceed €80,[6] the fees for the Dutch and Danish tests are fixed: the Dutch test costs €350 and the Danish test will cost about €400.

There are two important explanations for the relatively liberal integration abroad policy implemented in France. Firstly, the right to family reunification in France is codified in the French Constitution and thus cannot be made conditional upon passing a test or paying fees. Secondly, the reason why the French Government, according to Pascouau's interpretation in Chapter 4 of this volume, chose to introduce a language evaluation instead of a test lies in the wording of Article 7(2) of the Family Reunification Directive, which provides Member States with the possibility of requiring third-country nationals to comply with 'integration measures'. This wording clearly differs from the wording of the Long-Term Residents Directive (2003/109/EC), which opens up the possibility for Member States to require third-country nationals to comply with 'integration conditions'. It is therefore questionable whether Member States are allowed to make the right to family reunification, enshrined in Directive 2003/86, conditional upon success in a test. Furthermore, in a report to the European Parliament and the Council on the application of the Directive, the Commission stated that the measures

[6] Deutscher Bundestag, Drucksache 16/7259, p. 6.

should aim only at facilitating integration and not be adopted in order to pursue different aims.[7] From this point of view, it is questionable whether the Dutch and German integration requirements are compatible with the Family Reunification Directive.[8]

9.1 *The rationale for the introduction of language and integration tests*

Apart from the introduction of language and integration requirements as a condition for immigration in some of the EU Member States under consideration, Tables 2 and 3 below show that all the countries under consideration have introduced language and integration requirements in the host country (Table 2) and all countries, except Belgium, have introduced such requirements for naturalisation (Table 3). The introduction of language and integration tests, be they as a condition for immigration, after arrival in the host country, or for citizenship, has been officially justified on the basis of a civic republican concern about the promotion of active participation in the polity and civic society. In some countries, however, controlling immigration was also explicitly mentioned as a reason for introducing the requirements. In Austria, Denmark, France and the Netherlands, the link between integration requirements and migration control was publicly mentioned in official discourses. In France, this became apparent from statements made by the rapporteur of the Parliament that the goal of the integration evaluation abroad, which was introduced in 2007, was to manage migration flows. Since Article 8 ECHR often stood in the way of the non-renewal of a residence permit based on failure to attend mandatory language training courses within the framework of the integration contract, the introduction of mandatory language courses as a condition for obtaining a visa would be a more efficient mechanism for controlling immigration. In the explanatory memorandum accompanying the Dutch Integration Abroad Act, which introduced the integration abroad examination, it was stated that reduced immigration would be an effect of the integration examination, which is a mechanism for selection. But reducing immigration was not mentioned as a goal of the Act.[9]

---

7 Report from the Commission to the European Parliament and the Council on the application of Directive 2003/86/EC on the right to family reunification, COM(2008) 610 final, 8 October 2008, pp. 7–8.

8 Denmark is not bound by the Directive.

9 Second Chamber, 2003–2004, 29700, no. 3, p. 15.

Table 2: Integration requirements in the host country

	Integration requirement?	Content[10]	Leading to test?	Who pays?	Consequences of not complying with requirements
Austria	Since 2002.	Knowledge of German at level A2. No duty to attend a course.	Knowledge of German proven by a diploma from a certified language training institute or the successful attendance of an integration course of 300 hours.[11]	The immigrant pays. The course costs around €1000.[12]	Refusal of permanent residence permit.
Belgium: Flanders	Since 2003: integration courses; compulsory for certain categories of newcomers after signing a personal contract of civic integration.	Language course consisting of 120 to 240 hours of language tuition. 20 hours of vocational counselling. Civic course in immigrant's native language.	No; participation in 80% of the courses is required. Possibility of introducing tests is discussed.		Fine between 50 and 5000 euros. Possibility that non-compliance will be taken into account when applying for social benefits.
Belgium: Wallonia	Since 2006: Wallonia introduced reception programmes consisting of French language courses and civic information.		Reception programme not mandatory.		

[10] For an overview of the levels of language proficiency in the Council of Europe's Common Framework of Reference, please see annex 1.

[11] "Successful attendance" means attendance of the lessons and successful exam at the end of the course.

[12] There is a voucher system operated at federal level, and some provinces (e.g. Vienna) also operate a supplementary voucher system. If the exam is taken (or the course ends) within 24 months after immigration, the immigrant only pays 50% of the costs of the course, the rest is covered by the voucher. Otherwise the voucher loses its validity and the immigrant pays 100%. The city of Vienna pays an extra voucher of €300 upon completion of the course.

Table 2 (*cont.*)

	Integration requirement?	Content	Leading to test?	Who pays?	Consequences of not complying with requirements
Denmark	Since 1999: 3 years' introduction programme offered to foreigners legally residing in Denmark 2002: individual contracts 2006: integration contracts.	1999: 'Action Plan', including Danish course, based on abilities of individual 2002: duty to participate actively in introduction programme. 2006: activities laid down in integration contract: foreigners should make an effort, take responsibility and demonstrate their will to integrate, find employment and become self-sufficient. 2007: having held a full-time job for a period of 2.5 years and Danish language skills at level B1 or A2 if supplemented by knowledge of English language at level B1.	1999: only active participation in programme was required 2002: introduction of language test requirement 2007: examination at fixed level (B1/A2 combined with English language examination at level B1). See previous column.	Government, if participants are comprised by introduction programme; for participants who have not followed the language courses an exam fee of 1000 DKR (about 650 euros) may be charged.	1999: active participation in language course is condition for permanent residence Since 2002: failure to fulfil obligations of contract: reduction or suspension of 'introduction aid'[13] and no access to permanent residence. 2007: passing of integration exam a condition for permanent residence permit and cash benefit.
France	Since 2003, condition of 'republican integration' for persons applying for residence card. Since July 2003: possibility of integration contract for all foreigners applying for a residence permit	Integration contract implies voluntary commitment to follow language courses of a maximum of 400 hours (if necessary), training regarding French institutions and values of the	Language course leads to oral and written tests. Level of tests is lower than level A1 of CEF.		Failure to fulfil obligations of the integration contract taken into account when renewing integration contract for first time.

[13] Introduction aid is an unemployment benefit for foreigners, which is below the level of unemployment benefits for Danish nationals.

Table 2 (*cont.*)

	Integration requirement?	Content	Leading to test?	Who pays?	Consequences of not complying with requirements
	Since January 2007: conclusion of integration contract compulsory for all persons admitted to France for the first time and wishing to reside there on a long-term basis Since 2007 integration contract for the family.	French Republic and attending an information session on daily life in France. 2007: integration contract for the family: the obligation to attend a training course on the rights and duties of parents and compliance with compulsory school attendance by children.			Failure to fulfil integration obligations for the family may result in suspension of payment of social security benefits for the children or other economic sanctions against the family. Failure to respect the contract may also be taken into consideration when renewing the residence permit.
Germany	Since 1978, language skills Since 2005, Attending an integration course is a condition for permanent residence permit.	600 hours of language tuition + 30 hours of civics education. Since 2008: 900 hours of language course hours for persons requiring more extensive training + hours of civic education raised to 45.	Yes; until January 2008 the language test was optional. Since 2008, language test is compulsory + introduction of civics test.	2005: Government, immigrant pays €1 per hour taught in integration programme. Costs of tests covered by government.	Since 1978, refusal of permanent residence Since 2005, participation in course taken into consideration when renewing temporary residence permit (sanction not applied in practice) + reduction of welfare benefits. Successful participation in course (reaching level B1 and passing civics test) condition for issue of a permanent residence permit.
Hungary	Yes, since 2008; only for applicants for international protection, recognised refugees and temporary or subsidiary protected migrants.	Participation in language training and integration courses.	Regular examinations during language course.	Partly by state budget (refugee authority) and partly by other contracting partners (NGO, church,	Refugees and persons with temp. or sub. protection: obtaining subsistence allowance in first 24 months depends on participation in 520-hour.

Table 2 (*cont.*)

	Integration requirement?	Content	Leading to test?	Who pays?	Consequences of not complying with requirements
				municipality) if service contract requires own contribution. Refugee authority may use support from the European Refugee Fund.	language course. Subsistence allowance after recognition after 25–48 months depends on cooperation with employment service and participation in re-training or vocational training courses for at least one year or community service of at least 3 months.
Latvia	Since 2006.	Basic knowledge of the Latvian language tested by examination.	Yes.	Immigrant pays for the language test.	Passing the examination is a condition for obtaining a permanent residence permit.[14]
Netherlands	Since 1998.	1998: following an integration programme 2007: formalisation of requirements. Knowledge of language at level A2. Knowledge of Dutch society.	1998: programme led to test, but test meant to measure language skills 2007: passing of integration examination, consisting of 'central part' (computer-based language and knowledge of society tests) and 'practical part' (role-plays and portfolio).	Since end of 2007: government, pre-2007: immigrant.	1998: no legal consequences 2007: refusal of application for permanent residence; Financial sanctions (fines and reduction of social benefits).

[14] Furthermore, in Latvia, next to the tests for a permanent residence permit which have only been introduced in 2006, language tests, the level of which might have been much higher, for practising certain professions have been applied long before.

Table 2 (*cont.*)

	Integration requirement?	Content	Leading to test?	Who pays?	Consequences of not complying with requirements
UK	Yes, since 2007.	Knowledge of language and life in the UK.	Knowledge can be proven in 'Life in the UK' test or by advancing one level in a language with citizenship course.	Immigrant.	Application for indefinite leave denied.

As Perchinig has argued in Chapter 1, in Austria integration requirements were introduced under the influence of the right-wing FPÖ, which later divided into two parties, FPÖ and BZÖ. These parties promised to control immigration. Since 1998, applicants for naturalisation must prove they have sufficient knowledge of German. The latter requirement was reinforced in 2005 and, in 2006, knowledge of Austria's democratic order and history was added as a requirement for naturalisation (see Table 3). The explicit argument of reducing the number of naturalisations was used, especially after it became apparent that becoming an Austrian citizen had become an 'escape route' for bypassing the quota system for family reunification of third-country nationals, which did not apply to Austrian nationals.

In Denmark, the Danish People's Party (*Dansk Folkeparti*, DF) also championed the introduction of mandatory integration requirements. Since the Danish minority government, which has been composed of conservatives and liberals since 2002, depends on the support of the DF, migration and naturalisation policies have increasingly taken a more restrictive turn. The Aliens policy adopted by the new government in 2002 aimed at limiting the number of migrants. To that end, a Danish test was made a condition for permanent residence in 2002. In 2007 a genuine integration test at a fixed level was introduced. Furthermore, whereas a language requirement has been applied for naturalisation in Denmark since 1849, proof of knowledge of Danish by providing an examination certificate became a necessary condition in 2002. In addition, the level of language proficiency was raised to level B1. Since, in the opinion of the DF, this level would not be sufficient, the level of language proficiency for naturalisation was raised to level B2 in December 2005. At the same time it was decided that applicants for Danish nationality also have to prove their knowledge of Danish culture, history and society by passing a citizenship test.

Additionally, the Danish Aliens policy of 2002 aimed at controlling immigration, nevertheless the preparatory report of the Bill introducing the immigration test in 2006 stated that the purpose of the test was to enhance a foreigner's successful and rapid integration into Danish society. Furthermore, the Minister for Integration, when asked whether she expected a decline in the numbers of applications for family reunification, stressed that the purpose of the test was not to limit the number of applications for family reunification, nor did she expect a distinct decrease, see Chapter 3, page 129, with footnote 45. It remains to be seen whether this expectation will be met, particularly in the light of noticeable decreases in the Netherlands and Germany (see below).

In spite of official justifications for the integration requirements in terms of promoting integration, the aim of controlling migration is often confirmed by the fact that failure to comply with the integration obligations results in the refusal of a (permanent) residence permit or citizenship, or in the imposition of financial sanctions. These sanctions are currently applied in all countries under consideration. Integration contracts are presently required in Germany, France, Austria and Denmark (Table 2 above). Germany was the first Member State to require language skills for the issue of a permanent residence permit (Groenendijk, Guild & Barzilay 2001). Since 1978 having a command of the German language is a condition for obtaining a permanent residence permit. The Residence Act of 2005 required applicants for a permanent residence permit to have "sufficient knowledge of the German language" and "basic knowledge of the juridical and social order and living conditions in Germany". Only migrants who have participated successfully in an integration course, in other words those who have passed a language test at level B1 of the CEF and a civics test, can obtain a permanent residence permit.

In France the *Loi Sarkozy* from 2003, required an active commitment on the part of newcomers to attend language courses and a training course regarding French institutions. As Pascouau has noted in Chapter 4, integration contracts evolved in 2005 and 2006 and, in 2007, were extended to migrants' families. The official justification for the introduction of the integration contract for the family, which obliges parents to attend a one-day training session on parents' rights and duties, was to help parents address the specific difficulties they face when confronted with a new society, the rules of which are not easy to understand and are historically conditioned. But such an argument not only does exaggerate the differences between non-nationals and nationals and the distinctiveness of French norms and ways of life, but it also tends to conceal the extent to which the disciplinary powers of the state extend into the private domain.

By contrast, an integration contract is not provided for in the UK; migrants wishing to obtain a long-term residence permit have to take examinations covering linguistic skills and knowledge of life in the UK. The same applies with respect to naturalisation. In the following table (Table 3), we summarise the language and integration requirements for naturalisation in the countries under consideration.

Table 3: Integration requirements as a condition for naturalisation

	Integration requirement?	Language requirement[15]	Knowledge of society requirement	Leading to test?
Austria	Yes.	1998: 'Sufficient knowledge' of German 2006: Fulfilling requirement for permanent residence or diploma at level A2.	2006: basic knowledge of Austria's democratic order and the history of Austria and the respective province.	Yes; knowledge of Austria tested in multiple-choice test.
Belgium	No, proof of 'willingness to integrate' abolished in 2000.	No.	No.	No.
Denmark	Yes.	Since 1849. 2002: level B1 2005: level B2 2008: level B2 with mark 4 (replacing mark 2).	2007: introduction of knowledge of Danish culture, history and society 2008: Multiple-choice questions and answers no longer accessible beforehand.	Yes, both requirements are concluded with test.
France	Yes.	1945: applicant for naturalisation has to prove assimilation into French society. 2003 + 2006 reinforcement of this condition by requiring proof of knowledge of French language.	No.	No.
Germany	Yes.	2000: 'sufficient knowledge' of German 2007: oral and written knowledge of German at level B1.	2008: knowledge of social and juridical order and of living conditions in Germany.[16]	Yes, since 2007 language skills demonstrated by diploma; 2008: *Einbürgerungstest.*
Hungary	Yes.	Strong command of Hungarian language to pass examination and for naturalisation procedure.	1993: examination of constitutional issues.	Yes; oral and written test.

[15] For an overview of the levels of language proficiency in the Council of Europe's Common Framework of Reference, please see annex 1.

[16] In the test, however, the questions do not regard the German social order. Instead, the test focuses to a very large extend on questions about politics, rights, history, and geography.

Table 3 (*cont.*)

	Integration requirement?	Language requirement	Knowledge of society requirement	Leading to test?
Latvia	Yes.	Yes.	Basic provisions of the Constitution, text of the national anthem and history.	Both requirements tested in naturalisation tests since 1994.
Netherlands	Yes.	1985: adequate spoken Dutch and social contacts with Dutch nationals 2003: oral and written knowledge of Dutch (A2).	2003: knowledge of Dutch society.	2003: naturalisation test costing €260 2007: replacement of naturalisation test with integration examination (see Table 2), costs starting at €230.
UK	Yes.	1981: knowledge of English, Welsh or Scottish Gaelic 2005: formalisation of the requirement.	2005: introduction of requirement of knowledge of 'Life in the UK'.	2005: proving knowledge of language and life in the UK through 'Life in the UK' test or by progressing one level in a language and citizenship course.

With the exception of Belgium, all other countries under consideration in this volume demand that immigrants meet civic orientation and language requirements in order to gain full and formal admission into the political community. Citizenship has become more communitarian and civic republican in character (see van Oers in this volume; Introduction). In Austria and Denmark, political parties with a right-wing aliens policy campaigned for the introduction of these tests. By contrast, in the other countries under consideration, the influence of right-wing parties appears to have been absent. Again, the introduction of the integration requirements for naturalisation was officially justified in terms of promoting integration. Immigration control concerns, however, once more appear to have played a prominent role. In Germany, for example, the upgrading of the language requirement for naturalisation to a B1 level in 2007 and the introduction of a naturalisation test in 2008 was justified on the basis of the need to facilitate the integration of migrants. In addition, however, despite official justifications, concerns about the need to prevent 'naturalisation tourism' have led to the formalisation of the language requirement and the ensuing pressure on the more liberal *Länder* to adapt to the practice of the *Länder* that operated a stricter naturalisation policy. Similarly, although the introduction of a stricter language and integration test in the Netherlands in 2003 was justified in terms of facilitating applicants' insertion into Dutch society and increasing their awareness of their rights and duties, the fact that certain MPs had argued that the acquisition of Dutch nationality had been made "too easy" indicates that limiting access to Dutch nationality was also an aim of the introduction of the new naturalisation test. In the UK, the language of improving social cohesion and strengthening the sense of community belonging featured prominently when the New Labour government introduced the Nationality, Immigration and Asylum Act 2002.

In Hungary the introduction of an examination on constitutional issues as a condition for naturalisation in 1993 was justified on the grounds that it would be legitimate to expect applicants for naturalisation to show their attachment to Hungary by passing an examination. In reality, however, concerns relating to growing immigration led to the desire being expressed by all political parties to restrict the possibilities for acquiring Hungarian citizenship. Ethnic Hungarians are generally exempt from taking the examination, thereby lending credence to the argument that the examination was introduced in order to make it more difficult for non-ethnic Hungarians to naturalise.

Notwithstanding the discursive link between integration requirements and social cohesion, Michalowski correctly points out that the actual effectiveness of the integration requirements for migrant integration and social cohesion is difficult to establish. Quite often, in the name of integration, migrants are either left with an inferior legal status or are simply excluded from entry to the country altogether. Hence, "the focus of integration policy is no longer on the equalisation of opportunity, but rather on the discouragement and penalisation of migrants who do not possess certain attributes" (Ryan 2008: 312). The question whether integration tests function as a mechanism for selection and exclusion and for 'thickening' political belonging, thereby demonstrating a shift towards a more communitarian understanding of citizenship, can be more fruitfully addressed by examining the effects of the new integration requirements on the acquisition of a permanent residence permit and citizenship.

9.2 *The effects of the language and civic integration requirements*

Given the recent introduction of integration tests, it is impossible to predict with certainty the effects of formalised testing schemes on the behaviour of potential applicants and the level of their integration into the host society.

However, throughout the discussions in this volume the contributors have pointed out that the new civic requirements have resulted in reductions in the number of applications, be they for residence or citizenship. This is hardly surprising since the formalisation of the tests has coincided with a rise in the level of required knowledge of the language and of the host society (e.g. Denmark and the Netherlands) or with the introduction of other obstacles, such as high fees or a six-month waiting period after a candidate fails the test (e.g. the Netherlands until 1 April 2007).

In Austria, naturalisation tests were formalised in 2006. The 2006 Act has had a dramatic effect on the number of naturalisations. Compared to 2006, there were 46.5% fewer naturalisations in 2007. This indicates that the main objective of the Act, reducing the number of naturalisations, has been achieved, although the decline may also be due to a certain extent to a combination of the waiting period of ten years and the immigration peak in the first half of the 1990s. To what extent the decrease in the number of naturalisations can be ascribed to the introduction of the naturalisation tests, however, is unclear, since neither the number of candidates nor the success rates of the tests are published. Furthermore, the 2006 Act also tightened the requirements regarding income and residence, which makes that the formalised naturalisation test is not the only reason for the lower number of naturalisations.

In Denmark, however, a causal link between the introduction of a stricter language requirement and a decline in the number of naturalisations can more clearly be established. The introduction of a stricter language requirement for naturalisation in 2002 led to a decrease in the number of naturalisations. Compared to 2002, the year in which most applicants had their application processed under the old rules, the number of naturalisation dropped by 65% in 2003 when the language requirement at level B1 became effective, but this decrease was only temporary in nature. The subsequent tightening of the requirement in 2005 to level B2, the highest in Europe, is expected to have a more permanent effect. In the years 2007 and 2008, the numbers of naturalisations were 66% lower than in 2002.[17] The new restrictions in 2008 may accelerate the decline in numbers.

Germany was the first country to require language skills for the issue of a permanent residence permit and it introduced a language requirement as

[17] Statistics concerning the two other Danish integration tests, namely the immigration test as a condition for family reunification and the integration test as a condition for permanent residence and cash benefits are not available, since, at the time of writing of this book, the former test had not yet been introduced and the latter had only been effective for a short period of time.

a precondition for immigration for ethnic Germans in 1997, extending this condition to their family members in 2005. In 2000, it appeared that less than half of the candidates passed the language test and numbers published in 2005 showed that only 25% of the family members of ethnic Germans passed this test. In the meantime, the introduction of the immigration test for family members of foreign residents and German citizens has started to produce similar effects. In the first eight months of 2008, 41% of the tests taken were unsuccessful and the number of visas issued dropped by 24%.

In the years 2005 and 2007, Germany introduced the requirement of knowledge of the German language at level B1 for permanent residence and naturalisation respectively. The comparatively high German language requirements have been justified by the objective of making migrants independent actors in daily social interactions as well as in the professional sphere. In the first nine months of 2008, 50% of the test candidates failed to reach level B1. Hence, when the first persons subject to the law of 2005 start applying for permanent residence in 2010, half of the course participants might experience difficulties in obtaining a permanent residence permit if the German administration does not come up with a flexible solution. In the first nine months of 2008, 50% of the test candidates failed to reach level B1.

The reform of German nationality law in 1999 aimed at increasing the number of naturalisations. The number of naturalisations, however, only increased temporarily and shortly after the reform they decreased again. It is expected that the increase in the required level of language skills in 2007 and the introduction of the *Einbürgerungstest* in September 2008 will lead to a further decrease.

In Hungary, there are no official statistics regarding the number of candidates for the examination on constitutional issues or their pass rates. It is estimated that 60–70% of all candidates pass the examination. This means that between 30% and 40% of all test candidates will have to put their naturalisation application on hold.

In Latvia, the naturalisation tests introduced in 1994, which cover language and history and which have been simplified over the years, initially did not seem to form a barrier to naturalisation. In 2004 and 2005, less than 5% of all knowledge test candidates failed the test, but this number rose to 17.8% in 2008. Similarly, whereas 10% and 16% of all test candidates failed the language test in 2004 and 2005 respectively, this number rose to 21% in 2007 and almost 28% in 2008.

In the Netherlands, newcomers have been required to follow an integration programme since 1998, which ended with a test that was meant to measure the level of language skills of the course participants, but did not have any legal consequences. Level A2, the intended achievement level, was not attained in many cases in practice. This knowledge did not prevent the Dutch government from introducing a naturalisation test as a condition for naturalisation in 2003, which required language skills at level A2 and knowledge of Dutch society. The introduction of this test led to a dramatic decrease in the number of naturalisations. The numbers of naturalisations fell by more than 50% in 2004 and 2005 compared to 2002. Furthermore, in the period from April 2003 and September 2006, less than half of all those who registered to take the naturalisation test actually passed the test. Mention should be made of the fact that one-third of the immigrants who presented themselves as potential candidates eventually did not participate in the first part of the test. Research conducted in 2006 (see Chapter 2 Van Oers) demonstrated that immigrants were put off by the high price of the test (€260) and the absence of any possibility for preparation, which made reluctance to pay the high price even greater. The replacement of the naturalisation test by the integration examination in April 2007 has not led to a rise in the number of naturalisations. This effect was in any case unintended, since price, level and the possibilities for preparing for the integration examination are more or less identical to those of the naturalisation test.

In the UK, on the other hand, the introduction of the 'Life in the UK' test in 2005 does not seem to have had a negative effect on the number of naturalisations, which have constantly been rising. One possible explanation might be that the UK does not require a uniform standard of language skills or knowledge that has to be acquired by all future British citizens. Those interested in obtaining British citizenship and, since 2007, permanent residence, can choose either to sit the 'Life in the UK' test or follow a 'language with citizenship' course, during which they have to proceed from one level to the next. Looking at the pass rates for the 'Life in the UK' test per nationality, however, the test seems to have a negative effect on the naturalisation of certain migrant groups, family migrants and refugees in particular.

Finally, in Belgium and France the introduction of integration requirements have not led to a decline in the number of applications. In Belgium, fulfilling integration requirements is not a condition for obtaining any type of legal residence. Whereas in Flanders the policy of *inburgering* is mandatory for certain groups of migrants, successful participation in the integration trajectory is not assessed on the basis of test performance, but on mere participation in the three different programmes of the trajectory, namely, language courses, civic orientation and vocational counselling. This does not mean that a migrant's failure to participate is not penalised in some way; it might lead to the imposition of a fine or impact on social rights. In Wallonia, on the other hand, participating in the reception programme is not compulsory for newcomers.

In France, failure to fulfil the obligations does not stand in the way of the issue of a (permanent) residence permit, but it might affect migrant residence rights in other ways. Deliberate failure to respect the obligations set forth in the integration contract or the integration contract for the family may lead to non-renewal of the residence permit.[18] Even though it is still too early to draw conclusions on the effects of the integration contracts, it should be noted that the system of integration contracts remains quite flexible either in terms of content or in terms of effects.

While the actual effect of the integration requirements on migrant integration is difficult to establish at this juncture, the contributors to this volume have pointed out that, notwithstanding the official aim of facilitating migrants' integration into the host society, language and integration requirements prevent migrants from accessing a more secure residence status or naturalisation, and hence serve as a means of prolonging their exclusion.

We may therefore wonder whether the introduction of the integration requirements was not intended to serve the often-concealed aim of controlling the level and type of immigration. Especially when examining the Dutch and German cases, this tends to be the case. In Germany, past experiences with the language test for ethic Germans and their families did not stop the government from introducing a language and integration test for the family members of foreigners and German citizens. Furthermore, despite the decline in the numbers of naturalisations after the introduction of a language requirement in 2000, the government decided to tighten this requirement and to introduce a civics test for permanent residence and naturalisation in 2008. Similarly, in the Netherlands, the fact that many participants in the integration programme of the 1998 Newcomers Integration Act did not manage to reach level A2 did not prevent the Dutch government from requiring this level for naturalisation in 2003. Since the Dutch government did not use the opportunity to reverse the negative effects produced by the test when it was replaced in 2007, the conclusion can be drawn that controlling immigration and reducing access to citizenship might also have been a goal of the naturalisation test As research conducted in the Netherlands in 2006 (see Chapter 2) pointed out, the naturalisation test constituted a particularly high barrier for certain groups of immigrants, such as those with a low education level or income. Even though the other countries applying a citizenship test have not followed the extreme Dutch example, in that they do provide for preparation possibilities and offer the test at a reasonable cost, tests are likely to produce discriminatory effects for categories of immigrants in weak socio-economic positions.

[18] The possibility of non-renewal only exists in case the permit is renewed for the first time.

9.3 *Broadening the debate: human rights and pluralism*

According to human rights law, states must strike a fair balance between the competing interests of the individual and the community as a whole. Although, as a principle of customary international law, states can freely control the entry and residence of aliens into their territory, their power must be exercised in line with the rule of law and in accordance with their human rights obligations. In introducing integration tests and the civic integration programmes, the nine EU Member States mentioned in this volume do not seem to have paid attention to human rights or nationality law perspectives. Republican and, more recently, increasingly communitarian perspectives have prevailed. Without doubt, states' interests in controlling public expenditure and securing social harmony are legitimate interests, but it is questionable whether the interests of resident immigrants who, perhaps as a result of illness, age, poor educational background, etc., do not live up to the ideal of 'immigrants with good integration potential', have been sufficiently taken into consideration.

Once admitted to a state's territory, aliens in principle enjoy the same human rights as citizens. Differential treatment is permitted, but only in so far as it has an objective and reasonable justification. If not, it gives rise to discrimination. "No objective and reasonable justification" means that the distinction in use does not pursue a "legitimate aim" or that there is no "reasonable relationship of proportionality between the means employed and the aim sought to be realised" (see, for instance, the case of Abdulaziz, Cabales and Balkandali v. the United Kingdom: Judgment of 28 May 1985, Series A, no. 94, paragraph 72). It is doubtful whether there is "a reasonable relationship of proportionality" between integration tests as a condition for family reunification, a permanent residence permit and/or citizenship and the aim of improving immigrants' integration if groups of immigrants with a poor education, low income, etc., remain unable to meet the conditions and are thus excluded from access to family reunification, a permanent residence permit and/or citizenship. Although there is no 'human right' to family reunification as such nor to the acquisition of a secure status, arbitrary denial thereof may, according to the case law of the European Court of Human Rights, raise questions regarding Article 8 of the European Convention on Human Rights (ECHR) on the right to private and family life, in which case the non-discrimination provision in Article 14 of the ECHR applies.

It is true that certain rights may be reserved for citizens, but it must be borne in mind that, in return, the international community has aimed to ensure that every individual has a citizenship and thus, citizenship rights in his or her 'own country'. This aim was emphasised after World War II when the international community decided that it would never again experience the disregard and contempt for human rights that it had witnessed in the preceding years, when denaturalisation and denationalisation had been powerful weapons in the hands of totalitarian regimes (Arendt 1951). It was recognised that citizenship/nationality has a human rights perspective and, in 1948, the Universal Declaration of Human Rights (UDHR) proclaimed that "Everyone has the right to a nationality" and that "No one shall be arbitrarily deprived of his nationality or denied the right to change his nationality". In the subsequent years the UN's International Law Commission engaged in work on avoiding and reducing statelessness. The Conventions relating to the status of refugees (1951) and of stateless persons (1954) prescribe that the contracting states shall, as far as possible, facilitate the assimilation and naturalisation of refugees and stateless persons (Article 34 and Article 32) and the Convention on the Reduction of Statelessness (1961) imposes obligations on states to ensure certain stateless persons' acquisition of a citizenship/nationality. To this end, the Final Act recommends that persons who are stateless de facto (refugees) as far as possible be treated as persons who are stateless de jure.

States that make the acquisition of nationality/citizenship conditional upon passing language and societal knowledge tests at a level that certain groups of resident immigrants – and in some countries even immigrants' descendants – will never be able to pass, seem to have disregarded the aforementioned human rights principles and obligations. It should not be forgotten that the non-discrimination principle does not prohibit states from treating groups differently in order to correct 'factual inequalities' among them; indeed, under certain circumstances a failure to correct inequalities through different types of treatment may, without objective and reasonable justification, give rise to a breach of Article 14 of the ECHR (see *Case of Andrejeva v. Latvia*, 18 February 2009, § 82).

Therefore, language-learning facilities should be made available for immigrants, fees should not pose insurmountable barriers and language and societal knowledge testing, if any, should only test immigrants' relative competence. If testing at a fixed level is maintained, provision should be made for exemption for groups of people who, through no fault of their own, will not pass the tests.

This approach seems to be supported by the most comprehensive convention on citizenship, the 1997 European Convention on Nationality (ECN). The convention imposes legal obligations on the state parties to base their nationality law on a number of principles, including the UDHR principles that "Everyone has the right to a nationality" and that "Statelessness shall be avoided" (Article 4).[19] These principles have provided the inspiration for the substantive provisions of the Convention, including Article 6(3), which states that state parties shall provide in their internal law for the possibility of the naturalisation of persons lawfully and habitually resident on their territory. A former member of the Expert Committee that drafted the Convention, the Committee of Experts on Nationality (CJ-NA), has argued that lawful and habitual residence is no longer a condition for the acquisition of a host state's nationality, but rather "a ground for becoming entitled to the right to acquire that nationality" (Autem 1999).

The only fixed requirement for naturalisation is the ten-year maximum period of residence. However, as stated in the explanatory report to the ECN, paragraph 51, state parties may, in addition, fix other "justifiable conditions for naturalisation, in particular as regards integration". Most countries require applicants for naturalisation to have some knowledge of their official language. The question is what degree of knowledge of the language is it reasonable to require? It is fairly certain, as stated in a report on Conditions for the Acquisition and Loss of Nationality, drafted by Andrew Walmsley and adopted in 2002 by the CJ-NA, that requirements for knowledge regarding the language, culture and history of the country of which the applicant is seeking citizenship should exclusively be used and regarded as an element for integrating non-nationals and should not be used as a discriminatory means for a state to select its nationals. Elements of a state's law regarding integration should not be contrary to an individual's human rights nor be discriminatory, nor should 'integration' be interpreted as being the same as 'assimilation'. 'Integration' does not mean taking up living habits or religion or similar aspects, but means the ability to live together and requires tolerance from individuals towards others, despite the fact that they are different.

This perception is in line with the famous advisory opinion from the Inter-American Court of Human Rights, in Proposed Amendments to the Naturalization Provisions of the Constitution of Costa Rica, Advisory Opinion OC-4/84, January 19, 1984. The Court felt compelled to emphasise that in practice, and given the broad discretion with which tests may be administered, the risk is present that such requirements will become the vehicle for subjective and arbitrary judgments as well as instruments for the implementation of

[19] Among the countries dealt with in this book only two, the UK and Belgium, have neither signed nor ratified the ECN that entered into force 1 March 2000. The convention is ratified by 19 European states and among them Austria, the Netherlands, Hungary, Denmark and Germany (in the period 1 March 2000 – 1 September 2005). Nine states have signed but not (yet) ratified the Convention, among them France and Latvia.

discriminatory policies that, although not directly apparent on the face of the law, could well be the consequence of its application. Hence, there is a need to reflect on and debate contemporary discourses and conceptualisations of integration (Carrera 2006: 19–20). After all, contemporary uses of integration may not correspond to 'social inclusion', equal treatment and non-discrimination.

The pluralist perspective

While civic integration programmes are based on the assumption that societies are homogenous, distinctive and unified, one may start from a different premise; namely, the premise that political communities are neither static nor undifferentiated entities. Rather than being a reflection of pre-political commonalities, such as blood ties, ethnic origin, culture and shared historical experiences or distinctive communities of shared values, political communities are essentially the product of political processes, power relations, institutional design and strategic adaptation to exogenous and endogenous pressures. Pluralist perspectives have emphasised the constructed and process-related nature of political communities by putting emphasis on social interactions, complex processes of institutional design and the maintenance and evolution of schemes of human cooperation (Honneth 1998; Habermas 1998; Young 1990). Pluralism thus eschews notions of organic national communities and essential identities. Since political communities are not conceived as communities of fate or communities of character, that is, as historically ongoing associations having a common purpose or life, and collective identities are not seen as reflecting essential attributes and timeless qualities, the social and political inclusion of newcomers is not seen as threatening the alleged unity and cultural homogeneity of the community, nor does it threaten its national identity. Demoi are heterogeneous and differentiated in many respects, but neither heterogeneity nor differentiation undermines the stability of the polity or the political understanding of membership (Kostakopoulou 2001, 2008). Accordingly, polities ought to design flexible policies that welcome all those who become enmeshed in networks of cooperative interaction, work for the well-being of the commonwealth and share its burdens, and to rethink their concept of membership in ways that accommodate human mobility.

Human mobility has been, and continues to be, an inescapable fact and needs to be channelled responsibly and constructively in order to ensure the maximisation of its productive and creative energies. It is debatable whether the traditional liberal, civic republican and communitarian understandings of citizenship can adequately capture the dynamics and potential of mobility. Ideological narratives about the alleged destiny of the nation, discourses about the need to maintain the 'social cohesion' of the host country and, above all, the securitisation of migration, that is, turning migration into a security issue threatening the survival of societies (Weaver 1995, Huysmans 2006) preclude credible policy options. But policies based on respect for human beings and for diversity can make a difference. Such policies would need those in power to recognise that host countries have the positive duties to provide a favourable context for reception, to facilitate migrants' settlement, assist with their adjustment, understand their vulnerability and to ensure their socio-economic and political inclusion. But they also have the negative duties to refrain from imposing arbitrary distinctions and disseminating negative views, such as the view that migrants are uninvited, unwanted, a threat and a problem, and to refrain from reinforcing stereotypes and interfering illegitimately with their personal autonomy. Similarly, newcomers have a duty to contribute to the commonwealth, to share its burdens and to be law-abiding. But they do not have to abandon their identities or reject their value systems in order to conform to the attitudes and cultures of the host community. Pluralism thus leaves little room for 'authentic' cultures and 'true' members. Instead, it is characterised by dialogic exchanges and an "ethic of openness to unassimilated otherness" (Heller and Feher 1988; Parekh 2000), with a view to fostering inclusive and pluralistic communities in which people are treated as respectful participants and as equals.

Bibliography

Arendt, Hannah: *The Origin of Totalitarianism*. Harcourt, Brace and Company, New York, 1951. Autem, Michel: The European Convention on Nationality: Is a European code on nationality possible? in 11th European Conference on Nationality, "Trends and developments in national and international law on nationality" (Strasbourg, 18 and 19 October 1999), Proceedings, p. 32.

Carrera, Sergio: A Comparison of Integration Programmes in the EU, Trends and Weaknesses, Challenge Papers no. 1/March 2006.

Groenendijk, Kees, Elspeth Guild & Robin Barzilay, *Le statut juridique des ressortissants de pays tiers résidents de longue durée dans un Etat membre de l'Union européenne*, Report for the European Commission 2000.

Habermas, J., *The Inclusion of the Other*. Cambridge MA: MIT Press, 1998.

Heller, A. and Feher, F., The Postmodern Political Condition, Cambridge: Cambridge University Press, 1988.

Honneth, A., 'Democracy as Reflexive Co-operation: John Dewey and the Theory of Democracy Today', *Political Theory* 26(6), 1998, 763.

Huysmans, J., *The Politics of Insecurity. Fear, Migration and Asylum in the European Union*. London: Routledge, 2006.

Kostakopoulou, T., *Citizenship, Identity and Immigration in the European Union: Between Past and Future*. Manchester: Manchester University Press, 2001.

Kostakopoulou, T., *The Future Governance of Citizenship*, Cambridge: Cambridge University Press, 2008.
Parekh, B., *Rethinking Multiculturalism*, London: Palgrave, 2000.
Ryan, B., Integration Requirements: A New Model in Migration Law, *Journal of Immigration, Asylum, and Nationality Law*, 22(4) 2008, pp. 303–316.
Weaver, O., 'Securitisation and Desecuritisation' in R. Lipschutz (ed.) *On Security*. New York: Columbia University Press, 1995, 46–86.
Young, I. M., *Justice and the Politics of Difference*. Princeton: Princeton University Press, 1990.

Annex 1

Levels of language proficiency in the Council of Europe's Common European Framework of Reference[1]

Proficient	C2	Can understand with ease virtually everything heard or read. Can summarise information from different spoken and written sources, reconstructing arguments and accounts in a coherent presentation. Can express him/herself spontaneously, very fluently and precisely, differentiating finer shades of meaning even in more complex situations.
User	C1	Can understand a wide range of demanding, longer texts, and recognise implicit meaning. Can express him/herself fluently and spontaneously without much obvious searching for expressions. Can use language flexibly and effectively for social, academic and professional purposes. Can produce clear, well-structured, detailed text on complex subjects, showing controlled use of organisational patterns, connectors and cohesive devices.
Independent	B2	Can understand the main ideas of complex text on both concrete and abstract topics, including technical discussions in his/her field of specialisation. Can interact with a degree of fluency and spontaneity that makes regular interaction with native speakers quite possible without strain for either party. Can produce clear, detailed text on a wide range of subjects and explain a viewpoint on a topical issue giving the advantages and disadvantages of various options.

[1] http://www.coe.int/T/DG4/Portfolio/?L=E&M=/main_pages/levels.html, site visited on 31 July 2009.

Van Oers, Ersbøll and Kostakopoulou, A Re-definition of Belonging?, pp. 333–334.

User	B1	Can understand the main points of clear standard input on familiar matters regularly encountered in work, school, leisure, etc. Can deal with most situations likely to arise whilst travelling in an area where the language is spoken. Can produce simple connected text on topics which are familiar or of personal interest. Can describe experiences and events, dreams, hopes & ambitions and briefly give reasons and explanations for opinions and plans.
Basic	A2	Can understand sentences and frequently used expressions related to areas of most immediate relevance (e.g. very basic personal and family information, shopping, local geography, employment). Can communicate in simple and routine tasks requiring a simple and direct exchange of information on familiar and routine matters. Can describe in simple terms aspects of his/her background, immediate environment and matters in areas of immediate need.
User	A1	Can understand and use familiar everyday expressions and very basic phrases aimed at the satisfaction of needs of a concrete type. Can introduce him/herself and others and can ask and answer questions about personal details such as where he/she lives, people he/she knows and things he/she has. Can interact in a simple way provided the other person talks slowly and clearly and is prepared to help.

Index

Immigration and Asylum Law and Policy in Europe

1. E. Guild and P. Minderhoud (eds.): *Security of Residence and Expulsion*. 2000 ISBN 90-411-1458-0
2. E. Guild: *Immigration Law in the European Community*. 2001 ISBN 90-411-1593-5
3. B. Melis: *Negotiating Europe's Immigration Frontiers*. 2001 ISBN 90-411-1614-1
4. R. Byrne, G. Noll and J. Vedsted-Hansen (eds.): *New Asylum Countries? Migration Control and Refugee Protection in an Enlarged European Union*. 2002 ISBN 90-411-1753-9
5. K. Groenendijk, E. Guild and P. Minderhoud (eds.): *In Search of Europe's Borders*. 2003 ISBN 90-411-1977-9
6. J. Niessen and I. Chopin (eds.): *The Development of Legal Instruments to Combat Racism in a Diverse Europe*. 2004 ISBN 90-04-13686-X
7. B. Bogusz, R. Cholewinski, A. Cygan and E. Szyszczak (eds.): *Irregular Migration and Human Rights: Theoretical, European and International Perspectives*. 2004 ISBN 90-04-14011-5
8. H. Battjes: *European Asylum Law and International Law*. 2006 ISBN 90-04-15087-0
9. Elspeth Guild and Paul Minderhoud (eds.): *Immigration and Criminal Law in the European Union: The Legal Measures and Social Consequences of Criminal Law in Member States on Trafficking and Smuggling in Human Beings*. 2006 ISBN 90-14-15064-1
10. Georgia Papagianni: *Institutional and Policy Dynamics of EU Migration Law*. 2006 ISBN 90-04-15279-2
11. Elspeth Guild and Anneliese Baldaccini (eds.): *Terrorism and the Foreigner: A Decade of Tension around the Rule of Law in Europe*. 2006 ISBN 90-04-015187-7
12. Steve Peers and Nicola Rogers (eds.): *EU Immigration and Asylum Law: Text and Commentary*. 2006 ISBN 90-04-15374-8
13. Prakash Shah (ed.): *Law and Ethnic Plurality: Socio-Legal Perspectives*. 2007 ISBN 978-90-04-16245-7
14. Bruno Nascimbene, Massimo Condinanzi and Alessandra Lang: *Citizenship of the Union and Free Movement of Persons*. 2008 ISBN 978-90-04-16300-3
15. Evelien Brouwer: *Digital Borders and Real Rights: Effective Remedies for Third-Country Nationals in the Schengen Information System*. 2008 ISBN 978-90-04-16503-8
16. Nils Coleman: *European Readmission Policy:Third Country Interests and Refugee Rights*. 2008 ISBN 978-90-04-16554-0
17. Sergio Carrera: *In Search of the Perfect Citizen? The Intersection between Integration, Immigration and Nationality in the EU*. 2009 ISBN 978-90-04-17509-9
18. Jan Niessen and Thomas Huddleston (eds.): *Legal Frameworks for the Integration of Third-Country Nationals*. 2009 ISBN 978-90-04-17069-8
19. Galina Cornelisse: *Immigration Detention and Human Rights. Rethinking Territorial Sovereignty*. 2010 ISBN 978-90-04-17370-5

Martinus Nijhoff Publishers – Leiden · Boston

20. Ricky van Oers, Eva Ersbøll and Dora Kostakopoulou (eds.): *A Re-definition of Belonging? Language and Integration Tests in Europe.* 2010. ISBN 978-90-04-17506-8

21. Bernard Ryan and Valsamis Mitsilegas (eds.): *Extraterritorial Immigration Control. Legal Challenges*. 2010. ISBN 978-90-04-17233-3

Martinus Nijhoff Publishers – Leiden · Boston